MY BROTHER'S ROAD

To Alec,

In memory of Garlen and Aram

||||||||||||||||||||||||||||||||||||||||||||||||||||||||

My Brother's Road

AN AMERICAN'S FATEFUL
JOURNEY TO ARMENIA

||||||||||||||||||||||||||||||||||||||||||||||||||||||||

Markar Melkonian

with
Seta Melkonian

I.B. TAURIS
LONDON · NEW YORK

Reprinted as a paperback in 2007 by I.B.Tauris & Co Ltd
6 Salem Road, London W2 4BU
175 Fifth Avenue, New York NY 10010
www.ibtauris.com

In the United States of America and Canada
distributed by Palgrave Macmillan a division of St. Martin's Press
175 Fifth Avenue, New York NY 10010

ISBN 978 1 84511 530 2

A full CIP record for this book is available from the British Library
A full CIP record is available from the Library of Congress

Library of Congress Catalog Card Number: available

Typeset in Book Antiqua by JCS Publishing Services,
www.jcs-publishing.co.uk

Printed and bound in India by Rakesh Press

Contents

Preface to the Paperback Edition

S ince the first edition of this book appeared in 2005, the rich have become richer in my brother's adopted homeland of Armenia, and the poor are still poor. Neither war nor peace reigns in the ravaged mountains where Monte died; Armenians still control those mountains, but the two sides to the conflict have not put down their guns.

On January 23, 2007, however, something remarkable took place. In Armenia's capital, Yerevan, in a scene reminiscent of a funeral I had attended almost fourteen years earlier, thousands of demonstrators gathered in public squares to commemorate the death of another Armenian. At the same moment in Istanbul (800 miles to the west of Yerevan) Turks were bearing that Armenian murder victim's body through the streets and proclaiming him a hero in Turkey.

This time, though, it was not Armenians but Turks bearing the hero's body through the streets, and the city was Istanbul, not Yerevan. Four days earlier, Hrant Dink, aged fifty-three, had been felled on Halaskargazi Boulevard in Istanbul, with two 7.65-millimeter bullets in his head. His seventeen-year-old assassin explained that he had killed Dink for "insulting Turks."

For more that ten years, Dink had edited *Agos*, a bilingual Turkish and Armenian newspaper published in Istanbul. Over the course of those years he had received threats from Turkish nationalists, who viewed him as a traitor for describing the Armenian "tragedy" as a genocide. In October 2005, a judge had handed him a six-month

suspended jail sentence for violating Article 301 of the Turkish Penal
Code, which makes it a crime to insult Turkey, the Turkish government, or the Turkish national character.

Hrant Dink and Monte Melkonian never met in life, and it's not clear
that they would have liked each other if they had met. Dink stood up to
the Turkish regime and its Chosen People creed, but he abhorred the
assassins of Turkish diplomats. Their acts, he felt, only stoked more
blinding hatred. For his part, Monte might have viewed Dink as foolish
for kowtowing to pro-Western reformers in Turkey. Monte believed
that Ankara's officials were enemies not just of Armenians and Kurds
but of most Turks, too.

But Monte and Dink also had things in common. Both men
encouraged what they called "Armenian–Turkish dialogue," and both
had grown impatient with super-nationalist compatriots who always
portrayed things in black-and-white terms, as Armenians-versus-
Turks. Dink opposed French legislation making it illegal to deny the
Armenian genocide, and Monte would have recoiled in disgust at
hypocritical French legislators for whom the Armenian genocide represented just another handy hurdle to erect in the path of Turkey's
membership of the European Union. The French law violated the freedom of speech that Monte had defended, and for which Dink died.

It did not surprise me that Hrant Dink was killed. After all, many
martyrs had preceded Dink, including his cousin Nubar Yalimian, a
supporter of TIKKO, the Turkish Workers' and Peasants Liberation
Army. What did surprise me, though, was that tens of thousands of
Turks followed Dink's casket for miles through the streets of Istanbul,
to the Holy Mother of God Church in the Kumkapi district. Thousands
of these marchers chanted in Turkish, "*Hepimiz Ermeniyiz*," "We are all
Armenians." Confronted with this massive display of decency, even the
angriest of Monte's compatriots have reason to pause and reflect. With
his blood, perhaps, Dink has written his most eloquent argument for
dialogue.

Hrant Dink died believing that it is time for Armenians and Turks to
put aside their hatred and seek common ground. I wonder how many
of the demonstrators in Yerevan appreciated that this was Dink's message for them. Monte's story is very different from Dink's, more
circuitous and paradoxical. But at the end of the day, this was his message, too.

PROLOGUE

Funeral, 1993

W hen I picked up the phone on the morning of June 12, 1993 and heard my sister's voice, I figured she was calling about our brother, Monte. He was 8,000 miles away, on a warfront in the former Soviet Union, and we were trying to send him a batch of walkie-talkies. "The walkie-talkies probably won't be necessary," Maile said, her throat catching. Then she informed me that my only brother had been killed that day in a skirmish at the foot of distant mountains, in the Republic of Azerbaijan.

Such a strange fate for the kid in cutoffs—my little brother, eighteen months younger than me, with whom I had shared long summer days swimming in the irrigation ditches of our native San Joaquin Valley. But this was not the first time I had heard a rumor of his death: over the course of fifteen years, I had heard that he had been shot by a sniper, hit by an artillery round, buried under rubble in the wake of warplanes, and dispatched by a fusillade from airport police. This time, though, I knew the bad news was true. I asked Maile the first two questions that came to mind: how long did it take him to die? And: was he shot in the back? She didn't have an answer to either question.

A couple of days later, I was standing in the streets of Yerevan, the capital of Armenia, with Maile, my mother, my father, and my brother's good friend from Visalia, our hometown in the middle of California. As we headed for the state funeral, mourners began pulling me aside to share their suspicions. "Your brother was killed in an ambush," one said, "They were waiting for him." Another one claimed that an assassin had collected a reward for the killing, while someone else swore that the Turks had something to do with it. And then one of the mourners whispered that my brother had fallen into a trap, a trap set not by enemy soldiers but by men close to him.

The rumor of betrayal was not far-fetched. Over the years, Monte had run afoul of many people—not only Turkish, Israeli, and US intelligence agencies, but also ultra-nationalist compatriots, former cohorts in a self-styled Secret Army, local gangsters and warlords, and who knows who else—and he had survived perhaps a dozen lethal traps.

The "official" version of Monte's death only heightened my suspicions: my brother, a wily veteran of 100 battles, was supposed to have been killed in a deserted village after he walked up to an enemy tank and mistook enemy soldiers for his own men. To further fuel my suspicions, I knew that several close military and political leaders in Armenia had been killed under suspicious circumstances. Whether they had been victims of a power struggle or of the hired guns of "family businessmen," one thing was clear: their killers were not the enemy that faced them on the other side of the minefields.

But if Monte had been betrayed, then the question arose: who among the multiple candidates had done the deed?

Images that I had tried for years to banish from my imagination loomed back into view: there was Monte, alias Saro, peering through sandbags in Iranian Kurdistan. Then came Monte, alias Abu Sindi, huddling with Yassir Arafat under a hailstorm of shrapnel in Beirut. Then there was Monte, prisoner number 752783, alone in a dark cell in a prison outside Paris. Next came Monte, now alias Timothy Sean McCormick, collecting soda bottles on the street after a rally for Slobodan Milosevic, the new leader of a Yugoslavia that was sliding into madness. And finally, there was Commander Avo in the distant mountains of Karabagh, peering through binoculars at a battlefield strewn with buckled armor.

On the morning of the funeral, June 19, 1993, a shell-shocked soldier met us on the steps of the morgue. He had spent the night there, a self-appointed sentry sleeping fitfully on the stone stairs, wailing and chanting oaths. We climbed the steps and entered the chill of the refrigerated vault. Monte's body, clad in crisp camouflage, lay in a shallow casket of unfinished planks on a metal shelf. The woman in charge had wrapped his head with gauze just above the eyebrows, to conceal the deep cleft across his right temple, the result of a shell fragment that had crushed his skull a week earlier. Someone remarked that with his head wrapped that way the only sign of the wound was a badly chipped upper front tooth. But the chipped tooth, I knew, was no war wound:

twenty years earlier, he had slipped on a rock at his favorite swimming hole in California's Sierra Nevada mountains.

Later that morning, eight of Monte's comrades-in-arms slung rifles off their shoulders to take up the casket. We followed them to Officers' Hall, in the middle of Yerevan. For four hours, thousands of ragged mourners filed past the casket, as a reed flute droned through the hall. Unemployed factory workers in shabby jackets, gaunt peasants, and fatigue-clad fighters paid their respects to the thirty-five-year-old military commander, whom they knew as Avo. So did the President of Armenia and his ministers in Italian suits, as well as representatives from the country's major political parties, and guests from Iran, Lebanon, Syria, and France. Russian officers swept kepis off their heads before entering the hall. The US ambassador to Armenia, Harry Gilmore, arrived after the nearest of kin had been ushered to a back room for tea, and left before we reemerged into the hall.

According to the *Los Angeles Times*, some 100,000 mourners followed the casket through the streets that afternoon. Local journalists had exaggerated when they put the number at 250,000, but who could count those who thronged Republican Square to follow the caisson through streets freshly washed and patched for the occasion? Who could count the mourners who lined the road for six kilometers to a cemetery on a hill stippled with the graves of casualties of the most vicious war raging on the ruins of the Soviet Union? And what about the thousands who stood for hours under the sun at a gravesite piled chest-high with carnations and red roses?

To American eyes, the wire service photographs must have presented just another mob scene from some sad and unpronounceable spot in the Caucasus. At the edge of the open grave, a cowled priest brandished his miter like a sword, as old women in black wailed and children barely old enough to speak hung their heads. Unshaven fathers who had wept for their own dead sons wept again. I emptied the remaining bullets in the clip of Monte's rifle, twenty-one of them, firing bursts into the air, conscious all the while that my brother would not have approved of this wasteful, needlessly dangerous display. Incense spiraled to the sky.

In Armenia, Monte had spoken very little about his life. It was not surprising, then, that rumors abounded — rumors about him fighting in the streets of Tehran and Beirut, and in the hills of Kurdistan and Afghanistan; rumors of bombs in bistros, assassination plots in Greece and Italy, and prison strikes in France. There was a dark rumor, too, of a teenage girl shot in the back seat of a car in Athens. But no one, it seemed, could tie the rumors together into a single story. Once, when a persistent reporter had tried to get the inside angle on the mysterious commander, Monte had turned and walked away, saying: "Whoever knows me knows me."

In the final years of his life, when military duties demanded his all, he had left it to others to describe him. In Washington DC, a mouthpiece for the fledgling Republic of Azerbaijan obliged, describing him as a "terrorist with a criminal background." US State Department employees dubbed him a threat to national security, and an FBI agent quoted by a *Los Angeles Times* reporter described him as a soldier of fortune who simply liked killing people. More than one peasant in the southern Caucasus declared him a saint, "our holy son," and a *New York Times* correspondent quoted an Armenian who called him "the best god we ever had."

Few people at the funeral, however, knew that the commander whom they called Avo was once a multilingual student of archaeology who had turned down graduate work at Oxford University to fight in revolutionary Iran and war-torn Lebanon. Still fewer knew — or cared, perhaps — that their hero had once been a Little League pitcher with a blazing fast ball in small-town California.

The last time I had seen my brother alive was the summer of 1991, when I had come to the Soviet Socialist Republic of Armenia to hold a cross over his head and the head of his bride in an ancient chapel carved into a mountain of volcanic rock. A few days after the wedding, Soviet Armenia had disappeared from the maps, along with the Soviet Union. That visit had been the first time I had seen my brother since early 1981: for ten years, our only contact had been letters passed through the hands of couriers and prison censors. The only exception was a telephone call I had made in 1989 from a public phone in Athens, Georgia to a PLO office in South Yemen. I had dropped 108 quarters into the phone and stood there for twenty minutes, as our time-delayed words crashed into each other somewhere over an ocean or a continent. Despite the static, the happy rush of words came across as if we had just spoken the day before. "*Hey, how's it going?*" Monte had drawled, still the kid in cutoffs.

And yet Monte was always changing, taking on new identities, new passports, new residences. Somehow, he had come to lead 4,000 fighters of "the most battle-hardened and fanatically motivated fighting force in the former Soviet Union," as an unsympathetic journalist described the army of Mountainous Karabagh. And yet again, on the eve of a battle less than three months before his death, an interviewer for PBS had described him as "a gentle Californian." Despite all the changes and the oceans that separated my brother from me, despite the years of silence and our differences of focus and temperament, I've hoped that the interviewer was right.

Now, standing at the gravesite, I've tried to recall just what had prevented me, his only brother, from visiting him during his most desperate years. What had prevented me from at least delivering a couple hundred unsolicited dollars every now and then? Yes, I had been busy chasing paychecks. And yes, the anti-Turkish oratory echoing around Monte, and the reports of atrocities and counter-atrocities by Azeris and Armenians had sapped whatever faith I had left in the people he had sworn his life to defend. But standing at the edge of his open grave, the best of these excuses struck me as shameful. The question rebounded with greater urgency: *how could I have convinced myself over the course of the last ten years of my brother's life that I was too busy to find out who he had become?*

Ever since the funeral, I've met men, and some women too, who have counted themselves in the ranks my brother commanded. Others have named their streets, schools, and babies after him, and tattooed his name on their hands and arms. Half the adults in Yerevan, it seemed, had come into contact with him. A Russian general told a television interviewer, quite inaccurately, that they had first met when Monte had been a slayer of Soviets in Afghanistan. A one-legged woman claimed that Monte had rescued her from a minefield. The child of a peasant recalled his "amazing simplicity." And yet so much remained uncertain, obscure. Contradictory stories surrounded Monte, and for every claim it seemed there was an equal but opposite claim. So where did the truth lie? Was he temperate or was he a vodka guzzler? A communist to his dying day, or a reborn nationalist? A defender of captives or a slitter of throats? A dutiful son and brother, or an outcast from his family? As the rumors have proliferated over the years, my need to separate fable from creditable report has only grown.

For a time my brother's journey became my journey. I joined him behind sandbags in Beirut and took up a rifle in southern Lebanon. I didn't stay long—only a year perhaps, off and on. But it was long enough to attract the attention of the FBI and police departments in the US. After years of opened letters, tapped phones, and FBI skullduggery, I've acquired a certain reserve, a certain reluctance to publicize the details of my life and my brother's. For the sake of this story, though, I've had to overcome this reserve, which had become second nature to me.

But how could I possibly tell Monte's story when, except for a brief visit in 1991, I had been absent for the last ten years of his life?

A solution to this problem—or at least the nearest thing—presented itself to me, in the person of Monte's widow, Seta. Monte had shared most of the years of my absence with Seta, and with her he had shared his thoughts and the dangers of the journey. So with this, I set out to find my brother's story.

Monte had lived on the move, through a dozen countries, with a dozen aliases and a dozen forged passports. He had spent half of his years in refugee slums, guerrilla bases, safe houses, prisons, and remote trenches. He had shared his journey with many people, good and bad, but he had left too many places in too great haste. It was not until several years later, after research and revelations, that Seta and I could begin to retrace the steps that led to the top of the rocky hill where he was buried that hot spring day.

This book, then, is what I am left with after six years of searching for an answer to the question that my brother's funeral had only posed more clearly: how did he die, and who killed him, enemy or "friend"? Even more urgently, though, this book is the result of my search to find out who my little brother Monte had become.

ARMENIA AND THE MIDDLE EAST

'Armenian Homeland' according to Monte's map (The Right to Struggle, p.49)

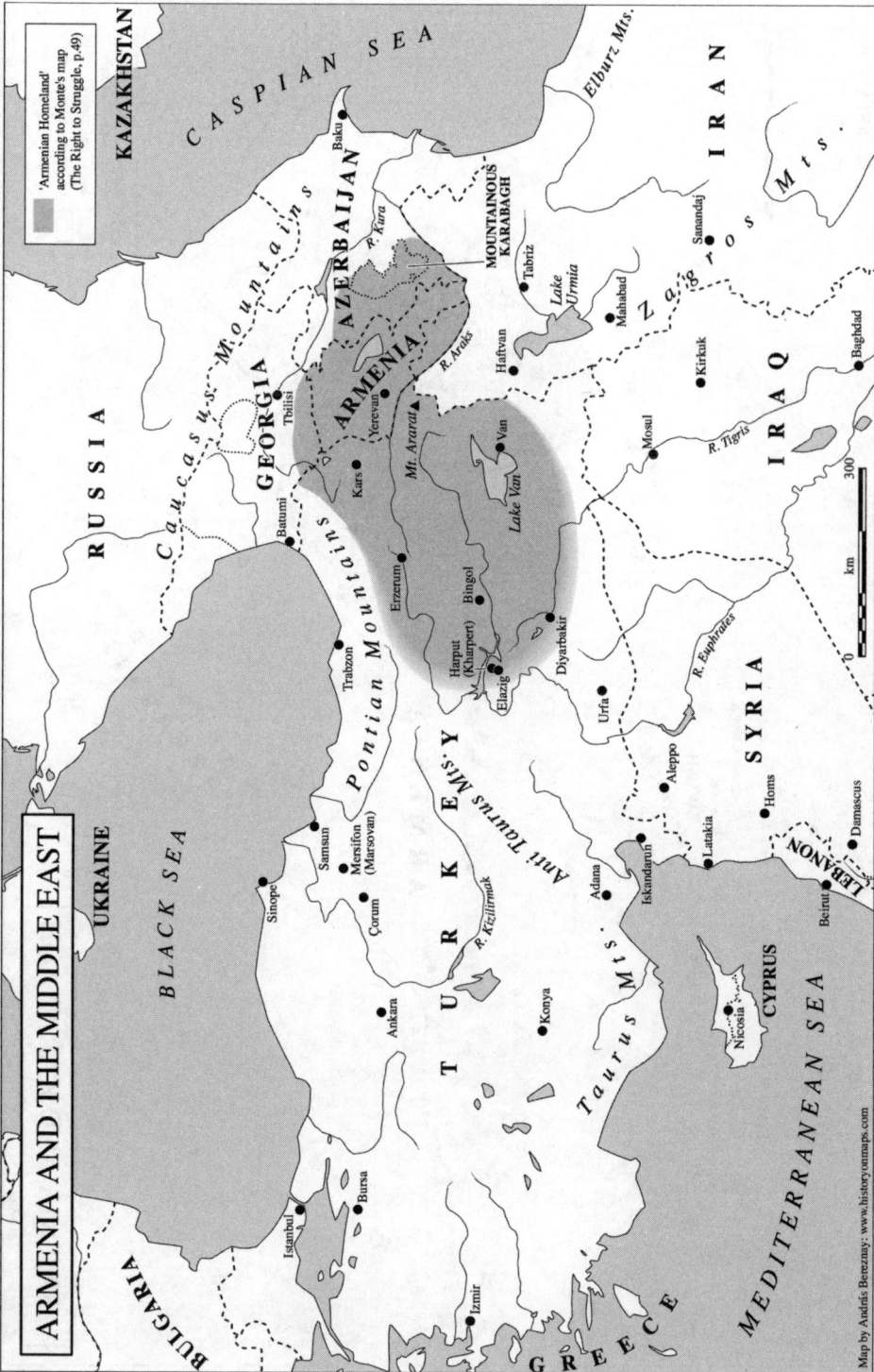

BULGARIA

UKRAINE

RUSSIA

KAZAKHSTAN

BLACK SEA

CASPIAN SEA

GEORGIA

Tbilisi

Batumi

Trabzon

Samsun

Mersifon (Marsovan)

Sinope

Çorum

Ankara

Istanbul

Bursa

Izmir

Konya

Pontian Mountains

Caucasus Mountains

AZERBAIJAN

Baku

ARMENIA

Yerevan

Kars

Mt. Ararat

Erzurum

Bingol

Harput (Kharpert)

Elazig

Djyarbakir

Urfa

Van

Lake Van

Hatvan

MOUNTAINOUS KARABAGH

Lake Urmia

Tabriz

Mahabad

Sanandaj

IRAN

Elburz Mts.

Zaggros Mts.

Kirkuk

Mosul

Baghdad

IRAQ

R. Tigris

R. Euphrates

R. Araks

R. Kura

Anti Taurus Mts.

Taurus Mts.

R. Kizilirmak

Adana

Iskandarun

Aleppo

Latakia

SYRIA

Homs

Damascus

LEBANON

Beirut

CYPRUS

Nicosia

MEDITERRANEAN SEA

GREECE

TURKEY

300

km

0

Map by András Bereznay: www.historyonmaps.com

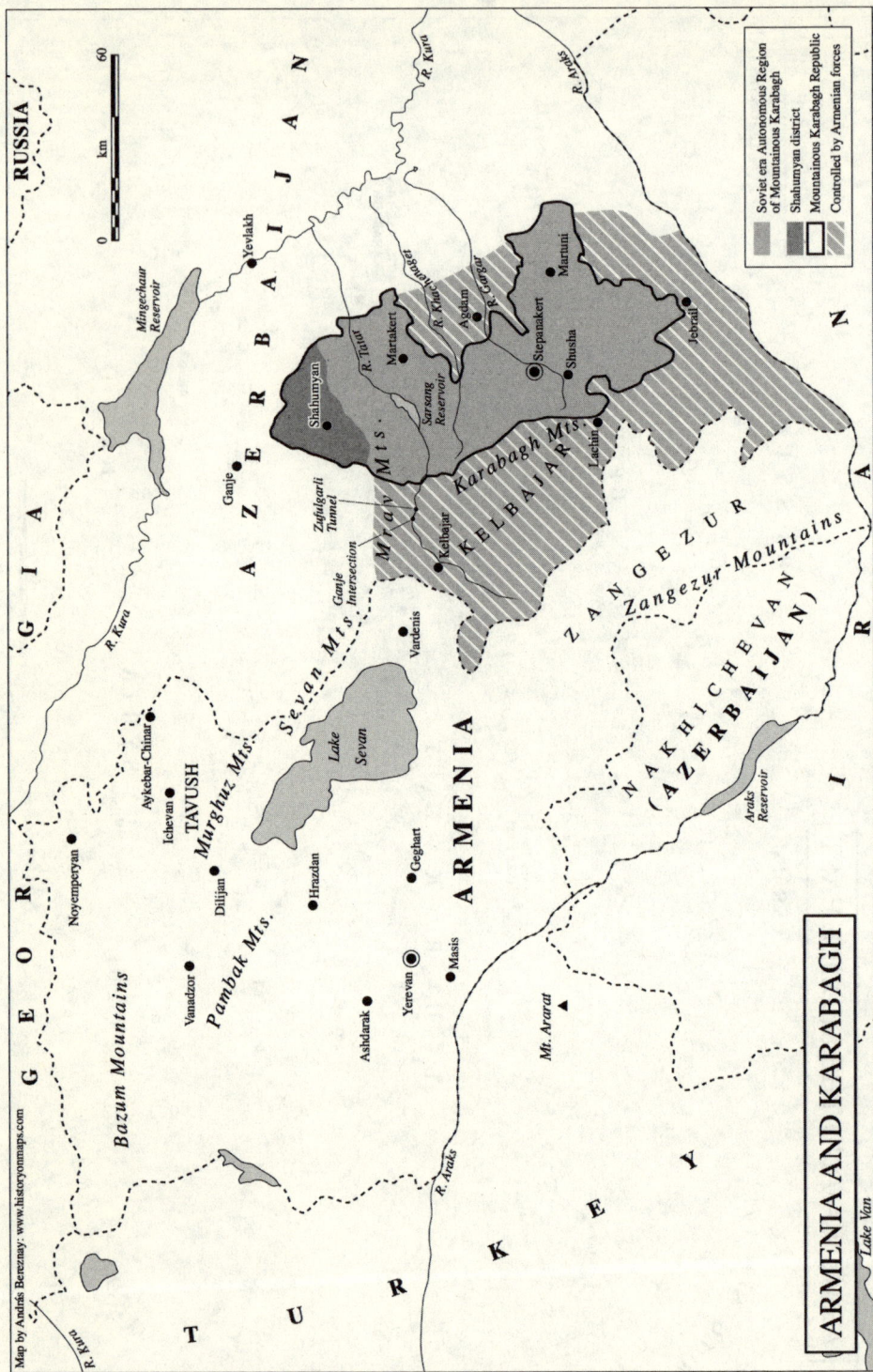

ARMENIA AND KARABAGH

Map by András Bereznay: www.historyonmaps.com

Legend:
- Soviet era Autonomous Region of Mountainous Karabagh
- Shahumyan district
- Mountainous Karabagh Republic
- Controlled by Armenian forces

RUSSIA

GEORGIA

AZERBAIJAN

ARMENIA

TURKEY

IRAN

Mingechaur Reservoir

Yevlakh
Ganje
Aykehor-Chinar
Ichevan
TAVUSH
Murghuz Mts.
Dilijan
Vanadzor
Pambak Mts.
Hrazdan
Bazum Mountains
Noyemperyan

Sevan Mts.
Lake Sevan
Vardenis
Geghart
Ashdarak
Yerevan
Masis
Mt. Ararat

R. Kura
R. Kura
R. Araks
R. Araks
R. Kura

Shahumyan
Mrav Mts.
R. Tatar
Martakert
Sarsang Reservoir
Karabagh Mts.
KELBAJAR
Kelbajar
Zaglugari Tunnel
Ganje Intersection

R. Khachin
R. Gargar
Agdam
Stepanakert
Shusha
Lachin
Martuni
Jebrail

ZANGEZUR
Zangezur Mountains
NAKHICHEVAN (AZERBAIJAN)
Araks Reservoir

Lake Van

km
0   60

N

MOUNTAINOUS KARABAGH

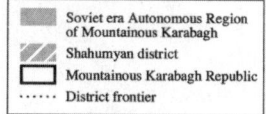

Soviet era Autonomous Region of Mountainous Karabagh
Shahumyan district
Mountainous Karabagh Republic
District frontier

Geteshen
Erkej
Manashid
Mardunashen
Bozluk
Karashinar
Shahumyan
Verishen
Gulistan

R. Tatar

AZERBAIJAN

Mrav Mts.

MARDAKERT DISTRICT

Aghdaban
Sarsang Reservoir
Mardakert
Haterk
Kedavan
Charekdar
to Kelbajar
Janyatagh

R. Khachenaget

Karabagh Mountains

Nareshtar

Agdam
R. Gargar
Yusufjanli

ASKERAN DISTRICT
Merzuli
Khojalu
Gulabli
Mehdishen
Avdal
Ashan
Cheyl Heights
Pertashen
Mughanlu
Kurapatkino
Avdur
Stepanakert
Amiranlar
Karadaghlu
Gishi
Martuni
Ghooroochookh Peak
SUSHA DISTRICT
Shusha
MARTUNI DISTRICT
Jardar
Vesalu
Alibali
Majgalashen
Lachin
Amaras
Krasnyi Bazar
Ghajar
Lachin Corridor
Fizuli

Goris
ARMENIA
HADRUT DISTRICT

Hadrut
Horadiz

Z A N G E Z U R

Jebrail

Gubatli

0   km   15

Map by András Bereznay: www.historyonmaps.com

||||||||||||||||||||||||||||||||||||||||||||||||||||||||||||||||

PART ONE

Choosing Ancestors

||||||||||||||||||||||||||||||||||||||||||||||||||||||||||||||||

||||||||||||||||||||||||||||| **1** |||||||||||||||||||||||||||||

Small Town Kid

C rouching behind sandbags in the rocket-scorched lobby of an apartment building, my brother Monte gave me a quick lesson on street fighting: at the first sound of gunshots, he advised, dash for cover. These are the seconds when most of the people who are going to get shot will get shot. Then "pep yourself up fast" he said, bouncing slightly on bent knees and fanning his fingers in front of his chest to emphasize the point. "You need to summon all your energy, and you need to do it *fast*."

It was east Beirut, spring 1979, and Monte and I were young and strong and eager for the good fight. We had come to civil-war Lebanon to help defend our fellow Armenians in their beleaguered neighborhoods there. On the other side of the Sinn el-Fil Highway, snipers who belonged to a rightwing Lebanese gang called the Phalange took up positions around pickup-mounted machine gunners. Rifles crackled back and forth across the post-apocalyptic cityscape. For the next two days, from May 9 to 11, our militia position saw the heaviest fighting in Lebanon that week, as both sides sowed the rubble with thousands of cartridges. Phalangist gunners wheeled in recoilless rifles and rocket-propelled grenades, while our comrades taped dynamite to the inside of tires, lit long fuses, rolled the tires across the street, and watched the enemy scatter like chickens. Once, as Monte pulled his Kalashnikov out of a hole in the rampart to reload, a sniper's bullet whizzed through the hole. During another spate of fighting, he ducked into an abandoned building and sprinted down a hallway, one step ahead of a long burst from a heavy machine gun, which punched through the cinderblock wall like a sewing machine needle through flannel.

Ten years later, Monte wrote of his years in Beirut that "It is perhaps strange that I stayed alive." Looking back, it strikes me as a miracle that my little brother ever reached the age of thirty-five.

We were born a year and a half apart in Visalia, California, the Walnut Capital of the World. Twenty-two miles north lay Kingsburg, the Watermelon Capital, and five miles beyond that lay Selma, the Raisin Capital. The town ended at our driveway. To the east, beyond our fence and the alfalfa field, lay peach and walnut orchards, and then the orange groves that banked against the foothills of the Sierra Nevada mountains. There were other Armenian families in Visalia, mostly recent spillover from the old "Armenian colony" in nearby Fresno. But they were scattered around town and the surrounding farmland, and it never occurred to us that they made up anything like an "ethnic community."

Visalia might have laid claim to some measure of charm in the late 1950s, when its population was less than 20,000 and a toddler could assume that the solar system orbited the one water tower he had ever seen. The movies just opening at the Sequoia motor theater had closed months earlier in San Francisco and Los Angeles, and Mearle's Drive-In, with its pink exterior and its giant neon soda, was the perfect emblem of small-town California. The Mom-and-Pop storefronts on Main Street, however, had already begun losing business to the liquor stores, supermarkets, and muffler shops that leap-frogged each other south along Mooney Boulevard, deeper and deeper into cleared farmland and toppled groves of valley oak.

Zabelle Melkonian gave birth to her third child and second son at Visalia Municipal Hospital at 4:50 a.m. on November 25, 1957. Her husband, our father Charlie, considered naming the seven-pound fifteen-ounce boy Marvin, but opted instead for Monte. He wanted a short name, he said, one that would "sound good over loudspeakers" — preferably loudspeakers in a baseball stadium or a sports coliseum. In keeping with family custom, Monte received no middle name. Mom described the new arrival in the baby book: "Very affectionate and loving. Happy but can be very fearless and aggressive when reproached." Although she registered his complexion as "fair," he darkened to a shade of cocoa that once prompted an apartment manager who took him for a "colored boy" to evict him from an unofficially segregated swimming pool.

Dad had risen from farm worker to self-employed cabinet-maker before becoming a father. Mom, formerly an elementary school teacher, turned to full-time mothering. For years, Dad handed Mom twenty-five dollars a week for groceries and clothes. By 1963, she had become so embarrassed about showing up at the neighbor's house to watch the Mercury space launches that she insisted on buying a television set. When times got leaner, she saved a few dollars by quitting her bowling team. Yet somehow our parents managed to insulate us from the financial insecurity of those years.

Mom reminded us time and again how fortunate we were to have been born in the United States. She set aside our grandmother's heavy blankets from the Old Country in favor of light American-style bedding, and she taught us to pull the sheets taut, like the skin of a drum, across the mattress Monte and I shared, and to secure it with crisp hospital corners. In this way we distinguished ourselves from our second-generation Okie playmates, whose beds even at high noon resembled nests of matted linen.

On Sundays, our protestations notwithstanding, Mom dressed us like pint-sized busboys, in button-down shirts, double-knee pants, wing-tip oxfords, and clip-on bow ties, and marched us to Sunday school at the nearby "American" Presbyterian Church. We were two kids with butch haircuts clutching blue tithing envelopes, each containing a dime. At Sunday school, we heard Bible stories that bolstered our conviction that the first shall be last, and the last shall be first.

For a boy growing up in the Walnut Capital of the World, it was consoling to learn that the nearby Sierra foothills had once served as a place of refuge for train robbers, cattle rustlers, and latter-day Robin Hoods. We had seen faded photographs of the baby-faced outlaws clutching holster buckles and Winchesters, and we had heard some of their names, too: Black Bart, Jesse James, the Dalton boys, and others. We had heard that once, long ago, a posse had returned to Fresno with the head of the greatest desperado of them all—Joaquin Murieta. But we had hoped that the report was just so much bluster, or a lie concocted for reward money, and that Murieta and his gang had escaped safely to Mexico.

Looking back, what I recall were the cartwheels, leapfrog, hide-and-seek, dichondra-flower necklaces, impetigo, stubbed toes, and games of chase lit by the summer sun. Digging holes for hideouts was a process imbued with infinite significance, though our work collapsed with the first heavy rain. Straddling boughs, we gnawed nectarines amid luminescent leaves and dancing shadows. We slid down grassy slopes on flattened cardboard boxes, wrestled in flooded orchards, and chased quail, jackrabbits, and bluebelly lizards through trellises. On summer evenings, we would stretch on warm asphalt, stare at the stars, breathe the fragrance of orange blossoms and weed oil, and listen to the whistle of distant trains.

On June 5, 1965, our lives would change. That was the day a young man in a Corvair ran a stoplight and slammed into our father's Econo-line van. Dad languished in bed for months, recovering from back injuries and a spinal fusion. When his doctor announced—rashly, as it turned out—that he would never be able to work again, he liquidated the carpentry business that he and his brother Sam had worked seventy-hour weeks to establish. As soon as he got out of traction, Mom dutifully returned to the sixth grade classroom to teach, while Dad took on the housework and cooking.

In those days, we ate a lot of rice pilaf, stuffed grape leaves, and an improvised soup our father called *chorbah*. He also served cracked wheat pilaf—sometimes too often for our taste. But we knew we had to finish what was on our plates. We didn't need reminders of starving children in India to convince us that it was bad luck to waste food: hushed references to starvation in the Old Country did the job.

Monte was a curious kid, always ready to learn something new. In fourth grade, he and his buddy Joel underwent a day of testing and emerged "Mentally Gifted Minors." As "MGMs" they were entitled to cigar-box butterfly collections, evenings of star gazing, and weekend fossil hunts with their favorite teacher, Mr. Clifford.

Somewhere along the line, my brother came to the conclusion that if humans have souls, then so must the rabbits, turtles, gophers, and pigeons that foraged and fluttered around the backyard. Thus it was only fitting that wooden crosses should sprout under the orange tree where we wrapped our dead pets in rags and buried them. Later, Monte claimed that as a boy he had believed not that he would one day swim like a frog and fly like a hawk, but that he actually could grow up to *be* a frog or a hawk. Throughout his life, he retained this belief in the radical reinvention of the self.

And change he did, from an early age. One morning, despite Dad's aversion to guns, he gave us each a clutch of coins, to spend a penny a bullet at the rifle range at Camp Tulequoia in the Sierras. There, Monte discovered he was a pretty good shot with a bolt-action .22, and after-wards he begged in vain for a rifle of his own. In the third grade we joined the Cub Scouts, where we learned how to "walk like an Indian," noiselessly rolling heel to toe. But Monte soon grew bored of the marshmallow men, balsa wood rockets, and whittling projects, and so he quit the Scouts, never having exceeded the rank of Wolf. He never forgot his troop yell, though, and years later, in the wee hours of guard duty in Beirut, he recited it for his fellow militiamen: "Two, four, six, nine / We are pack three-one-nine / Den Two—Better'n you!"

In the spring of 1966, Monte started Little League. He was the second-shortest kid on the team, but he commanded the pitcher's mound with focus and maturity. The faster I threw, the wilder I got. Not so with Monte: as a rule, he threw hard, fast, and "right down the pipe." Some players at that age copied the mannerisms of their favorite figures—Marichal's high kick; Mays' hat throwing; Clemente's tortured English. Monte's performance, though, was all his own: an austere sequence of businesslike motions, nothing feigned or balked. He had no slider, no change-up, no knuckle ball—just a curve for special occasions and a fast ball, and that was it. But the fast ball was searing. After a particularly sharp smack, the catcher would bolt to his feet, throw his glove in the dust, and shake his swollen hand. Although Monte was too young for the majors, my major-league coach, Mr. Simmons, would sneak him onto the field every now and then, to pitch an inning or two. At the end of the game, we would tuck our mitts under our arms and trudge home across the playingfield, sno cones in hand, crunching gopher mounds with our cleats.

After two successful seasons in Little League, Monte told Dad that he didn't care to try-out again. Just as he was heading into the best years of Little League, it seems, he had lost interest in playing the game. Some kids quit because they were no good at it, but Monte quit because it was no longer a challenge. In the years to come, I would see him do this time and again.

Monte was an easy-going, happy-go-lucky kid. He was hard to rile, but once riled, all bets were off. What made his rare flare-ups especially dangerous was that anger seemed to increase his focus, accuracy, and speed. One summer afternoon, during what was supposed to have been a friendly water balloon fight, I smacked him between the shoulder blades with a big one. He wheeled around and grabbed up a metal hose nozzle. I was running fast when I saw him wind up for the hurl. I leapt into the air to elude the rocket, but it nailed my right hip and I came down writhing. It had been a skillful shot, no doubt about that: throwing as hard as he could, he had hit the center of a moving mass at perhaps forty feet. I still have the crescent-shaped scar on my hip.

Although we settled the matter without resorting to adult mediation, he never apologized for it. Aside from this and a couple of less serious episodes, Monte did not have much to apologize for. Still, I don't recall one instance in those early years when he ever apologized for any act, even in the face of threats and punishment. In addition to his rarely riled but devastating temper, he was obstinate: there was a point beyond which he would not budge, regardless of the consequences. Apology was something he would have to learn in adulthood.

When it came to stubbornness, Monte had a topflight role model in the person of our gristly Uncle Armen "Brick" Kiramidjian. The wiry, tattooed fruit-farmer smoked three packs of Lucky Strikes a day, flicking the ashes onto his pocked wood floor, despite the protestations of the women of the family. He guzzled his own homemade wine, too. It was amber, slightly milky, and smelled like kerosene. He never bothered to strain out the gnats before bottling his vintage, but it went over well with his friends, just the same.

We spent many a weekend afternoon and part of our summers at Uncle Brick's "ranch" at the corner of Chestnut and Jenson streets, surrounded by forty acres of table grapes and free-range peacocks. Sometimes our second cousin Stacy would hand us the reins to her pony and we would trot around bareback. When the thermometer rose to the hundreds in the afternoon, all the cousins would splash around in a mud hole fed by an irrigation pipe near a eucalyptus tree.

Back in Visalia, we found ourselves in less pleasant predicaments from time to time. Once, as Monte and I were playing catch in a field, an Anglo kid pedaled up on a fancy Stingray bicycle and announced that Mexicans were not allowed on the field. That boy was looking for a fight: everyone knew full well that the polite word for Mexicans was "Spanish." Although he had clearly thrown down the gauntlet, I felt at cross-purposes: on the one hand, I was not about to try my luck with this guy, he had several years on us (Monte and I were then ten and eleven, respectively), and a big physical advantage. But I did not care to leave the field with my tail between my legs, either. Fortunately, Monte didn't wait for his big brother to sort it out. He casually informed the bully that we were not Mexicans but—Hawaiians! I'm not sure how seriously he took his own claim: maybe he was thinking of the stories Mom had told us about teaching third grade at a sugar cane plantation in Paauilo, on the Big Island, before she was married. Or maybe Monte was just bluffing himself and his brother out of a pinch. At any rate, the bully, suddenly confronted by a couple of swaggering *malahinis*, retreated in confusion.

As far as our ethnic background was concerned, we had this vague sort of understanding that we were Armenians. But what that meant wasn't clear: outside of the kitchen, our parents weren't especially informed about the subject, and there were no grandparents around the house to fill us in. Our only living grandparent was Mom's mother, Grandma Jemima, and since 1964 she had been living at an old folks' home east of Fresno in a eucalyptus grove behind a rickety cedar barn that looked like a shipwreck. Almost every weekend for three years, until Grandma's death, Mom would usher us into her room and we would kiss a cheek that grew paler and gaunter with each passing week. Then we would run outside to catch bluebelly lizards.

The home was full of brittle Old Country types — gnarled Armenians with a language and tears we didn't understand. They played pinochle, and one of the best players was a man with pointy ears who had a head like a medicine ball, and a permanent scowl. Moneybags, they called him, and he was rumored to have buried riches someplace, maybe in the Old Country. Several of the crones rocking on the porch had weird blue tattoos on their chins and the tops of their hands. Another old lady in black, Mrs. Cloud, also had a tattoo, but it was on her forearm. She claimed that it was her own handiwork, that she had punched it into her own skin using a nail and an ink of ashes mixed with spit. The tattoo read: 1915.

"*Eench unem?*" She asked in her mother tongue, "What else could I do?"

Mrs. Cloud did not otherwise seem insane. So it was hard for Monte or me to decide what to think of such stories.

A Riddle

S omewhere in the back of his mind, Dad wanted to get back into farming. After making a bit of money on the stock market in the late 1960s, it seemed the time had come. I was twelve and Monte was eleven in early 1969, when Dad asked us whether we would prefer to trek through Europe for a year or to move to a house on a ten-acre emperor grape vineyard near the Sierra foothills. With visions of horse trails unfurling through trellises, we loudly endorsed the vineyard idea. Besides, we didn't want to leave our pets and our friends for a year in boring old Europe. Our vote, however, counted for little. Mom and Dad had both been afflicted with itchy feet since youth.

Dad drew out the money he had put aside for our college educations, packed us into the yellow Buick, and headed east on Highway 10. In New York we boarded our first airplane — an Icelandic Airlines propjet headed for Keflavik. A few days later, in Luxemburg, Dad picked up a Volkswagen camper with an oval international license plate, and for the next fifteen months we wandered 41,000 miles through forty-one countries in Europe, North Africa, and the Middle East. We sometimes slept in hotels, but more often Dad would pull into a campground or an empty field beside the road. One morning we woke up in the middle of a Gypsy camp. Our parents shared the camper's foldout bed, Maile slept in the hammock in the pop-up top, Marcia slept in a hammock slung across the front compartment, and Monte and I shared an orange canvas tent. After some practice, we could pull the tent off the luggage rack and pitch it in about five minutes.

In Amsterdam, Dad introduced himself to a big, mustachioed rug merchant whose name, as it appeared on the sign over his establish-

ment, ended with an "i-a-n," like ours. Pleased to meet fellow Armenians in that city of strangers, the merchant invited us into his store for coffee. Seated on the low couch called a *sadir*, and surrounded by rugs and hookah pipes, he was jovial enough, until the conversation turned to his family history. Then his face suddenly darkened, as he described a scene of Turks stabbing family members with swords and bayonets. He pressed the palms of his hands together and raised his eyes to heaven, in mock prayer: "The priest told them they'd be saved if they prayed." He shifted his gaze to Monte and me and then sawed one hand across the other, as if carving salami: "The Turks came to the church and butchered them there, while they were kneeling in prayer." Then he leaned forward and spat out: "*God* killed them! *Jesus* killed them! The *cross* killed us!"

Monte and I sat frozen in embarrassment for this man's blasphemy. We looked at Dad. Though not a churchgoer, he had seemed at all times to be on cordial terms with "the Good Lord." On this occasion, though, he just drew his lips against his teeth and looked sad. Dad didn't talk about these things much, but he once told us that our Old Country ancestors had been killed because their religion forbade them to fight back. We imagined sheep kneeling under an axe blade. It was not clear whether Dad considered this sort of behavior admirable, stupid, or both.

The further south we drove, the cheaper food got. We settled for a few months in an apartment in Spain, at El Grão de Castellón, a fishing town on the Mediterranean Costa del Azahar.

One drizzly afternoon, Monte and I ran with the bulls in Burriana, a town just south of Castellón. I'm not sure why our parents, normally so strict, had allowed us to climb over barricades into narrow streets with rampaging bulls. Not even the most permissive fathers of our wildest friends would have allowed such a thing. But Dad was one of those people who liked to repeat the dictum that begins "When in Rome..." and he might have thought that running with bulls was a rite-of-passage for Spanish boys. At twelve and thirteen years of age, though, Monte and I were the youngest members of the all-male crowd of runners.

Suddenly, somehow, we found ourselves alone, sprinting down a narrow street, pursued by a lean young bull. We ran hard, looking for a ledge to jump on, somewhere safe from the bull's horns. When we came to a cross street, Monte ran straight ahead, but I ran to the right.

Turning the corner, I slipped and fell on the wet cobblestones. I looked up, as the bull came around the corner. It stopped and lowered its horns. I remember the animal's pathetic and beautiful eyes, the wet muzzle, steam from its nostrils, and the sound of raindrops on the cobblestones. Less than a moment later, Monte ran up to the bull, waving his arms. It turned and trotted after him. I had seen a bull fatally gore a *matador* in Zaragoza, and so I was pretty sure that my quick-thinking little brother had saved me from grievous injury, at the least. We regrouped, clambered over the barricades, and never ran with the bulls again.

Dad arranged for us to take Spanish-language lessons at Academía Almi, a small technical school in Castellón. Once during conversation practice, our teacher, a pretty college student we addressed as Señorita Blanca, turned to Monte and asked "*¿De donde vienes?* Where are you from?" Monte responded that, of course, he was from California. Señorita Blanca cocked her head. We didn't look like the towheaded American kids in the movies. "I mean, where did your *ancestors* come from?" she asked. By this time, Monte and I probably could have pointed to a spot on a map of the Near East. But what stumped me, and probably him, too, was that this young lady, a Spaniard whom we had known for weeks, had suddenly revealed that her image of us was not at all like our image of ourselves. She did not view us as the Americans we had always assumed we were. The rest of that day, and in the days and months to come, Monte pondered Blanca's question *Where are you from?*

In the spring we packed up the camper and hit the road again, this time heading east, towards the Holy Land. Somewhere on the road between Italy and Bulgaria, Mom resolved to make the trek to her ancestral town in Turkey. The old folks had called the town Marsovan, but the map showed only a Merzifon. By this time, Monte and I were curious. To the extent that either of us had grasped anything of our "ethnic heritage," we had been mildly embarrassed about it. To us, the Old Country was a dark, stale place that we associated with bitter, wrinkled olives, weeping old women, and cigars on Uncle Jack's breath. But now we wanted to take a closer look.

When Dad explained to a tourist official in Istanbul why he needed road maps of eastern Anatolia, the official shook his head gravely and issued a one-word travel advisory: "Kurds!" Recently, Kurds had stopped yet another bus to shake down the passengers at gunpoint. Long-distance calls were not going through because Kurds in telephone company uniforms had cut down several kilometers of phone line and reeled it up to the mountains, where they were holding it for ransom. They had attacked policemen, too. When it became clear that Dad was determined to make the trip, the tourist official advised him at least not to travel after sundown.

Monte found it amusing that these Turks nursed such a dread of Kurds. Kurds, it seems, were born mean and did not bathe often enough. They were Turkey's *bandidos*, its Comanches, its bad conscience. On the basis of all the nasty stories we heard about Kurds in Turkey, Monte took an instant liking to them. Like Joaquin Murieta's gang of California Robin Hoods, the Kurdish bands might also have been pursuing a program loftier than mere larceny.

To Monte's chagrin, we still had not encountered any ferocious brigands by the time we arrived in Çorum, hundreds of miles northwest of Kurdistan. We spent the night in that town, where the men wore baggy pants with cleverly placed holes in the pleated crotches. Early the next morning, after rice pudding for breakfast, we set out to the northeast. From Çorum it was only forty miles to the dot on the map designated "Merzifon." It was a sunny Friday morning, and the road wound through fields of opium poppies. Boys herding buffalo by the side of the road munched poppy bulbs as if they were apricots.

We were still hundreds of miles west of the ancient land of Armenia, but this part of Turkey was what Mom's side of the family called the Old Country. This was it!

As we approached Merzifon across meadows where sheep had grazed for centuries, neat houses and tile roofs stippled one hill and then several, like red and white lichen. I didn't notice the city wall, which had been so prominent in turn-of-the-century photographs of the city. A government pamphlet reported the population of Merzifon as 23,475 — about the same as Visalia's population when we had left a year earlier, and about the same as Marsovan's population eighty years earlier. Among the 10,000 Armenians in Marsovan at the end of the nineteenth century was our maternal grandfather, Misak Kiramidjian. His future wife, our Grandma Jemima, spent the first three years of her life there, too, until 1883, when her father hauled her off to Fresno, 8,000 miles away.

On top of a hill on one side of the town stood a cluster of large European-style buildings. This at one time had been Anatolia College, founded by Yankee missionaries. As a child, Misak had dreamed of enrolling in the college, but as he reported many years later, an avaricious brother-in-law had dashed his dream by "taking me out of school and keeping me in his store for eight years as a very young boy with no pay." Mom and Dad had wanted to take a look at the campus, but the former college was now an army garrison, and visitors were not welcome.

Driving into Merzifon's central square, Mom recognized the little clock tower, still ticking seventy-four years after Misak had left the city. It was just as her father had described it. Dad pulled over to record the scene on Super-8 film. A dozen years later, this scene appeared in a documentary film about immigrants in Fresno. In the course of blowing Dad's film up to 16-mm and converting it from color to grainy black-and-white stock for the documentary, the footage looks as though it were shot sixty or seventy years earlier. But even viewing the original color footage, it's hard to fix a date to the scene: a horse-and-carriage taxi, a donkey with a saddle, and passers-by in the baggy pants called *shalvar*s float in and out of the frame like tropical fish.

By the time Dad returned his camera to its case, a huddle of men and boys were ogling our exotic camper. We sightseers were the spectacle, and they, the "natives," were the curious on-lookers. Scanning the square, Mom noticed several pinkish garments hanging out to dry near a low brick building. They were the same as the bathrobe her mother, our Grandma Jemima, had used as a tablecloth for special occasions! Mom scrutinized the building with the robes hanging from it. Grandma Jemima had heard her parents describe Marsovan's domed bathhouse, or *hamam*, and she in turn had described it to her daughter, our mother, with remarkable accuracy.

One passer-by, noticing Mom's interest in the bathhouse, suggested that if she wanted a bath, there was a newer facility down the street. Mom, however, was interested in the old *hamam*. She and our sisters proceeded to the women's side and entered the antechamber, which was dark and steamy and smelled like a church. Sleeping babies hung from nets like hams curing in a smokehouse. The main room contained a shallow pool, where a burly woman was bearing down with both fists on a younger woman's scalp, working sweet-bay soap into her hair, as if kneading bread. For generations women had gathered here to relax, gossip, and arrange marriages. Heaps and heaps of soft skin had slid over the marble pool enclosure, rubbing it smooth and shiny. Mom recalled hearing that women from the wealthier families enjoyed the privilege of sitting nearer to the spout, where the water was clear and hot.

By the time Mom and our sisters emerged from their self-guided tour of the bathhouse, Dad was relearning the half-forgotten Turkish he had spoken as a boy in Fresno. Monte and I stood to the side self-consciously, while Dad talked with the curious townsmen who had gathered around our camper. One of his interlocutors might have recognized the word *Ermeni*, "Armenian." In any case, someone shouted to another man: "Go get Vahram." I remember being surprised that townsfolk would readily have identified one of their fellows as an Armenian. The second man returned with Vahram Karabents, a slim man in his fifties. Speaking Armenian, he invited us to his house.

Karabents climbed into the front seat to give directions. The camper bounced through narrow streets of packed dirt and cobblestone bordered on both sides by the walls of houses. Every now and then, we would glimpse a large wooden door at the end of a side street. Monte leaned towards the window of the camper. It was easy to see the outlines of crosses that had been crudely chiseled off the doors. In fifty-five years, those who had moved into the houses of their massacred or deported Armenian neighbors had not bothered so much as to refinish these doors properly, to plane down the chiseled-off crosses, or even to paint over the splintered evidence of prior ownership!

When Mom told Karabents that her parents were both from Marsovan and mentioned their family names, he recognized several of the names and knew where they lived. He directed us to Grampa Misak's old family home, and we gazed at it from the street. It was a corner house, just as the old folks had described it. The first floor was built of stone and plaster, and the top story was of wood and plaster. A balcony with a grape arbor hung over the street. The thick, ropelike vines that twisted up to the arbor looked as though they might have been planted by its previous residents, sixty years earlier. Though the house was poorly maintained, it clearly was occupied.

Mom and Dad were more than curious, but a house tour was out of the question. It would have been worse than awkward to knock on the door and ask the current residents for a tour of the house — especially if they turned out to have moved in after its original owners, Mom's forebears, had been deported or killed.

Further down the street, Karabents pointed out the place where Grandma Jemima's family home had stood before it was burned down. Only a wall remained. As we turned a corner, Monte noticed a strangely familiar structure behind another wall festooned with gaudy movie posters. It was unmistakably an Armenian church, with its steep roof, transepts, and curved apse. Or at least it *had* been a church. More recently, it seemed to have served as a movie house, although it didn't appear to have been in use for a while, even in that capacity. If Monte did not know then, he found out later that both of Grampa Misak's parents had been buried in the yard of an Apostolic church in Marsovan, where our Grampa's father had served as a married priest. So perhaps the remains of our great-grandparents lay in that very churchyard, surrounded by faded movie posters.

When we arrived at Karabents' house, our host led us through the front gate. Chickens skittered across the courtyard. Karabents' wife Ardemis and his mother Hripsime welcomed us, their unexpected guests, into their hearth. It was spotless, with a dirt floor wiped shiny with brooms. Our hosts appeared to be genuinely happy to see us. We were visitors, yes, and for this fact alone we deserved effusive Middle Eastern hospitality. Their congeniality, however, was of the special sort that Armenians reserve for their compatriots.

We took our seats on low couches. In the corner was a sink on a low platform. Karabents' wife lit a fire in a brazier and drew water from a hand pump into a copper kettle with a long handle and a tapered neck. This kettle, or *jazvah*, was identical to the one Mom kept on top of the stove at home. Our host heated tea water, and in keeping with custom, she served Mom and Dad immediately.

Karabents was a cooper who had fallen on hard times. No one was buying wooden kegs anymore, so the family survived on remittances from a son working in Germany. At some point, one of our hosts mentioned that their family name used to be Ben Ohanian. Dad asked, and they denied that they faced any discrimination from their neighbors. On the contrary, they got along well.

But who or what did our hosts consider themselves to be? Their neighbors knew them as *Ermenilar*, Armenians, but their hearth provided little evidence of this. There were no Madonnas, crucifixes, or saints on the mantle. On the other hand, there were no Muslim adornments, either—no verses from the Qur'an or photos of Mecca. There were little more than a few rugs, some lace, and some copper trays. Our hosts didn't speak Armenian in the streets, of course. But it was not clear that they spoke Armenian at home, either. For all we knew, this was the first time in years they had uttered those hard consonants, so different from mellifluous Turkish.

Our hosts claimed that there were no Greeks at all left in Merzifon, and only three Armenian families. Then someone, either Mom or Dad, asked why it had changed. Karabents' aged and bent mother looked genuinely puzzled. "One day all the Armenians left, and we found ourselves with only Turkish neighbors." She wiped the palms of her hands against each other, then held them up for us to see, and leaned back: "I don't know how it happened."

Mom and Dad had an idea how it happened: they had heard the stories the old folks in Fresno had told. They knew why Merzifon had the same size population in 1970 as it had eighty years earlier: there was the little matter of the massacres and deportations of Armenians that had taken place in the town periodically, between 1894 and 1918. What baffled us was how these few Armenians and no others had remained in Marsovan after it had become Merzifon. And this led to a scarier question: what had they done to survive?

Mom and Dad finished their tea and announced that it was time to leave. There were no campgrounds in Merzifon, so we would have to drive fifty miles to the Black Sea port of Samsun before sundown. Back in the idling camper, Karabents gave Dad directions to Samsun, while Mom bade her last goodbyes to our guests. Just then, an old woman patted Mom's arm as it rested on the passenger-side window. The woman opened her thin hand and held it out. She was begging for money. In our shiny camper and Spanish shoes, we must have presented a good prospect for a few coins. But who did she think we were?

The beggar was just an old woman, wearing rags in the town of her birth. Yet were it not for the fact that her tribe had deported and massacred our ancestors, we would not have been looking down at her from the seats of that camper. Indeed, she herself might have benefited in some way from the outrages. For all we knew, her father, uncle, or brother might have pilfered a clock, a rug, or a bicycle from an abandoned house. Maybe she had enjoyed a movie or two at the church-turned-cinema. Or perhaps, as a result of deportation and massacre, she could sit in warmer water at the *hamam*. Indeed, she herself might with her own hands have ...

Suddenly, Dad's eyes flashed. He raised the back of his hand, in a threatening gesture. "*Yok!*" he shouted, "No!"

Mom glowered at her husband: she was just an old woman!

Dad turned away from the old woman and twisted the steering wheel with his fists: how many Armenians in Marsovan fifty-five years earlier had begged for their houses, for their lives, for the lives of their children? And now this old Turkish woman was begging coins from *us*?

That evening, we pitched our tent in an empty campground outside Samsun. A warm breeze was blowing. My brother and I lay on our backs as the sun set and listened to the call to prayer from a minaret in the distance. Months later, after returning to the town of our birth, we would feel out of place. Perhaps the feeling would exceed the reality, but even downtown would seem smaller and dustier than we had left it.

Two years after the visit to Merzifon, Mom received a letter from a lonely old lady living in a retirement home in Nicosia, Cyprus. Sirouhi Benlian knew the Kiramidjian family from Marsovan, where she had been raised, and she had gotten our address through Mom's older brother, Uncle Ludwig. Her letter, dated September 6, 1972, confirmed dark suspicions. It read, in part:

> You mention the name Ben Ohanian, and that only three families remain in Marsovan. I suppose you do not know why only three families remain out of the 17,000 Armenians who were massacred and deported in the cruelest manner, according to Turkish government order. Ben Ohanian was a spy, a traitor. The Turkish government promised to save his life and those of his family if he acted as a spy. So Ben Ohanian went through the streets from morning till night, with a Turkish policeman. He pointed to the houses where Armenian men were kept so that they may be sent to the mountains, valleys and deserts to be killed in the cruelest way. He betrayed Armenian women, saying they had money and jewelry. Thus women were left without the means of subsistence. He betrayed Armenian girls, because Armenian girls were raped & some were forced to marry Turks.

The eagle, according to the proverb, is killed with an arrow guided in its course by her own feathers. Sirouhi wrote that once, she and a Greek companion had been making their way through a street in Marsovan, when a gendarme in the company of the traitor had ordered them to stop. "Ben Ohanian" — probably the patriarch of the Ben Ohanian family — "must have betrayed me," she wrote, because the gendarme had accused the girls of being daughters of the Benlian family. Sirouhi, who had happened to be dressed like a Greek at the time, denied her Armenian parentage, and began to speak Greek with her companion. "With God's help," she added, "I even scolded them." Meanwhile, two "well-dressed Turks" who had happened on the scene assured the gendarme that Sirouhi was indeed a Greek. Ben Ohanian and the gendarme apologized and went away. As for the "well-dressed Turks," the letter continues: "… they were speaking about the Armenian massacre & deportations, and I heard one say to the other: 'The salt of this town were the Armenians.'"

Years later, long after Sirouhi's letter had confirmed our suspicions, Monte described the visit to Merzifon as a pivotal event in his life. His wife Seta once explained to a journalist that her future husband "saw what he had lost" that day. She may have been right, although I don't recall him reacting dramatically to the events as they were taking place. And later, when he and I compared recollections of Merzifon, I don't remember him ever having condemned the Karabents family either. Not even their patriarch, "the traitor Ben Ohanian."

For my part, I doubt that Monte had had an epiphany in Merzifon. Perhaps what he had confronted that day, or in solitary reflection some time thereafter, was a riddle—the intolerable ambiguity of a defaced wooden door, a hearth with a bare mantle, and an old woman holding up the palms of her empty hands.

Stories of Forebears

When we returned to California in the late summer of 1970, Monte cut himself off from former playmates and set out to answer Señorita Blanca's question: *where did you come from?* At the threshold of his teens, he started reading the *World Book Encyclopedia* and the Bible, and voluntarily attending the American Presbyterian Church. The fruit of his early research took the form of a rambling but sternly moralistic jumble of book-learned history and stories of places visited. Every now and then he would raise his head from his writing-pad to ask my opinion about a passage. "Instead of writing 'bad,'" I shrewdly counseled, "write 'imperialist,' or 'totalitarian.' Something like that." After poking the last period into his pile of papers, he plopped 100 pages of scribbly cursive onto his eighth grade teacher's desk. The dumbfounded teacher scrawled a red "A+" at the top of the first page and probably didn't even bother reading the thing. I don't recall the essay's title, but it earned my brother a Good Citizenship Award from the American Legion. His head was barely visible above the podium when he accepted the citation.

For a while, Monte and I considered a career as priests. As descendants of "the first Christian nation," I suppose we felt especially qualified and responsible to spread the Good News. We were already convinced that Copernicus and Darwin had barred Aquinas' rational route to faith, but after reading Miguel de Unamuno's *La agonía del cristianismo* in Mrs. Ortiz's Spanish literature class, Monte was ready to go the route of Saint Benedict or Kierkegaard, to commit "intellectual suicide" for the sake of salvation. But he was not willing to be taken for a chump. In the course of several seasons, the golfers at First Presbyterian and the fashionable Jesus Freaks at our high school sapped our ardor. What the heck did their Yankee-Doodle flag-waving have to do with the carpenter from Nazareth, anyway?

Monte fixed his gaze firmly on this side of eternity and redoubled the search for his origins, weaving himself, his grandparents, and their parents' parents into an unbroken narrative that wound back through the ages, from the San Joaquin Valley to the Armenian plateau. According to Herodotus, we were descendants of Phrygians who had migrated from Thrace to Asia Minor. Whatever the factual merits of this story, it seems to have met the need of some Armenians who liked to think of themselves as long-lost Europeans, rather than western Asians. But Monte came to accept a more recent account, which made him a descendant of hill tribes native to "the lands of Nairi," around Lake Van in what is today eastern Turkey. Around 870 BC, leaders of these hill tribes established a unified state with the capital at Tushpa, the site of the modern-day city of Van. The Assyrians called this state *Urartu*, which might later have evolved into *Ararat*, as in Mount Ararat, the biblical resting-place of Noah's Ark. Around 590 BC, the invading Medes destroyed the central government of Urartu, and according to the account that Monte came to accept, the earliest Armenian kingdoms rose from the ruins of that state.

Down through the centuries, Persians, Romans, Byzantines, Arabs, Seljuks, Mongols, and Ottoman Turks invaded, fought over, and divided Armenia. By 1375 the last independent Armenian kingdom had fallen, and invaders had come to outnumber Armenians throughout most of their ancient homeland. Foreigners ruled, yet generations persevered into modern times as they had for centuries, plowing, sowing, and reaping.

In his early teens, Monte began to think of his grandparents' lives and his own life, too, as an extension of this saga. But clearly, his connection with his ancestors consisted of something other than a pure bloodline: Dad's side of the family had broad-faced, narrow-eyed Mongolian features; some of Mom's cousins were freckle-faced redheads, and Armenians from the town of Kharpert had a reputation for being so swarthy that Fresno Armenians referred to their Black neighbors as "People from Kharpert." Years later Monte concluded that, "In centuries past, as today, culture rather than genetic lineage has come to define the Armenian people, the Armenian nation."

For all his emphasis on "culture" rather than genetics, it might seem strange that he would write: "Like many other Armenians I don't speak

Armenian, but I consider myself an Armenian." By his early teens, in any case, he had resolved to learn the language. Before bounding off to school in the morning, he would open his grandmother's velour-bound New Testament and read out a couple of pages line-by-line. He didn't understand the words he was reading, but at least he taught himself the angular Armenian script that had helped preserve his tribe's identity ever since the fifth century.

Like Greeks, Bulgars, and Arabs, Armenians, too, describe their five centuries under Ottoman domination as the darkest of dark ages. In the latter half of the nineteenth century, tensions grew between Ottoman authorities and the subject nationalities of the empire. And so it was that, in 1895, Turks in Marsovan attacked their Armenian neighbors, pillaging stores and houses, and killing 109 townsfolk. The pogrom in Marsovan was part of a much wider series of massacres, which in turn was a prelude to even bloodier massacres twenty years later. It was the last round of massacres, from 1915 to 1918, that Sirouhi Benlian mentioned in her letter about "the traitor Ben Ohanian."

Mom's father, Missak Kiramidjian, survived the pogrom in Marsovan, but spent three months in prison because of his involvement in what he later described as "a secret Armenian revolutionary society." When his jailers released him from prison, they ordered him out of the land of his birth. So on March 9, 1896, he boarded a French ship at the Black Sea port of Samsun and left behind what he described as the "snake pit" of Old Country politics. In keeping with the Armenian dictum, *Oor hats, hon gats*, "Go where the bread is," he ended up in Fresno, where he bought a ten-acre muscat vineyard and cured his first crop of raisins with advice from Old Country friends. There, too, he married Jemima Seropian, who presented him with three sons and one daughter, our mother, who was born on August 16, 1920.

Years before Misak arrived in Fresno County, his future in-laws had already built a small commercial empire there. Documents at the County Hall of Records indicate that Jacob Seropian, Grandma Jemima's uncle, was the first Armenian to buy land in the county. After working at odd jobs in and around Worcester, Massachusetts for several years, Jacob headed west on the advice of a doctor who prescribed a dry climate for his respiratory complaints. When he stepped onto Fresno's plank sidewalks in 1879 or 1880, it was the hot, dusty home of only a thousand souls.

Mom stood guard over Jacob's reputation as the patriarch of the Armenian colony in Fresno, firing off indignant letters to journalists who reported that some other clan—the Nishikians or the Normarts—had settled there first. Monte, however, never shared her eagerness to claim Jacob as an ancestor. To him, his great-greatuncle was just one of the first of a long line of emigrants who managed to swindle themselves out of their heritage in exchange for a mess of pottage called the American Dream. Monte preferred the rough red Esaus to the smooth, clever Jacobs: those who refused to leave their homeland until they were forced out might have shown less foresight than the early emigrants, but Monte valued stubborn attachment to land over that sort of prudence.

Jacob's brothers and half-brothers, four of them in all, joined him in Fresno in 1881. Soon they began writing letters to friends and relatives in Marsovan, describing Fresno as a Garden of Eden where grapes grew to the size of a fist, eggplants weighed in at ten pounds, and watermelons swelled to the size of canoes.

To Mom, the story of Jacob's half-brothers, George and John, was as dramatic and instructive as anything that moved the pen of Horatio Alger: with money the brothers had made peddling fruit on the streets of Fresno, they began packing raisins and figs. By sulfuring the figs and curing them in a salt solution and steam, they could ship them with minimal spoilage to distant markets. When the Southern Pacific Railroad raised its freight charges, John Seropian calculated that it might cost him less to haul his fruit to San Francisco by mule team. He and his brother hired twenty mules hitched to two wagons, loaded them with seven tons of figs, raisins, and oranges, and sent the caravan 210 miles over the Pacheco Pass to San Francisco. The San Francisco *Examiner* sent a reporter and a photographer to document this "bold protest" against Southern Pacific's greed, and the news spread far and wide. Other farmers followed the Seropian example, and before long sugar baron J. Claus Spreckels subscribed $2 million to build a competing railroad. The new San Joaquin Railroad reached Fresno in 1896, breaking the Southern Pacific monopoly in the valley.

At the height of the season, the Seropian brothers employed 800 workers, packing and shipping fifteen carloads of dried peaches, apricots, pears, plums, raisins, or figs a day to markets in Chicago and points east, including England, Holland, France, and Germany. Their empire, however, was short-lived. After a series of lawsuits, differences with business partners, and inexplicable fires, they lost their packing house in 1904.

Everyone, of course, has illustrious ancestors with poignant life stories. The stories about Mom's side of the family were supposed to end in triumph of one sort or another: the triumph of Jacob Seropian, the lone pilgrim who lived just long enough to welcome his Old Country kin to the New Eden; the rags-to-riches saga of the Seropian brothers, who beat the Southern Pacific monopoly and rose from the status of street vendors to become owners of an enormous packing house; and the miraculous survival of an ancient people, delivered from death in the Syrian desert to the verdant San Joaquin, where, by dint of hard work, thrift, and foresight, they overcame native prejudice to reap their rewards as raisin packers and green fruit farmers.

Upon closer inspection, though, these stories seemed to mask futility and lives lived too long: George and John Seropian lost their packing house and were reduced to the status of a hermit and an employee of a rival fruit shipper. The sons and daughters of the pious "pilgrims" from Marsovan shrugged off church-going altogether, and an ancient Christian faith that had persevered throughout sixteen centuries of persecution evaporated like dew under the San Joaquin sun. And even Jacob, who died before his thirty-sixth birthday, had spent the last years of his life homesick for the Old Country and full of self-pity.

Compared to Mom's side of the family, Dad's side was anything but illustrious. Mom used the word *adep-sus*, Turkish for "uncivilized," to describe her in-laws. As far back as anyone can remember, our Melkonian forebears had been peasants, so when Dad's parents came to America, they naturally worked in the fields. Although they spoke two or three languages plus a little Kurdish, they never learned English, and they never learned to read or write in any language. They signed mortgages with unsteady Xs.

Dad's father, Ghazar, was an orphan who was born around 1875 in the village of Kharasar, near the town of Kharpert, in the heartland of ancient Armenia. Shortly after his fourth birthday, his older brother sold him as a bonded servant to a sheep farmer. Faced with induction into the Turkish army during the Balkan wars, Ghazar, his wife Haiganoosh, and the two of their five children who had not died of tuberculosis hopped aboard a French ship at the port city of Samsun. Arriving in New York in 1913, Ghazar bought a big bag of bread for their train trip across the new continent. By the time they reached California, the bread was so hard that they had to soak it in water to break it.

The family moved into a clapboard water tower on an acre of farm-land outside Fresno. Haiganoosh's eighth and last child arrived before the midwife, so she delivered it herself on the kitchen floor. She cut the cord, washed and nursed the infant, buried the placenta, mopped the floor, and had a hot meal on the table by the time her husband came home from the fields that evening. They named the child Garabed, after one of their three children who had died of "consumption" in the Old Country. That was April 27, 1919. As the baby of the family, our father was spoiled: he didn't have to start picking figs until he was four years old. On the first day of school the teacher asked the barefoot boy his name. An older sister, who by then spoke some English, answered for him: "Charles." From then on, he answered not to "Garabed" but to "Charlie".

The Melkonians pruned, picked, and packed whatever crop was in season: grapes, apricots, peaches, figs, tomatoes, and — worst of all — the acidic okra that left fingers cracked and bleeding. In the evening, Dad's mother would listen to Turkish singers on the old phonograph and sigh, "How can people so cruel sing so sweetly?"

Ghazar's watchword was *hamperootyoon*, patience. He died on September 1, 1948 in the back seat of his daughter's '38 Chevy, with a bag of peanuts in his lap and a peaceful smile on his face. Monte loved Dad's description of old Ghazar, squatting on his haunches in the evening hours, rolling cigarettes and chuckling as he watched Meli, his beloved Guernsey cow, graze. My brother never saw a photograph of Grampa Ghazar, but he carried this mental picture with him throughout his life.

As much as Monte enjoyed these stories, it was the larger national narrative that fired his imagination. He scoured bookshelves for additional information, starting with our parents' library. Somewhere between *Robinson Crusoe* and *The Human Comedy*, he found a dusty book entitled *Armenia and Her People, or the Story of Armenia by an Armenian*. The author, Reverend George H. Filian, had been an old friend of our maternal grandfather, Grampa Misak. Filian's book appeared in 1896, just as Sultan Abdul Hamid's campaign of annihilation of his Armenian subjects wound down. His description of a massacre at the mountain town of Sassoun is by no means the most lurid passage in the book:

> They tortured their victims like Indians or Inquisitors, in every fash-ion of lingering death and torment that makes the heart sicken and the blood run cold to read of. Crucifying head downward, and pouring

boiling water or ice-cold water on them, leaving them so till death came; flaying alive; cutting off arms, feet, nose, ears, and other members, and leaving them to die; thrusting red-hot wires into and through their bodies. They pulled out the eyes of several Christian pastors, said "Now dance for us," poured kerosene on them and burned them to death.

Fourteen-year-old Monte sat alone in a dark room and read the book from cover to cover. For a couple of days he was quieter than usual. The salacious descriptions of Turkish sadism did not disturb him as much as the descriptions of the "piteous," "hysterical" passivity of the victims. Filian likened Armenians to cattle, lambs, and chickens, and when farm-animal similes did not suffice, he ploughed the vegetable kingdom: Armenians were "fodder"; Turks cut off their heads like onions, "plucked" them, and crushed them "like grapes during the vintage." What struck Filian as admirable about Armenians — that they "sharpened their intellects rather than their swords"; that they "learned to make money" and refused to "train themselves in the use of arms"; that they embraced missionaries and European dress; that they hid behind "the great Christian powers" and exulted in "refinement" and "delicate sensibilities" — all of these behaviors struck Monte as ignoble and disgusting.

A quarter million Armenians died in the massacres Filian described, and four times that number would soon die in another round of massacres launched by another Turkish regime. 1915 — the year that Mrs. Cloud, the lady in the old folks' home, had carved into her forearm — was the year the second round of massacres began. It was the year Mrs. Cloud had seen her father, brother, husband, and son chopped with axes, and it was the year the military police marched her into the Syrian desert to die. And the old ladies with the blue tattoos? They were death-march survivors, too: Kurds, Circassians, or Bedouins had picked them up in the desert, adopted them, and tagged them with tribal tattoos. Later, these women fled from their adoptive tribes one by one and ended up in Fresno, each with her own untold story.

Mom's predecessors had left the Old Country before the first round of massacres in the 1890s, and Dad's predecessors had left just before the second round, from 1915 to 1918. For years we had assumed that both sides of the family had survived fire and sword, and had crossed the rivers of blood more or less unscathed. In time, though, Monte discovered that this was not true: Grampa Ghazar's village, Kharasar, had disappeared from the maps, along with dozens of other Armenian villages in the district of Dersim, as well as the entire Armenian Quarter of Kharpert. Mom's side of the family included early casualties of the purifying century, too: in a letter of November 10, 1972, Sirouhi Benlian, the old lady in Cyprus, described how one of Mom's aunts "... was lying very sick in bed, and the devil Turks—wolf Turks—broke the door of the house and cut her body into pieces while alive!" The aunt's husband and their only child, a son, were murdered, too, and a brother and other family members disappeared, never to be seen again.

"You know," Mom once said, lowering her voice to a near whisper, "If those terrible massacres hadn't taken place, you kids would not have been born in this wonderful country." Aside from this, Mom and Dad maintained near-total silence on the point. Mom's comment had made me wince, and I suspect it had had the same effect on Monte, too. Her point, I suppose, was that we should thank our ancestors for their sacrifice for us. But didn't Mom's claim in some strange way make the "wolf Turks" the unwitting instruments of our bright futures in America? And if so, wouldn't that mitigate their crime, at least to some tiny degree? But this thought was intolerable.

Life in the Walnut Capital of the World, moreover, did not strike Monte as adequate compensation for the damage done. It astonished him that, after a regime had killed more than a million people and deported the survivors from their own homeland, there didn't appear to be anything in the way of compensation or even consequences for these crimes, and no movement to reclaim the stolen land.

Apparently, Monte was not the only one to feel this way. One morning I showed him a story that had caught my eye in a local newspaper: on the afternoon of January 27, 1973, an old man had rung the switchboard operator at the Biltmore Hotel in Santa Barbara, to report that he had just killed two men. Mehmet Baydar, consul general of the Republic of Turkey in Los Angeles, and vice-consul Bahadir Demir, lay in expanding puddles of their own blood, both shot in the head with a .38 revolver in sunny California, a three-hour drive from Fresno. The assailant, Kourken Yanikian, was a man in his seventies who, according to the reporter, had never forgiven the Turks who had decapitated his brother and killed twenty-three members of his family.

Monte skimmed the newspaper story, his forehead knitting tighter with each line. Then he set the paper down without comment.

PART TWO

Departures

4

The Open Road

I n the fall of 1972, when I was sixteen, my buddy Frank and I were
doing footwork for the United Farm Workers union, the UFWA,
which was organizing contract-renewal strikes. It seemed like the
right thing to do: our native Tulare County was one of the richest counties in the San Joaquin Valley in terms of farm production, but it was
one of California's poorest counties in terms of persistent poverty. The
county's poorest residents, of course, were (and are) the farm workers
who produced its wealth. Fresh from the picket lines and wide-eyed, I
would describe to my brother scenes of County Sheriffs in powder-blue
shirts clubbing strikers, and of union storefronts peppered with bullet
holes. Monte would listen but would barely raise an eyebrow. At the
age of fourteen, he had his nose in the encyclopedia and his mind on
other things.

Monte kept his hair short and his nose out of trouble, and to his eter-
nal credit, he never donned the *de rigueur* flare-leg pants. His record of
sobriety was almost unblemished, and would remain so throughout his
life. He had been drunk only once in his life, on *sangría* during a long
lunch in Spain, and he had never so much as touched a tobacco cigarette to his lips, let alone one of the marijuana cigarettes that so many of
his classmates carried in their shirt pockets. Austerely attired in sneakers, jeans, and a tee shirt, he strode with a long, brisk gait through
French IV, trigonometry, Hobbes, Locke, and Pascal. In tenth grade, he
charged an astronomical twelve dollars an hour for private math tutorials, and earned as much in a couple of evenings as I earned all week
loading trucks with a forklift before and after school.

By the end of Monte's sophomore year in high school, his teachers reported that he was bored. Having completed all of the coursework by mid-term, he would just sit in the back of the room whispering with exchange students in Spanish or French. The school principal suggested that he pack off to college early, but Dad demurred: his second son was already one of the youngest kids in his class, and there was no need to rush things. It was then that Dad's friend, Roy Sumida, struck on the idea of sending the likeable kid as an emissary to Visalia's sister city in Japan, Miki City, a tool-production center near Osaka. Monte, for his part, was excited by the prospect of living on his own in a foreign country for a few months. Mr. Sumida made the arrangements by ham radio, and so in the summer of 1973 the fifteen-year-old boarded a Japan Airlines flight for Tokyo.

For the next months, he spent evening hours sparring and practicing karate with the Miki City police department. He learned that when he fixed his eyes on a distant point, his extended fist could support a seemingly unbearable weight. He also studied traditional fencing, or *kendo*, and received as a gift from his instructors a suit of armor with "Melkonian" written in *romanji* script across the lacquered breastplate. His study of *bushido*, the warrior's way, reinforced his conviction that self-discipline and hard work, rather than bounce and bluster, were keys to sustaining spontaneity and a truly individual style.

At the end of the sister city stint, Mom and Dad received a letter from Monte, informing them that he would be spending the coming year with a friend's family in Osaka. After a few months in Osaka giving private English lessons, Monte had put aside enough money to take a jaunt through Southeast Asia. In a breathless letter posted in early March, he noted that in Singapore, "The contrasts between the old & new, Chinese & Indian, & poor & rich in that place was too much to believe." The next stops were Malaysia, Thailand, and then "the filthiest, stinkiest place in that area," Vietnam. At barely sixteen years of age, Monte knocked around Saigon while artillery thudded in the distance and the National Liberation Front closed in. When Monte left Vietnam, he left behind another lie: he hadn't met anyone there who had even pretended that the Yanks had come to fight for their freedom.

In Hong Kong and Taiwan, Monte ate "turtle soups and baked snakes like crazy," as he described it in a letter to the folks, then he headed to South Korea. There, he stayed a few days at Sung Kwang Sa, a Seon Buddhist monastery near Seoul, where the monks spent most of their time reading sutras, meditating, and chanting.

The abbot of the monastery, a slight, bespectacled priest with a feathery white goatee, presented his guest with a robe and dubbed him *Koma Henji*, "Egg of a Monk." It was the first of a long series of sobriquets that Monte would receive in the coming years. The abbot liked the Egg: few others at the monastery were ready, as this strange boy clearly was, to climb a hundred-foot pole and then take a step into thin air. It must have been a letdown when Monte declined his invitation to stay at Sung Kwang Sa to become a full-fledged monk. Before Monte left, the old priest dipped his brush in ink, painted the Chinese character "Buddha" in bold strokes on a large silk scroll, and handed it to Monte as a going-away gift.

A little over a month later, my brother descended the disembarkation ramp at Bakersfield Airport. He was wearing a batik shirt and a flight bag over his shoulder, and I noticed that he loped across the tarmac on the balls of his feet with a new, springy gait. No longer the second runner-up runt of the class, he now stood medium-height in a crowd of Yankees.

In the coming months, he completed his straight-A career in high school, took calculus, psychology, and American government courses at a junior college, taught Spanish at a private grammar school, and attended Dr. Sidney Chang's History of China course at Cal State Fresno. He lead the Mt. Whitney High School quiz bowl team to a twenty-two-to-twelve victory over cross-town rival Redwood High, and towards the end of the school year he received a Bank of America Achievement Award "for Distinguished Performance, the Promise of Future Success, and Service to Society."

Monte and his buddy Joel spent warm weekends rock-climbing at Mineral King and Sequoia National Parks and swimming in the Kaweah River. One day in the summer of 1975, the river's current swept him off his feet and he fell face-first onto a boulder, breaking his nose and a big chip off his front upper tooth. Henceforth, his ear-to-ear smile bracketed by dimples was something to behold, revealing as it did a big white triangular tooth, front and center.

In the last days of that summer, Monte entered the University of California as a Regents' Scholar. He began his studies as a mathematics and history double major, but after excelling in four higher math courses, he switched to an individualized major in Ancient Asian history and archaeology. He told me he had changed majors because he was "antsy" to graduate as soon as possible and to re-enroll in the school of life. So even as dozens of other brash young math whizzes in the Bay Area were setting the groundwork for the personal computer revolution and multimillion-dollar fortunes, Monte set out in a different direction, heading towards a less metaphorical sort of revolution. He would never look back long enough to regret it.

At the slightest provocation, Monte would toss a toothbrush and a few history books into a flight bag, sling it over a shoulder, and head for the highway. While his fellow students were poring over textbooks in the library, he would be hunkered down on a freeway on-ramp, headed north or south between San Francisco and Mexico with a cardboard sign announcing "ANYWHERE BUT HERE." To him, as to Basho, Whitman, Jack London, and other poets of the road that he read, freedom was first and foremost freedom of movement, and the best picture of freedom was the open road.

Once, Monte and Joel hopped on a flatbed train car in the Oakland freight yard and showed up in Los Angeles eighteen hours later covered with soot from head to toe, their hair sticking out like wattle. At the end of the journey, Monte described being jolted awake by a long, piercing whistle and opening his eyes in pitch darkness, to find himself on his back, hurtling through a tunnel. He held his hands in front of his face, but could see nothing. "For a split second," he reported to me still awed, "I was sure I was dead! I thought, 'So *this* is what it's like to be dead!'"

Long before his second year at Berkeley, Monte had already identified himself as a "diasporan Armenian," an Armenian living outside the historic Armenian homeland. Accordingly, he did not describe himself with the standard ethnic designation "Armenian-American," but instead used the term "American-Armenian." It seemed trivial at the time, but in retrospect it's clear that for him the substantive in his self-description was "Armenian." His American nationality—the recent result of accident and genocide, both in the Old World and in the New—was just a dead-end detour, or even a "false identity," as he put it more than once.

Monte would always have a hard time convincing ultra-nationalist Armenians that his "patriotism," as he called it, had nothing to do with membership in a Chosen People. On the contrary. Before he was twenty, he had traveled enough roads and read enough books to have figured out that most people on Earth were poor, voiceless, and dispossessed in one way or another. Subservience and oppression were the normal state of affairs in Asia, Africa, Latin America, and Ireland.

Those who were *not* normal were the rulers and beneficiaries of the wealthiest and most powerful empire ever, the United States of America. Thus, by placing his tribe, the Armenians, in the large camp of *victims* of Chosen People and divinely anointed nations, Monte was connecting himself to a global community of peoples that was much larger than the Yankee nationality of his birth and citizenship.

These were heady days for a brash and astute young man. The example of Vietnam was ever-present in Monte's thoughts, and it appeared as though the winds of freedom were filling red sails from Angola to Nicaragua. Reports of strikes, armed clashes, and mass demonstrations in Turkey, notably the huge May Day, 1977 demonstration in Istanbul's Taksim Square, seemed to confirm the growing strength of revolutionary forces in that country, too. Meanwhile, something was stirring just to the east of Armenia: Iranian students at Berkeley buzzed with the rumor that the Shah of Iran's Peacock Throne was tottering. If the unthinkable were to happen—if in the coming years Shah Reza Pahlavi's CIA-installed tyranny in Tehran were to fall—this would have an uncertain but in any case enormous impact on the entire region, including Turkey.

Change was in the air, so as a matter of provision Monte began attending a Turkish language class. The accent, declensions, and vocabulary came easily to him, and he learned to his surprise that much of the background noise at family get-togethers and at the old folks' home had in fact been Turkish, not Armenian.

Monte met Turkish students through the language class, but he kept a reserved distance: their internationalist rhetoric, he suspected, masked a leftist variety of Turkish nationalism, or worse. He could not forget the betrayals of the past—and in particular, the fact that the Young Turks who ordered the genocide in 1915 had come to power promising reform and claiming friendship with Armenians. Monte had more sympathy for the Kurds, who had been rebelling long before we had trekked through Anatolia from Merzifon seven years earlier. But he couldn't ignore the fact that some Kurds, too, had helped massacre Armenians. Left to their own devices, he concluded, Turkish and Kurdish revolutionaries would never concede anything but bad-faith pledges to Armenians.

Monte's mistrust of Turkish and Kurdish revolutionaries, together with the feeling that storm clouds were gathering over Iran and Turkey, instilled in him an increasingly urgent feeling that "time is not on our side," as he put it more than once. It seemed to him and to many of us that Turkey was already teetering on the brink of the insurrection, and that "Sooner or later," as he wrote, "there will be a socialist revolution in Turkey." Indeed, Monte was desperately worried that the revolution would take place *too* soon, before Armenians could muster their own forces to back up their demands when the dust settled. He was not yet clear what those demands should be, but he was sure that there should be demands.

Because times seemed so desperate in 1977, Monte seized all the more eagerly on reports of attacks against Turkish officials, embassies, and airline offices in Europe by mysterious assailants calling themselves "The New Armenian Resistance," "The Armenian Secret Army," and "The Justice Commandos." The newspapers described the attacks as terrorism, but Monte preferred the term *armed propaganda*. In half-whispered discussions with pacifist Armenians at Berkeley, he argued that Turkish diplomats were legitimate targets of such attacks. After all, as representatives of the Turkish government, those diplomats were direct beneficiaries of the Armenian genocide, even as they continued to deny that the genocide had ever taken place. Moreover, the regime they represented had slaughtered thousands of Kurds, destroyed their villages, criminalized their language and culture, and jailed and tortured thousands of dissidents, both Kurdish and Turkish. Those diplomats hadn't been born into their offices: at some point, each one of them had made a decision to do what he was doing, and to stand for what he stood for. It was entirely fitting, then, that they should be held accountable for their decisions and actions. Indeed, it was an outrage that they had gotten away scot-free with so much evil for so long.

When the Armenian pacifists claimed that such attacks were pointless, Monte insisted that they served the very useful purpose of "waking up" the youth. And when the pacifists objected that the attacks would turn public opinion against Armenians, he replied in his emollient voice that the Turks never seemed to fret overly much about international condemnation. They hadn't fretted much when they butchered Armenians and stole their land, nor when they slaughtered Kurds, or annexed Arab Iskenderun, or invaded northern Cyprus, or bullied Greece in the Aegean. They simply went ahead committing their crimes and getting away with them, one after another. So, evidently, public opinion wasn't worth very much: "We should just ignore public opinion and do what we've got to do," Monte concluded.

In fall 1977, a couple of Berkeley students, including Armen S., one of Monte's pacifist friends, sent out mailers announcing their intention to reactivate the hitherto-dormant Armenian Students' Association (ASA) on campus. A few days later, when thirty or so students arrived at the university's Tan Oak Room where the first meeting was to take place, a scruffy youth in rubber sandals met them in the hallway and handed each a packet of explosives recipes photocopied from the *Anarchist Cookbook*. In the second issue of the ASA newsletter, contributor Judy Sanoian recalled the scene: "Who can forget what was, for most of us, our first glimpse of Monte, passing out xeroxed bomb literature at the first ASA meeting. You have to admit, it made an impression."

On October 3, 1977 at 3:50 a.m., a blast blew the front door off the Brentwood residence of Stanford J. Shaw, a history professor at UCLA. The improvised pipe bomb shattered the door, blew a three-foot hole in the wall, broke windows, threw bricks and stucco into the front yard, and scattered books around the living room. Fortunately, no one was injured. "I guess I gave too many Fs last quarter, huh?" Shaw quipped to reporters, before canceling his classes and taking a leave of absence from the university. But low grades probably were not the reason for the blast: Shaw and his wife had recently published a two-volume *History of the Ottoman Empire and Modern Turkey*, in which they described the wartime genocide of Armenians as a myth concocted by "Entente propaganda mills and Armenian nationalists."

FBI agents and police investigators snapped into action. They questioned dozens of Greeks and Armenians in Los Angeles and the Bay Area, tapped phones, read mail, infiltrated ASA meetings, and threatened non-citizens with deportation. Needless to say, Monte was a prime suspect in the bombing. His self-inflicted *coup de grace*, of course, was the open distribution of bomb-making instructions, but he had probably attracted police attention months earlier, due to his association with Cypriot, Iranian, and Palestinian activists at Berkeley. In any case, the investigators came up empty handed — and for good reason: as far as I know, Monte had no connection to the bombing in Brentwood.

Even as the police and FBI tried through intimidation and thinly veiled threats to isolate radicals like Monte, events conspired to anger and embolden his peers. In those days, one of the main concerns of the student association was an obscure "study of genocide" prepared by the United Nations Commission on Human Rights' Sub-Commission on the Prevention of Discrimination and Protection of Minorities. Paragraph 30 of the study mentioned Armenians as the first victims of genocide in the twentieth century. Turkish authorities had taken it upon themselves to demand that the reference be deleted from the final study. Many ASA members were at first bewildered and then infuriated, when "their" US government joined Ankara in opposing Paragraph 30.

Armenian students became more assertive on the Berkeley campus. At a January 16, 1978 meeting of ASA executives, Monte proposed that they sponsor a small display of books, photographs, and cultural artifacts at U.C. Berkeley's Doe Library. As soon as the library accepted their proposal, Monte and ASA President Jack Zarkarian set about collecting material for the exhibit. When the display opened on March 17, it consisted of several cases filled with yellowing books, old photographs, and a few other borrowed artifacts relating mostly to handicrafts, architecture, and church history. One of the display cases contained information about the Armenian genocide.

The display did not attract much attention until a Turkish student noticed it and alerted the Turkish Consul General in San Francisco, Mustafa Asula. The Consul promptly telephoned head librarian Richard Dougherty, and asked him to remove all material relating to the genocide. Passing through the lobby a couple of days later, Monte noticed that part of the display had disappeared, and that the emptied display case had been filled willy-nilly with items removed from other cases.

University spokesperson Ray Colvig defended Dougherty's action, describing the display as "inflammatory." Monte, in turn, pointed out that library officials had reviewed and approved all the material in advance, including the items they had later removed. When it became clear that university officials would not replace the items in the display case, Zarkarian, Monte, and other ASA members responded by setting up a card table in front of Sproul Hall, with photographs and photocopies of the censored material.

The display on the card table in front of Sproul Hall drew much attention from passers-by, and soon other campus groups joined the protest, too. Eventually, the Academic Senate's Committee on Academic Freedom agreed that "external political pressure" had been exerted on the library staff, and that such pressure constituted an infringement on academic freedom. A few days before the exhibition's closing date, library officials replaced the confiscated display items. When the dust settled, Dougherty resigned as head librarian and Asula was transferred to Libya.

Some ASA members viewed the Doe Library controversy as a moral and public-relations battle of epic proportions. Monte, however, dismissed it as little more than a brief distraction from his thesis research and preparations to graduate. By mid-March, he had resigned from the ASA, to concentrate on completing his graduation thesis.

Monte completed his undergraduate coursework and his honors thesis in two and one-half years. Barely twenty years old in the spring of 1978, he was now ready to move to "a higher level of commitment," either as an archaeologist or as a militant in an as-yet unspecified "armed struggle." For a while, it was not clear to me which path he would choose: archaeology or armed struggle? What was clear, however, was that both paths required fieldwork. And as he indicated in a letter to his sweetheart ten years later, he was eager for that:

> There are people who think they can understand a situation from afar. I'm not one of them. It is true that you can understand a lot of things by reading and listening to other people, and get an idea. But that's not enough. To really be able to understand, you should have experience, you should live through it.

When the department of archaeology at Oxford University accepted him as a doctoral student, one might have thought that the question of archaeology or armed struggle had been resolved in favor of archaeology. But this would have been too hasty a conclusion. As Monte explained to me at the time, archaeological fieldwork would be the perfect cover to reconnoiter in eastern Anatolia, to gain a detailed knowledge of the terrain, languages, and resources at hand, and in that way to prepare the ground for the armed struggle—whatever that would entail. I concluded, then, that my brother wanted to pursue both paths, archaeology and armed struggle, simultaneously, the former as a means to the latter, in the manner of that earlier Oxford student and enemy of Turkey, T. E. Lawrence.

One hundred objections immediately leapt to mind, of course, including doubts that the Republic of Turkey would ever permit the firebrand of the Armenian Students Association at Berkeley to conduct research in Urartuan archaeology there. Such "details" notwithstanding, Monte had at least set his priorities. A dozen years later, he explained his reasoning:

> For me, everything was so simple and logical that it was even mathematical: diasporan Armenians live outside Armenia because the genocide took place, and they were obliged to leave the country.

Today, they can't go back because the Turkish government has a colonial, exploitative, chauvinist, and genuinely fascist nature. Therefore, our nation should carry out an armed struggle over there, in order to achieve any tangible rights. And every Armenian patriot, including me of course, should go and participate in that struggle.

"Yes," he added, "it was that simple for me."

Simple or not, what strikes me as remarkable about my brother's account of how he set out on his path is that it consists entirely of calculations of what he *ought* to do. It is as if there were no doubt in his mind that, once he had determined what his trajectory *should* be, he could and would stick to it, no matter what. In this instance, however, it was much easier to determine what should be done than to do it. Especially since Monte, this California Quixote, this kid barely out of his teens, had concluded that the right course of action was to join non-existent battle ranks to fight one of the largest and most powerful armies on earth.

Pilgrimage

O ne mid-April morning in 1978, an engineering student answered a knock on the door of his second-story flat in Bromley-by-Bow, in East London, to find a young man standing there in "some sort of Mexican shirt," as he later described it. "Hi! I'm Monte Melkonian, from the US," the stranger blurted. "I'm Vahé Berberian's second cousin. He said you'd be happy to see me."

Nejdeh Melkonian opened the door wider and replied that yes, he was indeed happy to meet the stranger. The self-invited guest had the gift of bad timing, though: he had arrived unannounced just a few days before Nejdeh's first-year engineering exams. Still, they were both Melkonians, and sameness of surname called for hospitality, even in the absence of any evidence that they were remotely related.

When Nejdeh welcomed him in Armenian, Monte could only return the greeting with an embarrassed smile. Nejdeh's eyes narrowed, as he wondered what sort of compatriot couldn't even respond to a simple greeting in the mother tongue. Monte's red-faced reaction, however, convinced Nejdeh that the visitor felt terrible about not speaking Armenian. Monte spoke Spanish and Japanese nearly fluently; he read French and spoke some Turkish, too, but he still couldn't speak more than a few words of his mother tongue. The task at hand, as he · explained to Nejdeh, was to learn the language in short order.

Nejdeh invited the stranger in, and Monte rehearsed his itinerary, such as it was: he knew from experience in Spain and Japan that the quickest way to learn a language was to immerse oneself in the culture. His first destination, then, should have been the Soviet Socialist Republic of Armenia, the smallest of the fifteen republics that made up the

Soviet Union. There, even the Russians spoke Armenian. So far, though, his attempts to obtain a Soviet visa had failed, so as an alternative he had decided to hitchhike to Athens and then to catch a flight to either Tehran or Beirut, depending on the price of the airfare. Only after inspecting the large and embattled Armenian neighborhoods in both of those cities would he decide where to stay longer, to learn the language.

Learning the language, however, was not the only reason for heading to the Middle East. "I try to be as logical as possible in deciding how to participate in our struggle," he explained to a friend years later:

> I just looked at a world map, saw that Turkey has no border with the USA, and noticed that in 2 nearby countries (Lebanon & Iran) there were 2 large Armenian communities already engaged in their own self-defense and more closely implicated in our patriotic struggle. So I very logically decided that to maximize my efficiency in the struggle I had to go to that region.

These communities were "implicated" in the coming struggle, presumably, because their proximity to the Turkish-occupied Armenian homeland made them ideal recruiting grounds—and perhaps launching bases, too—for the clash he envisioned.

For the next four days and three nights, Nejdeh ignored his impending finals and Monte cancelled his visit to Oxford University, as they discussed life and the coming "patriotic struggle." Finally, Nejdeh accompanied his new friend to Dover, where Monte hopped on a ferry to Calais.

One week later he reached Lebanon. Arriving in Beirut on April 15, 1978, he lugged his pack across the dilapidated terminal lobby and then hailed a taxi that zigzagged around bomb craters under fluttering green and red banners. Militiamen at a checkpoint waved the taxi through the no-man's-land near the sandbagged National Museum at the Green Line crossing, and suddenly the green and red banners disappeared, replaced by white banners that read: "Syrian occupiers out of Lebanon!" and "Say No to the destructive Left!" Here, then, were the two sides in the Lebanese civil war: the loose coalition of leftists, Muslims, and Palestinians on the west side of Beirut, and the Gallicized right-wing "Christians" on the east side. Before long, Monte would discover that the array of parties in the Lebanese civil war was more complex than these labels implied.

Crossing the bridge over the Beirut River, the taxi crawled with the traffic down narrow Mar Yousef Street and pulled to a stop in front of a shabby storefront, literally a hole in the wall. Monte yanked his bags out, loped through the open door, and introduced himself to a smiling smoker behind an orange formica counter. Daniel M., the thirty-some-thing proprietor of Pholidisc, made his living selling bootlegged audiocassettes of popular music. A friend of a friend in Los Angeles had given Monte his address as an initial contact in Bourdj Hamoud, the Armenian quarter in east Beirut. Daniel put his guest up for a couple of nights, while he arranged for other accommodation. Soon, the newcomer began spending nights at a nearby Armenian militia post, the Nigol Touman Club, on the eastern edge of Bourdj Hamoud. There, he practiced field-stripping a Kalashnikov blindfolded (a feat school-boys in Lebanon could perform in a few seconds) and learned the lay of the land. After a couple of weeks, the younger militiamen at Nigol Tou-man Club came to accept Monte as a comrade in arms, a fellow guard in the Armenian militia

With a population density of 60,000 inhabitants per square mile, Bourdj Hamoud and its environs were home to some 150,000 Arme-nians, or about 80 per cent of the neighborhood's population. Officially, the three main Armenian parties — the Social Democratic Hunchaks, the liberal Ramgavars, and the ultranationalist Dashnaks — had proclaimed themselves neutral in Lebanon's civil war. Despite their official neutral-ity (or rather *because* of it), the residents of Bourdj Hamoud depended for their security on the armed vigilance of the Armenian militia, which protected Bourdj Hamoud against the right-wing militias that sur-rounded the neighborhood on all sides except the sea.

The Armenian militia was small and it lacked the heavier armaments of its adversaries: unlike the other militias, the Armenians set up no roadblocks, they kept their rifles out of sight during the daytime, and their guards wore no uniforms, opting instead for disco slacks and tight shirts. But what they lacked in firepower, they made up in their reputa-tion as fierce fighters, a reputation Monte would confirm soon enough. In other ways, though, the Armenians of Bourdj Hamoud fell short of Monte's expectations. Instead of the race of tough, cool combatants that big-talking immigrants in California had described, he found a tribe of insomniacs who spent their days haggling, dreaming of America, and spoiling their sons with candy-coated almonds and spaghetti westerns.

For their part, some of the older guards at the Nigol Touman Club eyed the newcomer with the suspicion reserved for adventurers who have come from afar to "experience" the daily danger that the natives had long since grown sick and tired of. Or was there another reason why he had left California, the fantasy destination of most of Lebanon, for this embattled slum? Rumors circulated that he was on the lam, that he was dodging a debt, that he was a CIA agent, a KGB agent, or the agent of some other nefarious group. The janitor at the guard post even whispered that he was "from the BBC." Others—perhaps most of the adults he met—concluded that he was a fool, rather than a knave. Understating the point a dozen years later in his autobiographical *Self-Criticism*, Monte wrote that "… it was a little difficult to gain the confidence of some Armenians" in Lebanon.

The disappointments only fueled Monte's impatience. He was still sleeping on someone's sofa when he began hatching plans to prepare for that unspecified but imminent patriotic struggle. It occurred to him that Ainjar, an Armenian village in Lebanon's Bekaa Valley, would be the perfect site for a military training camp, a destination for recruits. He had visited Ainjar with his parents eight years earlier, and since then he had reconstructed it in his imagination as a new Sparta. Its inhabitants, after all, were the proud descendants of the 5,000 men, women, and children who in 1915 had defended their summit of Musa Dagh, Moses' Mountain, above their ancestral villages near the Gulf of Iskenderun in southeastern Turkey. For fifty-three days (not the forty days of Franz Werfel's 1933 novel, *The Forty Days of Musa Dagh*), they had resisted the Turkish onslaught, until, on the morning of September 12, 1915, they flagged down a French warship, the *Guichen*, which evacuated the survivors to safety. Eventually, the French government relocated them to Ainjar, a malaria-ridden swamp at the foot of the Ante-Lebanon Mountains in the Bekaa Valley. In short order, the refugees built houses along neat streets and turned the swamp into a trout farm and orchards. With such a heritage, Monte reckoned, the descendants of these refugees were prime candidates to host a recruitment center for "the patriotic struggle."

At the first opportunity, he caught a ride with a friend headed to Ainjar. From the summit of Sannin on the Beirut–Damascus highway, the green-and-gold quilt of the Bekaa Valley resembled the view of the San Joaquin Valley from the Tejon Pass. Descending from Sannin and crossing the valley headed east, the conical cupola of an Apostolic church loomed into view above green apple orchards, framed by the graceful arches of a ruined eighth-century Arab palace. This was the village of Ainjar.

Monte pitched his training camp idea to Vahé Ashkarian, the village chief: the village council, he suggested, should set aside several acres of land for a collective farm, or *kolkhoz*, which eventually would support itself by agricultural production. When not farming, youths from Beirut and all points of the diaspora would receive military training and a proper patriotic education.

Ashkarian listened politely, and then referred the crazy kid to Sarkis Zeitlian, a Dashnak Party boss in Beirut. When Monte met with Zeitlian in Beirut a few days later, the portly honcho did his best to suppress a smile and then dispensed vague assurances that only inflamed Monte's impatience. Behind Zeitlian's condescending grin, however, Monte discerned fear.

These were perilous times for Dashnak leaders: for decades, their party had been the main political force in Bourdj Hamoud, but now the largest right-wing force in Lebanon, Pierre Gemayel's Phalangist militia, was challenging their power by demanding protection money and political supremacy over the Armenian neighborhood. Meanwhile, "armed propaganda" attacks against Turkish targets by mysterious Armenian assailants were churning up the emotions of the most committed sons and daughters of Dashnak families. For decades, Dashnak folklore had glorified young avengers like Arshavir Shiragian and Soghomon Tehlirian, who half a century earlier had assassinated high-ranking Turkish officials responsible for the Armenian genocide. Now, upstart hit squads, notably the Secret Army, were loading pistols again, adding new verses to the old ballads, and leading children away from the Dashnak fold like Pied Pipers.

In the face of these woes, Dashnak leaders were not overjoyed when an unkempt Anglophone proposed that they create a new center of militancy smack in the middle of their fiefdom, Ainjar! Such were the times, though, that they could not simply laugh off Monte's proposal. The party's bases of support in the large Armenian communities of Iran, Syria, and Lebanon were eroding as a result of political upheavals and emigration to the West. In this charged atmosphere, restive members of the party's own Youth Federation liked the training camp idea when Monte described it to them. So if Zeitlian were to reject the proposal outright, he would further damage the party's waning reputation as the guardian of the national cause. Under these circumstances, Zeitlian apparently decided to string Monte along until he cooled off or disappeared, as the hotheads always did.

And sure enough, Monte did disappear: after seven unproductive weeks in Lebanon, he left for Iran. There, he hoped he would have better luck applying for the Soviet visa he had failed to get in Beirut, thanks to poor phone lines and the gun battles that had closed the Soviet embassy on the western side of the city.

Arriving in Tehran for the first time, Monte found himself in an atmosphere very different from the chaos of Lebanon. Tehran was eerily quiet and orderly. A clerk at the Continental Hotel directed the newcomer to Sipan Union, a Dashnak community center, where his new friends addressed him as "Saro." Apparently, some of the local Dashnaks who had been in contact with their counterparts in Beirut suspected that the pseudonym was an attempt to conceal the fact that Monte was the same young man who had been giving party officials headaches in Lebanon. But actually, his new friends at Sipan Union had simply "Armenianized" his name: the word *sar* means "mountain," and hence "Saro" was a close-enough approximation to "Monte."

Monte soon found out that the Armenian community in Tehran consisted of two distinct class milieus: a petty-bourgeois milieu, centered around the affluent neighborhoods of Vila, Firdauzi, and the northern sections of the city, and a working-class milieu, located in the gritty, crowded neighborhoods of Zarkesh, Heshmatieh, and Majidieh. The working-class Armenians lived among Muslims and mixed Farsi words with their mother tongue. Their petty-bourgeois compatriots, by contrast, considered themselves more European than Iranian, even though their families had lived in Iran for centuries. At their wedding receptions, tuxedoed baritones transformed shepherds' songs into booming arias.

Since Monte did not come across as a crazy person or a loser, rumors spread among the staid types that he was evading arrest in his country of birth, or that he had come to shop for a "pure" wife to take back to the States. Others suspected that he was a provocateur or a spy. Among working-class boys, however, the feeling was different: Monte, a college graduate from the United States, had left the land so many Iranians yearned to reach, to live among them in the country of their birth. His presence in their homes and neighborhoods ennobled these familiar places and reassured them of the significance of their own daily lives.

Monte's most immediate priority, even before learning his mother tongue, was to repay a student loan debt of $2,000. Indebtedness was a form of dependency, and he hated dependency. He soon landed an English-teaching job at the Iran-American Association language school on Los Angeles Street in downtown Tehran. The director of the school paid native teachers poorly, but foreign teachers like Monte received the rather high wage of seven dollars an hour.

As the summer passed, Monte's letters began to reveal second thoughts about graduate school. In a letter to his parents dated July 29,

1978, he wrote: "My plans for next year have been changing a lot." Mom started to worry.

At about this time, Monte decided to renew his expiring Iranian visa by exiting the country and then re-entering it with a new visa. But where could he exit the country? The northern border with the Soviet Union was all but sealed, and the western border with Iraq was a battlefield waiting to happen. After the run-in with Consul Asula in San Francisco, furthermore, he was not about to cross into Turkey. So he set his sights on the next-nearest border — the border with Afghanistan. Early in the month of Ramadan, he stepped onto a rickety bus packed with pilgrims headed east. Most of the passengers were making a 500-mile journey to the third-holiest site of Shiite Islam, Imam Reza's tomb in the city of Mashhad, near the Afghan border. They might have assumed that their travel mate, with his beard and broken Farsi, was a fellow pilgrim from some hinterland village. Monte reinforced this impression by hopping down at bus stops to join them in prayer by the side of the road.

From Mashhad he bussed it another 200 miles over rocky terrain to Herat, in Afghanistan, and from there the bus bumped over another 600 miles of rocks to Kabul, where he took care of his visa business. Before returning to Iran, he visited Bamyan, which he described in a letter to his parents as "one of the most impressive ancient sites I've ever seen." "The two huge (44 meter) rock-hewn Buddhas with the fresco-covered caves all looking out on snow-capped mountains and a weathered Mongol fort were almost like Disney World," he wrote. He would have been disgusted to learn that twenty-three years later, the American-supported Taliban would deface the frescos in Bamyan and demolish the magnificent fifth-century sculptures.

In all, Monte had spent less than a week in Afghanistan, but the journey and the country had made a big impression on him. "I've learned a lot about Muslim brotherhood," he wrote to me a few days after returning to Tehran.

In another letter not long after that, he described the "most amazing things" he had witnessed after returning to Tehran:

> The demonstrations in Tehran involved about half a million people who walked through the streets throwing flowers to the police and kissing the police on both cheeks while saying "Brothers don't kill brothers." I watched this demonstration for three hours and the police were crying. Two police were crying so much that they got on their motorcycles and deserted their posts.

The country was standing up against the invincible Shah! A few minutes after eight in the morning of Friday, September 8, 1978, as Monte and a couple of friends were returning to the neighborhood of Zarkesh, a wave of humanity suddenly swept into them head-on. Monte and his friends sprinted against the current, until they arrived, panting and wide-eyed, at Jaleh Square, in southeast Tehran. The square smelled like benzene and appeared to be sprinkled with sawdust. "Bodies were all over," Monte reported in another breathless letter to his folks. Later, he learned that the Shah's soldiers had opened fire on thousands of demonstrators in the square that day, spraying them with assault rifles, while Cobra helicopters hovered overhead. The letter continued, admixing common accusations with first-hand testimony:

> Bulldozers went in and scooped corpses into dump trucks, which took them to a huge hole where they were all buried—some people were wounded, but not dead when they were buried. After the bodies were removed water trucks sprayed the streets, and by the next day you couldn't tell anything had happened (except for broken windows).

As news of the Shah's massacre at Jaleh Square spread, so did strikes by thousands of oil workers. The massacre had set a cold fire burning in Monte and now the unthinkable was suddenly thinkable. As soon as he had saved enough money to settle his student loan debts, it was time to settle a score with his boss, the imperious director of the Iran-American Association School, who had been paying native Iranian teachers poorly and was taking bribes. Monte approached other teachers and proposed that they jointly demand a minimum monthly salary. When the director heard about this he tried to bribe Monte into silence, but the fledgling labor organizer only redoubled his efforts. Finally, he convinced twenty-four out of twenty-eight teachers at the school to hand in their resignations. "Everyone at the school was just accepting the injustices he would pull until I straightened them out," he crowed.

Monte would like to have stuck around to witness the demise of the Shah, whom he described in a letter as "one of the biggest criminals in the world and certainly the biggest criminal in Iran." By mid-September, however, he had heard reports that things were "heating up" in Lebanon, as the Phalangists closed their grip around Bourdj Hamoud. Monte had other reasons to hightail it back to Lebanon, too: for one thing, Tehran was crowded and expensive. Besides, the Iranian Armenians' singsong dialect was unfamiliar, and he preferred the Western dialect that his grandparents had spoken. Most importantly, though, he had resolved to contact the Secret Army, the most active of the hit squads that were attacking Turkish diplomats. In its few short years of existence, the group had fired the imagination of young Armenians throughout the Middle East, sweeping aside five decades of political lethargy in the diaspora. It was time to check out the Secret Army.

Just before returning to Lebanon, Monte waited in a long line at a bank to withdraw $1,800 to pay off the last of his personal debts. The throng of frantic customers clamoring to exchange their Iranian rials for dollars was an omen of big changes to come. Monte packed his bags, caught a nineteen-hour bus ride from Tehran to Abadan, and then hopped on "a small, leaky 60 foot boat" for a thirty-seven hour jaunt to Kuwait. After a two-hour flight from Kuwait City, he arrived in Beirut on September 17, glad to be back.

Soon after Monte crossed the Green Line and plopped his bags down at Daniel M.'s flat, however, the Phalangists and their former allies, the Syrian Army, began lobbing artillery rounds at each other, and the shells from both sides rained on Bourdj Hamoud. As 155-mm rounds and Katyusha rockets smashed walls around him, Monte joined a huddle of civilians in the cellar of Airplane Building, a multi-story apartment building on the eastern shoulder of the Sinn el-Fil Highway. The building took its name from the crudely sculpted airplane that spanned the ceiling of the foyer. For eight days straight, from October 1 to 8, rockets and shells roared overhead like locomotives hurtling through a tunnel in both directions. When they slammed to earth, high-rises, warehouses, and factories folded flat like wet cartons. During lulls in the shelling, Monte and his fellow guards crawled out of the cellar with shovels, to help bury the dead in parking lots and fields.

After the echo of the last explosion, Monte emerged from the cellar again and scanned the rubble. It was hard to believe that the eight-day bombardment had claimed only 300 lives. Monte joined a cleanup crew, and when the last of the corpses had been scooped into garbage bags and hauled away, he landed a job as an assistant jack-of-all-trades, replacing shattered windowpanes, charging up stairwells with bags of cement on his back, and repairing roofs. He put his rock climbing skills to work, too, scaling the shakiest and most perilous heights, including the steeple of the Catholic church.

In late 1978, he began teaching English and coaching basketball at the Torossian Junior High School, an Evangelical school near Bourdj Hamoud. By this time, Monte had received rudimentary training with the Dashnak militia. He sometimes spent the night at the Nigol Touman Club, the Armenian guard post near the junior high school, but he preferred guard duty at Airplane Building, on the front line against the Phalangists. Perhaps thirty meters away, on the other side of the Sinn el-Fil Highway, stood a Phalangist militia center. During night watch at Airplane Building, Monte and the other guards would lean their Kalashnikovs against a wall and take potshots at rats with a pellet gun. The one who brought down the largest rat would treat the others to sheep's head soup at sunrise.

Monte did not have guard duty on the last day of 1978, when his friend Hagop Stepanian and Hagop's wife Manushag invited him to Ainjar for New Year's Eve. When the entourage pulled up to Manushag's family house that day, her second-youngest sister, Seta, opened the door to find a wild-looking young man in a blue jacket standing there holding a box of strawberries. More than anything else, she noticed his bright eyes. As soon as Monte laid eyes on her, his face lit up, despite himself. They introduced themselves, and she invited him in.

Seta stood nose-high to Monte and she was as sleek as a deer. Her fair complexion contrasted to her straight hair, black as obsidian, and large eyes to match. She had a long straight nose and strong, almost masculine hands. Monte liked the fact that she kept her nails short, and that she was wearing practical pants on New Year's Eve, instead of a frock. "How old are you?" he asked.

"Fifteen," she said.

Monte was surprised at how well this village girl spoke English. She mentioned that she sang in the church choir, too, and had helped to found a troupe that danced the traditional dances.

Monte frowned thoughtfully: "How old did you say you were?" He wasn't sure he had heard her right the first time.

"Fifteen."

She was a quick study!

Returning to Beirut after two nights in Ainjar, Manushag prepared yogurt soup for dinner. She knew that Monte loved that dish, but he didn't eat much. "Why no appetite?" Manushag teased, "Are you in love?" The question startled him and he paused to reflect on how his actions had so revealed his feelings. Whatever plans he had, they did not include falling in love. He reminded himself that he must remain single, footloose, and committed only to "the patriotic struggle" — a struggle which, parenthetically, did not yet exist.

One of Monte's buddies at this time was a skinny machinist and Kung Fu movie fan who swaggered down the streets of Bourdj Hamoud with a Chinese "potato-masher" grenade stuffed down his pants. I'll call him Basel, though this is not his real name. Basel personified working-class Lebanon: his arms were flecked with scars from the lathe to which he devoted his days instead of school, and although he was fiercely loyal to his ethnic community—in this case, the Armenians—he also nurtured a deep cynicism towards its chubby, complacent leaders.

At a pinball arcade one evening in early 1979, Basel introduced Monte to an urbane, neatly groomed young man named Alec Yenikomchian. Here was an unlikely trio: Basel, a scraggly high-school dropout with a grenade in his pocket; Monte, an eager California kid with a degree in archaeology; and Alec, the well-bred son of a respected physician.

Despite Alec's aristocratic bearing, he was a good listener and he had a sense of humor, too. A student of economics at the American University of Beirut, he would greet pretty classmates with a gallant half bow and a playful *Comment allez-vous, mademoiselle?* which he pronounced with a slight lisp. In his teens, he had hung out at pinball arcades with other members of the Dashnak Party's Zavarian Youth Group. As the sex banter had given way to discussions about the Palestinian resistance and the coming revolution in Turkey, their circle of friends had expanded. By his early twenties, Alec had connections in the Dashnak Party, the PLO, Kamal Jumblatt's Progressive Socialist Party, and who knows what else. He seemed at all times to have the inside scoop on intrigues in high places, and to conceal this knowledge behind a nonchalant poise.

Despite their different backgrounds, Basel, Alec, and Monte shared a feeling for the urgency of the times. When Alec declared that the coming years would be "the most crucial years in Armenian history since the genocide," Monte nodded his agreement. The Iranian revolution was shaking the balance of power in the region, and the Cold War had heated to a slow simmer along Turkey's eastern border with tiny Soviet Armenia, the last vestige of the ancient homeland where Armenians still controlled their own fate. Within the borders of Turkey, Maoists had declared "liberated zones" in eastern Anatolia, while strikers and demonstrators paralyzed the cities, and Kurdish guerrillas fanned out across the mountains. An opportunity was opening up—one unique and unrepeatable opportunity—to join the revolt against Ankara and to reclaim at least part of the ancient homeland Armenians had lost sixty-five years earlier.

Without fighters on the ground in the Republic of Turkey, however, Armenians would never be in a position to enforce their demands when high tide washed in, as it surely would. But where would the fighters come from? The few Armenians left in Turkish-occupied Armenia couldn't even raise their heads, let alone wage a war against the mighty Turkish army. Several thousand Armenians lived in Istanbul, 600 miles to the west of their occupied homeland, but they were hopelessly docile. Recruits for the struggle, then, would have to come from either Soviet Armenia or the diaspora. Soviet Armenia, however, would not openly support this war, at least in its crucial initial stages: Soviet leaders might love the prospect of "border rectifications" with Turkey, and they might love to remove Turkey from the NATO orbit, too, but the fear of an all-out war or a nuclear exchange along the highly militarized border with Turkey erased Soviet Armenia from the picture, along with the prospect of Soviet assistance.

That left the diaspora—especially the Armenian minorities of nearby Iran, Syria, and Lebanon—as a recruiting ground for the coming struggle against Turkey. Only youths in these communities had remained close enough to their land and culture to join the coming battle in large numbers. Thanks to war, economic problems, and poor leadership, however, young people were deserting these communities in droves, headed for distant Paris and Los Angeles.

To stanch the flow of emigration, and thus to safeguard recruiting prospects for the patriotic armed struggle, the youth needed inspiration and leadership. They needed an "armed vanguard," a militant organization that fixed its gaze on Turkish-occupied Armenian lands. Moreover, since the waves were washing higher in Turkey every day, the vanguard would have to be built *soon*. If they missed this unrepeatable opportunity, then the entire nation—not just the diaspora, but Soviet Armenia, too—would be condemned to increasing demoralization, emigration, and assimilation. "And if this happens," Monte concluded, "the white massacre of our nation will have succeeded." (He used the term "white massacre" to distinguish it from the bloody massacres that had claimed a million victims in the first two decades of the century.)

Thus, the stakes could not have been higher: the future of the Armenian nation—not just the diaspora, but the entire nation of 6 million people—depended on developments in Armenian neighborhoods in

Iran, Syria, and Lebanon in the next several years. However convoluted this line of reasoning may appear in hindsight, Alec and Monte had independently followed it to identical conclusions. The challenge, then, was to create an armed vanguard that would inspire and guide the youth—and to do so quickly.

In the spring of 1979, my sister Marcia and I stood on a highway on-ramp in Central California and stretched our thumbs to hitchhike to Los Angeles International Airport, 200 miles to the south. We were headed to Beirut to see our brother Monte. After a year of rumors that had placed him everywhere from the scene of a massacre in revolutionary Iran to a basement under rubble in Beirut, Marcia wanted nothing more than to see for herself that he was all right. My purpose, on the other hand, seemed less clear. Was I going to Beirut to bring my brother back to civilization, or was I going to join him on the edge?

Marcia and I caught a Freddy Laker flight from Los Angeles to London, and then bought British Airways standby tickets for the five-hour flight to Beirut. On March 24, our plane skidded to a stop on the pitted tarmac at Beirut Airport. We dragged our packs and suitcases through the vacant, cave-like terminal and then walked a while to find a taxi driver, an unshaven fellow in a natty jacket, for the ride to Bourdj Hamoud. When the driver heard our destination, he looked embarrassed and shook his head no. In his country, he explained, he could not drive the eleven kilometers across town for fear of being killed because he was a Muslim. He gave us a short lift to another unshaven fellow leaning against another old Mercedes, and asked the Christian driver to take us to east Beirut.

As we headed north towards the city, I stared out the window, trying to notice everything. Beirut had changed since our first visit in the Volkswagen camper nine years earlier. Back then, I hadn't noticed the tin roofs of Bourdj al Brajneh, the vast Shiite slum that sprawled out from the pines along the road from the airport. Now, the Holiday Inn was a sniper's nest, Colonel Sanders had a rocket hole in his face, and even the traffic cops carried assault rifles. Fresh water bubbled up through cracks in the streets from shattered pipes below, while the breeze blew the stench of raw sewage that washed onto the beaches. Shimmering Beirut was as beautiful as ever, though; perhaps even more beautiful, for all her vulnerability and suffering.

We passed the grim gunmen at the Museum crossing, and then the taxi crawled with the traffic down Mar Yousef Street, into the heart of

Bourdj Hamoud. When we arrived at the Pholidisc storefront, Monte's friend Daniel plucked the cigarette from his mouth and rose from his orange formica counter with a smile. After our greetings, I asked: "Where's Monte?"

"You never know where Monte is from one minute to the next," Daniel said, winking. The remark confused me, but I tried to keep a polite smile. He sent someone to locate our brother and invited us to his place for dinner. Once we made it to Daniel's flat, his wife made coffee and he sent a neighbor to pick up an order of take-out chicken. We had finished our coffee and half of the chicken by the time Monte finally strode through the door. He looked whiskery, wild, and happy to see us. We hugged and drank ouzo, and he introduced Marcia and me to friends who kept sauntering into Daniel's flat throughout the evening.

Towards the end of the evening, we thanked Daniel and followed Monte one or two blocks in the warm darkness to his six-story apartment building. Earlier that year, Monte had moved out of the Stepanian apartment into a comfortable apartment near to the school where he worked. As soon as he shut the door to his apartment, his mood changed from jovial to serious, and after Marcia flopped into bed he became downright morose. Opening a box from a closet, he showed me copies of extortion letters that he had sent to shop owners in the name of a Secret Army. "*What?!*" I shout-whispered, as a prelude to reminding him that the real Secret Army probably wouldn't be happy to discover that he was using their name in an extortion racket. He then pulled a Remington shotgun from the closet and explained that he had invested the extorted funds in firearms, to be used to advance the Secret Army's publicized aims. His eyes burned like embers through a glaze of welled-up tears, as he whispered, "We're planning something."

I gaped at him, stunned. "We"? Who was this "we"? "Good guys," no doubt. Wasn't that how he had described his Berkeley buddies to me—and me to them, too? Monte had a habit of exaggerating the virtues of his buddies, including his brave, brilliant brother, me. That much was clear. But now it sounded as though he was talking about joining some sort of group kamikaze operation!

Monte never filled me in on what exactly it was he had in mind. Perhaps he had no particular operation in mind at all. Perhaps he had simply curled his toes over the edge and was ready to jump—to bomb an embassy, to assassinate a diplomat, to hijack an airplane … to do anything, as long as it made a loud bang. In any case, I shouldn't have been so surprised about the intensity of his commitment. Even before

he had left Berkeley, he had made this quite clear: "You'll *never* understand our willingness to die for our people!" he had once snapped at a
longhaired pacifist. At the time, it had come off as mere rhetorical
excess, but he had probably been dead serious even then.

I rubbed my eyes with thumb and forefinger and tried to regain my
composure. More of his compatriots dreamed of America than they did
of Armenia, I said, trying my best to reclaim my authority as the older
brother. And if he got himself killed, they were more likely to laugh at
the "jackass martyr" than to follow his example.

The next morning, after feeding melon rinds to the pet tortoise on his
balcony and then instructing us to "Never jump when you hear a bang,
just keep cool," Monte took Marcia and me on a tour of Bourdj
Hamoud. Walking down a city street, he directed us to watch for movement above the first floor of surrounding buildings. He also advised
me, for the sake of not drawing attention to myself, to walk with arms
dangling at my side. I looked around, and he was right: the Lebanese
did not stride, stroll, or loiter as I did, American-style, with hands in
pockets.

We walked the perimeter of Bourdj Hamoud in the Lebanese manner, as our brother pointed out Syrian Army roadblocks, Phalangist
posts, knots of Saudi soldiers from the Arab League, and the occasional
Lebanese Army post. "Memorize their uniforms," he advised sternly: it
could be disastrous to mistake a Phalangist checkpoint for a Syrian
Army post. The easiest militiamen to identify were former Lebanese
President Camille Chamoun's Israeli-trained Tigers, in their tight,
stripy French camouflage. Monte pointed out an intersection near Sinn
el-Fil where these dapper dandies had once stacked the bodies of the
women and children they had slaughtered.

The morning after our tour, one of Monte's superiors at the Junior
High School, a Maronite bureaucrat named Khalil K., treated us to a
breakfast of raw sheep's liver, complete with a lecture on the advan-
tages of exterminating Palestinians. According to this educator,
Lebanon's problems could be traced to the day the blighted race of Palestinians invited itself to his country. Khalil had no love for his patrons
"the Jews," of course, but he spelled out his priorities, raising an index
finger for emphasis: "I would rather be the slave of a clever man," he
announced, "than the master of a race of donkeys." This, Monte and I
agreed, was the sum-total of Levantine wisdom: one must either be a
slave or a master. There was no third option.

"This war is insanity," Monte had told me the night I had arrived in Bourdj Hamoud, "It's brother killing brother, without rhyme or reason." Before long, however, he would conclude that, although there may not have been good *reasons* for the war, there were *explanations* for it. And one of the explanations involved an attempt by a few plutocrats to continue running the country like their own private shop, at the expense of the poor and voiceless majority of both Muslims and Christians.

We had not yet been in Beirut for a month when one of Chamoun's Tigers took aim at yet another Armenian youth and "made his mother cry," as the locals put it. Ever since we had first arrived in Bourdj Hamoud, Daniel had extolled the wisdom of the Armenian policy of neutrality in Lebanon's civil war. When we joined hundreds of others in the street for the Tiger victim's funeral, though, we began to understand that neutrality, too, had its cost. After the mourners had walked a couple of blocks, a line of guards shunted the women aside, while the men closed ranks shoulder-to-shoulder and continued down the street. As the all-male phalanx approached a Tiger militia post, scores of Armenian pistols went into the air, as if on cue, and started crackling. On a balcony directly above the Tiger post, a muscular compatriot charged a machine gun and fired long bursts into the air, as a hail of spent cartridges and ammo belt links clattered like a drum roll on the tin roof of the post below. The procession wound through Bourdj Hamoud, to a cemetery in the ruins of the former Shiite neighborhood of Naba'a. There, a priest thrust a crucifix towards heaven like a sword and reminded us that the man he was burying was a martyr: *Mah eemat-syal anmahootyoon eh*, he intoned, repeating the words of the fifth-century Armenian chronicler, Yeghishe: "Death knowingly grasped is immortality."

The funeral was deadly serious theater, but the message did not seem to have reached its intended audience. Returning from the cemetery, Monte and I watched an enemy Land Rover race back and forth on a dirt street, right in the middle of Bourdj Hamoud. Monte muttered an obscenity in Arabic. In due time, he would find a way to send a louder message to Chamoun's gang.

All the while, another sort of drama was unfolding on the streets, as Phalangists stopped Armenians at road blocks, beating some, ransoming others, and confiscating cars. Their message was simple: either put money in our till or leave Lebanon. One day, as Monte walked through a Maronite neighborhood during a period of heightened tension,

Phalangist militiamen grabbed him and bundled him off to the *Consul Militaire Kataib*, a courtyard arcade in a largely deserted seaside district called Qarantina. Monte's captors pushed him into a cell that had one small window near the ceiling. Through the window, he could hear waves crashing and feel a warm breeze. One of the captors accused him of being a Palestinian with a forged US passport. He then charged his pistol, put it to Monte's head, and pulled the trigger.

Click. No bullet in the chamber, ha ha.

They then stood him in front of a security officer, who thumbed his confiscated US passport and asked him what the hell he was doing in Lebanon. Monte explained in French that he was visiting friends, teaching, and researching his area of interest in archaeology. The officer leaned back in his chair and smiled. "Tell me something about archaeology, then," he demanded. Monte immediately launched into a lecture on Perso-Medean archaeology. The Phalangist rolled his eyes. "OK, OK ..." he said, returning the US citizen's passport. They released him with a stern warning.

By May 14, newspapers reported that Camille Chamoun, the silver-haired warlord in coke-bottle glasses, had mediated yet another cease-fire between the Armenians and the Phalangists, and the dispute had been resolved. Monte, however, remained skeptical. And sure enough, before a month had passed, the Phalangists and the Chamoun gang had killed another four unarmed Armenians.

Long before this, Monte had resolved to arm himself. As he explained to a pacifist friend several years later:

Exploitation and oppression are in themselves forms of violence, and to defend myself and others, I will leave all my options open, includ-ing violent options. This is natural, and the way things go. I don't care whether someone has been born into a position of oppression or if he has "worked" his way there. If he oppresses, he oppresses. If he refuses to correct his behavior the easy way, then we'll just have to do things the hard way. It's as simple as that.

"You can find anything in Lebanon, even bird's milk," Daniel had told us. Monte confirmed the adage when he perused the inventories of local arms dealers. He bought two Czech machine pistols for starters, and a couple of F-1 grenades. "A gun is a tool," he used to say, "Differ-ent guns are useful for different jobs." Accordingly, he had a machinist thread the barrel of his 7-mm Unique pistol, and then purchased sev-eral items of unknown manufacture, for which the title "silencer" was not especially appropriate. The first time we test-fired one of these items on his balcony, the neighbors across the hall burst through the door, convinced that something awful had befallen us. Removing ourselves to a wooded hillside to test another one, we had to hurry away when the first couple of pops attracted a curious kid to the test-fire spot.

Some of our fellow guards at Airplane Building liked Monte's gungho spirit. He would show up on time and chipper, to cover for militiamen who excused themselves from guard duty complaining of stomachaches and domestic duties. To others, though, Monte was bad news. One evening, as we sat at a small restaurant eating fava beans, a fellow militiaman staggered through the door and swayed in front of us. He smelled of booze. We were troublemakers, he slurred, kids who had appeared on the scene one fine day, all charged up and ready to fight. But Bourdj Hamoud was his *home*: his family and job were here, and he was trying to build a future for his children. He wanted us to understand that, unlike us, he couldn't afford to sit around all night itching for a chance to charge a rifle.

For the next month, Marcia, Monte, and I worked to save money for airplane tickets, to return stateside for our parents' surprise twenty-fifth wedding anniversary party in Fresno. Marcia sewed jeans in a cellar sweatshop during the daytime and turned Monte's big dining room into a modern dance studio in the evening. Teaching took up most of Monte's time, and I worked as an assistant to a pastry baker in the morning, taught English at a business college in the afternoon, and gave private English tutorials at night. By late June, we had saved just enough money for the airfares. Monte set his pet tortoise free, and the three of us returned to the United States to attend the anniversary party.

I dressed in a three-piece suit on the day of the surprise party, and Monte wore his best button-down shirt and corduroy pants. When our folks entered the rented hall in Fresno and saw all four of their sons and daughters assembled there, they cradled our faces and kissed us on the forehead, one by one. A little later, Dad asked Monte about his graduate school plans. "I already have too much education for what I want to do," Monte replied. He had made his final decision to abandon archaeology and to focus on changing the future.

During the month of July, Monte visited friends in San Francisco and Los Angeles and closed his bank account. On the way to Los Angeles International Airport in early August, I drove him to a discount store to purchase gifts for friends in Iran. With his daypack stuffed full of oven mitts, he boarded a Freddy Laker flight to London and bade goodbye to the country of his birth forever.

6

Time of Turmoil

B y the time Monte returned to Tehran on the night of August 8, 1979, a revolution had taken place in his absence. It had been less than a year since he had left Iran on the leaky boat to Kuwait, yet Tehran seemed like a new city. "It is a very, very free atmosphere, and there are absolutely *no* soldiers in the streets," he wrote in a letter dated August 15. "People are much happier now." Monte's friends at Sipan Union greeted him with smiles and slapped handshakes.

Warmth and idealism suffused the crowd at Sipan Union, as did rumors about the Kurdish rebellion in western Iran, just across the border from occupied Armenian lands in Turkey. Since leaving Berkeley, Monte had tried to surmount his distrust towards Kurds. He had read somewhere that the Kurds who had taken part in the genocide were from clans led by men who owed their allegiance not to their own people, but to Turkish leaders in Istanbul. After betraying their Armenian cousins, these leaders betrayed their own brothers and sisters by siding with the Turkish army that massacred and deported Kurds in the 1920s and 1930s. Since then, even Kurds from the offending clans had come to view Armenians as fellow victims of their mutual Turkish enemy.

If the rumors of the Kurdish rebellion turned out to be true, exhilarating questions would follow: had the Kurds in Iran succeeded in establishing their own government? And if so, what were the chances that their insurrection would spill over the border to the 12 million Kurds on the Turkish side? And if those prospects were good, could Armenian recruits form their own group and join the insurrection?

It was time to visit Kurdistan.

Two days after arriving in Tehran, Monte, his new friend Vahig, and ten other friends in their late teens and early twenties hired a couple of cars and headed from Tehran to the city of Mahabad in Iranian Kurdistan. Passing through the city of Tabriz on their way, they heard about an Armenian volunteer organization called Land and Culture, which had undertaken some sort of project in the region of Haftvan, on the Salmast Plain. The Land and Culture bivouac was on the way to Mahabad, so Monte and his friends decided to stop there for a visit. When they arrived without notice on or around August 11, the camp leader, Raimond Kevorkian, was supervising a crew of thirty young volunteers, mostly from France, who were reinforcing a stone-and-adobe wall around an old church. It was a modest but useful task, so after a few words with Kevorkian, Monte rolled up his corduroy pants and started hauling adobe in a wheelbarrow.

For the next four mornings, he and Kevorkian rose early to mix the adobe before the other volunteers emerged from their tents. They flooded the mud pit, tossed in straw, sloshed barefoot in the mixture, and talked as they treaded in place. As Monte described his abiding vision of a *kolkhoz*-cum-training camp in Ainjar, it occurred to Kevorkian that the young man was rehearsing a future role.

Fewer than a dozen Armenian families lived near the church in Haftvan. They worked the fields as their ancestors had for centuries, in striped wool bloomers, sheepskin caps, and long skirts. Monte visited a total of two dozen largely Armenian villages in Iran, including Gyardabad, near Lake Urmia, and the village of Peria, near Isfahan. In letters to his folks he described these villages, with their mud-brick houses and yards full of cattle and sheep, their bread ovens and butter churns, their wool dying and carpet weaving. He also described the stubborn destitution of village life amid the natural beauty, and a monotony born of poverty that ground the imagination to dust. "Only two out of 24 had schools," he reported of the villages, "and only 8 had electricity." It was even more depressing to discover that, of the 20,000 Armenian peasants who had lived in and around Peria twenty years earlier, 12,000 had moved to Soviet Armenia, while many others had abandoned their ancestral villages to look for jobs in Isfahan and Tehran.

After four or five days at Haftvan, it was time to continue the journey south to Mahabad. The entourage announced their arrival to rebel leader Ghani Booloorian, who had recently emerged from twenty-eight years in one of the Shah's dungeons. They also introduced themselves to Dr. Abdul Rahman Ghassemlou, the highest-ranking leader of the

Kurdish Democratic Party in Iran. With some 15,000 men in arms and eleven tanks, the KDP was the most powerful organization in Iranian Kurdistan. Ghassemlou's tie and suit jacket did not impress Monte, though, nor did his claim that Kurds were "true Europeans" surrounded by Asiatics. It was the long-lost European story again—the same old story he had heard from Armenians and Lebanese Maronites. Vahig told Ghassemlou that he and his friends wanted to go to the front, but when he mentioned that one of his friends was from the United States, the Kurdish leader's smile disappeared and he snapped, "We don't need any more fighters at the front."

Monte and his entourage enjoyed a better reception from Komala, an organization dedicated to autonomy in Iranian Kurdistan. The leader of Komala, a fifty-seven-year-old Sunni religious scholar named Sheikh Ezzedin Hosseini, invited the youths to sit with him on the floor around a tray of tea. The sheikh spoke in sincere generalities about Armenian–Kurdish relations and offered to provide arms and training to his Armenian brothers, if they so wished. Monte took an instant liking to the sheikh, with his white turban, horn-rimmed glasses, green robe, and graying beard. For years after meeting him, Monte would greet comrades with a *temmenah*, touching fingers of the right hand to the forehead and then placing the open hand on the heart.

Two nights later, a rumor reached Kurdistan that fighting had broken out in Tehran. Monte and friends rushed back to the Iranian capital, determined to join the battle on whichever side they deemed more "progressive." When they reached Tehran on August 17 or 18, however, they were disappointed to find out that the rumors of battle had been exaggerated. The Revolutionary Guards had already quelled leftist demonstrations, and an uneasy quiet had settled on the streets.

Not long after returning to Tehran, Sipan Union began buzzing with rumors of yet other battles: in Lebanon, Phalangist gunmen had leveled their weapons at Bourdj Hamoud again. "Knowing the guards in Bourdj Hamoud and the situation in Lebanon," Monte later wrote in his *Self-Criticism*, "I knew that they needed moral and political backing." He resolved to return to Beirut as soon as possible, but not before he and his friends slapped together a solidarity demonstration in front of the Lebanese consulate in Tehran. Prominent Armenians in the Iranian capital did not welcome news of the planned demonstration: the last thing they needed was a crazy American kid churning up young blood among Armenians in post-revolutionary Iran. The night before the demonstration, fliers appeared in Armenian neighborhoods denouncing "adventurists" in the community and insinuating that an American spy was in their midst. The next morning, Monte grabbed a bullhorn and mounted a jeep to address several hundred young men in front of the consulate. It was a minuscule demonstration by Iranian standards, but it was spirited, and it further antagonized Dashnak leaders, both in Iran and in Lebanon.

In a Dear Everyone letter to his folks, Monte jotted a couple of casual lines about his junket to Kurdistan and the demonstration in front of the Lebanese consulate in Tehran. The letter overcame Mom's prodigious ability to convince herself, despite mounting evidence to the contrary, that Monte was headed to graduate school and a respectable academic career. The way she saw it, her bright but naive son had adopted a cause that had made him an easy target for manipulative fanatics. He had fallen headfirst into the snake pit of Armenian politics. She began writing letters imploring him to return home.

To Monte, though, there was no such thing as returning home. In one sense, home was Armenia, a place he had never been to before. In another sense, home was wherever he happened to be.

Monte left Tehran for Beirut on September 16, two days after the end of the latest round of Phalangist–Armenian fighting had wound down. The roadblocks along the Green Line that separated the airport and west Beirut from the east side of the city had just reopened when he crossed into Bourdj Hamoud. As soon as he eased his flight bag off his shoulder, he was surprised to learn from a friend that his cousin David had landed in Lebanon a couple of days earlier. With a fresh degree in political science and a desire to learn first-hand about the civil war, David had begun learning his first lesson before he had had a chance to unpack: claiming that Armenians had assisted the Palestinians, Phalangist gunmen had killed four members of the Bourdj Hamoud militia, kidnapped Armenian families, bombed shops, and dragged women from their cars to shoot them on the side of the road. Once again, Armenian leaders rushed into negotiations with the Phalangists and handed them one concession after another. By the end of the negotiations, twenty-five Armenians lay dead, their killers remained unpunished, and David burned with rage.

Immediate events only confirmed the futility of appeasement. One afternoon not long after a ceasefire agreement, a hulky Phalangist strode into the middle of the Sinn el-Fil Highway and began shouting obscenities and threats at residents of Airplane Building. The men of the building were off at work, and the women were alone with their children. Peeking over the balcony, Manushag Stepanian, now eight months pregnant, spotted several armed Phalangists approaching her building. She grabbed her husband's walkie-talkie and called for help from Arakadz Club, the local militia center. The Club dispatched two unarmed youths to investigate, but when the youths arrived to find Phalangists firing into the air, they weren't sure what to do.

To their relief, Monte had already arrived on the scene, and he was all business. Loading a rifle, he threw himself against the sandbag barricade in the lobby of Airplane Building and fired a couple of shots across the Sinn el-Fil Highway. As the Phalangists retreated to the far side of the highway to take cover, Monte dashed crouching to the other end of the barricade and fired a burst, and then he scurried to the middle and fired a couple of shots from there, too. From the Phalangists' perspective on the other side of the highway, it must have appeared as if a full detail of guards were defending the building. Monte kept up the illusion for about an hour, "jumping right and left like a monkey," as Manushag later described it, and holding the Phalangists at bay until the men of Airplane Building returned from work and reinforcements arrived from the Club.

From that day on, the ladies of Airplane Building—Ghonushu Arsho from the fifth floor, Batta Marie from the sixth floor, Digin Marie from the seventh floor, and the others—viewed their crazy young compatriot with a mixture of gratitude and maternal protectiveness. He had taken the matter in hand decisively and with a level head, defending them when the honchos at the Club had failed in their advertised role as protectors of the neighborhood.

In early October, Monte and Cousin David lugged their bags from the comfortable, well-appointed apartment near Torossian Junior High School and dropped them on the floor of a grimy, shattered sixth-floor apartment in a half-collapsed concrete high-rise diagonally across from Airplane Building. Artillery had pummeled the south side of the building the year before, reducing that section to chunks of concrete walls, ceilings, and floors dangling mid-air from tangled steel rods. The electricity bill still arrived in the name of a Lebanese Shiite who had been driven from the building three years earlier, and the apartment had neither glass panes in the windows nor running water. The pipes didn't drain either, even after Monte emptied a wine bottle full of undiluted hydrochloric acid down them, so he and David peed in the rubble of the collapsed portion of the building, stepping carefully, at the risk of falling from a crumbling ledge or dropping six floors through a shell hole.

On weekends, Monte and David started meeting with a small group of friends at a dacha in the mountain village of 'Aley, overlooking Beirut. It must have been reassuring to roast chestnuts on a diesel stove and talk politics with thoughtful compatriots who were also trying to think things through. Monte did more listening than talking in 'Aley, but the meetings helped to clarify the "minimal goal" of the coming struggle, which he had begun calling the "patriotic liberation struggle." He had never accepted the grandiose Dashnak pipedream of a "Free, United, and Independent Armenia," along the fanciful lines of the unratified 1920 Treaty of Sevres, but he never averted his eyes for a moment from Turkish-occupied Western Armenia, either. In 1984, he would help draft a declaration of purpose that would reflect his conclusions five years earlier in 'Aley:

> As a very minimum, we declare that any diasporan Armenian must have the right to freely return to "Western Armenia" (i.e., those areas of the Armenian homeland currently under the direct jurisdiction of the Turkish state), and to establish herself as a native there, enjoying equal and full political, economic, national, and human rights on par with all other inhabitants.

The only hope for achieving even this minimal goal was for Armenians to establish themselves as a fighting force on the ground in "Western Armenia." But how to infiltrate a fighting force into Armenian lands occupied by the second-largest NATO army?

Even as Monte pondered this large question, he faced daily danger just trying to get from point A to point B in Lebanon. Every time he passed a Phalangist checkpoint on the way to 'Aley or west Beirut, he was taking a risk: Monte's passport carried Iranian visas, and the Phalangists despised the Khomeini regime in Tehran. Dashnak hostility had escalated, too, ever since his involvement in the anti-Phalangist demonstration in Tehran the previous September. Monte was no longer welcome at the Club; conversations stopped when he entered rooms, and former friends kept their distance. One day, as he passed through the Maronite neighborhood of Ashrafiyeh, a sniper's bullet just missed — close enough for him to feel the swish.

In the coming weeks, the bad blood between Monte and the local honchos would further curdle. One morning in early 1980, Secret Army graffiti and posters appeared on shrapnel-pocked walls around Bourdj Hamoud, and the morning after that, staff at Torossian Junior High School confiscated Secret Army fliers that someone had placed on the students' desks. The appearance of Secret Army fliers at the school where Monte taught only confirmed suspicions around Bourdj Hamoud that he was a member of the faceless group. At the same time, it convinced Monte that the Secret Army was drawing near. He hoped that a recruiter would contact him soon.

As his relationship with the local Dashnaks deteriorated, so did his picture of Ainjar: beneath the ranunculus-carpeted idyll lay a rural ghetto run by party bosses. Still, Monte continued to visit his friends in the village, arriving unannounced and accepting anyone's invitation to spend the night. He would call at the Kabranian house, too, although by this time Seta was away, attending a girls' high school near Beirut.

On February 12, 1980, Monte and Cousin David were sipping beers at their friend Nazo's house in Ainjar, when three Dashnak militiamen walked in. They didn't look happy. Monte listened quietly as one of them, a youth named Vartkes, ordered him to leave the village and never return. At that, David leaned over the table and shouted in English, "*Fucking Dashnaks!*" One of Vartkes' friends pushed the table over on its side. Monte held his cousin back with an arm, then looked Vartkes in the eye and calmly agreed to leave in the morning. No, Vartkes insisted, he must leave immediately. Monte repeated that he would leave the next morning. Vartkes paused for a beat, and then headed to the door with his cohorts in train. Once outside, one of the other militiamen proposed returning to Nazo's house to bundle Monte and David out of Ainjar that same evening. Vartkes shook his head. That wouldn't be necessary: Monte had told them he would leave the next morning, and so he would. He may be a troublemaker, but he was also a man of his word.

On February 18, about a week after his eviction from Ainjar, Monte returned to his apartment from a militia meeting to find the door splintered and ajar, and his few possessions strewn across the floor. Papers were missing, too, including several issues of *Hay Baykar*, an incendiary tabloid published by Secret Army supporters in Paris. More infuriating, however, was the disappearance of a manuscript and artwork for a book Monte had spent months working on, a book of stories and drawings by his Torossian School students about life in Bourdj Hamoud during the war. He would never recover that manuscript.

When I returned to Beirut on April 4, 1980 and lugged my pack past the splintered door, I didn't think I'd ever get used to the dust that billowed through the broken windowpanes from the street below and coated every surface in the apartment. There I was, on another one of my rescue missions. This time, if I could not convince Monte to leave Lebanon altogether, then at least I would try to move him to west Beirut, beyond the range of Phalangists and Dashnak bosses.

One of the first things Monte did after I plopped my bags down in his apartment was to give me a tour of the kitchen. "We have running water," he said, hoisting a blue plastic bucket. "You take this, run down six flights of stairs to the cistern, fill it up, and run back up six flights of stairs. Get it? Running water!" Next, I learned to my alarm that Monte planned to covertly photograph militia posts around Bourdj Hamoud with the 35mm camera he had asked me to bring. He and some "good guys" needed the photos, he said—to plan a putsch against the Dashnak leadership of the community!

Then I noticed that Cousin David was now packing a nickel-plated .357 Python revolver. Monte had made a couple of new purchases of his own, too, including an Afarov light machine gun, a clunky relic of the Great Patriotic War, which he kept under his convertible sofa. He had also bought a G-3 assault rifle, complete with bayonet and incendiary grenades. The rifle, which fired the expensive .308 NATO round, struck me as a rather impractical purchase. When I asked why he had paid good money for the thing, he explained that since the G-3 was the standard-issue rifle of the Turkish Army, learning to operate it was a way of knowing one's enemy. I stared at him and thought to myself: "My God, this guy thinks he's going to be fighting the Turkish Army before they adopt a new service rifle!"

In his *Self-Criticism*, written ten years later, Monte described his Bourdj Hamoud days as "a time of great turmoil," and "a very important period of maturation." More than one commentator has suggested that the Marxism that he had begun to profess by this time was just a fashionable jargon that he had added on to his nationalistic core beliefs, but this was not the case. Although he never studied Marxism systematically, he had read and appreciated the odd Marxist classic by this time, notably Engels' *Socialism, Utopian and Scientific*, and Lenin's *Imperialism*. As a student of Armenian history, moreover, he was well aware of the pivotal role of class struggle throughout the centuries, from the fall of the Urartuan kingdom in 590 BC, through the peasant revolts of the Middle Ages, right up to the Soviet period. Dialectics made perfectly good sense to him, too: he was, after all, an aficionado of Chinese natural philosophy and of the Indian logician Nagarjuna, with his twelve categories of negation. All of this, plus a short attention span when it came to supernatural bosh disguised as Great Truth, pushed and pulled him to Marxism.

The way Monte saw it, class struggle always takes place within a larger story of an ethnic culture, or a people. In the Armenian case, this larger story spanned not only two dozen centuries, but also thousands of miles of diaspora. Thus, Monte described Armenians in Bourdj Hamoud first and foremost as part of the Armenian people, and only secondarily as one of a dozen confessions and ethnic communities in Lebanon.

This was a point of contention between us. Once, we tussled over a statement by Danny Chamoun, the chief of the Tiger Militia: angered by Armenian resistance to paying the Tigers' "taxes," the ex-president's son complained that Armenians in Lebanon had "treated the country like a hotel," rather than their home. Neither Monte nor I disputed this claim, but we evaluated it differently. To my way of thinking, the most serious problems Bourdj Hamoud faced were *Lebanese* problems, which needed to be solved in Lebanon, together with other Lebanese. Monte, by contrast, viewed Lebanese Armenians as Armenians first and foremost. To him, their unwillingness to put Lebanon first was evidence of a praiseworthy ethnic stubbornness. Returning to this topic years later, he wrote that Armenians of the diaspora, including those in Lebanon, "must *by definition* envisage an eventual change of address." Monte, of course, envisioned a change of address to Turkish-occupied Armenia, but as I irritably reminded him, Armenians in Lebanon were far more likely to change their address to Los Angeles than to their ancestral homeland. This observation never had much effect on Monte: he had convinced himself that, given the opportunity, many of these emigrants would reverse the westward drift and head to Armenia.

For all his focus on "an eventual change of address" to historic Armenian lands in Turkey, I would soon find out that Monte was immersed in Lebanese politics, and in an alarming way, too. At first I had assumed that the explosives in his refrigerator—loops of cordite, dozens of blasting caps, and fifteen kilos of mud dynamite, all hidden behind green beans and goat cheese—had been earmarked for a role in his dormant coup plan. After a while, though, I began to suspect that Monte's story about the coup plan had been a ruse, to conceal some other, even darker purpose. When my curiosity finally overcame my sense of dread, I confronted him with my suspicion—and soon regretted it. Monte explained in an off-handed manner that he and a couple of "good guys" had been meeting with a certain Palestinian who had provided explosives training and had offered logistical support for behind-the-lines operations against the right-wing militias. The Palestinian, a low-ranking Fatah contact named Abu Nabil, had offered money, too, but Monte had turned down the offer, stressing that his motives were purely patriotic: Tel Aviv was Ankara's strategic ally, and Camille Chamoun, one of Tel Aviv's collaborators in Lebanon, had distinguished himself as an enemy of Palestinians and Armenians alike.

Monte and one of his new confederates had spent the night of March 12 in a garage near Bourdj Hamoud, rigging a Volkswagen with high explosives. The next day, he had parked the car on the side of the Dora–Junieh Highway. Then, laying in wait with a remote detonator, he had set off the bomb just as Chamoun's motorcade approached. The explosion gouged a large crater in the road, sent Range Rovers flying, and killed one of Chamoun's bodyguards. Monte had hoped that this attack would kill Chamoun and push the Tiger militia into a turf war with their nominal allies, the Phalangists, thus weakening the right-wing militias in relation to the left-wing "patriotic forces" with whom we all sympathized. Ever the survivor, though, Chamoun emerged from the smoke with only light wounds. Although he publicly blamed Palestinians for the attack, he must have suspected his rivals, the Phalangists. If so, his suspicion was wrong in this case, but it was not unwarranted: within the coming year the Phalangists would decimate the Tigers, killing hundreds in the process and distinguishing themselves as the worst of Chamoun's many enemies.

"*What?!*" I exhaled as Monte brought me up to date on his latest plot. I told him that he must desist immediately. His nickel-and-dime extortion scheme the previous year was one thing, but rigging car-bombs to kill a ruthless warlord who had informants and operatives all around us: this would endanger not only himself, but everyone who came into casual contact with him …

I closed my eyes and rehearsed in my mind how I would inform my dear Aunt Vickie that her son David had died in a Lebanese torture chamber. I had to get Monte and David out of Bourdj Hamoud fast. Living under the thumb of the Phalangists and the Chamoun gang was making them crazy. In the days that followed, I awoke early and took a taxi to west Beirut, where I looked for a job and an apartment and cast about for a plan—any plan—to move them to safety there.

I also resolved to keep a closer tab on my brother's movements. One day in early May, David and I tagged along with Monte to a meeting at a friend's apartment in Naba'a. On the way, Monte explained that we were headed to an appointment with someone who wished to discuss "revolutionary ideas" with us. When we arrived at the apartment, our friend's mother introduced us to a wiry man smoking Winstons in the sitting room. He was wearing dark slacks and a long-sleeved dress shirt with the top buttons unbuttoned, in the manner of an off-duty shop-keeper. His name, our hostess said, was Minas Ohanian. When he rose and stepped forward to shake our hands, the top of his long head did not come much higher than my shoulders, and when he sat back down, he smiled, revealing bad teeth. It was hard to guess his age, what with his pasty, acne-scarred face, his low gravelly voice, his strange accent, and his shock of black hair. He claimed he was an airplane mechanic and a "crazy revolutionary." "Crazy?" someone asked. "All revolution-aries are crazy," he replied, doing a Levantine impersonation of a film noir tough guy.

"I don't think so," Monte responded, "Revolutionaries aren't crazy at all."

We began munching pumpkin seeds, while Monte posed questions to Ohanian as if he were drawing them from a memorized list. He wanted to discuss the national question, Soviet Armenia, and Iran. He also wanted to discuss the April 6, 1980 press conference in Sidon, in which masked representatives of the Secret Army and Abdullah Ocalan's upstart Kurdistan Workers' Party (Partia Karkeran Kurdistan, or PKK) had pledged to cooperate in the war against Ankara. Our new acquaintance, however, had little interest in geopolitics or Armenian–Kurdish solidarity, and I wasn't hearing anything in the way of "revo-lutionary ideas" from him, either.

After about an hour, when we had piled the ashtrays high with pumpkin seed shells and Monte seemed to have reached the end of his questions, Ohanian leaned back in his chair and said he'd like to con-tinue the discussion at another venue. As we rose to take our leave, he cracked a joke that I don't recall, and then broke into a crooked smile, revealing his teeth again. They seemed to have been ground down to about half their full length and fused together by brown crud, to the extent that it was hard to tell where the gums left off and the teeth began.

Walking back to the apartment, Monte was quiet. He must have sus-pected that this strange man was a Secret Army recruiter, and that our meeting had been something like a job interview. I didn't know it then, but he and Ohanian had already made arrangements for their next meeting.

A couple of days later, we found ourselves driving with Ohanian in his lime-green BMW to a partially destroyed gas storage facility near Bourdj Hamoud, by the sea. We sat on pipes, beside a spherical storage tank that had collapsed like a giant gourd years earlier when an artillery round had hit it. The tangle of pipes and valves, the crushed storage tank, and the roiling sea beyond—we were in the middle of Hieronymus Bosch's Hell, and our host, Minas Ohanian, in his safari jacket with sleeves folded up, was one of its denizens. His teeth looked even worse in broad daylight.

Now it was his turn to pose questions. "What do you want to do with your life?" he asked. Monte explained in a low, calm voice that he wanted to work to liberate occupied Armenian lands in Turkey. They explored this idea a bit further, then our host brought the interview to a close with another joke I don't recall. He drove us back to Naba'a and left us on the shoulder of the Sinn el-Fil Highway.

A few days later, Monte rushed to yet another appointment, this time without David and me. Soon after Monte and Ohanian greeted each other near the lighthouse in west Beirut, a young Libyan concierge nabbed them and delivered them to a Palestinian security officer in the area. Little did the Libyan know that he had taken into custody a personal friend of Colonel Qadhafi. When the security officer discovered Monte's US passport, he triumphantly phoned Yassir Arafat and announced that he had captured an American spy. Arafat cut him off: "Why is it," he asked, "that every time you call me you've got another story about a spy you caught?" As Ohanian listened with a bemused smile, Arafat ordered the officer to release the suspects immediately.

The appointment that day had not gone well. But despite all the confusion, Monte had managed to tell Ohanian that he wanted to join the Secret Army, to dedicate himself full-time to its work.

Alec had already met Ohanian months earlier, and he, too, was thinking about joining the Secret Army. Even without knowing about Monte's relationship with Abu Nabil and his involvement in the attempt to assassinate Chamoun, Alec had concluded that Monte's life was in imminent danger in Bourdj Hamoud. He knew that the Dashnaks had broken into Monte's apartment and had kicked him out of Ainjar, and he knew about the sniper bullet in Ashrafiyeh, too.

A couple of evenings after the ill-fated meeting with Ohanian in west Beirut, a high school student appeared at our door, breathless and wide-eyed. We had to leave Bourdj Hamoud, she said, and we should start packing at once: they had received word that soon—perhaps even that evening—Dashnak gunmen would break down our door and try to kill us. As soon as she left, Monte pushed a clip into his pistol.

A week earlier, as it turned out, he had finally summoned the courage to ask Seta out on a proper date, which they had set for that very evening. The proposal had surprised Seta: until that moment, she had thought of Monte as a friend and a mentor, not a romantic interest. Monte was supposed to pick her up at the Stepanian's apartment in Airplane Building, but when the appointed hour passed, Seta began to worry. One of her older sisters had warned her that American men were as fickle as American women were fast. Still, she didn't want to believe that she had made too much of Monte's attention ...

That evening, Monte, David, and I packed our bags. David would lay low at another apartment for the night, but my brother and I stayed put, to avoid raising suspicions. Monte spent a sleepless night in the hallway cradling his pistol, while I lay on my bedroll a few feet away with a pistol under my pillow and a grenade under my blanket. I was relieved at least that my brother's career as a car-bomber was over, and that we would soon be leaving east Beirut.

At six in the morning on May 25, 1980, Monte followed two blocks behind me as we walked through the rubble, past closed shops, and over the bridge that connected Bourdj Hamoud to the rest of Beirut. Reunited at the taxi stand on the western bank of the Beirut River, we bade goodbye to brave, generous Bourdj Hamoud. A few moments later, Alec picked us up in his white Peugeot, and we headed to west Beirut.

PART THREE

The Secret Army

7

Underground

As we ducked into the Peugeot, I glanced sideways at Alec. He was a good-looking young man with a crescent of black hair across his forehead, and he was smiling at me with a knowing twinkle in his eye. We sat silently as he navigated the debris-strewn Corniche-el-Nahr, past the sandbagged museum at the Green Line, past the black flag fluttering from the minaret of Abdul Nasser Mosque, down a narrow side street, and into the desperate cinderblock maze of Beirut's Fakhani slum. Pulling up to a stone wall with "Piss here" spray-painted in Arabic over a Phalangist symbol, we grabbed our few bags and crossed the street in front of a fire station. Alec nodded to guards at the entrance of a dank lobby, and we strode up six flights of stairs, two stairs at a time, to arrive puffing at a door with two blue eye decals pasted over the lintel, to ward off evil. The door opened onto a narrow foyer leading to a room that was empty except for a few pieces of furniture, scattered firearms, and framed photographs of Secret Army martyrs on the wall. Someone had hung a rubber skeleton from one of the framed photos. A heavy blue door led to another room beyond the kitchen area. We would come to call this flat the Seventh Floor.

After a couple of moments, Minas Ohanian jaunted through the door with a satchel under his arm and a Winston in the middle of his crooked smile. He greeted us without removing the cigarette, made a joke, opened the blue door beyond the kitchen, and disappeared behind a large desk piled a foot high with multicolored passports, embossing stamps, and official-looking papers in an assortment of scripts. After rummaging around the office for a few minutes, he left.

As the smoke from his Winston curled into a question mark and dissolved, it occurred to me that the Seventh Floor was not merely a safe house, as we had assumed at first, but actually the nearest thing to a headquarters that the Secret Army had. Even more disappointing was the correlative realization that Ohanian—the joker who, no doubt, had hung the rubber skeleton from the photo—was not a low-level operative: he was the masked spokesman at the joint Secret Army–PKK press conference in Sidon a month earlier, the wiry one who had introduced himself as Hagop Hagopian. He *was* the Secret Army!

Hagopian's real name—or rather his original name—was Harootyoon Takooshian. He was born in the late 1940s in Mosul, Iraq, one of at least three children of Mugurdich and Siranoosh Takooshian. According to Secret Army hagiographers, the boy had run away from home at the age of fifteen, and by the age of sixteen he had joined a small Palestinian group called Abtal al-Auda, "Heroes of the Return," which soon merged with Dr. George Habash's Arab Nationalist Movement and a couple of smaller groups to form the Popular Front for the Liberation of Palestine, the PFLP.

At the fringe of the PFLP, young Harootyoon apprenticed himself to his most important mentor, Wadi Haddad. The "terrorist mastermind" Haddad set up a "Foreign Operations Branch" of the PFLP in July 1968, with himself as its leader. From a closet-sized office papered with airline itineraries, he meticulously planned an attack on Zurich Airport in 1969, then a hijacking at Dawson's Airfield in Jordan in September 1970, followed by other operations. And throughout it all, Harootyoon was at his side, quaffing every lesson like a siphon.

After King Hussein's massacre and expulsion of Palestinians from Jordan in 1970, Haddad and his apprentice made their way to Lebanon. Eventually, the apprentice became one of Haddad's right-hand men and participated in several operations, including a hijacking at Athens Airport and a February 6, 1974 takeover at the Japanese embassy in Kuwait. By then, his new acquaintances knew him as *Mujahed*, "Holy Warrior." These new acquaintances included Popular Front militant Leila Khaled, Japanese Red Army leader Furaya Yukata, and a round-faced young Venezuelan named Ilyich Sanchez Ramirez, better known as "Carlos." In the early 1970s, the PFLP foreswore hijackings and declared Haddad's Foreign Operations Branch illegal. Haddad's group continued operations independently until 1974, when it dismantled itself in the face of internal dissension.

At about the time old man Yanikian shot two Turks in Santa Barbara, Abu Iyad, one of the founders of the Fatah guerrilla movement, asked

Hagopian why no one had yet founded an Armenian group similar to his own Palestinian Black September splinter group. Palestinians were looking for allies in Lebanon, but beyond this self-serving consideration, Abu Iyad and other Palestinian leaders sincerely considered themselves friends of Armenians: the two peoples had shared a bond of suffering at the hands of the Ottoman Turks, and in the twentieth century both had been deported *en masse* from their respective homelands.

Monte would later claim that Hagopian had taken up Abu Iyad's challenge solely in order to satisfy his lust for money and power. Since Hagopian had little formal education or professional training, opening his own little Beirut-based "revolutionary movement" might have seemed like the best route to personal wealth and power. But this version of things ignores the fact that many of Hagopian's equally unschooled and less agile contemporaries excelled at professions that were considerably easier, safer, and more profitable than the career path he had chosen.

Hagopian's first task was to establish connections in the Armenian diaspora, to cover the logistical costs of his group's inaugural "armed propaganda" operations. He approached Dashnak bosses in Lebanon for assistance, explaining his proposal in Iraqi Arabic mixed with Palestinian colloquial dialect and broken Armenian (he had attended Armenian elementary school in Mosul, but had forgotten much of the language through disuse). The bosses greeted his proposal with the same lack of enthusiasm they later displayed towards Monte's *kolkhoz* idea, and Hagopian quickly saw the futility of pressing the point.

Hagopian, a high-school dropout, nurtured a deep but uneasy respect for "intellectuals," and when he found himself surrounded by educated and articulate Arab militants his insecurity grew. Perhaps for this reason, as well as the need to connect with donors, he approached Kevork Ajemian, a middle-aged novelist, bookstore owner, and strident nationalist. Hagopian, an eerily accurate judge of character, immediately perceived that Ajemian craved recognition. Ajemian, for his part, saw in Hagopian a man of action who could put ideas—in this case, Ajemian's own ideas—into practice.

They convinced a couple of local businessmen to advance start-up funds for the group. Now that the Man of Action and the Intellectual had sponsors, they needed foot soldiers. Ajemian introduced Hagopian to several young men, among them a tall, handsome but wan sixteen-year-old named Hagop Darakjian. Soon after their first meeting, Hagopian and Darakjian carried out the group's inaugural action—the

January 20, 1975 bomb attack at the offices of the World Council of Churches in west Beirut. A communiqué attempted to provide a rationale for this unlikely target: by facilitating Armenian emigration from the Middle East to assimilation in the West, the Council had implicated itself in a "white genocide" that would gut the oldest and strongest Armenian communities of the diaspora. At first, Hagopian thought of claiming responsibility for this attack in the name of "The Kourken Yanikian Group," but later he came to favor the grand conspiratorial title, "Armenian Secret Army." The next four attacks—all bombings against Turkish diplomatic and private interests in Beirut—were carried out in the name of the ASA, but shortly after that, Ajemian convinced Hagopian to amend the group's title, to emphasize its proclaimed goal of liberating Armenian lands in Turkey. So, beginning with an August 7, 1975 bomb attack that damaged the Turkish second secretary's car in Beirut, communiqués appeared above the ungainly signature, "Armenian Secret Army for the Liberation of Armenia." Thus, in one title, Ajemian and Hagopian managed to combine bombast with perseveration.

News of the Secret Army's several bomb attacks thrilled Bourdj Hamoud's youngsters, who had heard patriotic ballads from the cradle. Since the beginning of the war in Lebanon, they had watched their parents emerge mouse-like from basements after artillery barrages to sift through the uninsured ashes of their shopkeeper dreams. Now, fifty years since Tehlirian, Shiragian, and the other avengers of yore had laid down their pistols, Dashnak honchos worried that the old revolutionary ballads had become advertisements for the party's impotence. In an attempt to stanch the foreseeable hemorrhage from their Youth Federation to the Secret Army, the party's bureau secretly set up a rival assassination squad. And so it came to pass that, in October 1975—two and one half months after the Secret Army's first operation—the Justice Commandos of the Armenian Genocide gunned down a Turkish ambassador in Vienna and issued their own communiqué for the occasion. Four months after that, on February 16, 1976, Hagop Darakjian shot and killed Oktar Cirit, the first secretary at the Turkish embassy in Beirut, with a silenced pistol. With this, the Secret Army and the Justice Commandos began in earnest their competition to chalk up the most dead diplomats.

Soon, the Justice Commandos mounted assassination and bombing operations in Paris, Vatican City, and Madrid, claiming the lives of two more Turkish ambassadors, two family members, and two chauffeurs.

These attacks came at the price of antagonizing the Dashnak Party's Cold War patrons in the West, but they reassured increasingly restive Youth Federation members that the party had not entirely forgotten its original charter as a guerrilla organization. Hagopian, however, turned his rival's successes to the Secret Army's advantage: as soon as he got wind of a Justice Commando attack, he would phone the press agencies to claim credit for it in the name of the Secret Army.

While the Secret Army–Justice Commandos rivalry had been heating up, Hagopian had spent a year unrecognized in a rented house right in the middle of the Dashnak fiefdom of Ainjar. His tranquil life was interrupted in late 1976, however, when a KGB operative peppered his Fiat with a machine pistol, hitting him with twelve slugs in the neck and shoulders. The attack seems to have been part of a factional dispute within one or another Palestinian splinter group that Hagopian had long since quit. Hagopian somehow survived the attack, and Abu Iyad arranged for medical treatment in Yugoslavia.

In his absence, Darakjian assumed full charge of the Secret Army. During that time a dozen or so "part-time" recruits drifted into the group. *Tezoog*, or "Dwarf," specialized in the production of homemade detonators, and another recruit named Raffi was the designated communiqué writer, because he had attended a bit of college. By this time, Abu Iyad had arranged for the group to use the Seventh Floor flat in the security headquarters building of the Palestine Popular Struggle Front, across the street from the Fakhani fire station.

Wadi Haddad died of cancer in an East German clinic, just a few months after planning an October 1977 hijacking of a Lufthansa flight to Mogadishu Airport in Somalia. Meanwhile, in a hospital in Yugoslavia, Hagopian met his future wife Marija Odak, a Serbian nurse from Zagreb. Marija had a daughter, Toani, whose father, she claimed, was a debonair Japanese pilot. After Hagopian's six-month convalescence, the mother and daughter accompanied him to west Beirut.

Thanks in large part to Hagop Darakjian, the Secret Army continued to generate headlines. From August to October 1978, Darakjian traveled across Turkey, leaving behind a trail of six or seven bomb craters, including one in Ankara at a monument to Kemal Ataturk, the founder of the Republic of Turkey.

In 1979, Hagopian established several important contacts among Armenians in Paris. The most important of these contacts was Ara Toranian, co-founder and publisher of *Hay Baykar*, the radical tabloid that had initially been printed with Jean Paul Sartre's help on the *Temps Modernes* press in Paris. Hagopian also contacted a clutch of self-styled Maoists in France who would phone in credit for their bomb attacks using the name New Armenian Resistance. Among other pyrotechnical activities, the NAR had bombed the Soviet Information Office in Paris and an Aeroflot office in Brussels.

The April 6, 1980 press conference in Sidon, in which the Secret Army and the Kurds of the PKK pledged to join forces against Ankara, further stoked the imaginations of young Armenians impatient with the big talk and no action of their elders. By mid-1980, Hagopian was ready to expand operations. But in order to do so, he would need to recruit a group of "full-time" members. Since Monte had no immediate relatives within range of Phalangist or Dashnak retaliation, and since he had already distinguished himself as a fighter in the militia, he was a prime candidate for recruitment.

Months before his induction into the Secret Army, Monte "already had some intimation that ASALA lied a lot in its communiqués and pamphlets," as he wrote in his 1990 memoir, *Self-Criticism*. "But in a way," he wrote, "I wanted to convince myself that there were real Armenian revolutionaries behind these actions." If there were revolutionaries behind the assassinations and press conferences, there weren't more than a dozen of them. And that was hardly an army, secret or not. To try to build a movement from this "rinky-dink operation," as Monte later described it, would be like starting from scratch.

The Secret Army's meager membership was as disappointing as the rubber skeleton was disconcerting. Details like the rubber skeleton and the evil eye decals on the lintel above the entrance to the Seventh Floor gave the place the juvenile feel of a boys' clubhouse. And when Hagopian opened his mouth, he did little to dispel that impression. When Monte asked him why he had tacked the skeleton to the photo frame, Hagopian growled through his crooked smile: "That's how we're all going to end up." It was a line worthy of a villain in a spaghetti western, but entirely unworthy of a revolutionary leader. Later, Hagopian would admit that his purpose was not to liberate Armenia but merely to "make noise" (*tsayn hanel*).

But Monte saw an advantage in the very fact that the Secret Army had no clear political goals. Precisely because the group was inchoate, it would be that much easier for him and like-minded recruits to mold it into a genuine revolutionary organization. Even the group's silly name didn't bother him: "No big deal," he shrugged, "We can change that later."

Taking a step into thin air, he handed his passport and guns to Hagopian and made out a will bequeathing to the Secret Army all $800 he had to his name. When Hagopian locked the passport and money in the big green safebox in his office, Monte abandoned his plan to visit Soviet Armenia in mid-June—or any time soon. More than ten long years would pass before he would set foot in Armenia for the first time.

Monte scanned his address book for names of personal contacts that might prove useful in the new work he had undertaken. One of these contacts was a certain Cindy A., a Fresno native and "good guy" whom Monte had met in Berkeley. Insinuating that Monte's high opinion of the young lady had a romantic component to it, Alec teasingly began calling him *Abu Cindy,* "the Father of Cindy." Hagopian took up the nickname, too, and to Monte's annoyance it stuck, eventually appearing on ID cards, police reports, and published articles as "Abu Sindi."

David concluded that it was time to bring his eight-month visit to an end, so he returned to the United States. From where Monte stood, however, there was no going back. Hagopian began grooming him and Alec as his successors, to assume leadership of the Secret Army in the likely event that he were killed. He trotted them from office to office in Fakhani, introducing them to personal contacts, including PLO chairman Yassir Arafat and George Habash, General Secretary of the PFLP. The meeting with Dr. Habash confirmed Monte's long-standing admiration for him. The Palestinians arranged for Monte, Alec, and other Secret Army recruits to receive special weapons training. Occasionally, Hagopian accompanied them to the firing range to supervise training sessions himself. Once, he instructed Monte and Alec to kneel on the ground facing each other about a foot apart, and then he lowered his .38 and fired round after round between their noses, until they no longer blinked.

During another training session at a Fatah firing range near Chatila refugee camp, they were surprised to be joined by a tall Teuton toting an Austrian sniper rifle equipped with a Polaroid camera that could record a "hit" through the scope. It was unusual to see a blond in a Palestinian camp, especially one with a gun, so Monte assumed that he was a member of the Red Army Faction or the Revolutionarer Zellen, or some other German "frontline organization." The Teuton introduced himself in English as "Hell." It was a strange nickname. Palestinian fighters adopted *noms de guerre* that translated as "Freedom," "Struggle," "Return," and other abstract nouns, but Monte had never heard of this one before.

Monte and Alec fired a few rounds from Hell's rifle. Even in the hands of a novice, it was dead-on accurate at several hundred meters. Monte marveled out loud at how lucky he was to have survived past encounters with snipers.

In the coming weeks, Hell would call on Hagopian at the Seventh Floor from time to time, and the two of them would sit on a divan in the foyer and gossip like hausfraus. Although the German didn't discuss politics, Hagopian once told him in his broken English: "Mao Tsetung said that guerrillas should swim in the masses like fish in the sea. But what *we* need is to swim in money!" The two men chuckled, but when Monte overheard this, his stomach churned.

Hell and Hagopian also had some sort of running joke between them, which Hagopian abbreviated with the word *khanzeer*, Arabic for "pig." He would say the word and then smile his crooked smile. It was not until months later that Monte understood the "joke." On September 26, 1980, a bomb exploded at the Munich Oktoberfest, killing thirteen people and injuring seventy-two. The presumed bomber, one Gundolf Kohler, died in the blast. Self-identified authorities on such matters have described Kohler as "a Bavarian neo-Nazi who belonged to no organization," and "a lone wolf without an organization." As Monte came to realize, however, Kohler was a confederate of Hell's who had arrived at Oktoberfest carrying a bomb that he had been told was set to detonate after he made his getaway. Kohler, then, was what is technically known as a "pig" — an unwitting delivery system for a "pig bomb." He was Hell's *khanzeer*. And far from being a comrade from a "frontline organization," the tall, amiable Teuton with the fancy rifle was in fact Udo Albrecht, founder of a little setup called Freikorps Adolf Hitler, and collaborator with the 400 or so ne'er-do-wells of Karl Heinz Andreas Hoffman's Bavaria-based Wehrsportgruppe Hoffman. Hell was, as Alec put it, "a very dangerous man."

The neo-Nazi's presence at the Fatah base angered Monte: hadn't his friends died fighting against Hell's fellow fascists in east Beirut? Hell, moreover, was a *German* fascist — the sort of fascist our father and uncles had spent years of their youth fighting. Bullets were the most appropriate medium for interacting with the likes of them.

Fortunately for Hell, the bloodbath in Munich had blown his cover, and he disappeared before Monte or anyone else could take steps against him. He resurfaced shortly after that, when police seized him in West Germany, but as he pretended to lead them to a weapons cache near the East German border he bolted and sprinted to the other side.

There, East German police seized him, but somehow—either through incompetence or collusion—he slipped out of their grasp, too, and went deeper underground.

Hell's friendship with Hagopian raised further doubts about the Secret Army leader's integrity, but Monte did his best to resist these doubts. Times were desperate, and he was ready to push Brazilian guerrilla Carlos Marighella's message to its furthest extreme: "Violence before politics." Others concurred. "We love to hear those bombs going off," Tezoog the bomb maker told Monte, as he showed him how to tamp fulminate of mercury into brass tubes for detonators.

By the time I found out about Hell, I had a backlog of issues to raise with my brother. It wouldn't be easy to do that, though, since he lived in one place, while I lived in another: while he toiled away in the slum of Fakhani, I was teaching English and sleeping in a king-size bed in a penthouse in the glittery Hamra District. Every now and then we would meet at Fakhani or the American University campus to exchange a few words, but never long enough to sit down and talk.

Then Monte started disappearing for weeks at a stretch. In mid-July, about two months after he had joined the Secret Army, Hagopian handed him a falsified Iranian passport and an airplane ticket to Athens, and directed him in an off-handed manner to find a Turkish target there—any Turkish target—and hit it. These were the marching orders for Monte's first "foreign operation." After several fruitless days of walking past the Turkish embassy and changing shirts, he returned to Beirut to apprise Hagopian of the difficulties in Athens and to ask what he should do next. Flipping a hand, Hagopian told him to toss a grenade at the Turkish Airlines office and to get on to the next operation. Monte shook his head. He was not about to launch his career as an "armed propagandist" with such a slipshod stunt. After two frustrating days at the Seventh Floor, he boarded another flight to Athens, convinced that henceforth he would have to answer his own questions.

As luck would have it, the flight from Beirut to Athens contained a retinue of pastel-clad tourists from our old hometown, the Walnut Capital of the World. One of the Visalians, a Mrs. Smith, had been a speech therapist at Monte's elementary school fifteen years earlier, when she had tried without much success to cure him of a lisp. Recognizing her former pupil, the cry went up, "Hey, look everybody! It's Monte!" Slaps on the back, and *"Howya doin, Monte?"* filled the second-class compartment, as the aspiring political assassin with the Iranian passport cranked up his imagination to explain to his fellow small-town Californians what exactly he was doing on that flight.

On the evening of July 31, several days after Monte had returned to the Greek capital, a car with diplomatic plates pulled up in front of the Turkish Airlines office, near the spot where he was waiting. Through the darkly tinted glass, it appeared as though there were four shapes in the car, two in the front seat and two in the back. Two weeks had passed since Monte had first arrived in Athens, and he still had not carried out an operation. He walked up to the car, raised his 7.32-mm pistol, and shot the driver and the other passenger in the front seat. Then he twisted around to fire into the shapes in the back seat. As he turned from the car to make his escape, a young man pulled himself from the back seat holding his gunshot wound and sprinted after his assailant. Bystanders joined in the chase.

Dashing across a busy street, Monte slipped and his Seiko wristwatch clattered across the asphalt. It had been a gift from a Japanese friend who had inscribed Monte's name on the back of the movement. Monte pivoted in the middle of the street, searching for the watch among the gawkers and honking cars. He found it, snatched it up, and resumed his dash, pushing past pedestrians on the sidewalk, just ahead of several runners in hot pursuit. Panting hard, he dashed to the top of a knoll and shook off his pursuers in the park beyond the knoll.

The next day, he discovered from a newspaper story that the driver he had shot and killed was one Galip Osman, an administrative attaché at the Turkish embassy in Athens, and an agent for Turkish intelligence, the MIT. Great, Monte thought: one less Turkish spy. But he was not at all happy to learn that the wounded passenger in the front seat was Osman's wife, Sevil. And he was shocked to learn that the shapes in the back seat were Osman's sixteen-year-old son and his fourteen-year-old daughter. The daughter, Neslihan, had died of her wounds, and the bereaved son had sworn in the presence of journalists that when he grew up he would follow his father's footsteps into the MIT.

When Alec later asked Monte why in the world he had shot the boy and girl in the back seat, his comrade snapped, "I wasn't going to leave witnesses to identify me." "At any rate," he later wrote in a strange passage,

> … the special dark glass windows of the attaché's car obstructed the shooter's view of who was who in the car. If a clearer view had been offered the shooter (who thought there were other diplomats in the back seat), the girl's life would probably have been spared.

There was never any question in Monte's mind that the girl's father, the Turkish attaché, was a legitimate target: he had freely chosen to represent a regime that continued to occupy northern Cyprus, Arab Iskenderun, Kurdistan, and most of the Armenian homeland, and was in the process of killing thousands of Kurds, leveling hundreds of their villages, and imprisoning and torturing hundreds of union leaders, students, and other Turkish citizens. And on top of everything else, it would seem, the attaché was further culpable for having driven a car with tinted glass, thereby endangering his children by not having "offered" a clearer target to his assassin.

When I learned that my brother had pointed a pistol at a shape in the back seat of a car and had shot dead a fourteen-year-old girl, I could not shake the conviction that it would take a lot for him ever to redeem himself. As time passed, his expressions of regret became less glib. Five years after the shooting he described it as a counterproductive and indefensible crime, the likes of which should never be repeated, and for the next thirteen years he would attempt to prevent others from committing similarly cruel acts. This would be his gesture of compensation. But the compensation would never be adequate.

When Monte returned to Lebanon from Greece, I noticed that he had lost his smile. He joined a Palestine Popular Struggle Front camp in the desert south of the Bekaa Valley, near the village of Yanta. On his first night of guard duty, thousands of stars brighter than any he had ever seen filled the sky right down to the horizon. For the first time in months, he spent hours in quiet thought, interrupted only by the striped hyena, which whined in the desert like a crying child. After a bout of relentless calisthenics at sunrise, he spent the rest of the day kicking his knees up on the drill ground, scattering brass at the rifle range, crawling under barbed wire and gunfire, and somersaulting shirtless down slopes of sharp stones, thistle, and acanthus thorns.

Many of the trainees at the Struggle Front camp were *shibl*, or "cubs," in their teens. Some of them had literally run through the desert and crossed the Syrian border a few hundred meters east of the camp, to flee Syrian President Hafez al-Assad's crackdown against the Muslim Brotherhood in Syria that summer. The older trainees consisted of Arabs and Armenians, mostly from Syria, Lebanon, and Palestine. There were six Kurdish cadres, too, from Abdullah Ocalan's PKK.

At night, the Kurds actually dreamt about their suffering motherland, and as soon as they awoke they charged off to the drill ground. They dug foxholes with gusto and shouted *Thaura! Thaura!* "Revolution!" during assault practice, instead of the usual *Allahu Akbar!* "God is

Great!" When they picked the odd quince, they left coins for the farmer at the foot of the tree, and when a Druze farmer came to harvest olives at a nearby orchard they climbed the trees with buckets to help. Once, when the Kurd Suleiman broke a banana in half and absent-mindedly handed Comrade Hassan the smaller of the two pieces, his PKK comrade Terjuman demanded a round of criticism and self-criticism. Suleiman came clean with a self-criticism and a solemn oath never again to engage in such unseemly behavior.

After their initial amusement wore off, the scruffy, swearing, cigarette-smoking Arabs and Armenians at the camp began to feel self-conscious in the presence of the abstemious Kurds, with their internationalist songs, their allusions to German classical philosophy, and their constant focus on revolution. But Monte loved these goings-on. "These guys are like *gold!*" he effused.

Their enthusiasm was contagious. One by one, the smokers started tossing aside their cigarette rations after returning from the morning jog. All the comrades grimly huddled around the radio for news about the September 12, 1980 military coup in Turkey. Arab recruits volunteered to shoot Turkish diplomats. Before long, they were all stomping shoulder to shoulder under the sun, shouting in Arabic, Kurdish, and Armenian: "Return to the homeland!" "Struggle until victory!" and "We are *fedayees!*"

At Yanta, Monte felt that expansive feeling that comes with living and fighting together for a common purpose. It was a feeling for which the word "solidarity" is entirely too tepid. The simplest activities — squatting around a tray of lentils; tearing bread and handing it out; donating blood; passing the overcoat at the change of the guard — each of these gestures formed part of a daily liturgy that had nothing to do with egoism *or* altruism. Quite apart from the question of whether their goals were realizable, the new comrades had moved, if only for a few days or weeks, beyond the plodding mediocrity of shopkeepers and the crushing cynicism of Beirut. This was the way a revolutionary movement — a *struggle*, as Monte would say — was supposed to feel.

After the exalted atmosphere of the boot camp under the wide desert sky, it was depressing to return to the cramped, fuggy Seventh Floor, where no one but Hagopian seemed to have any idea what was going on.

In late summer, the first issue of the Secret Army journal, *Armenia*, appeared on glossy paper in broadsheet format, fresh off the Struggle Front's press. Hagopian had long believed that his group needed to publish a journal, to project a properly "intellectual" message to potential supporters. The emblem on the masthead showed a hand clenching a rifle, superimposed over a map that vaguely resembled Woodrow Wilson's fanciful frontiers of Armenia. It was a graphic reminder of how the trappings of violence crowded out sober discussion at the Seventh Floor.

Alec dubbed the first issue of the journal a "shit number," but Monte viewed the new journal as a precious opportunity to exchange ideas and to elevate the level of discussion. Hagopian had a habit of interrupting political discussions with snide jokes. To him, it was all *gur-gur*, "gossip." But now, thanks to the journal, recruits had a forum to discuss goals, strategies, and life experiences. Although *Armenia*'s print run never exceeded a few hundred copies, Monte knew that its readership would far exceed its print run. Secret Army supporters in Lebanon, France, and Iran would pass their copies from hand to hand, discuss its glaring defects, and demand more clarity. And this in turn would strengthen the hands of the only Secret Army members articulate enough to provide greater clarity: namely, Alec, Monte, and likeminded comrades.

Beginning with the second issue and continuing for the next twenty-one issues over the course of three years, Monte forfeited sleep to devote late hours to the journal. Almost all of his written contributions appeared anonymously, and some contained deliberately awkward and ungrammatical passages, as if they were stiff translations from another language. In one article, for example, he imagined a deceased father's words to his son: "I want you to keep your gun after getting it. I want you not to bargain. I want you to be a real struggler."

Although Monte saw great potential in the journal, other duties took precedence. In early fall, Hagopian sent him back to Europe, with orders to bomb the Turkish consulate in Geneva and to collect a "donation" from a wealthy Iraqi-Assyrian there. The Assyrian, a man named Victor Chayto, owned an upscale jewelry shop in Geneva. Sarkis Soghanalian, a Lebanese arms merchant and a CIA collaborator, had enlisted Chayto's help with arms sales to support Iraqi leader Saddam Hussein's war against Iran. Monte embarked on his assignment with a special zeal. He hated arms merchants, he detested Saddam Hussein, and he sympathized with Iran in its defensive war against Iraq. After the debacle in Athens he was determined to do a better job this time around.

Monte met Alec in Geneva, and they tailed Chayto so closely that they learned the songs he sang in the shower. One day in the course of Monte's rounds, he literally ran into an old acquaintance from Bourdj Hamoud while crossing a street. Girair, one of Chayto's bodyguards, blew Monte's cover with a big smile and a surprised "Hey, Monte!" as both did a double take in the middle of the street.

Grabbing a train at the Nyon station, Monte headed to Italy. Soon after that, on the night of October 3, two bombs exploded in Milan, one at a Turkish-owned shop and another at the Mondadori Press office. Both bombs, of course, were Monte's handiwork. The Mondadori bombing was a warning to the editors of the weekly magazine *Panorama*, who had violated an agreement with one of their writers, journalist Rita Porena, concerning an interview with Hagopian. Monte later described this punitive bombing as "anarchistic and Mafia-like."

The Milan bombs had caused no injuries. But Monte had no idea that yet another bomb had exploded that same night back in Geneva, and that it had claimed a victim. At 9:30 on the evening of October 3, as Alec hunched over a table in his room at the Hôtel Beau-Site in Geneva, a white flash engulfed the room. "I can't see!" he shouted to Suzy, a friend who had been in the room with him. Through the smoke and the smell of burned flesh she could make out his bloody face and the stump where a hand had been. Suzy was bleeding from slivers of brass shrapnel, too, but Alec's body had shielded her from the main force of the exploding Semtex that he had been assembling into a small bomb.

After the explosion, the manhunt was on for Monte, who had been spotted with Alec just a few days earlier. Fearing that the Lebanese secret police might take Monte's brother in for questioning, Hagopian ordered his own brother Ohan to fetch me from my apartment in west Beirut. When Ohan arrived at my door on the night of October 9, I had not yet heard about the explosion in Geneva six days earlier. But when he told me I had five minutes to pack all my things, I could tell it was no time to ask questions. I tossed my things into a bed sheet and hauled the bundle downstairs to Ohan's waiting Pontiac.

I had not seen my brother for weeks, so it was strange that he did not greet me with a smile when I arrived at the Seventh Floor. "What happened?" I asked, fearing the answer. "You should sit down," Hagopian answered. I glanced over at my brother, who nodded in agreement.

"A bomb went off in Geneva," Hagopian blurted, "Alec lost his eyes and a hand, and he's in prison."

Months earlier, Alec and Monte had made a pact that if one of them were captured the other one would try to spring him from prison. Monte had already taken the first step to pressure Swiss authorities to release his comrade. On the night of October 8 — almost as soon as Monte had returned to Lebanon — bombs went off at the Swiss embassy in Beirut, the Swiss ambassador's home, and the Swiss first secretary's car. I had heard the explosions from my apartment near Hamra Street, and when I heard the first sketchy report on Radio Monte Carlo the next morning, I had wondered why in heaven's name any of the dozens of armed groups in Beirut would bomb the Swiss embassy, of all places. Now, my brother was packing for Europe again, preparing to take the next step to fulfill his pact with Alec. Meanwhile, as Hagopian informed me and Monte agreed, I would have to remain at the Seventh Floor, to avoid possible detention for questioning in connection with any of this.

Since I was going to be their guest for a while, Hagopian invited me to join the Secret Army. When I refused, he berated me in front of my brother and several of his comrades, ascribing my reticence to laziness. When I turned and walked out to the balcony, Monte followed. "Never let anyone talk to you like that," he said, his eyes flashing. "*Never.*" We had switched roles: now *he* was the older brother, dispensing stern advice to me.

I felt terribly guilty that I was making myself a headache for Monte, even as he faced the task of springing Alec from prison. Since there was nothing for me to do at the Seventh Floor but to mope around all day, I resolved to make myself scarce. I had already received basic training in a Palestinian camp, so it seemed like a good time to follow up on my long-standing wish to volunteer for duty in the south, to help defend Lebanon against the Israeli invaders who regularly dropped bombs on refugee camps. I convinced Hagopian to dispatch me to the Struggle Front training camp near the Syrian border and then I transferred to a front-line position in the south, near Mount Hermon.

Meanwhile, Monte had left for Europe, to "apply pressure" on Swiss authorities. His task was imbued with a sense of heightened urgency: Ara Toranian had visited Alec in police custody and had reported that there was hope that partial sight could be restored to one of his eyes. Swiss authorities did not appear to be pursuing restorative treatment, though, and Monte concluded that they were deliberately denying Alec proper medical treatment, "to make him unable to continue his work to struggle for his people," as he wrote in an unsigned article in *Armenia*.

Monte believed that the sooner he could spring Alec from prison, the better the chances that Alec's sight could be restored, at least partially.

Hagopian, for his part, viewed Alec's incarceration as a challenge to the Secret Army's credibility and a test of the group's resolve. Within the next few days, plate glass began raining on streets in front of Swissair offices and other "Swiss interests" in London, Paris, Marseilles, Geneva, and Madrid. In the book *A Critique of Armenian Armed Action*, Monte lists a total of eighteen bombings and attempted bombings claimed in the name of a fictitious "October 3" group between October 12, 1980 and February 5, 1981. These bombs injured a total of twenty-one passers-by, four of them heavily. Surprisingly, though, they claimed no lives.

Since Monte had already been sighted in Switzerland, it would have been too risky for him to enter that country to mount operations: if he were arrested, Alec would be denied one more agent working for his freedom, and it would take that much longer to spring him. Through an Italian connection, he checked into a Red Brigades safe house in Rome and prepared further strikes against Swiss diplomatic and commercial targets in Italy. While laying low, he practiced Italian with his hosts. Before long, Red Brigades communiqués began repeating Armenian grievances against Ankara.

Upon returning from Europe, Monte assisted new recruits with their last wills and rededicated himself to the group for which his closest comrade had sacrificed his sight. He would arrive on time for appointments and take care of business. He no longer joined in the revolutionary songs, and when Arab comrades pouring tea asked how much sugar he took, he would grunt, "It doesn't matter." After departing without the usual salutations, his former friends would shake their heads: their amiable pal Monte had turned into Hagopian's humorless errand boy.

I didn't like the changes, either. One night my brother arrived at a Struggle Front base and called a meeting while I was on guard duty there. When I didn't show up at the meeting tent, he sent an Arab comrade to relieve me, but I refused to go: I wanted nothing to do with Hagopian or the Seventh Floor. Besides, duty as a guerrilla in southern Lebanon suited me fine: our purpose—to defend Lebanon against Israeli invaders or to die in the process—struck me as both honorable and realistic.

After a few minutes, my brother approached the guard post with a flashlight. Seeing him alone in the darkness, a wave of hopelessness washed over me. I had been having a recurring nightmare, a vivid one: in the dream, I would break the blue door to Hagopian's office, to find my brother standing at the threshold with a stump where his right hand had been. "They cut it off," he would say, at once apologetic and embarrassed. It was never clear who "they" were. Then bullets would begin raining on us from the hallway. I would fall to the floor, fire a few rounds from a pistol, and then turn to check on Monte. He would still be alive, but moving in slow motion, and the right side of his forehead would be missing. Bullets would continue hitting us as we writhed in our blood. The dream would end with one clear thought: *"We're dying like dogs."* For the next thirteen years, I would be haunted by the fear that my little brother would die a slow, gruesome death.

When I completed my tour of duty in southern Lebanon, I hoped to either volunteer for a second tour or to work with Mahmoud Labadi, the director of the PLO Information Office in Beirut. Hagopian, though, insisted that I either join his Secret Army or leave Lebanon. Monte interceded for me, but to no avail.

When I returned to the United States in early 1981, I sent word of my safe arrival to Hagopian, through a contact. I wanted to ease Monte's mind about that at least, but Hagopian didn't bother to share the information with him. After a couple of days with no word of my arrival, it occurred to Monte that Hagopian might have killed me. After all, he had heard Hagopian on the phone, threatening to kill Alec's Dashnak brother, so why not me, too? When Monte finally received news of my safe arrival in the States, he was relieved, of course, but doubts continued gnawing at him like a worm in a walnut. Until this point in time, he had viewed Hagopian as a misguided but reformable "revolutionary friend." Now it dawned on him that "it would be easy to become a 'jackass martyr'." He started sleeping with a pistol.

By this time, Hagopian was drinking half a bottle of whiskey a day, usually late at night. Not willing to risk being spotted by Muslim associates, he would send one of his new recruits to a liquor store to purchase the whiskey for him. It bothered Monte that two of these recruits, skinny dark Abu Mahmoud and brawny fair Lulu, had taken to addressing Hagopian as *Mu'allem*, "Chief."

After a hasty trial, Swiss officials expelled Alec from Switzerland. Zaher al-Khatib, a dashing young Lebanese parliamentarian and a leader of a small organization that called itself the Workers' League, arranged for Alec's February 12, 1981 passage through Beirut Airport.

Alec moved into a first-floor office in the Workers' League building, and community newspapers from Tehran to Los Angeles announced: "Alec is Free!" As the news spread, new recruits flocked to the Seventh Floor. The Secret Army rapidly gained scores of active members and thousands of supporters in a dozen countries, from Canada to India.

And yet, as the new recruits found out soon enough, the group remained a one-man shop: all orders emanated from Hagopian, all connections with other groups went through him, and he was accountable to no one. Journalists reported interviews with cowled "Central Committee members" who introduced themselves as Mihran Mihranian, Vahram Vahramian, and Murad Armenian. But behind the cowls and the pseudonyms was one man — Hagopian himself. Alec, Ajemian, and Monte begged him to form a real central committee, but Hagopian refused to relinquish his prerogatives as sole decision-maker. "This organization is like a whore," he once told me, smiling his crooked smile: "Lots of men come and go, but we stay put, right here." He had used the royal "we."

In mid-January 1981, Italian officials had asked a Fatah official named Hael Abdulhamid to help negotiate a "ceasefire" with the Secret Army. The Italians sent word that they were prepared to support Armenian demands for Turkish recognition of the genocide, in exchange for a Secret Army pledge to desist from bombings in Italy. Monte attended the first negotiations, which took place at the west Beirut home of another PLO official named Abu Hisham. Through their Palestinian intermediaries, the Italians proposed a number of "good faith measures," including the closure of transit centers for emigration from Soviet Armenia. Monte was not interested in cutting such a deal, but he proposed an alternative condition: in the interest of establishing "an atmosphere of trust," the Italian embassy should arrange for Alec's eye treatment in Italy. The day after Yassir Arafat conveyed the message to the Italian embassy, the PLO chairman's secretary informed Hagopian that the Italians had agreed to arrange for the treatment. Within a week, Alec was on his way to Italy, accompanied by family members. After ten days of treatment in one of the most modern hospitals in Italy, however, doctors concluded that the retinal nerve was irreparably damaged. Alec returned to Beirut resigned to total blindness.

Monte blamed the malign negligence of Swiss authorities for the fact that his friend had lost whatever had remained of his vision, but he blamed Hagopian even more. It was Hagopian, after all, who had dispatched Alec to Switzerland in the first place, thus endangering the Secret Army's best asset for the sake of a petty extortion scam. Alec was everything Hagopian was not: educated, articulate, fluent in Armenian, and well respected by Armenians and Arabs alike. Now, thanks to the explosion at the Hôtel Beau-Site and the attendant notoriety, Hagopian's main rival within the Secret Army was both blind and highly visible. It had all worked out so well for Hagopian: Alec had become a showpiece for the Secret Army, escorted to press conferences and led through funeral processions. Meanwhile, his injuries, together with the constant threat of arrest attendant with his notoriety, conspired to isolate him.

But even as Monte's doubts were growing, the Secret Army was riding a wave of popularity among Armenians in the Middle East. On April 24, 1981, Monte's friends in Tehran watched in shock as thousands of men, women, old folks, students, and even children grabbed up flags, banners, posters, and leaflets emblazoned with the Secret Army insignia and jammed the streets in front of the Turkish embassy. Undeterred by the Iranian Revolutionary Guards posted around the embassy to defend it, demonstrators scaled the fence and smashed windows. Confused, the Revolutionary Guards fired into the air, but this only fueled the teeming rage. When the Guards followed up with tear gas, the demonstrators set fire to their leaflets to burn the gas out of the air. They tore down the fence with their bare hands, swarmed onto the embassy grounds, hoisted down the Turkish flag, and burned it, while the staff inside the building trembled in fear.

When Monte heard about the demonstration in Tehran, he grabbed the phone and dialed up his friends there: "Congratulations!" he shouted. The spontaneous rage in Tehran confirmed what he had suspected for years: sixty-five years after the Armenian genocide, his compatriots had literally jumped at their first chance to lash back at the Turkish government. But what was even more encouraging was the fact that the crowd had switched its allegiance, if only for a few hours, from the Dashnak Party that had monopolized community leadership for six decades, to the unknown Secret Army. From then on, when Monte invoked "the potential of the diaspora," he would recall photographs of enraged masses marching through tear gas to pull down the fence around the Turkish embassy.

For months, Monte's hopes for the Secret Army had been locked in silent combat with his growing doubts about Hagopian. Now, even as the demonstrators in Tehran set his hopes soaring, Hagopian's erratic behavior was escalating. On May 28, 1981, a bomb exploded on the grounds of an Armenian community center in Paris, killing a neighbor's guard. On June 4, 1981, police dismantled a bomb planted at the entrance of an Armenian church on Rue Jean-Goujon, and the next day a bomb exploded in front of another Armenian church in Issy-Les-Molineaux, a suburb of Paris. Monte had begun to suspect that these bombings had not been the work of the "Turkish fascists" who had supposedly taken credit for them, but of Hagopian and his provocateurs.

On or around June 20, 1981, Alec arrived at the desert camp at Yanta, supposedly to boost morale there. In reality, though, the purpose of the visit was at long last to discuss doubts about Hagopian with Monte, who was at the camp at the time. The two comrades sat at the top of a limestone cliff behind the camp. While Monte looked out across the desert, Alec began describing Hagopian's lies, cruelty, and intransigence: the poorly planned operations, the staged bombings of Armenian targets in Paris, the broken agreements with allies, the bombs in bistros and metro stations, the senseless civilian casualties.

Alec paused for a response from Monte, but all he heard was the wind blowing through dry thistle. He resumed his report in a steady, factual voice: Hagopian abused volunteers, spread distrust among the ranks, and fraternized with the likes of Hell, the neo-Nazi. He refused to relinquish control over any important aspect of the Secret Army's work. He stood against the Secret Army's transformation into a genuinely revolutionary organization with an accountable, collective leadership and clear goals. Meanwhile, time was running out for Armenians who wanted to join the coming revolution in Turkey ...

Monte turned towards his sightless comrade, whose face was still flecked with green copper shrapnel from the explosion in Geneva.

After a moment, Alec heard soft sobbing. "What's going on?" he asked.

I had seen my brother shed tears before, but in all the years I had known him, I had never heard him cry. That day on the cliff at Yanta, Alec heard him cry.

Monte took a moment to collect himself. "The Armenian people," he said, "have lost their last hope."

8

Terrorist Suspect

O n the cliff at Yanta, Monte wept for a loss even more grievous than the spilling of innocent blood. He was convinced more than ever that the future of Armenia turned on the ability of his compatriots to fight in their own army for the right to return to the larger part of the homeland they had lost as a result of the 1915 genocide. The regime in Ankara occupied three-quarters of the Armenian homeland, and thus continued to thwart what Monte described as "the historical and cultural attachment" of Armenians to "their homeland *in its entirety*." If the occupation continued unopposed, then not only would Armenians of the diaspora face certain assimilation, but the resulting demoralization would also accelerate emigration from tiny Soviet Armenia, and the "white massacre" would have succeeded.

At some point after descending from the cliff that day in June 1981, Monte resolved to "solve Hagopian's problem," to kill the monster. Monte had sunk to the deepest depths of Grandpa Missak's "snake pit of Armenian politics," and there at the bottom, in a scaly coil, lay black-eyed Hagopian.

His plans were soon interrupted, though. Beginning on July 11, Israeli F-15s returned to Lebanon to drop bombs on the city of Sidon, as well as the market town of Nabatiyeh and the densely populated refugee camps of Ein el-Hilweh and Rachidiyeh. When the attacks began, Monte and perhaps eight other Secret Army fighters had been manning three of the Struggle Front's defensive positions—one near Hamra village and two in and around Kfar Tibnit, near Nabatiyeh. Israeli tanks squealed over the hills in the medium distance and Israeli helicopters hovered low overhead, dropping phosphor flares that threw flickering blue shadows over the boulders and brush around Monte's earthen bunker.

Armed with a map, binoculars, and a radio, Monte and his comrades went up against one of the mightiest armies on earth. Putting his math skills together with his military training, he radioed enemy coordinates to Palestinian rocket launchers and 130-mm artillery guns several kilometers behind the lines to the north. Then, as *Washington Post* journalist Jonathan Randal observed, the Palestinian gunners unleashed devastatingly accurate barrages against the invaders. They pummeled the militarized settlements of Qiryat Shemona and Nahariyya in Galilee, too, and on July 22 they scored direct hits on two Israeli tanks at the Khardali Bridge, near Monte's spotting position.

On July 24, the warplanes disappeared after a Saudi-brokered cease-fire, and the forward spotters at Kfar Tibnit emerged from their trenches. Monte lifted his eyes towards Galilee with the sun on his face. During the previous fourteen days and nights of bone-rattling artillery and aircraft bombardment, the Israelis, with their American-made F-15s and F-4 Phantom bombers and their French-built Mirages, had killed at least 450 people and wounded over 1,000. Many of these casualties had been Lebanese, not Palestinians, and the vast majority had been civilians. At the end of the battle, though, even the *New York Times* admitted that "the heavy Israeli attacks appear to have inflicted little or no military damage on the Palestinian guerrillas." Kfar Tibnit confirmed a lesson Monte had taken to heart years earlier, when he had reflected on his brief visit to Vietnam: determined fighters could hold their positions, damage a vastly superior enemy, and emerge unscathed.

After the Israeli retreat, Hagopian moved his wife and his stepdaughter Toani to a flat in Airplane Building in east Beirut, right across from the Phalangists' center on the Sinn el-Fil Highway. After a day at work, the Secret Army chief would drive home through Phalangist checkpoints at the Museum crossing and take a hot shower in his newly renovated bathroom. Then he would dress in a black faux-silk kimono, flop down on an overstuffed piece of upholstery from Gallery Khabbaz, and light up a Winston, while Marija poured him a whiskey and his increasingly estranged stepdaughter pouted around in slippers. This picture nauseated Monte: Hagopian's life was conforming ever more closely to the lives of the ruthless businessmen he so thoroughly resembled in other respects. Hagopian's new residence posed a more serious problem, too: now that the Secret Army chief rarely spent nights at the Seventh Floor any more, it would be even harder to eliminate him.

On top of everything else, Monte soon faced another distraction, when Hagopian assigned him the task of training four volunteers for a spectacular "armed propaganda" mission in a European capital. The operation would go by the code-name *Van*, an ancient Armenian citadel that lay in ruins in Turkey. Calculating that the Van Operation would "strengthen the progressive tendencies inside ASALA," Monte postponed his plot against Hagopian and focused on the task at hand with grim determination. Throughout August and September, Vazken Sislian, Kevork Guzelian, Aram "Anto" Basmajian, and a new recruit, Hagop Julfayan, trained at a new camp they had set up at Tellet el-Wardeh, the Hill of Roses, on the coast in southern Lebanon. The barracks was an old stone house at the end of a red dirt road that wended through olive and fig trees and stone terraces of grapevines. The four recruits had already received considerable commando training by late summer, when Monte accelerated the training to Olympic pace: running, calisthenics, group maneuvers, karate, pistols, special weapons, and explosives.

On September 24, 1981, the training paid off. Vazken, Kevork, Aram, and Hagop entered the foyer at the Turkish consulate at Boulevard Haussman 170, near the Opéra Garnier in Paris. They then extracted a Kalashnikov and pistols from a backpack, pulled pins from grenades, held the grenades over their heads, and proceeded to take over the consulate, room by room. A Turkish guard shot Vazken in the abdomen, but was immediately killed by return fire. Hagop Julfayan caught a bullet, too, but the comrades ignored the pain and blood loss for the duration of their siege.

As police and television crews arrived on the scene, so did angry Turkish immigrants. Before long, 500 Turks had congregated behind police barricades to demonstrate their support for the hostages, and 150 Armenian counter-demonstrators converged on the spot, to demonstrate their support for the commandos. Shoving matches turned into fistfights, as police tried to separate the two angry groups.

Meanwhile, inside the consulate building, the commandos released a mother and a child, and as soon as they determined that the vice-consul was losing too much blood from a gunshot wound he had sustained during the take-over, they released him, too. After holding the embassy for fifteen hours, and having made their point, the commandos laid down their arms. Several of the hostages insisted on shaking hands with their captors before they left the embassy building, and a hostage who had been wounded during the takeover told police, "I'm sure that the gunman didn't do it on purpose. The shot went off by itself." On videotape broadcast internationally, Vazken Sislian emerged from the embassy holding a gunshot wound in the abdomen with one hand, but standing tall and raising his other hand in a "V" for victory salute. French police cuffed the commandos and whisked them away to the Maison de Correction de Fresnes, a former Vichy concentration camp twenty kilometers south of Paris.

Monte considered the Van Operation to be by far the best operation the Secret Army had ever undertaken: it had required planning, martial skill, nerve, and quick thinking. One person had been killed — a guard who had opened fire first — but aside from the attackers themselves and the vice-consul, no one else had been injured. Valiant Vazken, Kevork, Hagop, and Aram galvanized the Armenians of France, as well as thousands of others across the diaspora who until then would never have thought of themselves as "terrorist sympathizers."

Meanwhile, Monte received marching orders for another "foreign operation." He arrived in Rome by train on October 13, checked into a hotel not far from the Turkish embassy, then drove a rented car to a pre-arranged location just outside the city to pick up a pistol from Italian comrades. The moment he laid eyes on the 7-mm automatic, though, he moaned, "This is a toy!" Since Turkish embassy staff had taken to driving armor-plated cars with bulletproof glass, the proper tool for attacking them would have been at least a 9-mm pistol with alternating teflon and dum-dum rounds. But instead, Hagopian had provided Monte with a small-caliber pistol. "They might as well have issued me a spear," he muttered.

On October 25, he dined at an empty cafe on a little island on the river near Piazza di Spagna, and then he strolled to a park near the Colosseum, absorbed in thoughts about architecture and the morals of various nations. He started to ascend some stairs leading into the park when he stopped in his tracks: he was standing in front of a Turkish consular official's car, one of the cars he had been shadowing for almost two weeks!

Monte hurried to his hotel room to fetch the pistol and set his jaw as he screwed on the silencer. This time he would shoot only an adult male in the front seat. By the time he returned with the pistol under his blue nylon jacket, he had devised a plan of attack and escape. He crossed the street, approaching the embassy staff car. Turkish embassy second secretary Gokberk Ergenikon, at the wheel of the car, noticed him approaching. The Turk started rolling up his window and went for his 9-mm pistol. Monte pulled his 7-mm from his jacket and pointed the silencer through a diminishing three- to four-inch opening in the window. Ergenikon fired a shot, hitting Monte's left forearm, and knocking his first shot off target. As the window closed, Monte squeezed off several more shots, but the 7-mm slugs did not pierce the bulletproof glass. He knew he had only grazed his target with his first shot, but it was no use to try to finish the job. The failed assassin buried the hand of his bleeding arm deep in his jacket pocket and sprinted from the scene.

Several days later, having escaped to a safe house in Milan, an Italian comrade drove him to Paris for medical treatment in another safe house. By the time the doctor in Paris unwrapped the towel, the slug had been in Monte's arm for five days.

Hagopian was in France, too. Having collected more donations for the Secret Army, he induced a reluctant protégé to accompany him on his November 11 return flight to Beirut. The Middle East Airlines flight log listed this protégé as one Dimitriu Georgiu, but his real name, of course, was Monte Melkonian. Against his better judgment, Monte had set aside his concerns about traveling on the forged Cypriot passport that renegade Palestinian ringleader Abu Nidal had provided. The plane idled on the tarmac at Orly Airport for an hour, until the airline staff asked passengers to disembark while a repair crew replaced the glass in one of the plane's windows. Hagopian and Monte ducked into a restaurant in the airport lobby. Suddenly, "Dimitriu Georgiu" heard his name announced over the PA system. Hagopian left the airport, while his protégé stayed and calmly finished the brunch he had ordered. A few minutes later, at 10:45 a.m., a plainclothes officer of the airport security police approached him, asking for his name and passport. Monte's forged Cypriot passport, it seems, bore a number very close in series to the similar passports of two Libyan suspects who had been arrested in connection with a recent bombing at a synagogue on Rue Copernic in Paris. (Monte's passport bore the number A328140, while the suspects who rented the motorcycle that transported the explosive in the Rue Copernic bombing carried passports with numbers A308747 and A303139.) The Rue Copernic bomb had killed four people, including a small child, and had wounded twenty-two others.

Airport security police reckoned they had nabbed *un gros poisson*, "a big fish" of international terrorism, and a check of the suspect's bags confirmed their suspicions. The bags contained Secret Army tracts, newspaper clippings about the Van Operation, 10,200 francs, and a couple of wireless microphones. At about 5:30 p.m., after several hours of fruitless interrogation, they formally arrested the suspect and drove him to the Palais de Justice. During a strip search there, they discovered a recent bullet wound in his left forearm, one that matched Ergenekon's description of the wound he had recently inflicted on his assailant in Rome.

Monte spent that night in cell 36 of the *dépôt*, a dungeon in the inner courtyard of the Palais de Justice. The next day, two bombs damaged the Air France office and the French Cultural Center in Beirut. A hitherto unknown "Orly Group" claimed responsibility for the attacks. On Monte's third day of incarceration, Ergenikon arrived in Paris to see if he could identify his assailant in a police line-up. Monte decided he needed a shave. For lack of a razor, he sharpened a butter knife against the walls of his cell, and then dragged it over his cheeks and chin. By the end of his shave, he looked as though he had emerged from a spat with a wildcat. Just before the police stood him in the line-up facing a two-way mirror, he slipped wads of paper into his shoes to appear taller, and then he stuffed something between his cheeks and teeth, giving his mug a jowlier contour. Ergenikon squinted at Monte and five other men in the line-up. After forty minutes, he fingered a warder at Fresnes Prison, a guy who did not resemble Monte in the least.

The police, whom Monte called *les flics* ("cops"), could not hold their suspect indefinitely for a mere passport violation, and it made little sense to provoke further bombings. So when the forty-eight-hour initial investigative phase (*la garde à vue*) lapsed, the Public Prosecutor's Department gave the order to let the suspect go. The *flics* were infuriated. Monte spent a night under police surveillance at the Orly Hilton, putting the bill on his own tab. If all went well he would be on the 11:00 a.m. flight to Beirut the next morning.

In the interim, however, the Saturday edition of *Le Figaro* had run a story on the detention of the terrorist suspect, hitting a sensitive nerve by associating him with the attack on Rue Copernic. Confident that the public mood had shifted, the *flics* grabbed Monte and handcuffed him again. In all, Monte would spend twenty-five nights in Division 2, cell 88 at Fresnes, the same prison where the four commandos of the Van Operation had been locked up.

Ara Toranian retained Patrick Devedjian, the Gaullist mayor of the Paris suburb of Antony, as Monte's attorney. Meanwhile, "Orly Group" attacks escalated as Hagopian applied more pressure for Monte's release. On November 13, 1981 a grenade injured a policeman driving on the Boulevard Périphérique near Porte de Charenton. The next day, a blast buckled sheet metal in a parking lot at La Bourdonnais near Les Vedettes de Paris. The day after that, four bombs scorched an Air France office, and branches of Banque Libano-Français, Union des Assurances de Paris and Fransabank, in the eastern suburbs of Beirut. The same day, yet another "Orly Group" bomb exploded at a McDonald's restaurant on Boulevard Saint Michel in Paris, causing no injuries, and on November 16, an explosion at Gare de l'Est wounded two passers-by. On November 19, French airport security shut down Orly Airport for an hour and declared a full-scale alert, after an anonymous caller claimed that the control tower was going to blow. A communiqué signed by the "Orly Group" threatened to kill French diplomats and to destroy an Air France flight in mid-air. Then, on December 3, 1981 Hagopian told reporters from a French weekly magazine: "Now we're ready to strike French authorities hard."

On December 7, 1981, the day before Monte's trial, the court handed down an edict forbidding him from ever setting foot on French territory again. After a brief trial, he received a four-month suspended sentence for possessing a falsified passport, and the next day (December 9), after deliberating for closer to two minutes than twenty, the judge ordered the terrorist suspect to be expelled from France. Police inspectors placed Monte on a flight to Beirut.

On December 10, Hagopian whisked the new arrival off to a press conference at the "Voice of the Workers" radio station. Secret Army militants flanked a figure in a black hood with ghoulish eye slits, whom they introduced as Dimitriu Georgiu. Then Hagopian pulled the hood off like a magician. Instead of a rabbit, he revealed Monte's close-cropped head. "Although Georgiu answered a few questions, the unidentified spokesman seems to have been in firm control of the proceedings," stated a report dated December 16, 1981 from the American embassy in Beirut.

Behind the poker face, Monte was livid. For almost a month, he had endured solitary confinement, long hours of interrogations, and threats, in order to conceal his identity and even his native language. He seemed to have convinced French police that his real name was Khatchig Avedissian, an Armenian born in Turkey and living in Lebanon. But now, not more than a few hours after his release, Hagopian had seen fit to advertise Monte's real identity to the international press corps in Beirut. Now that his identity was out in the open, Interpol,

Turkish MIT, and at least four other police agencies were out to get him. Monte Melkonian was a wanted man now, publicly identified and confined "for security reasons" to the Seventh Floor under the watchful eyes of Hagopian's henchmen, Abu Mahmoud and Lulu. Like Alec before him, Monte now found himself at the end of a short leash with few options: he had made himself the slave of a clever man.

Months had passed since he had first determined that Hagopian had to go—months of postponing the "definitive steps" he had to take against Hagopian. Israel's July 1981 invasion of southern Lebanon, the training of the Van commandos; the Rome operation, and Monte's arrest in Paris—this series of events had delayed the day of reckoning by more than six months. Now, with Monte confined to the Seventh Floor, and with Hagopian commuting from east Beirut, it would be much harder to eliminate him. On top of that, the Secret Army chief had acquired the habit of disappearing for days at a time on "business trips" around the Mediterranean, coming and going without notice. It was as if he smelled danger at the Seventh Floor.

Monte would have to continue biding his time, going through the motions of discharging his duties, while waiting for an opportunity to strike. But each training session he conducted, each communiqué he wrote, and each extorted "donation" he collected only bolstered Hagopian's position, misled more youths, and endangered more innocent lives.

Almost four months had passed since Monte had returned to Beirut from Paris and had silently sworn to "solve Hagopian's problem" quickly. Soon, however, he would have to postpone the final reckoning yet again. On March 31, Mom, Dad, Marcia, and Maile stepped off a silver passenger jet onto the tarmac at Beirut Airport, after a forty-five-minute flight from Cairo. Lulu met them at the airport and drove them by a circuitous route to Fakhani. When they plopped their bags down in the Seventh Floor, Monte greeted them with a big smile and bear hugs. He looked good—bathed, tan, and fit in his jeans, tee shirt, and rubber sandals.

They unpacked their bags. Dad had brought a bag of home-cured gebrail raisins, and Mom had brought dental floss, toothpaste, two new pairs of Levi jeans, and new underwear. Their son was grateful for the raisins and the toothpaste, but he didn't need the jeans, the pair he was wearing still had much life left in it.

They spent most of their week-long visit in one room, catching up on news about family and friends, while young men and women rushed to

and fro, huffing, puffing, and lugging guns. Mom and Dad slept on a
divan, while the others slept on couches and the floor. Mom could not
fathom why her son would choose to live in these cramped, charmless
conditions. She reminded him that, in the course of "doing his own
thing," he had caused her countless sleepless nights. Wincing, Monte
informed her that he was not "doing his own thing"; he was performing a national duty: "This is a fifty-year struggle," he said, "If your
generation had started it years ago, we'd be that much further ahead."

"Struggle?!" his father exhaled, "What struggle? We were trying to
get *food* to eat!"

This was perhaps the closest thing to a heart-to-heart talk that Monte
and his father had ever had. They didn't talk much about Monte's
plans, though, and once it became clear that he was not about to be dis-
suaded from his calling, the arguments ceased and conversations were
pleasant. Monte laughed at jokes, but Maile noticed that he never let
loose with a deep belly laugh, as he formerly had done. He seemed
distracted.

In the meantime, Hagopian had returned from his latest business
trip. When the elder Mr. Melkonian first laid eyes on the Secret Army
chief in his blazer, he turned to his son, nodded his head in Hagopian's
direction, and said: "That guy's a little Napoleon." Hunching his shoulders to suppress a burst of laughter, Monte put his finger to his lips:
"*Shhhh!*" Hagopian treated the guests politely but not warmly.

After much lobbying, Hagopian permitted Monte and his guests a
couple of hours of sightseeing in Beirut before they parted ways. The
family talked and munched on green almonds as they strolled along the
palisade overlooking the Mediterranean Sea at dusk. The next morning,
Monte saw them off for their return flight to Cairo.

"He said he was following his principles," Dad told a journalist ten
years later. "What could we do?" Once, when I brought up the subject
of Monte's dedication to his cause above personal safety, Dad sighed,
"It's one of those things ..."

Now that his parents and sisters had left and were safely out of retaliatory range of Hagopian's henchmen, Monte dug his fingernails into
his palms and rededicated himself to "solving Hagopian's problem."
He was now ready to pay a higher price to get rid of Hagopian. That
higher price would involve killing not just the main target, but if necessary Lulu, Abu Mahmoud, and anyone else who got in the way, too. In
late May 1982, he hurriedly booby-trapped a barracks room at the Hill

of Roses, just ahead of a visit by Hagopian. After rigging the bomb, he concealed the detonator under a cloth in an adjoining room. When Hagopian entered the booby-trapped room, the time was right. Monte pushed the button … *but the bomb didn't detonate!* He punched the button again. *Nothing.* In his rush to rig the bomb, he must have left a loose wire connection to the detonator.

Monte quickly and covertly disassembled the booby-trap, then retired to the toilet and hit his head with his fist. Athens, Rome, and now this! That made three assassination attempts that he had botched — or four, counting the car-bomb attack in early 1980 that had killed Camille Chamoun's bodyguard, but had failed to kill the warlord himself. Thanks to the fact that Monte had failed to attach one wire from a battery to a detonator, Hagopian had survived without even being aware that someone had tried to kill him.

Monte had already abandoned the first condition he had placed on his decision to assassinate Hagopian — namely, the injunction against killing anyone but his main target. Now he was ready to jettison the second condition, the condition of secrecy: he was ready to kill Hagopian "in front of everyone, if necessary."

"Very, very, very unfortunately," Monte lamented in his *Self-Criticism*, even this last desperate plan would come to nothing. Another storm was approaching, one that would "turn Lebanon upside down," as Monte would later describe it. Even in his distracted state of mind, the warning signals were obvious: Palestinians of the West Bank had exploded in mass protests, US military aid to Israel had increased by several hundred million dollars during the first quarter of 1982, and Ariel Sharon had returned from Washington DC after five days of discussions with Secretary of State Alexander Haig. Clearly, another Israeli invasion was in the offing.

Hagopian disappeared, and Monte made his way south to the camp on the Hill of Roses. On June 1, the aircraft carrier USS Kennedy took up a position off the Lebanese coast. Then, in the pre-dawn hours of June 3, Monte watched from a trench as a line of Huey helicopters approached his hill, growling like bears. The long-awaited invasion had begun.

Monte and a handful of Secret Army comrades ducked into orchards and vineyards, as southern Lebanon came under two days of bone-jarring bombardment. Then, at eleven in the morning on June 6, thousands of Israeli troops backed by warplanes, ships, tanks, and heavy artillery, began pouring across the border from Galilee and squealing up the coastal road in a solid column of motorized armor. The Syrian Army retreated to positions north of the Beirut–Damascus Highway in the Bekaa Valley, and as usual, Arab diplomats did little more than exercise their jaw muscles in the UN General Assembly, while the United States vetoed even the most insipid Security Council objections to the invasion. In a flash, several thousand poorly trained Lebanese and Palestinian defenders armed with rifles and rocket-propelled grenades faced 90,000 invading troops, 1,300 tanks, 1,300 APCs, and 12,000 troop and supply trucks. With over 600 combat aircraft, including Phantoms and 120 of the latest F-15s and F-16s, the Israelis monopolized Lebanon's airspace, and thanks to Israeli gunships and the US 6th Fleet, they had sewn up the coast as well.

For the defenders, Beirut represented the only hope of sustained resistance. Monte and his comrades trudged north with heavy packs, evading helicopters and warplanes. On June 9, they arrived at Zaher al-Khatib's family estate in the hills northeast of Sidon, to regroup. The next day, nine Secret Army recruits, joined by Workers' League comrades and a couple of Palestinians, continued their trek north. Arriving in an abandoned mountain village, Monte proposed setting up an ambush against the advancing Israelis. His experience as an artillery spotter at Kfar Tibnit the previous summer was fresh in his memory: as he later summed it up, "The rule is that one must attack, cause harm to the enemy, and retreat with no losses."

One of the Palestinians in the group glowered at Monte. "You're crazy!" he shouted, "You're going to get us all killed!" Everybody knew that enemy warplanes would swoop down at the first report of gunshots, to napalm the landscape. Ignoring the Palestinian's protestations, the Secret Army and Workers' League comrades began setting up firing positions along the road. Exasperated, the Palestinian grabbed Monte's Kalashnikov and tried to wrench it from his hands. Monte held on, and the two engaged in a tug-of-war. Suddenly, an Israeli helicopter descended from nowhere like a huge spider, sending a squall of dust billowing over them. The guerrillas ducked behind a wall and continued their tug-of-war there, pushing and pulling with gritted teeth. Although they evaded the chopper, it had scuttled the ambush plan, resolving the dispute in the Palestinian's favor. They had to leave the village quickly: for all they knew, the chopper pilot had already radioed for an airstrike, and warplanes were on the way.

By the time Monte and his comrades completed their twenty-seven-hour trek to Beirut, the refugee camps of Ein el-Hilweh, Rachidiyeh, and al-Bass had been reduced to fields of twisted metal, pulverized concrete, and corpses. When the invaders arrived at the southern out-skirts of Beirut, however, they stopped. Despite their overwhelming military advantage, they would not push into west Beirut by land, as long as several thousand lightly armed Palestinians remained in the city to defend it. Instead, Menachem Begin cut off food, water, electric-ity, and medical supplies to west Beirut, and then the Nobel Peace laureate ordered saturation bombing of the city from air, land, and sea. Four hundred tanks, 100 heavy artillery pieces, offshore gunboats, and one of the largest airforces on earth began dumping thousands of tons of munitions, including white phosphorus, cluster bombs, and airburst bombs, onto the 500,000 civilians of west Beirut.

Throughout July, Menachem Begin transformed west Beirut into a charnel house. Casualty figures published in the West put the death toll that summer at 17,825. Another half a million had been driven from their homes in the south of Lebanon; 30,000 were maimed, and the country had sustained untold billions of dollars of property damage. According to the International Red Cross, the vast majority of the vic-tims were civilians, and a large proportion were children.

On the other side of the ledger, Monte's comrades had somehow managed to kill several hundred armed Israeli invaders that summer, and the number was steadily rising, even after Begin "redeployed" to less vulnerable positions. Reagan sent in the Marines, and his special envoy Philip Habib promised that the United States would now defend the same Palestinian refugees who had just suffered so terribly at the hands of America's proxies — but only on the condition that PLO fight-ers would leave Beirut. When Arafat accepted the deal, Israeli Defense Minister Ariel Sharon proclaimed: "We have done a service to the world. Israel has driven international terrorism from Lebanon."

As the Israeli siege ground on, Monte commanded a position near the Cadmus Hotel, where he and a handful of Secret Army guerrillas manned a single 120-mm cannon to defend their stretch of beach against an amphibious landing. The Seventh Floor had been empty since the first days of the invasion. For weeks, the Secret Army had been preparing for the inevitable exodus from Beirut, hiding weapons and burning documents on the balcony, including Monte's thick notebooks on Turkish history. Explosives and guns had already been distributed among the recruits, smuggled through Israeli and Phalangist lines, and hidden in homes in east Beirut. In late August, Hagopian and other Secret Army members followed the last of their arsenal out of west

Beirut, through Israeli and Phalangist checkpoints "with the greatest of ease," as Monte noted, thanks to "Israeli and Phalangist incompetence."

The invasion stoked Hagopian's paranoia and sadism, and the ensuing confusion provided the cover he needed to shore up his control of the Secret Army. In mid-July, he ordered Lulu and a new henchman, Ramez, to execute Nishan Dadourian, a blind man whom Hagopian had abducted and kept tied up in a small room, apparently for no other reason than that he had been a friend of a certain Hamo M., a potential rival with close connections with the Iraqi Baath Party and Fatah. Ramez and Lulu took turns firing a Czech 7.65-mm machine pistol into the blind man's head, neck, and back at point-blank range. Because of the low-powered firearm and Dadourian's powerful build, they fired thirty-five rounds before they were sure he was dead. The executioners then heaved the body into a car and dumped it somewhere in the rubble of the bombardment.

Soon after Dadourian's murder, the Secret Army chief ordered the execution of another recruit, Sarkis Kiulkhandjian, whom Hagopian had grown to dislike. Ramez did it alone this time, with one 9-mm slug in the head. To complete the indignity, Hagopian then announced that Kiulkhandjian's corpse was his own, and that he himself had died during a bombardment. "Hagopian is dead—We are all Hagopians!" *Armenia* announced in bold letters, and Secret Army supporters from Los Angeles to Tehran requested church services for their "martyred leader." Emboldened by his faked death, Hagopian made his way to safety in east Beirut. Meanwhile, Monte and half a dozen of his Secret Army comrades remained at their posts in west Beirut until Yassir Arafat ordered them to evacuate the city, along with 7,550 PLO fighters and 1,000 Syrian soldiers.

The first group of these evacuees embarked on Saturday, August 28 from the port of Beirut as part of the Palestinian contingent. When they disembarked at the Syrian port of Latakia, Syrian authorities transported the non-Palestinians, including a small number of Kurds, Bengalis, and Eritreans, to the prison-like Hamuriah military camp near Damascus. Hafez Al-Assad had always been skittish about the presence of militants—even unarmed militants—on Syrian territory, and memories of his brutal confrontation with the Muslim Brotherhood two years earlier only underscored the necessity of keeping a close track on the evacuees from Lebanon.

At Hamuriah, Monte joined a huddle around a transistor radio, to listen to the first reports of the massacre at the Sabra and Chatilla camps. The news saddened and angered him, but it did not come as a surprise. He had assumed all along that Reagan's pledge to defend the refugees was worse than worthless, and he also knew from first-hand experience in Bourdj Hamoud that Israel's axe-wielding Phalangist proxies were capable of great cruelty. Now, well over 1,000 corpses — most of them women and children — confirmed his assumptions.

Most of Monte's fellow inmates sweltered for a month and a half at Hamuriah before their expulsion from Syria, but thanks to intervention by a Syrian Air Force "liaison officer," the Armenians spent only one week there, before moving to the Hotel Ramsis in Damascus. After ten days at the hotel, Monte, Ramez, and three or four other members of an advance party made their way to Lebanon's Bekaa Valley. On September 26 (less than a month after they had been evacuated from Lebanon by sea), they dropped their packs in a house in the Bekaa village of Al Marj, which they shared with Abu Nidal's group, the Fatah Revolutionary Council. In a published interview at the time, Hagopian (using yet another pseudonym) stated that henceforth the Secret Army and Abu Nidal's group should be considered one and the same organization. Monte never applied the term *comrades* to "Abu Nidal's boys," however: for one thing, he detested their patron, Saddam Hussein. For another thing, they couldn't keep their mouths shut, and they seemed incapable of abiding by even the most elementary security measures. And worst of all, outrages like the Rue Copernic synagogue bombing in Paris confirmed their criminal stupidity beyond any doubt.

After a couple of months in the Bekaa Valley, Monte rejoined Hagopian at a Damascus safe house on November 26, a day after his twenty-fifth birthday. By then, his isolation and his inability to "solve Hagopian's problem" were taking their toll. One December morning, he awoke to learn from another recruit that he had been talking in his sleep for an hour that night. The report shocked and worried him. Had he revealed his intention to kill Hagopian? It came as some relief to learn that he had done his sleep-talking in slurred English: who knows what Abu Mahmoud would have done if Monte had sleep-talked in intelligible Armenian. But had this been his first episode of sleep-talking? And why should he assume it would be the last?

After the sleep-talking episode, he was glad to return to the camp near Yanta, which the Struggle Front had abandoned in 1981. At the time, only a handful of residents were at the camp, including a tall Iranian teenager named Tavit Tavitian and an explosives trainer known as Khalil. Monte spent two months there, in a cinderblock barracks surrounded by snow, with little to do but ruminate. One day in February 1983, he happened to be crossing the Beirut–Damascus Highway near Deir Zanoun when he noticed a white Volvo approaching. It looked like Seta's father's car! It was cold, and his face was covered with a *kefiyeh*. He stopped in the middle of the road, and as the car passed, he caught a glimpse of Seta. As it turned out, she was home for winter break, and the family was on its way to visit friends in the nearby town of Zahle. The car passed close enough for Monte to touch, and as he watched it disappear down the icy road, another car almost hit him.

Monte stumbled off the road and trudged back to the barracks, deep in thought. Almost exactly one year earlier, he had shared a passionate kiss with Seta during a furtive meeting in the basement of a radio station in Fakhani. It was just a kiss and their meeting was brief, but Seta had taken a big risk by coming to Fakhani to search for Monte behind Hagopian's back. That kiss was Seta's promise—a promise to wait for him. But how long would she have to wait? Twenty precious months had passed—almost two years!—since Monte had resolved to kill Hagopian. Each of his successive plans had come to nothing, though, and Hagopian had emerged stronger than ever. Monte would have to try something new. At the risk of being betrayed, he decided to enlist confederates in his assassination plan.

As the snowy days and nights had passed, he had noticed that Tavitian and Khalil had begun muttering against Hagopian. When Monte cautiously approached them with his proposal to eliminate Hagopian, they nodded their agreement. The three conspirators then prepared "a rather serious plan" (as Monte described it in his *Self-Criticism*), which involved faking an accidental explosion in the munitions shed. It might be weeks or even months before they could coax Hagopian to come to the camp, though, "and until then," as Monte noted in *Self-Criticism*, "who knows what could have happened?"

By this time, Hagopian was taking steps to ensure that Monte would remain isolated and under his control. Knowing full well that police agencies monitored Armenian newspapers, he released a communiqué that claimed that Monte had been a member of the Secret Army team that had launched a bloody attack on Ankara's Esembogha Airport on August 7, 1982. This report was false, but by planting the story, Hagopian drew even more police heat on Monte, thus ensuring that his potential rival would remain isolated, underground, and under his thumb.

At the same time, Hagopian was isolating himself from former supporters. For years, Ara Toranian's *Hay Baykar* group in Paris had celebrated the Secret Army and its leader, Hagop Hagopian, as saviors of the Armenian nation. With each bombed cafe and airport lobby, though, the Parisians' misgivings increased. On March 21, Toranian discovered an unexploded bomb hanging from the floorboard of his Renault. He blamed Hagopian's provocateurs for planting the car-bomb, and the *Hay Baykar* group withdrew support for the Secret Army.

The tide had begun to turn in Tehran, too. At the huge April 24 rally in that city, fistfights broke out between Secret Army supporters and a reassertive Dashnak contingent. Meanwhile, Hagopian's non-Armenian allies were also having second thoughts. The PKK denounced the Secret Army's reckless attack at Esembogha Airport and the bombings in Europe, while the Struggle Front and larger Palestinian organizations opposed Hagopian's ever-closer relationship with the Palestinian renegade, Abu Nidal.

In several cities of the diaspora, however, the Secret Army's fortunes were improving. One notable case was Athens. The Secret Army enjoyed the sympathy of many Armenians in the Greek capital, and Premier Andreas Papandreou's Pan-Hellenic Socialist (PASOK) government, which was embroiled in a long-standing dispute with Turkey over islands in the Aegean, did not discourage that sympathy. From April to June 1983, half a dozen Secret Army members relocated from Damascus to Athens. A rumor circulated that Hagopian had used eleven pounds of gold bullion collected by Secret Army supporters in Iran as a down payment on a hotel near Athens. Meanwhile, a wealthy businessman from Kuwait proposed setting up a supermarket in Athens to provide the Secret Army with a reliable source of income. On June 15 1983, Hagopian, now an aspiring grocer, followed the other recruits to Athens, leaving Monte in the settling dust of Yanta with his defunct assassination plots.

Monte cursed himself for not having "thought more quickly" and for not taking drastic steps sooner. For over a year, he had been desperate enough to shoot Hagopian dead in front of a dozen witnesses if he ever got the chance, and to shoot anyone else who got in the way, too. Then he had taken the risk of revealing his designs to Tavitian and Khalil, to enlist their support. One last reservation had remained in place, though, and he was now prepared to relinquish even that: all along, he had assumed that he could kill Hagopian without killing himself in the process. Now he regretted having placed even this "unrealistic" constraint on his range of action.

9

Martyrdom

E ven as Secret Army veterans distanced themselves from Hagopian, youngsters continued to show up at the group's Damascus
safe house to dictate their last wills. The Secret Army never had
more than 100 full-time militants in the safe houses, training camps,
and sleeper cells at any given time, but "part-time" members outside
this core numbered hundreds more, and they could be found in Armenian ethnic enclaves everywhere from Moscow to Madras, and from
Toronto to Cairo. These supporters collected money, published bulletins, smuggled weapons and explosives, and arranged safe lodging for
militants. The outermost fringe of supporters merged into an expanding ring of sympathizers, thousands of them on six continents, who
subscribed to bulletins and donated money.

In Tehran, a group of Secret Army supporters had been staging burg-
laries and robberies, and sending the loot via courier to Hagopian, to
help finance Secret Army operations. But by the summer of 1982 these
supporters had polarized into two camps over issues of leadership,
aggravated by personality conflicts. On the verge of fistfights, they
agreed at last to send an emissary to Damascus to meet the Secret Army
leadership for the first time, to seek its mediation.

In November 1982, the emissary, a sandy-haired waif barely out of
his teens, borrowed his father's coat and set out south from a PKK base
in Urmia, western Iran. Garlen Ananian's parents had saved the life of a
Kurdish fighter who had caught a bullet in his thigh, and that fighter,
Samir, offered to repay the debt by escorting Garlen on foot to Damascus. Garlen and Samir trudged through mountains, blizzards,
battlefields, minefields, and deserts. They came under fire from Iraqi

soldiers and passed within twenty meters of a Turkish Army ambush near the Iraqi frontier. Samir noticed that after marching all day with a heavy pack, his comrade would eat little more than a piece of bread and a few dates. Garlen's chronic stomach problems grew worse and he began spitting blood. In mid-January 1983, after a trek of nearly two months, they arrived exhausted, sick, and hungry at the Secret Army safe house in Damascus.

Garlen had only a high school education, but he had devoured books on Armenian history and Leninism, in order to speak seriously of serious things. Now, after two long months of peripatetic reflection, he was bursting to discuss and resolve the controversies dividing his comrades in Iran. After a bite of bread, he broached these topics with one of his new acquaintances, a thirty-something recruit, intellectual-looking, with a goatee. The recruit stroked his goatee sagaciously and then proceeded to display an abject ignorance of every topic at hand.

Garlen frowned. Granted, the blockhead sitting in front of him was probably a new recruit. But how, he wondered, could the other comrades in the Secret Army permit even a neophyte or a low-level functionary to remain so ignorant? It didn't occur to him that the ignoramus with the goatee might be Hagop Hagopian, the Secret Army leader himself. Hagopian might have noticed Garlen's incredulous expression. In any case, he cut the discussion short, turning to Lulu and saying, "Take him to see Abu Sindi. He's in charge of relations with Iran."

Lulu drove Garlen to Yanta to confer with Monte, alias Abu Sindi. Arriving at the camp, Garlen recognized Monte from three years earlier, when a mutual acquaintance had introduced him as "Saro" to a group of skinny boys playing basketball in a churchyard in the town of Urmia, in western Iran. Nodding in the direction of Damascus, Garlen asked with unsmiling irony: "Who's the professor?" Monte cocked his head in puzzlement, then an expression of recognition came over his face and he burst out laughing. The goateed "professor," he explained, was not a low-level functionary but the entire one-man leadership of the Secret Army.

Garlen exhaled as if he had been punched in the chest. He had just spent two months stumbling with a stomach ulcer through a thousand kilometers of mountains, blizzards, and landmines, just to ask advice from an oaf who, as it turned out, was entirely indifferent to the issue! That night, Monte and Tavitian poured glass after glass of tea, while Garlen described every detail of the conflicts that had polarized the

Secret Army supporters in Iran. He continued pouring his heart out for a week, from the first cup of tea in the morning until they lay back and stared at the rafters at night.

Monte listened quietly for as long as he could. Finally, he whispered his intention to kill Hagopian. Garlen recoiled. He agreed with Monte's assessment of the Secret Army chief, but if he had such strong objections, then why didn't he just pick up and leave the Secret Army to start his own group? Monte shook his head. As long as Hagopian continued to breathe, his Secret Army would attack rival groups and obstruct the "patriotic liberation movement."

By this time, Hagopian's chief henchmen, Abu Mahmoud and Lulu, were acting more like prison guards than comrades. In late March 1983, when Monte and Garlen returned to the Secret Army safe house in Damascus, they locked Monte into a closet-size room adjacent to the water closet, and they locked Garlen into a crawl space above the bathroom. Garlen stayed in the crawl space for two months. When he began vomiting blood and passing bloody stools, Lulu took him to a doctor, who discovered three large ulcers that required urgent attention. Returning to the safe house, Abu Mahmoud shoved Garlen into the crawl space again without treatment.

Through the walls, Monte heard Garlen begging to be released, and then crying out in pain as Abu Mahmoud beat him to shut him up. Monte clenched his jaw shut: it would have been counter-productive to shout a protest. After another two weeks, Hagopian's henchmen pulled Garlen out of the crawl space and locked him in the room with Monte, who at the time had been laid out with a double bout of jaundice and typhoid. Monte could barely move, but Hagopian refused to allow him to seek medical care. Day after day and throughout the nights, Garlen brought him tea and bread, helped him to the bathroom, arranged his bedding, and did whatever else he could to ease his comrade's pain.

By this time, the controversy that had polarized the Secret Army supporters in Tehran now split the group into two hostile camps. When Garlen heard the news, he lowered his face into his hands. His mission to Damascus had been a complete waste of time. There was nothing for him to do now but return to Iran. He requested permission to return straightaway, and even offered to make the journey by foot again, to save on transportation expenses. But Hagopian denied his request and refused to release him.

Now, when Monte whispered, "There's only one cure for this sickness: a bullet in the head," Garlen nodded his agreement. He suggested that they try to get Hagopian to Iran, where it would be easier to kill him. This sounded like a good idea to Monte, too—if they could pull it off. Knowing Hagopian's weakness for women and money, Monte mentioned to him as if in passing that the Armenian community in Tehran was fertile ground for collecting money and for organizing a girl's group, too. Having thus convinced Hagopian to make the trip to Iran, Garlen then added in an off-handed way that it would not be necessary for Monte to accompany the Secret Army chief there. The reverse psychology worked: sure enough, Hagopian took one of Monte's passport pictures to prepare his traveling companion's Iranian visa.

Meanwhile, the Secret Army's body count was rising. On June 16, 1983, a religious youth named Mgo Madarian opened fire with a Chtair machine pistol and grenades in the Istanbul bazaar, killing two bystanders, wounding twenty-seven others, and "knowingly grasping death" in the process. In published photographs, Madarian's corpse lies face up in a puddle of blood with eyes open, his left hand still raised in a "V" for victory sign.

The bloodbath at the Istanbul bazaar only heightened the tension between Hagopian's henchmen and the other recruits at Yanta. When Tavitian fell into a quarrel with Lulu about letters to his family that Hagopian had confiscated, the Secret Army chief gave Lulu permission to shoot Tavitian if he caused further headaches. Sensing that he was in a precarious situation, Tavitian convinced a couple of other recruits to join him in a plot against Lulu. One of these recruits was a slender, clean-cut youth from Amman, Jordan named Aram Vartanian. At his first opportunity, Vartanian made the twenty-four-mile journey from the camp to Damascus to inform Monte of Tavitian's plot. It was simple: Vartanian would summon Lulu to the ordnance shed at the camp under one pretext or another, and then Tavitian would set off an explosion there in such a way as to give the impression of an accidental detonation. With one of the worst henchmen out of the way, it would be easier to eliminate Abu Mahmoud, and then Hagopian himself.

The whole thing struck Monte as "a very, very dangerous plan, with very little possibility of succeeding in its final aim," as he later described it. Although Hagopian was far away in Greece at the time, Monte knew that as soon as he got wind of the "accident" at Yanta, he would rush back to supervise an investigation, taking special care to ensure his own security. As alarming as Vartanian's news was, Monte knew he had to be careful how he reacted to it. He knew that, thanks to months of his own inaction, he had lost credibility in the eyes of Tavitian and his co-conspirators. As he put it, "They were thinking: 'If he knew what to do, why hasn't he done anything by now?'" By reacting too strongly against Tavitian's plot, Monte knew he could lose whatever scant influence he still retained, and as a result Tavitian "could do more dangerous, crazy, and extremely fatal things," including perhaps even turning his anger against Monte. Under these circumstances, Monte could not veto Tavitian's plan. He instructed Vartanian to tell Tavitian that he should proceed with the plan only if it were "well prepared and well concealed."

He would soon regret not having rejected the plan outright. When Vartanian returned to Yanta and repeated Monte's instructions, Tavitian interpreted the response as an unqualified green light. At 6:30 a.m. on July 15, while the recruits were squatting in a circle for tea, Tavitian walked up behind Lulu and leveled his Togarev pistol at his head. The other recruits in the circle fell silent in wide-eyed shock. When Tavitian pulled the trigger, though, the notoriously faulty pistol failed to fire. Everyone in the circle noticed the click except the intended target, Lulu. One of the recruits made a joke to break the tension. Lulu continued sipping his tea, and Tavitian walked away. Calling Vartanian away from the circle, Tavitian grabbed the Jordanian's 9-mm automatic, charged it, walked up to Lulu again, pointed the muzzle just above the nape of his neck, and squeezed the trigger.

Monte and Garlen were alone at the safe house in Damascus when Vartanian arrived breathless, to deliver the news. Monte had not yet recovered from jaundice, so he turned orange as he listened to the report: Tavitian had shot Lulu in front of six or seven witnesses, without preparing anything in the way of an escape plan, and at a time when it was impossible to strike Hagopian!

When Abu Mahmoud stepped through the door, Monte and Vartanian told him that Lulu had accidentally blown himself up while fooling around with explosives. Shaking his head, Abu Mahmoud muttered that he had suspected something like this would befall Lulu: his protégé did not know very much about explosives, and was careless. When Abu Mahmoud phoned Greece, though, Hagopian was suspicious. He ordered his henchman to go to the camp at Yanta with a camera and to photograph everything there. Abu Mahmoud made arrangements to leave for Yanta the next morning.

Meanwhile, Monte and Vartanian discovered Garlen's passport in a drawer and found some money too, which they divvied up between Vartanian and Garlen, to cover their escape. As soon as Abu Mahmoud would leave for Yanta, Garlen and Vartanian would pack their bags and make their escape. Monte, though, would have to beat Abu Mahmoud to Yanta, to make sure the others at the camp had their stories straight and had convincingly blown up Lulu's body to erase all signs of the bullet wound. Tavitian was so far out of control, and the other recruits were probably so preoccupied with escaping, that Monte could trust no one but himself to clean up the mess before Abu Mahmoud arrived. Since Monte did not have a passport to enter Lebanon, he arranged for a PLO escort to meet him at the Syrian side of the border early the next morning, to prevail upon authorities to issue him a *tsrih*, a special permit to enter Lebanon.

At daybreak, before Abu Mahmoud left for Yanta to investigate Lulu's death for Hagopian, Monte caught a taxi headed to the Lebanese border. When he arrived at the border checkpoint, though, the PLO escort was nowhere to be found. Without the escort he could not get a *tsrih*, and without that piece of paper he couldn't complete the last leg of his trip to Yanta. After waiting for three nerve-wracking hours, Monte helplessly watched an ambulance with Abu Mahmoud in the front seat pass through the checkpoint and zoom down the desert road towards Yanta. Abu Mahmoud was going to beat him to the camp! Monte's escort finally arrived a few minutes later, and he told the driver to put the pedal to the metal. If he could reach the camp before the ambulance left with Lulu's body, he might at least be able to check the wounds and tailor a story to fit them. But just before Yanta appeared on the horizon, Monte was horrified to see a cloud of black smoke hanging above the camp. Tavitian had just detonated the ordnance shed — a full day after Monte had told Abu Mahmoud it had been detonated — and the evidence was hanging above the desert like a banner for all to see! A few minutes later, Monte's Land Cruiser hurtled over an escarpment and jerked to a stop in the middle of the camp.

The place appeared deserted except for Tavitian, who approached the Land Cruiser with a strange smile. "Where's Abu Mahmoud?" Monte asked in a language his chauffeur did not understand.

Tavitian responded with an eerie nonchalance: "In the same hole that Lulu was in." After loading Lulu's body into the ambulance, he explained, the driver had left Abu Mahmoud at the camp, telling him that he didn't have permission to return to Damascus with anything but a corpse. Then, as soon as the ambulance had disappeared, Tavitian had put a bullet in Abu Mahmoud's head.

Monte was too stunned to strangle Tavitian. The other recruits at the camp had already fled—some to Palestinian organizations, some to Syria; others to Beirut, and others elsewhere. All that remained was for those who were left to try to escape. Vartanian had no travel documents, though, and when he tried to enter Jordan on someone else's unmodified Lebanese passport, border guards demanded a visa. He rushed back to Damascus, located the Lebanese owner of the passport, and asked him to get a Jordanian visa. Vartanian would have to lay low in Damascus for a week, though, until the Jordanian embassy prepared the visa.

Meanwhile, Garlen spoke with a friend who drove buses from Syria to Iran. The driver agreed to take him to Iran, but he would not be leaving for several days. Garlen handed him an envelope containing a letter addressed to "all the comrades" in Iran. In the letter, he explained that he would probably die soon. He asked his comrades to forgive his mistakes, and requested that if his remains were ever discovered, they should be buried in Armenia.

Monte knew that Hagopian was on his way back from Greece. Time was running out, and Monte would have to tie up loose ends fast. He and Tavitian gathered the rifles at the camp and lugged them several hundred meters, to a camp that belonged to a Turkish "independent left" group called Kurtulush. Until then, the neighbors had kept their distance: the Secret Army recruits didn't like Turks, and the Turks, for their part, viewed Hagopian's followers as a bunch of nuts. Monte explained to the bewildered Turks that a split had taken place within the Secret Army, thanks to internal opposition to indiscriminate attacks such as those that had taken place at Esembogha Airport and the Istanbul bazaar.

After stowing the guns at the Kurtulush camp, Monte and Tavitian set out for Damascus again, leaving the Turks behind, scratching their heads. If the two fugitives could get over the border into Syria, they might be able to make their way to Iran with Garlen. Arriving at the Syrian–Lebanese border, however, they discovered that, thanks to Palestinian in-fighting in a refugee camp near the Lebanese port of Tripoli, Monte could not approach Palestinian connections for a permit to cross the border into Syria. To make matters even worse, an Arab at the border who had heard about the killings at the Armenian camp informed Monte that pro-Syrian Palestinians were already searching for the killers. Hagopian's influence with the Syrian Air Force officer was paying off again.

Monte and Tavitian were stuck in Lebanon, where it was foolish to expect that they would not be caught and killed: this, then, was to be their fate, their *jagadakeer*—literally, "what was written on their foreheads." Monte consoled himself with the thought that at least Garlen and Vartanian had money and transportation arrangements, and were on their way to safety.

The comforting assumption was incorrect: Garlen and Vartanian were stuck in Damascus. For lack of any better option, they presented themselves to the priest at the Armenian church and asked for asylum. After taking them in, the priest asked an elderly parishioner to "Please take food to the boys." Soon word had spread around the neighborhood that two boys were hiding in the church. On or around July 26, Hagopian and a couple of gunmen burst into a small room in the back of the church, seized Garlen and Vartanian, and took them away.

Yanta had not been the only site of killing on July 15. That same day, a suitcase packed with an explosive charge and ten propane gas canisters had exploded at a busy check-in counter at Orly Airport near Paris, fatally shredding seven people and injuring dozens of others. When a caller claimed credit for the blast in the name of the Secret Army, revulsion spread among the group's erstwhile supporters in Paris. Despite Hagopian's rapidly ebbing support, however, the blast advanced his most immediate aim, an aim that was not obvious at the time: the Secret Army chief had become obsessed with scuttling a conference that had been scheduled to take place that summer in Lausanne, Switzerland. He had originally encouraged the Second World Congress on the Armenian Question, but at the eleventh hour it had occurred to him that Ara Toranian's rival *Hay Baykar* group would be the chief beneficiaries of it. Hagopian ordered the congress organizer, a certain Reverend James Karnusian, to cancel the conference, but the Reverend refused. Infuriated, the Secret Army chief phoned a henchman in Paris and ordered him to plant a bomb that would kill as many people as possible. (It seems the henchman had intended for the bomb to explode in the hold of an airliner in mid-air, but it exploded prematurely at the check-in counter.) Just as Hagopian had hoped, the bombing generated enough disgust and fear to fatally cripple Karnusian's congress movement: in the aftermath of the bloody attack at Orly, not more than ninety conferees attended the Second World Congress, down from 400 at the first gathering.

A few days after the eruption on July 15, 1983, two strangers approached Seta's father, Bedros Kabranian, as he was washing his Volvo in front of the family house in Ainjar. One of the strangers wore the uniform of a Syrian army officer. The other stranger greeted Mr. Kabranian in a language the Syrian officer did not understand: "Monte sent me," the tall youth said, smiling broadly. "Pretend that you know me and that you've invited me for tea at your place." Mr. Kabranian smiled back and invited his two guests to sit with him in his parlor. Still feigning a jovial tone in front of the soldier and speaking a language the Syrian officer didn't understand, Tavitian told Mr. Kabranian that Monte had sent him to arrange for a meeting at a prearranged spot. On Tavitian's way to Ainjar, though, soldiers at a Syrian army checkpoint had become suspicious when they discovered that he was carrying a Palestinian ID card with an Arab name, but didn't speak Arabic. The soldiers had detained Tavitian and contacted the Syrian secret police, the *mukhabarat*. While waiting for the *mukhabarat* agents to arrive, Tavitian had told the Syrian officer that he wanted to go for a stroll, so they had walked together to the Kabranian house.

"Now Monte's going to kill me," Tavitian muttered under his breath. He had botched another plan, attracting the attention of the Syrian army and the secret police in the process, and dragging the Kabranian family into the mess, to boot. Soon enough, a couple of *mukhabarat* agents showed up at the Kabranians', and the master of the house cheerfully invited them to sit, too. Calculating that the army officer and the Syrian agents would be in a better mood after a couple of drinks, Mr. Kabranian brought out his best whiskey and poured big ones for the agents. When they had emptied their glasses, Mr. Kabranian announced that he had picked up a young hitchhiker earlier in the day, and that he now wanted to go check on him, to see how he was doing. After a few more drinks, Mr. and Mrs. Kabranian, their youngest daughter, and Tavitian piled into the Volvo. The Syrians followed them in a second car.

After a couple of kilometers, Tavitian instructed Mr. Kabranian to pull over to the side of the highway. As soon as the Volvo pulled to a stop at the village of Mejdal Ainjar, Monte hopped out of a parked car, where he had been waiting for a long time. He looked yellow and thin, but he was wearing his first smile in days. He bought bananas from a nearby stand and presented them to Mr. Kabranian and his unexpected guests, the Syrians. By that time, the Syrian agents were in too good a mood to be bothered with unpleasantness. After agreeing to meet

Monte there the next morning for "formalities," they left. As their car shifted to the top of the gear range and disappeared down the highway, Monte heaved a sigh of relief and turned to Mr. Kabranian: "I have something to tell you," he said, "but I should speak with Seta first."

Mr. Kabranian had a bad feeling that this strange young man was getting too serious with his second-to-youngest daughter. Monte was not exactly ideal son-in-law material: what could he offer his daughter, aside from danger? And what was his line of work, anyway? He was too logical and tough to be crazy, but just that sort of person was capable of doing the craziest things. Still, he was a smart young man, agile and disarmingly direct – and an American citizen with a college education, to boot ...

Mr. Kabranian sighed. As a father of six daughters, he couldn't help but like such a serious suitor: if nothing else, he would make a devoted husband. And maybe he would grow out of whatever it was that had propelled him into the unfathomable mess he now found himself in. He put a hand on Monte's shoulder. Seta, he said, was spending part of her summer break visiting with friends and relatives in Beirut. Monte could contact her through her sister, Manushag, who had a new number in west Beirut.

They bade him farewell at the side of the road.

Monte and Tavitian probably spent that night curled up in a field. The next morning, the Syrian police agents did not show up for the meeting at the arranged hour. Perhaps Mr. Kabranian had made them so comfortable with whiskey that they had forgotten the appointment. Monte heaved another sigh of relief, and then he walked to a nearby post office to use the pay phone. Around nine o'clock, Seta picked up the ringing phone at Manushag's apartment in Beirut. As soon as Monte heard her "Hello," he bubbled "Is it you? *At last!*" Seta smiled broadly and pressed the receiver to her ear. She was surprised, happy, and anxious to hear whatever Monte had to say to her.

"A blow-up has taken place," Monte told her. He wanted to explain more, but that would have to wait until they saw each other face-to-face. Until then, it was enough to hear her voice and to confess his love. Seta was so happy to hear his "I love you" that she ignored his ominous reference to "a blow-up."

Monte probably wouldn't survive the next several days, but at least he had confessed his love to Seta. He hung up the phone and took a taxi to Mr. Kabranian's workplace, the Park Hotel in the nearby town of Chtaura. They sat by the pool for a long time, as Monte described the events of the previous days. After hearing him out, Mr. Kabranian agreed to drive him to Ainjar to speak with the village leader, the local head of the Dashnak Party. They entered Ainjar at dusk that day, and Mr. Kabranian parked near the grocery store owned by Zaven Tashjian, Vahé Ashkarian's successor as village chief. Monte said thanks to Mr. Kabranian and disappeared into the darkness. It would be years before they would meet again.

Monte and Tavitian stayed at Tashjian's for two days, from July 20 to 22, while the village council consulted with party bosses in Beirut about their fate. The decision to grant them refuge was taken by Hrair Maroukhian, a member of the Dashnak Party's bureau, the party's highest decision-making body. In the coming months, the two fugitives would spend their days in small, dark rooms, with only each other as company. From time to time, they would change houses in the middle of the night, and militia guards would receive orders to be especially vigilant about suspicious activity in one area of the village, then another. The guards who carried out these orders included Vartkes, the young man who had expelled Monte and Cousin David from Ainjar three years earlier.

Even before Hagopian had returned to Syria from Greece, he had suspected that a split had taken place, and that Monte was behind it. The Secret Army chief knew Monte well enough to know that he could not remain "hiding in darkness" (as the Secret Army journal put it) for long. Hagopian would use Garlen and Vartanian as bait, to lure Monte into the open by provoking him into a rash attempt to liberate his comrades. The Secret Army journal, *Armenia*, began publishing photographs of the two beaten and starved captives. In one snapshot, Garlen sits against a wall in dirty pants with his arms tied tight behind his back above the elbows with wire. His face is swollen and bruised, a bloody rag lies on the cement next to him, and an automobile tire is visible at the left edge of the photograph. Monte knew what the tire was for: he could not exorcise the image of his comrade, strapped to the tire, being hoisted up and dropped to the concrete floor, over and over again. Garlen's groans and cries echoed in his head.

Monte was an animal thrashing against its cage. He tried desperately to send word to former colleagues still inside the Secret Army, to urge them to take steps to free Garlen and Vartanian. When no one stepped forward, he tried to convince Dashnak leaders to help him set up a raid to free his comrades from their mutual enemy. He argued and pleaded with them until he was hoarse, but his proposal was even easier to ignore than the *kolkhoz* idea five years earlier. Finally, for lack of any other option, he proposed to undertake a suicide operation alone against Hagopian. As long as the operation stood a chance of liberating his comrades and killing Hagopian, it would be worth it. Nobody but Monte believed that such an operation would amount to anything but an additional provocation, and so the Dashnaks barred him from undertaking it. Finally, Monte hung his head and slid to the floor. It was too late.

The killing of Lulu and Abu Mahmoud must have confirmed every paranoid delusion that Hagopian had ever nurtured. If there ever was a question of his sanity, the Secret Army chief now removed all doubt, as he spiraled down the neck of a whiskey bottle into madness. As a crowning testament to his sadism, he videotaped the interrogation and execution of Garlen and Vartanian and mailed the videocassettes far and wide.

Monte and Tavitian were still hiding in Ainjar in late summer 1983 when they received the news that their comrades had been executed. Monte's stomach buckled. He was at once livid, disgusted, and unutterably saddened. He loved Garlen like the younger brother he never had, and he reserved for Vartanian praise he had never used for anyone before or since: Aram Vartanian, he said, was a perfect soldier. Later, Monte would note that the documents from the Lebanese and Syrian ministries of health had accurately described the deceased, Garlen Yusuf Ananian, a Struggle Front fighter born in Urmia, as "a martyr."

For days, Monte could not bring himself to utter a word to the only other occupant of his small, dark room. It was that other occupant, Tavit Tavitian, who had pulled the trigger on Lulu and Abu Mahmoud, thereby sending Garlen and Vartanian, two of his dearest comrades, on the path to Golgotha. Tavitian had taken to eating furtively, hunched over his plate as if to protect it from attack. "I know I messed it all up," he admitted in his increasingly high-pitched voice.

Monte turned away in disgust. All he could think about, he later told Seta, was marrying her, having two sons, and naming them Garlen and Aram.

As angry as Monte was with Tavitian, he never blamed him publicly for the events he had set in motion by shooting Lulu on July 15. Both outwardly and in his heart, Monte accepted full responsibility for the catastrophe. His crime—and it was a grievous one—was to have waited too long. As he noted in his *Self-Criticism*, if he had only acted on his plans in May 1982, the lives of innocent victims at Esembogha Airport, the Istanbul bazaar, and Orly would not have been lost.

Hagopian, for his part, was determined to make sure that Monte wouldn't survive long enough to procreate or do anything else. In *Armenia*—the same Secret Army journal for which Monte had toiled for three years—appeared a photograph of a hand pushing a bullet into a revolver, with the menacing caption: "TRAITORS WILL BE PUNISHED." By this time, the ever-expanding circle of traitors to Hagopian included Ara Toranian and his friends, Dashnak leaders in Lebanon, Yassir Arafat and Abu Iyad, the Struggle Front, and the PLO. And at the head of the conspiracy was Monte Melkonian.

Speaking in Armenian on an audiocassette distributed among Secret Army sympathizers, Hagopian scoffed at Monte's denunciation of "antihuman acts" such as the suicide attacks and the Orly Airport bombing. If Monte was made of such softhearted stuff, Hagopian wondered out loud, then why had he "pumped bullets" into a fourteen-year-old girl sitting in the back seat of a car in Athens? No one in the Secret Army had ordered him to shoot the girl, and no one had forced him to undertake those early bombings in Europe, either. Was it not pure hypocrisy for a person with such a violent record to wrap himself in a fuzzy cloak and denounce the bombing at Orly Airport?

Once again, Hagopian had hit where it hurt. Monte had no reply to this jab—no reply, that is, except the penitence of renouncing past errors, and a public pledge to correct his actions. "I am guilty," he concluded,

> ... and if guilty people should be punished, there is no punishment too severe for me. I am honestly prepared to accept even the death penalty—but on the condition that the person executing me be someone who has tried as hard as I have tried to solve problems and to struggle, and who has made fewer mistakes than I.

I wasn't even vaguely aware of what had happened to my brother until late summer 1983, when a Secret Army supporter in New York, where I was living at the time, handed me an audiocassette of Garlen and Vartanian's "confessions." That evening I lay on my bed listening to Garlen's tortured words and Hagopian's low growls. The voices jumbled together into an impossible knot, and then the cassette ended with the strains of a mournful ballad dedicated to the memory of Lulu and Abu Mahmoud. Not long after that, I returned from work to find my third-floor apartment ransacked. My expensive movie camera had not been touched, but my personal papers were fanned out across the floor, and some of them were missing. Discovering my cassette player lying in the middle of a rumpled bedspread, I nudged it with a broom handle, to convince myself it was not booby-trapped. The NYPD crime report concluded that the burglars had lowered themselves into the apartment from the roof and entered through a window. After that, I began taking different routes to and from work and I resumed walking Beirut-style, keeping my eyes open for movement above street level.

Back in Ainjar, while Monte was moldering in a small room with boarded-up windows in an abandoned house near the trout farm, he suddenly leaped to his feet. Just beyond the walls of his room, on the street outside ... No, it couldn't be ... *but it was*! It was Seta's voice! She and a friend were discussing music as they strolled past Monte's hideout. Hailing her was out of the question: Monte couldn't risk revealing his location to Seta and her friend. Trying to catch a glimpse, he pressed his face against the crack between a window frame and the panel nailed over it, but it was no use. He pushed his ear against the crack. Even as Seta's voice faded into the distance, it pulled him out of a long, dark tunnel of despondency.

In late August, Seta returned to her studies at Yerevan State University in Soviet Armenia, with only a vague feeling that Monte was at the center of some dreadful occurrence. Half a year later, on March 3 or 4, 1984, the twenty-year-old student found a letter under the door of her dorm room in Yerevan. The letter, dated December 11, 1983, was a love letter: "I don't at all believe in the sixteenth century love stories, the stories in which love always causes pain," Monte wrote. "These things only cause me happiness."

There was not much else to cause him happiness: he was twenty-six years old and still "hiding in darkness"; his closest comrades had been tortured and shot; whatever dissidents remained within the Secret Army were too frightened to make a peep, and Hagopian was free to order more bombings in cafes and airport lobbies.

When Monte had first arrived in Ainjar, he had assumed that his days were numbered. He knew that Hagopian had eyes and ears in the village, and he was certain that it would only be a matter of time before someone spotted Tavitian and started whispering the sort of rumor that had led Hagopian to the church in Damascus where Garlen and Vartanian were hiding. Months had passed since then, though—precious months—and despite the fact that Monte and Tavitian remained "right under Hagopian's nose," it seemed that the Secret Army chief had lost their scent.

Meanwhile in Paris, Ara Toranian had been scraping together money to smuggle Monte and Tavitian out of Lebanon, to Europe. As soon as the funds came through, Tavitian packed his bags. When he left, Monte barely nodded good-bye: he cared only that Tavitian would never cross his path again.

Monte purchased a stolen French passport in the name of a Guy Jean-Claude V.-D., born February 10, 1941 in Paris, and attached his photograph to the inside page. On the morning of May 4, 1985, he pushed his papers and a few items of clothing into a couple of shopping bags and slumped into an automobile headed to Damascus Airport. After "hiding in darkness" for over twenty-one months (from late July 1983 to early May 1985), he was heading into the sun again. As the car gently rolled into the foothills of the Ante-Lebanon Mountains, he turned and glanced back at the patchwork of the Bekaa Valley. This had been his first view of Lebanon fifteen years earlier, on the same road, headed in the opposite direction. Now, it was the last he would ever see of that beautiful, suffering country.

1. June 1966. Monte, eight years old, up to bat for his Little League team, the Bears (courtesy of Melkonian family).

2. December 1969. Left to right: the author (aged thirteen), Monte (who had just turned twelve), unidentified burro and driver, Maile (aged fourteen), Marcia (aged ten). The photo was taken near Castellón, Spain (courtesy of Melkonian family).

3. Fall 1978. Members of the Armenian militia posing in front of Airplane Building in Bourdj Hamoud, Lebanon. Monte is standing in the back row on the far left, dressed in "some sort o Mexican shirt." Visible above their heads is the stylized airplane that graced the lobby of the building *(courtesy of Khajag Hagopian)*.

4. Fall 1978. Manning the barricades in the Bourdj Hamoud, Lebanon *(courtesy of Khajag Hagopian)*.

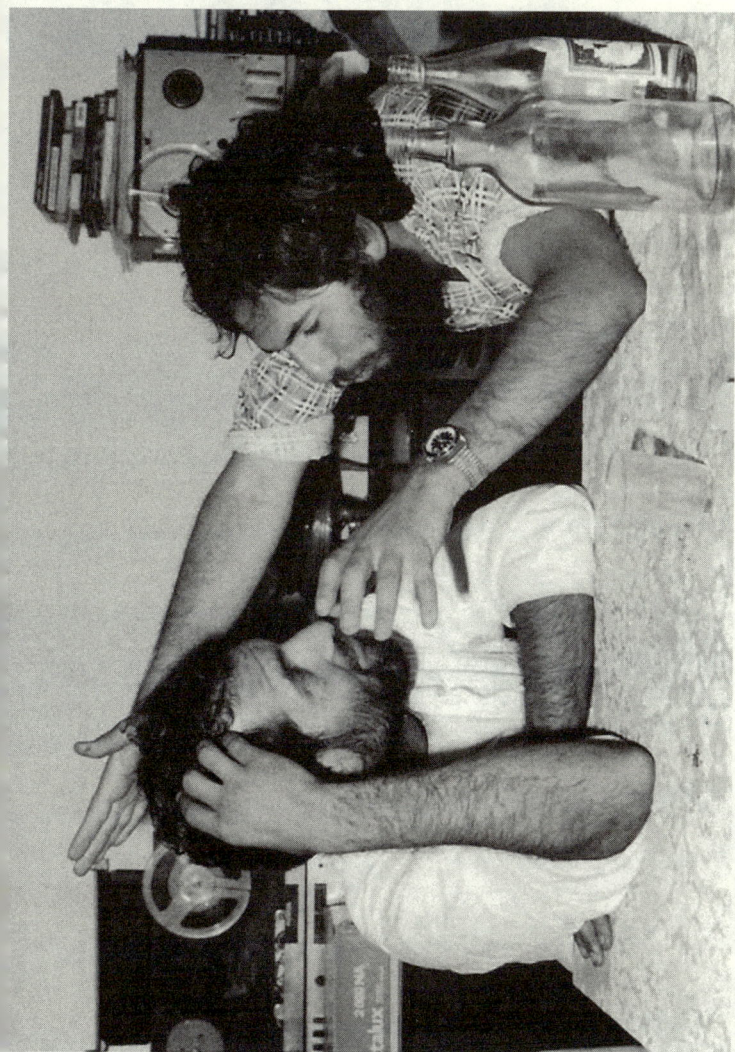

5. March 24, 1979. Monte (on the right) at a friend's apartment in Bourdj Hamoud, Lebanon, sets the author straight on a point. Monte's wild appearance, together with the empty bottles, might give the misleading impression that he had been drinking too much *arak*. Actually, he had just arrived late for dinner when our host snapped the picture (*photo by Daniel Madzounian*).

6. September 13, 1991. The Karashinar front, in the Shahumyan district. Monte (top row, centre) with fellow defenders *(photo by Myriam Gaume)*.

7. September 14, 1991. "Avo" napping after a battle in the village of Bozluk, in the Shahumyan district *(photo by Myriam Gaume)*.

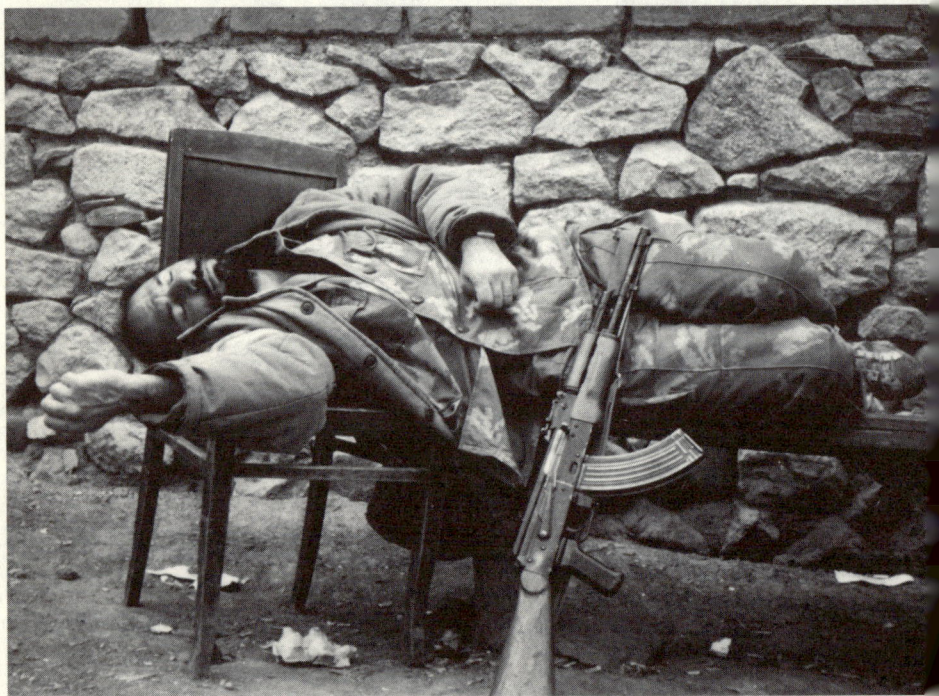

October 1992. Monte and Colonel Haroyan at the village of Mooshkabad, Mountainous
Karabagh (photo by Seta Melkonian).

October 1992. Seta and Monte on a hill near the village of Mooshkabad, Moutainous
Karabagh (courtesy of Seta Melkonian).

10. November 1992. Monte warms his hands in his room at the Graduate and Faculty Dormitory on Mashdots Boulevard in Yerevan, Armenia *(photo by Seta Melkonian)*.

11. January 1993. Trying out a sniper rifle. Left to right: Commander Avo, Saribeg Mardirosyan, Gomidas Avenesyan (photo by Max Sivaslian).

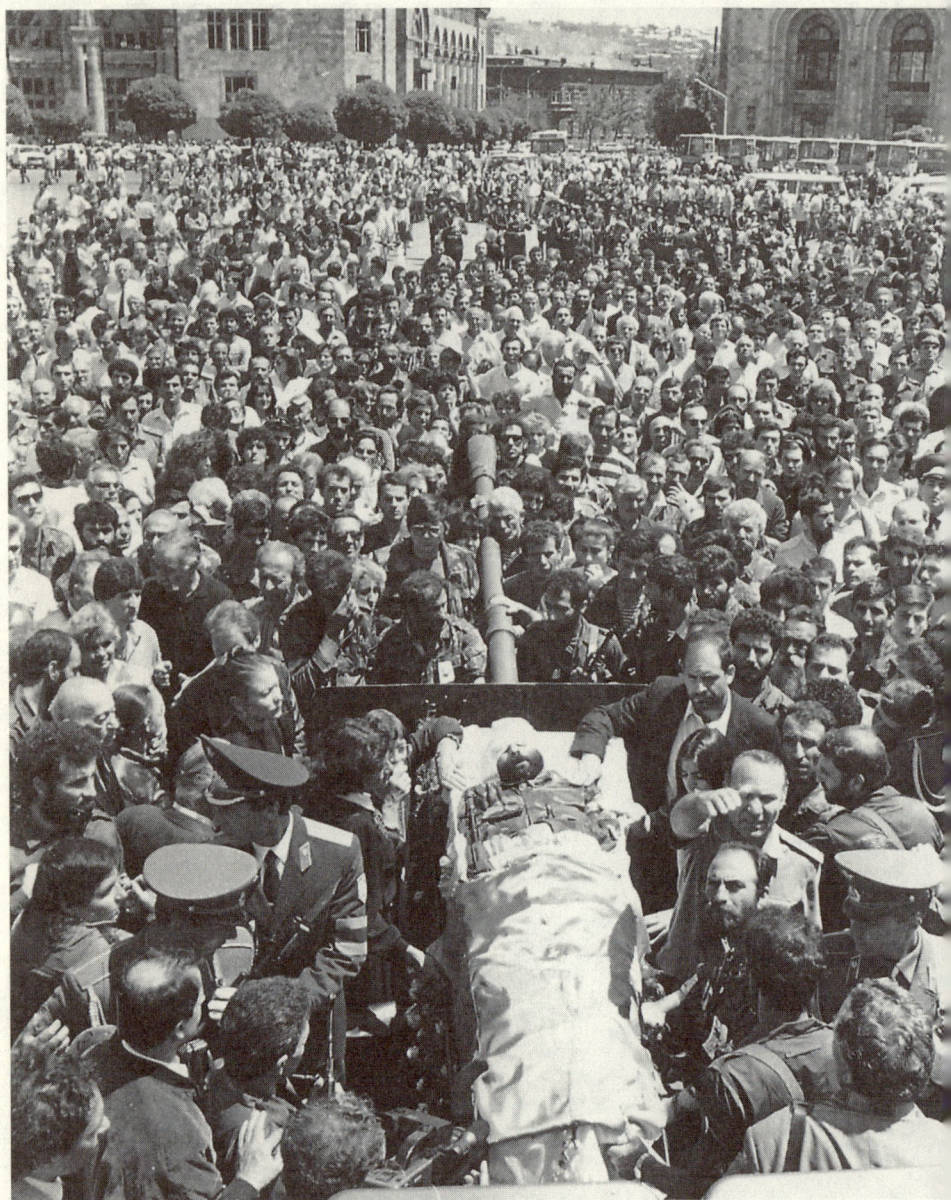

12. June 19, 1993. Monte's funeral procession through Republican Square in Yerevan, Armenia *(courtesy of the Monte Melkonian Fund)*.

PART FOUR

"Everywhere Walls"

Good-Doers

From Damascus, Monte flew to Amman and then to Madrid. On May 20 or 21, 1985, a comrade drove him over the border to France, where he lodged with an old man in Voiron, an Alpine town not far from the Italian border. Monte had wanted to proceed directly to Paris, to strategize with the comrades there and regroup, but his Paris comrades advised him to lay low for a while. Police in the French capital were on high alert after the most recent spate of bombings in cafes and metros, so the time was not right for a convicted terrorist to show his face on the boulevards, even in disguise. To make matters worse, Ara Toranian, the leader of the Paris group, had just survived his second car-bomb attack. Hagopian's enemies, including Monte, would have to tread lightly in France.

After a couple of months in Voiron, however, Monte could not be restrained. In July, he relocated to the Paris neighborhood of Montparnasse, where he billeted in a *chambre de bonne*, a closet-sized apartment with the toilet and shower down the hall. He did push-ups and sit-ups in his room, hundreds at a time, and walked or took the metro to meetings with Toranian's friends, where he bent their ears with every last detail of the Secret Army split. Through local contacts, he met secretly with representatives of the PKK, as well as with Corsican and Basque separatists.

By this time Monte was carrying an Italian passport under the name of Frederico Vella, as well as a US passport under the name of a certain Jack Daniel M., a resident of Indiana. Some of Toranian's friends took to calling him "Jacko." Monte kept his eyes open on the boulevards, and he kept an old Berretta automatic in his pocket, too. He would not repeat the mistake he had made five years earlier when, joining the Secret Army, he had handed his guns over to Hagopian. Monte made sure all the serial numbers had been filed off the Berretta. If he ever got a bead on Hagopian, he would take the shot, no matter what.

Monte now enjoyed what he later described as "the most favorable conditions for free activities since May 1980," when he had first stepped into Hagopian's shadow. Still, he was not an entirely free man in Paris: every time he ambled along a busy boulevard in his jeans and sneakers, he ran the risk of jogging the memory of any passer-by who had seen a published photo of "Dimitriu Georgiu" back in winter 1981. Three and one-half years of thinning hair on top of his head went some distance in the way of disguise, though, and as an added precaution he grew a bushy moustache. He assumed that French authorities knew he was in the country, but they didn't worry him much: not even the *flics*, as stupid as they were, would wish to arrest the one person best qualified to snuff their mutual enemy, Hagopian.

Procuring a driver's license under an assumed name, he drove to Lyons and Marseilles to reconnoiter for possible attacks against Turkish targets. One of Monte's Marseilles comrades, Levon Minassian, was a brusque, talented graduate student of sociology, a Communist student leader, and the most visible member of the local chapter of Toranian's group. Nicknamed *Shishko* ("Chubby"), he was Marseillais before all else, with all the bluster, bravado, and *joie de vivre* that being Marseillais entails. Shishko was out on bail, after his recent arrest for armed robbery: on the night of July 28, 1984, according to the indictment, he and five local rogues had waylaid an armored postal truck on the road to Pennes-Mirabeaux near Marseilles, and had made away with $1 million. Shishko denied the charge, claiming that on the night of the robbery he had been at a secret "political meeting," the details of which he was not at liberty to disclose. Monte had been laying low in Lebanon when he learned that his gung-ho comrade was sitting in prison at Avignon. He promptly wrote a one-page letter addressed to "Mr. Judge," the investigating magistrate in Shishko's case. The letter purported to confirm Shishko's alibi: "… we ourselves were with Minassian at Aix-en-Provence from the evening of Friday July 27, 1984 until the evening of July 28, where we had a long meeting." After assuring the judge that he was prepared to testify in court to this effect, Monte had added his thumbprint in ink to the bottom of the page, along with the signatures of his previous aliases, "Khatchig Avedisian" and "G. Demetriou." At Monte's insistence, Tavitian had also affixed his thumbprint and signature to the document.

Picking up the leaked news, the sensationalist paper *Le Quotidien de Paris* had run a story in late 1984 bearing the headline "The Summer Terrorist Meetings." According to *Le Quotidien*, Monte had been in the south of France caballing with other shady types, including Corsican separatists. Other news outlets had then picked up the story, and Hagopian's journal *Armenia* joined the fray, too, accusing "Mitterrand's phony socialists" of harboring Monte as part of a conspiracy to undermine the Secret Army. The accusations had stung the *flics* at the DST (the Direction de la Surveillance du Territoire) to the quick, since it was their job to prevent the likes of Monte from entering the territory of the Fifth Republic.

In mid-September, Monte and five or six comrades, including Shishko and Toranian, crammed into Monte's *chambre de bonne* to pose the ever-recurring question: *what is to be done*? They needed to prepare the ground for a new, more accountable successor to the Secret Army, but the question was, how to do it? The comrades who pushed their knees together in the room that day knew they were in a bind: on the one hand, a period of quiet regrouping and reorganization was long overdue; on the other hand, they needed to make a loud noise, to show that they and their fellow Secret Army dissidents were not just spoilers, but were capable of striking Turkish targets. For the past year, *Hay Baykar* had done little more than publish exposés of the misdeeds of the very Hagopian whom Toranian and his friends had extolled as a savior only a couple of years earlier. Now, disillusioned former supporters were drifting away, and Toranian and his friends, like their Dashnak rivals before them, had concluded that they needed selective but spectacular attacks against Turkish targets, to shore up waning support and rekindle lost enthusiasm.

Monte's attitude, though, was more subdued than the others at the meeting had hoped. He had learned the hard way that rushing headlong to "just do something" could often be worse than doing nothing. To him, the most urgent task was to restrategize, and to do it more realistically. In a letter to a friend written more than a year later, Monte would admit that he considered it "highly unlikely" that Armenians would ever succeed in reuniting even a small part of their Turkish-occupied homeland with Soviet Armenia. At the very least, though, the descendants of genocide survivors must win what the Turkish state had denied them for seven decades, namely the right to live on their ancestors' native soil, to "enjoy a collective cultural life and have all necessary political, economic, social, etc. rights that all other peoples in the region should share." This was Monte's "minimal goal." Unable to resist returning full circle to the "highly unlikely" scenario, though, he added: "The option of possible re-unification of *some* areas must be left open."

The conferees in Monte's room were in agreement about all of this, and they agreed on the need for a "vanguard" group, too. But when it came to the relationship between the vanguard and support groups, serious disagreements arose. Toranian and his friends envisioned a loose confederation of autonomous support groups throughout the diaspora. Monte, by contrast, argued for a single pan-diasporan organization, one that would unite all the local groups under one program and one "supreme body" (*kerakoyn marmeen*, in Armenian). Hearing this, Toranian blinked incredulously: hadn't their experience with Hagopian's one-man shop been bad enough? Wasn't it clear that the conditions of the diaspora would render such a supreme leadership little more than an open invitation to one-man tyranny?

Monte replied that members would exercise control by electing their own local deputies to a collective leadership. In any case, he argued, the scattered character of the diaspora demanded that they unite all their resources into one single organization. They couldn't afford to break the lines of command and to spread their meager resources thin, among twenty or thirty far-flung groups, each with its own leadership and program. Shishko tried to patch over the dispute with generalities and shrugs, but both sides became more intransigent, and they adjourned several hours later with headaches.

Monte reckoned that the ever-pragmatic Toranian would set aside his objections and fall in line with the idea of a single pan-diasporan organization, if only someone could pull off a spectacular operation, to reinvigorate *Hay Baykar* supporters. He would keep his eyes open for a Turkish target, while at the same time forging ahead with the more important task of working out a new program for the vanguard.

During his years underground, and especially during the last two years as a fugitive from Hagopian, Monte had become anxious to undertake a comprehensive study of Armenia and the Armenian diaspora, past and present. This study, in turn, would be the basis for the vanguard's manifesto. Entering the Bibliothèque Sainte-Geneviève with a falsified library card, he read the eight-volume work on Armenian history prepared by the Academy of Sciences in Soviet Armenia. He jotted down a topical outline for his own historical study, and then enlisted comrades in Paris, London, Beirut, and Toronto to contribute chapters. I was living in San Francisco that fall when I began writing the sections on philosophy and Armenian immigration to America.

For weeks, Monte had been weighing the pros and cons of testifying for the defense in Shishko's upcoming robbery trial. He didn't want to see Shishko slammed behind bars, but he understood that testifying in France would be a big risk. He doubted that the French government really wanted him behind bars — after all, he was the enemy of their enemy Hagopian. But he had been expelled from France four years earlier, and he didn't want to press his luck by flaunting his illegal presence in the country. When Shishko assured him that his testimony was necessary, though, Monte set his misgivings aside.

The investigating magistrate, an amiable gentleman named Jean-Jacques Bagur, agreed to attend a secret deposition, to record Monte's testimony about Shishko's whereabouts on the evening of the hold-up. The need for secrecy made the deposition arrangements a "slightly elaborate process," as Monte understated it. On October 28, two of Shishko's comrades, Bzdig and Sheytan, picked up Bagur, his secretary, and a stenographer, who were waiting at a pre-arranged location in Aix-en-Provence. The hooded "kidnappers" politely blindfolded Bagur and his retinue, and then drove a winding route through the mountains. They changed cars, drove some more, and finally pulled up to a house near Voiron, where Monte and Shishko were waiting. The stenographer set up her steno machine, and for the next ten hours Monte answered a long series of questions in his California-twanged French. Afterwards, the abductors again bundled up Bagur and his retinue and returned them in a dizzy state to the pick-up spot in Aix-en-Provence. Back in Voiron, Monte was relieved to have concluded his gentlemen's agreement with Bagur.

The "kidnapping" had proceeded without a hitch, except that the questions and answers had taken longer than initially planned. When the stenographer returned home late that evening disheveled from the trip, her husband demanded to know where she had been. After swearing him to secrecy, she told him. Her husband, who happened to work for the French intelligence agency, the DGSE (Direction Générale de la Sécurité Extérieure), promptly informed his superiors. Delighted to cast their rivals at the DST in a bad light, the DGSE officials then leaked the rumor to at least one conservative paper, and in no time at all the French public learned that a French judge, abducted on the territory of the Fifth Republic, had permitted the testimony of a wanted terrorist to be entered into court records. The leak seemed to confirm earlier (inaccurate) claims that Monte had been in France at least since late 1984, and it was another slap in the face to the DST. To compound the DST's embarrassment, Hagopian's journal *Armenia* denounced the Mitterrand government for turning France into "a haven for all murderers and traitors." The DST was now under great pressure to catch Monte.

Soon, Monte would raise the stakes even higher. During a jaunt to Marseilles, he had come to suspect that a Turkish merchant marine ship at anchor in the harbor—the *Yakdeniz* perhaps, or the *Mohac*—was loaded with military ordnance bound for Turkey. He checked arrival and departure schedules and began strolling around the harbor with a hidden camera. Monte was a strong swimmer and a quick study: even if he couldn't find a confederate, he was prepared to rig the bomb, snorkel into the oily water at night, and fasten the explosives to the ship's hull all by himself.

Blowing up an unmanned Turkish ship loaded with ordnance would make a dazzling, non-injurious, but very loud *bang*. Monte yearned to sink the ship, but doing it immediately was out of the question. Police were on high alert in the days leading up to Turkish Prime Minister Turgut Ozal's November 14, 1985 visit to Paris. Monte hated Ozal, a fat free-marketeer who had ridden a wave of blood to power after the 1980 coup. The fact that the Prime Minister flaunted his Kurdish background, even as he headed a regime that deported and terrorized Kurds, only made him a traitor in Monte's eyes, in addition to a tyrant. As much as Monte wanted to embarrass Ozal, however, he knew it would be foolish to try to strike a Turkish ship during the Prime Minister's visit to France: the *flics* had put Toranian and his friends under constant surveillance during Ozal's visit, and there would be heavy reprisals against them if the attack took place at that especially sensitive time.

Monte bided another month in Voiron, far from the heightened police vigilance in the Île-de-France. In late November, after Ozal had left France, Monte packed his toothbrush, his pistol, a couple of shirts, a pile of letters and notes, two or three books, and a bundle of wires and timers into a couple of plastic shopping bags and returned to Paris.

He had wanted to move back into his previous *chambre de bonne*, but on the way there he learned that the police had just arrested the interim resident for smuggling hashish. Rather than blundering into the middle of a drug bust, Monte judged that it would be safer to stash his shopping bags in a train station locker and curl up to sleep on a metro platform. But this, too, would be risky: after numerous bomb attacks in the metro, the cops were wary of dark-skinned vagrants.

Another comrade, alarmed at news of Monte's fate, approached a friend of his, asking her to host "an Armenian patriot" for just a few days, until other comrades succeeded in arranging more permanent lodging. Zepur Kasbarian, twenty-four, a Syrian-born grammar school aide, did not know Monte's whole story, but she would not allow a patriot to live like a *clochard*, a vagrant, on the streets of Paris. On November 24, Monte lugged his shopping bags up six flights of stairs and plopped them down in Zepur's cramped *chambre de bonne* at 51 Avenue de Saint Mandé in Montparnasse.

By giving the strange young man the only set of keys to her room, Zepur, a resident alien in France, ran the risk of deportation if arrested. She was also taking another kind of risk: in addition to being a patriotic Armenian, she was also a modest Middle Eastern woman, and a pretty one at that. But if she had any misgivings about sharing a twelve-square-meter room with a young man who had just spent two years in dark hideouts, she was relieved to discover that her guest was oblivious to her as a woman. He pulled off his jeans and shirt, stretched across the length of the room, chirped good night, and dozed off. To him, Zepur was a comrade, and that was that. Besides, he had his eye on another woman: "There are three billion females on Earth," he once told Seta, "but I don't care what 2,999,999,999 are about."

Monte's devotion to Seta posed its own problems. On his twenty-eighth birthday, November 25, 1985, he stood at a phone booth in the street and tried but failed to reach Seta in Yerevan, Soviet Armenia. Finally, he set good judgment aside and dialed Soviet Armenia from the phone in Zepur's room for the first and last time. The call would appear on Zepur's phone bill, but he would reimburse her in cash. When Seta picked up the phone on the other end of the line, they spoke for exactly one hour, from two to three in the morning, Yerevan time. Seta wished Monte a happy birthday, then they hung up and he dozed off, happy and content.

If the phone line had been bugged that night, it was not the only one. DST agents had staked out Toranian's *Hay Baykar* office, and when they noticed that one of Toranian's collaborators, a sandy-haired young emigrant from Soviet Armenia, was making calls from a pay phone across the street from the office, they bugged the line. The young man, Benjamin Keshishian, wanted to interview Monte for *Hay Baykar*. On the morning of Thursday, November 28, less than two weeks after Ozal's visit to Paris, Keshishian phoned Monte at another pay phone and scheduled a meeting for 11 o'clock that morning, mentioning their rendezvous site by name.

Monte arrived a few minutes early at the Brasserie Le Zeyer on Rue d'Alésia, and took a seat in the enclosed terrace. He was wearing thick-rimmed Lozza glasses and a maroon-striped pullover. A few minutes later, Keshishian greeted him and sat down across the table, with his back to the entrance. He had been seated for less than five minutes when, in the middle of a sentence, Monte calmly raised both of his hands into the air. Keshishian cocked his head. For a second he thought it was a joke, but when he turned his head, he was staring into the barrel of a pistol. Customers turned over tables and scattered, as seven plainclothes officers closed in. Keshishian jumped to his feet and grabbed a chair to hit the officers, who cocked their pistols, ready to fire.

"Take it easy," Monte told him calmly. "Put the chair down."

They cuffed the two suspects and led them to separate unmarked cars, which raced, sirens blaring, to the fortress-like Commissariat de Police on Avenue du Maine. There, the two suspects were questioned in separate cells. Leading the investigation was a middle-aged plain-clothes man of medium height and build who wore a big silver bracelet on his right wrist, emblazoned with "Philippe." Toranian and his friends had often sat in Chief Police Inspector Philippe Chicheil's office during interrogations, admiring the chart on his wall that demonstrated beyond a shred of phrenological doubt the Negroid origins of the Armenian cranium. By virtue of such "specialized knowledge," presumably, Chicheil headed up the section of the DST that dealt with Armenian matters.

In the late afternoon, Chicheil and two assistant inspectors pushed Monte into a car and dashed, headlights ablaze, to 51 Avenue Saint Mandé, to witness the search of Zepur's room. They reached the address at about a quarter after six in the evening and unlocked the door with the yellow key they had found in Monte's pocket. Entering the room, they pushed the suspect to the cot, where he lay on his stomach with his hands cuffed behind his back and a bemused half-smile on his face. While the inspectors turned the place upside down, Monte gathered his thoughts: DST agents must have followed Keshishian to Le Zeyer, and they must have located Zepur's place by tracing the phone call to Yerevan three days earlier. Monte had hoped that someone had somehow alerted Zepur, but alas, this had not been the case.

Half an hour into the search of the room, DST officers downstairs in the foyer cuffed and arrested her as she returned from work. They held her in the lobby, while the agents upstairs finished ransacking her room.

Chicheil's *flics* seized hundreds of pages of notes in Monte's hand, including names and addresses of Turkish consular staff in Paris and Lyon, and a long shopping list in four languages and three scripts, which included the following items: 100 kilos of high explosives, light mortars, and Sagger, TOW, Red-Eye, Stinger, and S-7 rocket launchers. They also seized Monte's Berretta, a soldering iron, an amp meter, "very high quality" matchbox delay timers, printed circuits and other electronic components, 3,000 francs (totaling about $450 at the prevailing rate of exchange), and falsified and stolen ID documents, including French, Italian, and US passports.

When asked about these items, the suspect responded "I have nothing to say." Nor had he much to say about other confiscated items, including a map of Marseilles harbor marked with Xs and eleven snapshots of the Turkish ship, the *Mohac*, at port. (In his final indictment, the prosecutor would confirm that the ship "regularly transports gunpowder and explosive or inflammable products." Henceforth, the *Mohac* would be the big fish that got away from Monte.) Later, when forensic chemists at the Central Laboratory of the Judicial Police claimed to have found traces of penthrite—an explosive—on wads of confiscated plasticine, Monte admitted that he had used the plasticine to simulate Semtex when demonstrating bomb assembly to comrades, but he denied that the material had ever come into contact with penthrite: "There's a rule among us: we don't fool around with explosives," he said, citing "precedents that have claimed the lives of militants."

Chicheil and his officers finally wrapped up the search at 8:45 p.m. Monte refused to sign the search report and he didn't raise an eyebrow in Zepur's direction when the *flics* pushed him through the lobby to the waiting car. Back at the Commissariat de Police, Zepur could hear the muffled voices of Monte's interrogators in the cell directly across the hall, and every now and then she would hear Monte's laughter echo down the hall. This was his way of refusing to answer a question. He claimed that he and his bags had been present in Zepur's room without her consent or knowledge. When DST interrogators showed Zepur a photo of Monte taken several years earlier, she claimed she didn't recognize him: the bearded youth with the full head of hair in the picture bore little resemblance to the thin, balding man who had shown up at her door.

Interrogation continued until November 30, at noon, when the initial investigative phase, the *garde à vue*, expired and the prisoners were taken to the Palais de Justice to be remanded to the fourteenth section of the Public Prosecutor's Department, Paris. The final DST report concluded that the arrest of Zepur, Keshishian, and Monte had prevented "the commission of a terrorist act."

On behalf of the Committee for Support of Armenian Political Prisoners (CSAPP), Toranian engaged one of the most renowned trial lawyers in France to head their defense teams. Henri LeClerc was a tall, imposing figure, impeccably suited, with a no-nonsense demeanor. A socialist who had been radicalized during the events of 1968, he had defended "progressive nationalist" Corsicans, Algerians, and former French-colonial Africans, as well as the Van Operation boys. Monte impressed LeClerc as a lucid, reflective militant who knew the limitations of "armed propaganda" within countries like France.

When Monte's lawyers presented their client in court, the investigating magistrate, Gilles Boulouque, was grim. Between bangs of a mallet, he charged Monte with possession and use of falsified documents to enter France, concealment of forged administrative documents, and illegal possession of explosives and a firearm. Boulouque was not impressed when Monte claimed that he kept the pistol for self-defense in the face of Hagopian's death threats. Like Zepur and Keshishian, Monte was also charged with participation in an *association de malfaiteurs*. Monte described the later charge as "the joker in the French penal code's deck." Its closest counterpart in the US criminal code might be "criminal conspiracy." Devised in the nineteenth century to imprison anarchists, the charge carried a maximum sentence of ten years.

The three suspects were denied bail, and Monte found himself in the hands of the same prison officials who, as he had put it in his previous incarnation as Dimitriu Georgiu, had "fed me to the ticks." On November 30, he emerged from a paddy wagon into the shadow of a five-meter high wall of ragged concrete topped with razor wire. It was an all-too-familiar sight: this was the same Fresnes Prison where, four years earlier, Monte, then alias Georgiu, had languished for a month. Built in 1881, the prison had the look of a Nazi concentration camp. And for good reason: between 1940 and 1944, Fresnes had indeed been a concentration camp and a trans-shipment depot for thousands of internees headed for Nazi death camps to the north and east. Since then, the prison, with its unpainted walls, barbed wire, and tiny windows, had seen little in the way of improvement.

As interminable as Monte's first stay had seemed, he knew he would be spending a longer time at Fresnes this time around. He was back in the "hole" again, and there he would remain, at least until his trial took place—whenever that would be. Guards led him down a corridor of slamming gates to a tiny, dingy cell. Only the dullest mottle of sunlight managed to filter through the layers of glass blocks, iron screens, and bars on the window. Back in 1981, he had spent four weeks in just such a total isolation cell. Now, as one of about forty prisoners among Fresnes' 4,300 inmates who were categorized as detainees under special watch (*détenus particulièrement surveillés*, or DPS prisoners), he would be spending seven more weeks in this prison-within-a-prison.

There were those who argued that his arrest was not in the best interests of France. In the second week of December, the weekly magazine *VSD* published an article by journalist Philippe Bernert, who noted that Monte condemned the Orly bombers and opposed attacks against civilian targets, and that he posed little threat to France. *Liberation*, however, quoted a DST spokesperson who cautioned: "This man isn't all that harmless."

Harmless or not, events were unfolding in France that would guarantee a long stay in prison. On Saturday, December 7, a homemade incendiary bomb exploded at the Galerie Lafayette on the busy Boulevard Haussmann, and fifteen minutes later a second bomb exploded at Printemps, a crowded department store on Haussmann. The explosions injured forty-one persons, twelve of them seriously, mostly from smoke inhalation and burns. According to news reports, French police believed that the bombings might have been the work of Monte's supporters, who, once again, were attempting to pressure authorities to release him. They would soon come to different conclusions, but by then public outrage would rule out any leniency towards accused Middle Eastern terrorists.

News of Monte's arrest had appeared in both the French press and Armenian-language papers, and to Mom's boundless embarrassment, one or two lines even filtered into Fresno-area papers. Her former friends were keeping their distance at Lions Club dinners and Sons of Italy dances. "Monte sends his love to all his relatives and friends," was all she wrote about her imprisoned son in her Christmas card of 1985.

By January 19, Monte had been transferred from his total isolation cell (92S) in Division 1 to Cell 79S in the solitary confinement section of Division 3, which was reserved for DPS prisoners. Solitary confinement was a big improvement over total isolation. His new accommodations included a tile floor instead of cement, and a six-by-twenty meter court for *promenade*, instead of the previous three-by-ten meter court. The best thing about his new location, though, was contact with fellow inmates. Although he was still alone in his new cell, he now took his exercise break with the other DPS prisoners. He was younger than the others, most of whom were convicted terrorists, gangsters, lifers, and escape artists serving long sentences. "Many of these are actually quite educated, intelligent, and nice," he told his skeptical parents in a letter written soon after his release from total isolation, "They can really teach you a lot and give good advice."

At about three in the afternoon on Saturday, January 25, a guard informed Monte that a visitor was waiting to see him. It was visiting day, and hundreds of people milled in and out of the stalls in the visitors' hall, but it wasn't difficult to pick out his father, in his cowboy boots and wide-rimmed hat. Dad picked out Monte, too, striding across the hall in his usual jeans and rubber sandals. Monte greeted his unexpected visitor with an ear-to-ear smile, but repeated the admonition that he had made in a letter: his father really shouldn't have taken the time and expense to make the trip, since there wasn't much for him to do.

"It's one of those things ..." Dad replied.

They remained standing throughout the visit, as they caught up on news of family and friends and discussed Monte's legal situation, but not the events leading up to his arrest. After thirty minutes, a guard sidled up to Monte to escort him back to his cell.

During their meeting, Monte had mentioned to his father that he had no valid US passport. Hagopian had confiscated his passport years earlier, and it had been lost or destroyed during an Israeli bombing. Without a valid passport, or without some other travel document, no country would accept him after his release from prison — whenever that would be. And without any place to go, French authorities might hold him in detention for years after he had served his sentence.

On a long shot, Monte submitted a passport application to Marvin Groeneweg, of the Office of American Services at the US consulate in Paris, on February 19, 1986. On January 13, 1987 he finally received a letter informing him that the State Department had "temporarily blocked" his passport application under a provision of Section 51.70 of Title 22 of the Code of Federal Regulations, which reads: "(A) a passport, except for direct return to the United States, shall not be issued in any case in which: (1) the applicant is the subject of an outstanding Federal Warrant of Arrest for a felony ..." On November 6, 1986, it seems, the US District Court in Fresno had issued an outstanding federal warrant for his arrest, for having possessed a stolen US passport at the time of his arrest in France. The charge, a violation of 18 USC 1543, carried a maximum sentence of five years in prison plus a $2,000 fine.

One of Monte's lawyers, a Mr. Bochet, contested this outcome at a passport denial hearing that took place at the US embassy on October 27, 1987, but to no avail. On February 11, 1988, Monte received a registered letter from the embassy informing him that they had upheld the decision to refuse him a passport, due to the outstanding warrant for his arrest. In a letter to his folks, he summed up the situation: "What all this means is that if I return to the US I will be arrested upon entry, and a legal process will begin."

Monte wasn't interested in returning to the United States, with or without an outstanding warrant. And he certainly was not interested in bouncing out of Fresnes and right into an American prison. "The best thing about the United States," he would say, "is Mexican food." Tamales in a prison cafeteria, however, were bound to be lousy. He would have to fight extradition to the United States, but without a valid passport it would be difficult.

Our sister Maile and a representative for the Committee for the Defense of Armenian Political Prisoners enlisted the help of a well-known Bay Area attorney, Charles Garry, to fight against Monte's extradition to the United States. Born Garabedian in Fresno, Garry had been a founding member of the National Lawyers' Guild and the defense counsel of choice for Black Panther defendants. Garry confirmed our suspicion that no one could guarantee what would happen to Monte if he were returned to the United States: once US officials had him in their clutches, they could slap him with additional, more serious charges. The more Maile and I reflected on this, the more ominous those possible charges became: Monte, after all, had been a prominent member of a "terrorist group," the Secret Army, which in July 1981 and then again in July 1982 had attempted to launch rockets at the US embassy in Beirut. Both attempts had failed, and Monte probably had not been involved in either of them. (He had been battling the Israeli army in southern Lebanon at the time of the first attempt, and he had been commanding a defensive position elsewhere in Beirut at the time of the second one.) Nevertheless, he never criticized these failed attacks—not even after the split, when he excoriated many other Secret Army operations.

Meanwhile, French politicians were on the campaign trail. Faced with upcoming municipal and presidential elections on March 16, 1986, contenders for public office were striking strident "anti-terrorist" postures. To complicate matters, President Mitterrand's government was deeply implicated in the very same sort of activity for which Monte had been charged: on July 10, 1985, a Portuguese journalist, Fernando Pereira, had been killed when the *Rainbow Warrior*, the flagship of the Greenpeace environmental group, had been bombed in Auckland harbor, New Zealand. New Zealand police arrested two French nationals, Dominique Prieur, aged thirty-six, and Alain Mafart, aged thirty-five, in connection with the bombing. Prieur and Mafart were both agents of the Direction Générale de la Sécurité Extérieure (DGSE), France's foreign intelligence-gathering apparatus, and Prieur was also a major in the French Army. In September 1985, *Le Monde* confirmed that senior French officials had ordered the operation as part of a campaign against Greenpeace, which had spearheaded protests against French atomic tests at Mururoa Atoll in the South Pacific. A New Zealand court established that Mafart and Prieur had entered a foreign country illegally with false passports, intending to sink a ship at harbor. As details of the plot surfaced in the international press, French authorities accused Monte of the very same offenses that their own agents had committed in New Zealand.

Despite tough talk from the police and the politicians, the terrorist bombings in Paris escalated. On February 3, a blast in a shopping center on the Champs Elysées wounded seven passers-by, and another bomb was defused at the top of the Eiffel Tower. On February 4, an explosion in the Gilbert Jeune bookstore at Place St. Michel wounded three browsers, and the next day a blast in the FNAC Sport shopping complex wounded ten more people. A self-titled "Committee for Solidarity with Arab and Near Eastern Political Prisoners" claimed responsibility for these bombs and demanded the release of three suspects from French prisons: Anis Naccache, Georges Ibrahim Abdallah, and Varoujan Garbidjan. Naccache, a Lebanese Arab, had attempted to assassinate Iranian dissident Shapur Bakhtiar; Abdallah was a member of a small anti-American group called the Lebanese Armed Revolutionary Faction; and Secret Army member Varoujan Garbidjan had been accused of responsibility for the bloody July 15, 1983 Orly bombing.

"This is exactly what I knew would happen—and exactly what I knew the DST was impotent to stop," Monte wrote of the bombings, "and the sad part of it is that I know very well that the worst is yet to come." Sure enough, on March 17, 1986, a blast on the TGV, the French high-speed train, injured ten people and heralded another spate of attacks. Three days later, another blast on the Champs Elysées caused two deaths and twenty-eight injuries, and that night a potentially devastating bomb was defused in the metro. In response to these attacks, the DST arrested some sixty-four suspects, mostly Arabs and Armenians.

By mid-April, five months after Monte's arrest, the judge in his case finally gave Ara Toranian's girlfriend Valerie permission to visit the prisoner as a representative of the CSAPP, the legal defense committee that Toranian and his friends had organized. For the next three years, Valerie would be Monte's only regular visitor, faithfully arriving once a week, on Mondays, Wednesdays, or Saturdays, for half-hour visits.

Monte received stacks of letters from supporters, including a drawing by a six-year-old, Philippe Levonic, of a stick figure with two strands of hair protruding from his head, standing next to an empty prison cell with a broken bar, and the caption: "*Tonton Monte* will soon get out." By Easter 1986, however, the prisoner had given up hope of an early release. His fellow suspect Benjamin Keshishian had been released from La Santé Prison after four months of detention, when the Public Prosecutor admitted insufficient evidence to prosecute him. But unlike Keshishian, Monte and Zepur were not French citizens. To make matters worse, French officials had made Monte's case a personal vendetta—payback for the Dimitriu Georgiu affair in 1981—and they wanted to keep him in the hole as long as possible. This accounted for what Monte believed were fabricated "traces of explosives" on the confiscated plasticine.

As the days and weeks passed, Monte's letters became more reflective. In a letter of October 12, 1986, he responded to news from his college buddy Armen S., hinting that former acquaintances in the States had disowned him:

> Believe me, I couldn't care less if people respect me or not. What is crucial for me is that I respect myself. Without self-respect I would become a wretched wreck. It is for self-respect that I work and live. Personally, I don't believe in competition with others, be it physical, mental, or any other form of competition. What I believe in is competition with <u>myself</u>. This is the hardest, most frustrating kind of competition, because it's impossible to outdo yourself. You always feel you could—and must—do better. I wouldn't say this is an entirely healthy approach to life, but it's the way I am now.

"This does not mean that I fully respect myself," Monte added in the same paragraph: "No, no, I've made too many mistakes and left too many problems unsolved to really respect myself."

In early November, Monte received notice that his trial would take place on November 28 — one year to the day after his arrest. Like many defendants in criminal trials in France, he was tried not by a jury but by a three-judge tribunal selected by the Ministry of Justice. At 1:30 p.m. on the day of his trial, a police escort brought him in chains to the 14th Chambre d'Accusation through an underground tunnel linking the Prefecture de Police with the Palais de Justice on the Île de la Cité. The moment he stepped into the packed courtroom of oak paneling and green wallpaper, supporters stood up and began clapping. One of the robed judges hammered his mallet and shouted: "Either be quiet or leave the courtroom!"

Monte took his seat to the left of the judges, behind bulletproof glass and between two gendarmes. His attorneys, LeClerc and François Serres, spoke for a total of perhaps twenty minutes. When Monte took the stand, he answered the questions of the defense and the prosecution in detail, with aplomb and a serious, precise demeanor. Addressing the judges directly, he told them: *Nous ne sommes pas des malfaiteurs. Nous sommes des bienfaiteurs*: "We are not *malfaiteurs* (literally, 'evil-doers'); we are *good*-doers." Later, in a letter to his parents, he regretted that his speech had been "a little weak," but others present that day came away with a very different impression. A young police reporter who until that moment had despised any and all "terrorists" left the courtroom after the trial with an impression of the defendant as an honest man, a man whose goals and actions were harmonious, and who was "prepared to go all the way."

After six hours, the court adjourned and Monte was informed that the final verdict would be handed down in fifteen days. The newspaper *Liberation* described the trial as a "dialogue of the deaf." The prosecutor's questions had struck Monte as incoherent and ill-informed, and Judge Boulouque's "extreme stupidity and idiocy" had left him shaking his head with disbelief.

Two weeks later, on December 12, 1986, authorities took Zepur and Monte to Paris for sentencing. Zepur received a two-year suspended sentence and a year on parole, and was released that night, after fifty-four weeks in Fleury-Mérogis prison, including a month in total isolation.

In spite of the prosecution's best efforts, Monte was not convicted of plotting to sink the Turkish ship. Instead, he was convicted of entering France illegally and possessing a falsified US passport and an illegal handgun. In his report dated December 12, 1986, the prosecutor recommended "imposing severe penalties upon Melkonian," but he added that Monte should be granted "the benefit of some respite in view of the ideological motivations that inspired his activity, and of the patent disavowal that he has shown for the blind terrorism of the ASALA of Hagopian." In the end, Monte received a six-year composite sentence — four years in prison plus a two-year suspended sentence — and after that, expulsion from France forever. The prosecutor's report also ordered him and Zepur to pay half of the Republic's court costs, amounting to 17,998.50 francs. Monte's lawyers thought this was a favorable outcome under the circumstances, but Monte considered the sentence "more insulting than anything else."

Returning to his prison cell after the trial, Monte hoisted himself up to the window to examine the adjoining courtyard: if it didn't rain, the ground would be dry enough for handball the next morning.

After handball the next day, he wrote to his parents: "I am absolutely amazed at stories about people who can't take it in jail. And it seems the worse the conditions are, the higher one's morale stays."

"As I said," he added, "the battle isn't over yet."

Serving Time

M onte passed most of his time at Fresnes Prison alone, in a succession of three-by-five meter cells. Each cell had a toilet and a
sink with cold water, a cot, a small light, a table, "a very barred
up window," and a heavy steel door with a peephole. Each morning a
guard would wake him up at seven with a *clang*, and then ladle a ration
of coffee or milk into a cup. After that, Monte would lower himself into
the narrow space between his cot and the wall and do sit-ups and push-
ups for seventy-five minutes. At 8:30, he would be marched out to
morning *promenade* in a five-by-eight meter exercise yard surrounded
by high cement walls. Returning to his cell at ten o'clock, he would continue exercising until noon. Like other DPS prisoners, Monte ate alone
at a far table in the cafeteria, under the watchful eyes of guards. After
lunch, he would read, write, and listen to news on his transistor radio
until the afternoon *promenade*, from 2:30 to 4:00. After dinner at 6:00, he
would return to his cell to read and write. When he had first arrived at
Fresnes, he had been allowed only one short shower a week, but in
March 1986 he started a two-shower-a-week regime. Since Monte spent
his days working up a sweat, the additional shower came as a relief,
both to him and to anyone in the vicinity.

Fresnes contained some 3,500 prisoners and 1,200 guards. "Most of
the guards are good people," Monte wrote on New Year's Day 1986. By
the following summer, however, he had changed his opinion of them.
Guards at Fresnes belonged to the hard core of the Forces Ouvrières, a
right-wing union made up in large part of policemen, security officers,
and prison guards. "Many guards are very racist," he explained to a
visiting documentary filmmaker, "and they occasionally use the most

insignificant pretext to beat on non-French prisoners, especially Blacks and Arabs." "As an Armenian," he added, "I am also subject to their racist hostility." This was especially true of the flint-faced guards in Division 1, where "the proportion of mentally disturbed guards is the highest." If the opportunity arose, Monte wrote, these guards would not think twice about killing an inmate.

But even the most rabid guards avoided crossing Monte's path. For one thing, the guards assumed—quite correctly in Monte's case—that DPS prisoners had friends with guns outside. For another thing, the guards feared inmates like Monte who spent their days lifting weights and building brawn. On top of that, Monte refused to take "medicine." Doctors at the overcrowded prison routinely sedated inmates, and Monte's refusal of sedatives just made him more difficult to control.

Monte spent afternoon *promenade* in "various discussions—mostly political—with the other prisoners," as he described it in a letter to the documentary filmmaker. When inmates would gather in a circle and talk about their wives and lovers outside, Monte would fall silent and think of Seta. He recalled a night he had spent on the veranda of her family's home in Ainjar. It was back in spring 1979. The sky had been full of stars and he hadn't been able to sleep. Watching the stars twinkle, he had resolved to confess his love the next morning. But by sunrise, he had lost his courage. Now in Fresnes, he would see neither Seta nor the night sky for what would seem like ages.

Thanks to the solidarity among inmates at Fresnes, especially the DPS prisoners, Monte promptly chalked up his first official offense. On January 22, 1986, only four days after his release from total isolation, a guard yanked a teething ring from a child's mouth during visiting hours, reducing the child and its mother, the wife of a fellow DPS prisoner, to tears. After *promenade*, Monte and five other DPS prisoners refused to return to their cells and announced that they would refuse food, too, until the division director, a Mr. Marchand, removed the offending guard. News of the hunger strike spread throughout the prison, and when several more DPS prisoners joined the rebellion, jittery officials announced that the offending guard would be transferred out of the division.

A second offense followed closely on the first one. One winter day in sub-zero weather, a moody guard dragged an elderly inmate with a tracheotomy down to the *mitard*—a damp, dark prison-within-a-prison, straight out of the imagination of Alexandre Dumas. Though well-appointed with rats, the *mitard* lacked windows, heating, running water, and a mattress. Monte and other inmates demanded that the prisoner be released from the dungeon. Fearing a confrontation that might spark a wider rebellion, prison authorities again relented, releasing the prisoner after two days in the *mitard*, instead of the full eight days.

In a Dear Everyone letter, Monte noted that five former inmates at Fresnes had become heads of state, mostly of African countries, and that more than forty years earlier one of his heroes, Missak Manouchian, had spent the last days of his life in cell number 354, just across the aisle from Monte's cell. Manouchian, a survivor of the Armenian genocide, had joined the French Communist Party in 1934 and rose to lead a band of 150 partisans during the Nazi occupation. His band derailed trains and killed more than fifty Nazis and Vichy collaborators before he and twenty-two of his comrades were captured in November 1943. They were imprisoned at Fresnes and shot as a group on February 21, 1944. "Being here," Monte wrote from his cell in Division 2, "is almost an honor."

But not quite. In a letter of July 12, 1986, Monte explained the need for constant militancy in the face of prison authorities: "If they sense the slightest weakness in a prisoner," he wrote, "they try to exploit it to the limit." Monte and the other DPS inmates resisted body searches, but they did not always succeed: "Often they would search my body in the lowest and most brutal ways," Monte wrote in his *Self-Criticism*. In a letter to his comrades in San Francisco, he wrote: "I've always been aware that anyone who plans to actively participate in our struggle should expect nothing but difficulties — huge difficulties." And in a later letter, he reflected:

> I think all judges should be forced to spend at least a year in prison before exercising their profession. This would make them more realistic. In many ways I am extremely glad that I've been able to have such an experience. I'd prefer not being here, but as long as I'm here I'm learning a lot.

Still later, when he learned that his father had been called up for jury duty in Tulare County, he advised him to "try to understand that sending someone off to prison for a long time usually just makes things worse."

In letters to her son, prisoner number 752783, Mom described how, ever since his arrest and imprisonment, she had finally managed to get a few nights of sound sleep. "At least you're safe in jail," she wrote, counting her blessings.

"Never, never say that," Monte snapped back in his next letter to her: "I know plenty well how to stay alive on my own. I don't need reactionary marble heads deciding what is or isn't good for me."

On Monday, February 9, 1987, a guard ushered Seta, recently arrived on a flight from Moscow, into the narrow booth in the visitors' hall where Monte stood. Broad smiles stretched across both of their faces. Monte had been writing to her in Yerevan, addressing long letters to "My Sweet Darling Seta," and signing off as "The one who adores you." For all the time they had known each other, they had hugged only once and had kissed no more than a couple of times, but his letters had confirmed his devotion. Seta hid the letters away like treasures, but she wasn't sure what to make of his plan for their future together, after prison: somehow, he claimed, they would make their way to their ancestral homeland inside the borders of Turkey, and there they would work, fight, and raise a family in frontline camps with warrior comrades. It was an endearingly crazy proposal. Seta's father had received suitors who had promised her a life of comfort and leisure, but she knew that she would feel safer in a guerrilla camp with Monte than in a quiet suburb with another man. She had come to Fresnes to tell him that she would wait for him, like the heroines in the stories she had heard as a child—the women who waited years for their warriors to return from the mountains.

The morning of Seta's last visit, Monte entered the visitors' hall determined to discuss a long list of urgent topics. But when he entered the booth and laid eyes on Seta, he couldn't resist stretching across the partition and kissing her. A guard knocked on the booth: "Melkonian!" Such contact was a violation of policy. The kiss lingered. Another knock, this time harder: *Melkonian!* Seta whispered onto his mouth that they should sit down, but he pressed harder against her lips. The worst they could do, he whispered, was to send him to the *mitard*.

"I don't want you to go there!" she moaned.

"I don't care. It's worth it. It's worth it," he whispered between breathless kisses.

Several weeks later, a story appeared in *Présent*, the newspaper of Jean-Marie Le Pen's xenophobic *Front National*, which reported Seta's visit to France as an example of Mitterrand's leniency towards terrorists. "I am so angry," Monte wrote in a letter of May 2, 1987, after hearing about the "exposé": the story of Seta's visit would surely reach Hagopian's ears, and as a result, "the danger her family faces will increase even more."

At the end of a long cold winter, Monte reported that, in the month of February 1987 alone, the prison population in France had increased by 1,400, or about 3 per cent. Cells in some prisons housed four times the number of inmates for which they were designed. "At this rate they're going to create huge problems for themselves," Monte warned. Sure enough, on July 11, 1987, women at Fleury-Merogis Prison refused to re-enter their cells after *promenade*. By July 14, Bastille Day, male inmates joined the strike, and rebellions spread to other prisons. A prisoner died while being forced back to his cell, and inmates at a prison near Marseilles torched and ripped apart a third of the institution.

On July 20, the strikes spread to Fresnes, where Monte was one of the planners and organizers of the "movement." Vans loaded with riot police converged on the prison, but the strike at Fresnes resolved itself without bloodshed. Tensions remained high, though, and sporadic flare-ups would continue for the next year.

On August 7, after Monte's role in the prison rebellion had become known, authorities transferred him without notice to Poissy Prison, a former monastery about forty kilometers northwest of Paris. At the new prison, Monte received a new prisoner number, 9111, but retained his DPS status. Poissy contained only about 400 inmates—less than one-tenth of the prisoner population of Fresnes—and conditions were better in other respects, too, including clean sheets once every two weeks, and one phone call a month. Monte even had access to an exercise room, and he enjoyed the unthinkable luxury of daily access to shower facilities. Best of all, he now ate in the refectory with a dozen other inmates around three tables. For twenty months at Fresnes he had eaten at a separate table, all by himself. "After eating alone for so long you realize how much meals are really a social occasion," he wrote in a letter of August 7, 1987 to his folks.

Monte's third winter in prison arrived and departed. On the morning of April 28, 1988, he received the best news of his life. He probably heard it first on a morning radio report, but remained skeptical until he carefully examined published photos in the newspapers and then confirmed it with Valerie: at 4:30 that morning, two young women and a wiry man in a dark jacket had stepped out of an apartment in Phaliron, an affluent suburb south of Athens, and headed to a car in the darkness, to catch a flight from Athens to Belgrade. Glancing to the side, the man spotted two figures approaching on the sidewalk, their faces covered with ski masks. Without putting down his valise, he turned to run, as the masked figures swung shotguns to their hips. The first round hit him in the stomach, and then three more shots rang out, as boar rounds the size of tire lugs hit his shoulder, abdomen, and the left side of his head, taking off part of his face below the eyebrow. He stumbled fifteen meters before slumping to the sidewalk near a garbage can. His assailants made their getaway in a minivan, leaving their victim sprawled on the sidewalk, his left hand stretched above his head as if waving farewell.

The victim, of course, was Hagop Hagopian, and one of the two women trembling on the dark sidewalk was Janet Hagopian, née Minasian, a young woman barely out of her teens. Hagopian had remarried after his first wife, Marija, had disappeared. Back in 1986, a Secret Army recruit had glimpsed among Hagopian's papers a snapshot of Marija sprawled on a blood-blotted bed. Hagopian might have flown into a jealous rage after discovering that she had been seeing other men in Bourdj Hamoud, or he might have killed her to remove an obstacle to marrying Minasian. In either case, his young new wife was now a widow.

So Hagopian was dead. But who had pulled the triggers? The Turks wouldn't have been able to track him down. Dashnaks might have done the deed, or rivals within the Secret Army itself. Shishko's boys were likely suspects, too, since they had been tailing Hagopian for months. Whoever the men in the ski masks were, one thing was clear: four rounds of boar ammunition had closed a long, sad chapter in Monte's life. Monte had lived under Hagopian's thumb for three years, and he had lived in Hagopian's shadow for another five years. Now, suddenly, a gust of freedom blew through his prison cell. When God wants to make a poor man happy, according to the Turkish proverb, He makes him lose his donkey and then find it.

Monte's bright mood darkened, though, when his old comrade Ara Toranian visited him at Poissy and announced that *Hay Baykar* was to cease publication. A few short years earlier, thousands of demonstrators had marched under the banner of the group that had formed around the tabloid. But ever since the Orly bombing, the group had lost members and community support, even as it tried to absorb the costs of attorneys' fees for Monte and other arrested militants. Now the coffers were empty, and Hagopian's death provided the final excuse to stop publishing the paper.

Monte received the news sadly, but he was in no position to oppose Toranian's decision. Hagopian was dead, but so was *Hay Baykar*, the flagship of "the progressive movement" for which Monte had had such high hopes. He lay awake at night and listened to distant train whistles. Now more than ever, prison walls pressed in, and inmate number 9111 took refuge inside his head.

Like the mountains of his homeland, Seta waited far beyond the walls of his prison cell. In a letter to her dated August 23, 1988, he wrote a love poem in Armenian, which he titled "Memories of You." As far as I know, it was one of only two poems he had written since elementary school, and it was his last:

> Everywhere walls and obstacles,
> Everywhere sadness and darkness,
> Everywhere cold and hostile —
>
> But I've found openness and light,
> I've found happiness and hope,
> I've found them in memories of you.

By this time, it was difficult even for Monte, a virtuoso optimist of the will, to find hope in anything but memories.

But just as his hopes for the "progressive movement" were fading, he noticed a flutter on the periphery of his vision. Months earlier, in late 1987, he had read and reread a brief newspaper report about a petition signed by several thousand Armenians in an isolated corner of the Soviet Union. The petition called for Soviet Armenia's annexation of the Mountainous Karabagh Autonomous Region, an Armenian-populated puzzle piece of 1,700 square miles, located within the Soviet Republic of Azerbaijan, just to the east of Soviet Armenia. Monte had long supported this demand, but it had been secondary to his main goal of self-determination for Armenians in the much larger part of their homeland within the borders of Turkey. Now, as his grander goal faded, he refocused on Mountainous Karabagh.

Monte scoured every newspaper that arrived in his cell, and twisted his radio dial up and down the shortwave spectrum like a safecracker. Through the squeaks and the static, he monitored broadcasts from near and far and began stippling notes in a neat, miniaturized script into a pocket calendar, recording events as they unfolded in Mountainous Karabagh. On February 20, 1988, he noted, 40,000 demonstrators — one-third of all Armenians in Mountainous Karabagh — had gathered in Stepanakert, the capital of the Autonomous Region, to demand secession from Soviet Azerbaijan and unification with Soviet Armenia. Meanwhile, in the Soviet Armenian capital, Yerevan, thousands of demonstrators, buoyed by Soviet leader Mikhail Gorbachev's new policy of *glasnost*, or openness, took to the streets to join their voices. Soon, the thousands became tens of thousands, then hundreds of thousands, chanting "Karabagh is *ours*! Karabagh is *ours*!"

Monte had never been to Mountainous Karabagh, but he knew its history and demographics by heart: for twenty-two centuries, Armenians had eked out a living on the volcanic soil of those mountains. By 1920, the newly independent Republic of Azerbaijan, a Turkic country, had laid claim to Mountainous Karabagh, despite the fact that more than 95 per cent of the population was Armenian. When Soviet rule spread to the southern Caucasus in the early 1920s, Stalin attempted to placate Kemal Ataturk's nationalist Turkey by leaving Mountainous Karabagh under the control of Azerbaijan, instead of attaching the region to Soviet Armenia. In the following decades, Armenians in Mountainous Karabagh repeatedly but vainly petitioned Moscow for redress of their mounting grievances: the few paved roads in the region bypassed Armenian villages; new jobs were few; electricity and telephone service were poor, and Armenian-language newspapers and school textbooks were scarce. By the late 1980s, only about 75 per cent of the region's 160,000 inhabitants were Armenian, while most of the non-Armenians were recently resettled Azeris. Like many of his compatriots, Monte viewed the relative decline in the Armenian population of the region as the result of an Azerbaijani policy of driving the native population from the land.

The demonstrators in Stepanakert and Yerevan demanded that Mountainous Karabagh be allowed to secede from Soviet Azerbaijan, to join Soviet Armenia. They invoked Article 70 of the constitution of the USSR, which described the Soviet Union as "an integral, federal, multinational state formed on the principle of socialist federalism as a result of the free self-determination of nations and the voluntary association of equal Soviet Socialist Republics." Azeri counter-demonstrators, on the other hand, denounced the demand, invoking Article 78 of the constitution, which stated that "The territory of a Union Republic may not be altered without its consent." Thus, the two sides pitted an irresistible force—namely the self-determination of the Armenian majority of Mountainous Karabagh—against an immovable object, namely the territorial integrity of Soviet Azerbaijan.

Seta joined the expanding crowd of demonstrators just down the street from her dormitory in Yerevan. Returning to her dorm room, she filled reams of airmail stationery with reports from the city squares, and mailed them to her fiancé in Poissy Prison. On February 26, she reported that almost 1 million people had filled icy Opera Square in Yerevan, to demand Mountainous Karabagh for Soviet Armenia. The Kremlin responded by invoking clichés about the fraternal relations of the Peoples of the Caucasus, and sending scared young soldiers into the streets with riot shields. Every step the Soviet authorities took only brought more demonstrators into the streets.

"Things have been accelerating at a much faster rate than I ever thought they would," Monte wrote, almost as a moan, in a letter of February 27, 1988. The next day, 260 miles to the east of Yerevan, in the miserable Azerbaijani oil town of Sumgait, marauding Azeri thugs began shattering plate glass in the shadows of smokestacks. For three days, they looted Armenian apartments, beat women with fists and metal bars, and killed twenty-eight Armenians, according to the official tally.

Even as mobs overwhelmed and attacked militiamen in Sumgait, rumors spread of collusion between the police and the Azeri rioters, whom Armenians now identified not as Azeris but as "Turks." By February 29, Sumgait was under curfew, but the riots had spread to other cities, as mobs wrenched thousands of Armenians from their homes in Azerbaijan. Television footage showed frail grandmothers with faces bruised and swollen from beatings steadying themselves as they emerged from planes at Yerevan Airport. The figure of the leering Turk loomed again. Meanwhile in Baku, Azeri speakers announced that Armenians, "a perverse and masochistic people," had incited the pogroms against themselves in order to crank up sympathy for their cause in Moscow.

By July 1988, a general strike paralyzed Armenia, and Gorbachev called troops into the streets of Yerevan. Tanks blocked off Opera Square, and the sky above the city throbbed with helicopters. Predictably, Gorbachev's attempt at intimidation backfired: on July 12, the regional government of Mountainous Karabagh announced its decision to secede from Soviet Azerbaijan and unite with Soviet Armenia, and by the end of the summer, Seta was reporting that the demonstrators in Opera Square had feverishly seized on slogans demanding that Armenia secede from the Soviet Union.

Shotgun skirmishes escalated in Mountainous Karabagh and along the border between the "fraternal Soviet republics" of Armenia and Azerbaijan. By late 1988, some 260,000 Armenians had been deported from Azerbaijan, mostly from Baku, and in the grim symmetry of the Caucasus, a roughly equal number of Azeris had been deported from Armenia. Finally, in his calendar entry for September 2, Monte wrote in small, careful letters: "No more belief in Glasnost in Armenia," and in an audiocassette message he recorded for Seta in November–December, he moaned, "Really, something very bad is happening."

Just when it seemed that nothing worse could happen, catastrophe fell on top of the on-going tragedy: at 11:41 a.m. on December 7, 1988, the ground in Armenia shifted in a most non-metaphorical way, and within ninety seconds collapsing masonry crushed the life out of 25,000 bodies. The earthquake leveled the Armenian town of Spitak and turned Leninakan, the country's second-largest city, into a cemetery. Half a million survivors huddled in the snow without shelter. In Yerevan, meanwhile, tracts appeared that claimed to quote a cable from Azerbaijan: "Congratulations on your earthquake. Nature has spared us the trouble."

"In prison everyone dreams of an earthquake," Monte had written more than a year earlier, in a letter of October 4, 1987, "because that's about the only thing that can bust all these walls at once." And later, in a letter of February 13, 1988, he had written: "We could use a nice strong earthquake over here. It would clear up the problem of all these walls. It's incredible the way they build nuclear power plants on earthquake faults but never a prison." On December 7, 1988, though, he changed his opinion of earthquakes. As if the loss of life, livelihood, and property was not catastrophic enough, Monte saw an additional threat: in a letter written three days after the earthquake, he warned that because of the earthquake, "there's a danger that people will 'forget'" about Mountainous Karabagh.

As it turned out, not even the earthquake survivors were in danger of forgetting Mountainous Karabagh. Homeless and cold survivors thronged Gorbachev when he reached the disaster zone three days after the quake. The survivors had spent three freezing nights in the open air. Their wives, fathers, and children lay unburied, and they were still sifting through the rubble of their shattered homes. But instead of greeting Gorbachev with pleas for help, they reviled him for his vacillations on Mountainous Karabagh.

"What?!" Gorbachev gasped, "The people are in mourning, and the first question they pose to me is about Karabagh again!" There, in the ruins at the earthquake site, the cosmopolitan General Secretary had received the most convincing evidence yet that he was hopelessly out of touch with his own citizens.

Meanwhile, in faraway Poissy Prison, Monte paced his cell back and forth, back and forth. He ached to grab a shovel and join an earthquake relief team. "I can't believe that I have so much strength, I can do so many things, and I'm shut up in these four walls," he lamented in a letter to Seta. He didn't know when he would be released from Poissy or where he would go from there. All he knew was that the date of his release, however imminent, would arrive too late.

According to French law, prisoners serving terms of four years or less are entitled to a three-month reduction of sentence per year. Moreover, a convict who had already served at least a year in custody could request that his last year's reduction be awarded in advance. Thus, convicts receiving four-year sentences routinely completed their term in three years. On the basis of this information, Monte calculated that if he were to serve the maximum term, he would be released in December 1988.

But where would he go from prison? French law prohibited his expulsion to any country that refused to accept him, or to any country that he refused to enter. The United States, of course, was more than willing to accept him. Two years earlier, Monte had received a letter from the US embassy in Paris guaranteeing that he would be issued a *laissez-passer* for the United States as soon as he was released from prison in France. Thanks to the federal charges against him, he would then face yet another jail term, this time in the United States. Even more ominously, federal prosecutors might slap him with much more serious charges, including terrorism and murder.

Monte and his defense committee braced against extradition to the United States and looked for an alternative country that would be willing to accept him after his expulsion from France. Turkish authorities had let it be known that they would be happy to receive him in Turkey, but Monte was not about to accept their invitation to the gallows. Greece was a more promising destination. A representative of the Pan-Hellenic Socialist government had whispered to a contact in Paris that if one day Monte were to find himself in Greece, police there would not pursue him. Despite the expression of solidarity, though, Athens would not issue him a *laissez-passer*. Indeed, not one friendly country was willing to issue him a *laissez-passer*. French authorities, who by now just wanted him out of their hair, were at a loss what to do.

As it turned out, Monte's hope for an early release in December was overly optimistic. He was still in Poissy Prison in early January 1989, when one morning he received a strange emissary at the visitor's hall. The visitor told Monte that he had come directly from the office of George H. W. Bush, the forty-first President of the United States, and that he would report back to the President when he returned stateside. He then explained that he had questions to ask, all of them connected to the December 21, 1988 explosion of Pan Am Flight 103 over Lockerbie, Scotland. The explosion had killed all 259 passengers aboard the Boeing 747, among them 189 US citizens, plus eleven people on the ground, and had given rise to what Rodney Wallis, Director of Security for the International Air Transport Association, called "the biggest murder hunt in history." The emissary wanted to know the identity of the bombers, and in particular, what connection, if any, Abu Nidal's Palestinian renegades had to them. If Monte would cooperate in the investigation, the emissary explained, then the US government would drop the federal warrant and charges against him, immediately issue him a passport, and permit him to enter the United States.

Monte still had no wish to return to the United States, but it was a tempting deal: with a valid US passport, he could leave France directly for Soviet Armenia and rejoin Seta there. He might have had information that his visitor would find useful, too: he later confided to Seta that the Lockerbie bombing bore the signature of Abu Nidal. But he was not about to help the Bush administration, not even to the extent of admitting his ignorance of the bombing. He hated the Lockerbie bombers, just as he hated the Orly bombers, because they shredded and burned innocents. For the very same reason, however, he detested the Commander-in-Chief of the US military even more. With his own hands, Monte had helped dig the mangled bodies of children from the rubble that US-made bombs and warplanes had left in Lebanon in 1981 and 1982, and with his own nose he had smelled the mountain of burning flesh that was the handiwork of America's Israeli proxies. After dedicating years of his life to opposing Hagopian's retail butchery, he was not about to make himself an accomplice of the wholesale butcher in the White House.

Monte sat stone-faced until the emissary finished talking, then he replied, "I have nothing to tell you." He pushed away from the table, stood up, and walked back to his cell.

On January 10, 1989, Monte was informed that he would be expelled from Paris to New York in three days. On the day of his scheduled expulsion, he wrote in a Dear Everyone letter: "I will refuse with absolutely all my force any attempt to send me to the US." At the bottom of the letter, he wrote: "I have no idea what's in store for me. I don't know when I'll be able to write again. Until then give everyone my very best regards and love."

A contact in France had already informed me through what we hoped was a secure phone line that Monte was in danger of being extradited to the United States. On a long-shot and for lack of any better ideas, I walked into the disheveled and bustling Nicaraguan embassy on New Hampshire Avenue N.W. in Washington DC without an appointment, to see if I could arrange for a *laissez-passer* and asylum for my brother. A distracted young staffer listened just long enough for me to drop the names of one or two sympathetic Sandinista officials with whom I had discussed the matter several years earlier in Managua, then he shook his head: his embattled people could not risk granting asylum to an American citizen with an outstanding warrant against him. Later, I learned that the US President's mouthpieces had floated the rumor that in addition to every other conceivable misdeed, the Sandinistas had somehow transformed Nicaragua into a rear base for Armenian terrorism. Like so many other charges against the Sandinistas, this too was a bald-faced lie.

Fortunately for my brother, I was not the only one on the case: his long-lost comrade Shishko had already been in action for months. A year and a half earlier, the Marseillais had jumped bail and fled to Greece and then Yugoslavia on falsified travel documents. (Over the course of the years, Shishko would come to possess no fewer than forty-seven passports, most of them forged.) In the meantime, a court in Aix-en-Provence had convicted him *in absentia* and sentenced him to life in prison. Now, as Monte's lawyers were fighting their client's extradition to the US by legal means, Shishko had embarked on a more direct manner of fighting extradition. Ever since his arrest in 1984, he had tried to explain to French officials that he, Monte, and their comrades opposed Hagopian because they opposed terrorist attacks that claimed the lives of noncombatants. Still, Chicheil and his *flics* would not budge from the opinion that each and every Armenian militant was by nature just as bloodthirsty and ruthless as Hagopian, and that Shishko and Monte's proclaimed opposition to blind terrorism had been nothing more than a flimsy excuse for a power grab within the Secret Army.

Shishko decided to turn the cynicism of the *flics* to Monte's advantage. Summoning all of his considerable theatrical talent, the Marseillais stood at a pay phone somewhere in Yugoslavia and growled at French officials through long-distance lines: if Monte were sent to the United States, he snarled, Parisians would "swim in French blood." And since he, Shishko, was facing a life sentence in prison, he didn't give a damn whether he died in the process of his bombing campaign. Or so he told the French authorities. In reality, of course, Shishko had neither the means nor the intention of carrying out his threat. The credibility of his bluff rested on the French authorities' inability to distinguish the motives of Secret Army dissidents like Shishko and Monte from those of Hagopian's henchmen. It was as if Shishko were telling the authorities: "OK, you were right all along: my friends and I are indeed ruthless bombers. So if you don't release our comrade, you can expect a bloodbath."

After this performance, Shishko then plinked more coins into the pay phone and dialed a round of numbers he hoped the *flics* had tapped. One of the numbers was a *Hay Baykar* comrade, a Mr. Apik Ch. With feigned exaltation, Shishko announced that unspecified negotiations had concluded successfully, and that Monte would soon be going to "a place where the camels are small" — an obvious reference to Yemen. (In reality, though, Yemeni officials had not been contacted, and they were entirely in the dark about this affair.) Then he delivered similarly elliptical messages to the PLO headquarters in Tunis and to an office of the Democratic Front for the Liberation of Palestine (the DFLP), an organization with close relations with the government of South Yemen. One can imagine bewildered secretaries on the other end of the line squinting into their receivers. One or more of these phone lines must have been tapped, since French authorities came to conclude that Shishko had indeed worked out a secret arrangement with Yemeni officials to accept Monte after his expulsion from France.

Monte stepped out of Poissy Prison on January 16, 1989. But since his expulsion papers had yet to be filled out and his destination had yet to be finalized, he went from prison directly to the depot at the *préfecture de police* near the now-familiar Palais de Justice. The news of Monte's release spread quickly, as friends from the defense committee, as well as journalists and admirers, descended on the Île-de-la-Cité. A growing line of well-wishers joined voices in the song *Pour toi Arménie*, a favorite of the French crooner Charles Aznavour.

By the end of his second day at the depot, the visiting room was the scene of a prolonged party. In an attempt to restore the appearance of sobriety, authorities bundled Monte off to a more remote setting, namely the Etape Coqvert, a luxury hotel outside Paris, in the Forêt St. Germain en Laye, a woodland inhabited by boars and foxes. Thanks in part to its isolated location, French authorities used the Coqvert as transit lodging for political hot potatoes, from Richard Nixon to Ayatollah Khomeini. Monte would spend the next eight days at the Coqvert, waiting to leave for parts unknown.

Security was heavy at the hotel, and Monte's every leisurely jog in the forest turned into a parade: first came the police car, then the gendarmes on motorcycles, then police on foot jogging ten steps ahead of Monte in his laceless running shoes, followed at the same distance by more police joggers and motorcycles. Having thus worked up an appetite, the ex-con would proceed to the restaurant with his entourage. Since the Fifth Republic was picking up the tab, Monte made a point of ordering the most expensive items on the menu, and ordering them in large quantities. He shared his lobster, *forêt noir*, and good wine with the gendarmes while they chummed it up around the white linen tablecloth.

Meanwhile, Shishko was creating more mischief with pay phones. In an attempt to stoke the fire he had already built under French authorities, he rang up one or two left-wing journalists in Paris, and tipped them off about Monte's extravagant accommodations at the Coqvert. The left-wing journalists then dropped in at a Paris cafe haunted by journalists from *Le Figaro*, *Parisienne Libre*, and *Le Quotidien de Paris*, and taunted their right-wing colleagues with the news that Monte Melkonian, a notorious Middle Eastern terrorist, was living high on the hog at a luxury hotel in the Forêt St. Germain, all courtesy of the French taxpayer. One of the journalists at the cafe then zoomed off to the Coqvert and tried to push his way into the hotel. When a gendarme slapped him across the face, the episode made a sensational lead for newspaper stories: the *flics* wine and dine a convicted terrorist, and then slap a Frenchman trying to inform his fellow citizens of how their tax money is being squandered. In the ensuing public furor, French authorities were ready to ignore formalities, cut corners, and do just about anything else to get Monte out of France post-haste.

And so it was that Shishko, a lone long-distance caller plinking coins into pay phones, outmaneuvered the DST and the French government.

On February 5, 1989, Monte boarded Air France flight 491, the weekly arc from Paris to Djibouti, via Jidda and Aden, South Yemen. With luck, he would be getting off at Yemen. If and when he arrived there, he was to contact one Mohammed Ali Mohammed at the PLO embassy. And if he were able to make that connection, Monte would then get himself to Armenia one way or another.

Realistically speaking, it was anyone's guess what would happen when flight 491 lifted off the runway in France. In an attempt to ensure the expellee's arrival in the People's Democratic Republic of Yemen, Shishko had insisted that one of his "boys" accompany Monte on the airliner. So when Monte took his seat in the idling plane, he sat between one of two DST escorts and an old acquaintance, in the person of the very same Bzdig who three and one-half years earlier had helped deliver Judge Bagur blindfolded to the deposition in the Alpine town of Voiron.

After three years and two months in French prisons, Monte bade good riddance to the Fifth Republic. His only regret was that the DST had refused to return the notes on Armenian and Kurdish history that they had confiscated at the time of his arrest.

The plane's engines rose an octave, and then it lurched towards a hazy horizon.

Wandering through Ruins

B
ack in September 1988, as the air was cooling into autumn at Poissy Prison, Monte had written: "This will be my last winter here. I need to go somewhere with a warmer climate." Now, five months later, he was to have his wish. When his plane touched down in Yemen, a Palestinian from the embassy explained to skeptical Yemeni airport officials that their unheralded guest with his halting Arabic was, somehow, a fighter for the Palestinian resistance. Monte woke up the next morning in a DFLP training camp.

On Saturday February 18, Seta arrived at Aden Airport without a visa. A stocky man with straight black hair walked up, introduced himself as Abu Maher, the Palestinian Consul, and offered his services.

Abu Maher drove her through the desert under the sparkling arch of the Milky Way and they pulled up to the gate of the training camp at about ten at night. After a moment, Seta noticed silhouettes in the moonlight. It was a group of men, most of them dressed in billowing white *abayyeh*s. Suddenly, her eyes fixed on one figure among the others, a figure in green running pants. She bolted from the car into the starry night. When Monte saw her, they lunged together and embraced.

Wordless and smiling, Abu Maher drove the couple back to Aden. He steered towards the bay, then down a narrow causeway leading to the Island of Chalets, a small peninsula of cream-colored cottages surrounded on three sides by the milky green water of the Gulf of Aden. A moment later, Monte unlatched the door of a chalet and dropped his bags.

After breakfast the next morning, Monte hit the lambent sand and dived into water for the first time in three and one-half years. "Oh, man!" he exhaled, "This feels *great!*" He beckoned Seta to join him, but the stingrays in the sand and the jellyfish bobbing on the waves put her off. Monte cocked his head. It was sad that his fiancée, a village girl from the Bekaa Valley, had never learned to swim. He would teach her soon, but perhaps this beach, with its unwelcoming marine life, was not the place.

On the morning of their twelfth day together, Monte checked their bill for the chalet and learned to his shock that it came to $1,200. Distraught, he and Seta relocated to an empty bedroom in the apartment of a young radio programmer at the Palestinian embassy. The couple scooted three sponge mattresses together on the floor to make a bed, and for the next month they slept there at the apartment, swimming at the beach across the street, cooking fish, and drinking papaya juice. Yemen was the nearest thing to a vacation for Monte in ten years.

One of those days, I plinked 108 quarters into a public phone in a university library in the United States and dialed a number in Aden. After a moment, I heard a *clomp-clomp* approaching the receiver on the other end, and instantly recognized Monte's footsteps. "Your Armenian's gotten a lot better!" he said, genuinely pleased. He sounded younger and more ebullient than eight years earlier, when I had last heard his voice. There was too much to talk about, and I was afraid of losing the tenuous phone connection, so I talked fast and tried to keep the conversation focused on the most urgent matters at hand—namely travel money, and how to get it to him.

Monte was impatient to become an active militant again, and Yemen was too far from Toranian's friends, Shishko's boys, and the other comrades in France. Monte had no clear idea of the steps to be taken next, but he knew at least that he needed to regroup with the old comrades as soon as possible. They needed to meet, to reassess their goals and strategies once again, in view of the rapid rise of the Karabagh Movement in Soviet Armenia. Perhaps they should found a new journal or form an altogether new organization.

Monte and Seta condensed their belongings into two big suitcases and two handbags, and Abu Maher lent them $300 for the airfare. Two months after he had arrived in Yemen, Monte and his fiancée left for Czechoslovakia. Seta was traveling on her Lebanese passport, but Monte was at a serious disadvantage: the only passport he had managed to get his hands on was a green Italian forgery that had been modified so sloppily that it was useless, and his only other travel document was an English-language fax from the Palestinian representatives in Yemen, asking whomever it might concern to expedite the carrier's passage to the PLO office in the Czech capital.

When their Malev Airlines flight landed in Prague, an emissary from the Palestinian mission greeted them at the airport and drove them to a small apartment in the city center. The next day, they walked from the metro station on Mustek Square to the Ambassador Hotel to meet an old friend. As they entered the lobby, a familiar voice called out: "Abu Sindi!" Monte and Shishko embraced, and the Marseillais shook Seta's hand.

The next day, the three fugitives strolled to a park to discuss their next move. Shishko had been trying to reach an under-the-table agreement with the rhetorically anti-imperialist PASOK government in Greece. He had asked a PASOK official for temporary asylum in Greece, just long enough to allow Monte and him to catch their breath and plan for their next destination, which they hoped would be Yerevan.

"We gotta get back to work," Monte kept repeating, "We gotta get going."

Before Shishko returned to Athens to resume negotiations with the Greeks, he showed Monte a tourist brochure of Dubrovnik, Yugoslavia. The idea of laying low there had merit: lodging would be cheap in Yugoslavia, and they would arouse little suspicion in Dubrovnik, a city flooded with tourists. Before heading to Yugoslavia, Monte handed his botched Italian passport to an Arab comrade, in exchange for a properly forged Irish one. For the next year and a half, he would be traveling under the improbable name of Timothy Sean McCormick, born February 8, 1954 in Dublin.

On May 20, 1989, Monte and Seta flew to Belgrade and after a couple of nights at a youth hostel there, they arrived in Dubrovnik by bus, still lugging two overstuffed suitcases. There on the shore of the Adriatic, Monte finally had the chance to begin revising essays that he had written over the years. He wanted to publish the essays together as a book about the national question and the Armenian struggle.

Dubrovnik was relatively cheap, but inflation soon started to take its toll on Monte's tiny budget. When contacts in France failed to wire an expected infusion of money on time, he and Seta collected soda bottles in parks and redeemed them at a mini mart for a pack of shell pasta. They collected more bottles the next day, but when they presented their treasure at the mini mart and it became clear that they were not returning the bottles from drinks they had purchased there, the owner chased them out of the store. Dejected and hungry, the couple strolled to a bakery to admire the buns in the window, steaming fresh from the oven. Monte asked the baker how much a bun cost, then he pulled all the coins from his pockets and counted them. It was not enough. "Sorry," he shrugged, and started walking away. The baker ran after them, took Monte's coins without counting them, and put a bun into his hand.

Returning to their room, they remembered that a Canadian tourist down the hall had lost her beach towel recently. Seta opened her luggage and pulled out two towels that a friend had given as a premature wedding gift. Monte knocked on the tourist's door, held the towel up to his nose to conceal an embarrassed smile, and offered it for sale.

This was where ten years of toil, agony, and danger had landed him: hawking his towel to a tourist. The situation struck him as funnier than it was sad.

When Monte finished correcting and editing his essays on the national question, he folded the papers in half and posted the bundle to me at a safe address in San Francisco. I received the essays in four hefty brown paper envelopes with Dubrovnik postmarks dated June 12, 1989. They came with a request to publish the material as a book, to foster more thoughtful debate and greater unity among comrades. I titled the book *The Right to Struggle*. Since several of the longer essays had been written collectively, Monte had asked that I publish the book either anonymously or under the name of a collective author. He did not want his name to appear as the sole author of the book. "What I think is essential," he explained, "is to present ideas and information—not to blow the horn of this or that personality."

I'm not sure why I disregarded his instructions. Maybe I thought they were the result of false modesty. After all, Monte clearly had authored the book: the entire manuscript was written in his spidery script, and his bone dry prose filled every page. Only later would I discover that I had made a serious blunder. But by that time the damage had been done: thanks to the fact that I had ignored Monte's instructions by naming him as the sole author, the book would provoke recrimination from the dwindling ranks of his comrades, who would accuse him of grabbing full authorial credit, when only partial credit was due.

When Monte mailed off the bundle of corrected essays in early summer 1989, though, he felt little more than relief. Without the bulky, incriminating manuscript in his luggage, it was now a bit easier to travel. He knew he couldn't stay in one place too long: The DST,

Interpol, and who knows who else, were on his trail. From Dubrovnik, he and Seta made their way up the Dalmatian coast and hopped a ferry to the island of Hvar, where they had heard of a cheap room for rent in a private home, an arrangement called a *soba*.

Their first morning in Hvar, Monte and Seta strolled to a sandy beach to resume swimming lessons. The lessons proceeded well enough, although Seta was not making much progress with freestyle. The next day they walked further, to a more isolated beach to skinny-dip, and they returned every day after that. Once, when food money had run low, he called Seta to show her a pretty fish trapped in a tidal pool. "It looks like we'll have dinner tonight," he exulted. He had already explained to Seta how to kill a fish quickly, by pushing its nose into the ground. Now he caught the fish, squatted, and looked into its eyes. Seta stepped back and averted her eyes, but when she opened them a moment later, she saw her fiancé striding towards her with empty hands. He had released the fish into the sea. "Let's let it go to live its life," he said, displaying his big white teeth. They went hungry that evening.

With each passing day, Monte felt worse about accepting money from his comrades to support his life as a fugitive. After months of tramping across borders, he wasn't any closer to Armenia than when he had left France, and by the end of summer, he was penniless. In a letter to me dated October 8, he swallowed hard and asked for "around $3000." The request surprised and embarrassed me: my brother had never asked his family for that kind of money before, not even as a loan. The very fact that he had asked this time was an indication of the urgency of the request.

That fall, Shishko met Monte in Yugoslavia, to discuss regrouping their comrades within a new organization, to be called the Patriotic Front for the Liberation of Armenia, the PFLA. Monte had long since abandoned the "stupid" and "very naïve" idea that he had pushed during the cramped meeting in Paris back in 1985, the idea of uniting all local groups across the diaspora under a single centralized leadership. It would be infinitely better, he and Shishko now agreed, to bring local groups throughout the diaspora under a loose umbrella organization with an elected coordinating committee that would funnel aid to the vanguard organization fighting in Mountainous Karabagh—and eventually in Turkish-occupied Armenia, too. The looser arrangement would vouchsafe the autonomy of each local group, while at the same time enhancing "efficiency in certain necessarily centralized domains of the struggle," notably the armed struggle.

Always worried that the police were closing in on them, Monte and Seta caught a train to Budapest, while Shishko returned to Greece using one of his forty-seven passports. In the Hungarian capital, Monte read newspaper reports that made him boil inside with equal parts of anger at Gorbachev and frustration at his own inability to participate in the unfolding events: on January 13 and 14, 1990, another round of anti-Armenian rioting had racked Azerbaijan, this time in the capital city of Baku. Thugs had beaten, burned, and stomped to death fifty-six Armenians, according to the official tally, and had expelled tens of thousands from their homes. Gorbachev ordered 20,000 Soviet troops to occupy the city on January 20. During the occupation, the troops killed 150 people, mostly Azeris, and wounded hundreds of others. In defiance of the Soviet leader's latest attempt at intimidation, Azeris tightened the rail and road blockade against Armenia, and the ranks of demonstrators in Baku's Freedom Square swelled.

After a month laying low in Hungary, and just as his Hungarian visa was about to expire, Monte began to worry that Seta might be arrested with him at a border crossing. His Irish passport was a good forgery, but after almost a year of crossing and re-crossing borders, customs officers were now squinting suspiciously at the collage of expired visa stamps that covered its pages. He decided for the sake of security that he should cross the border into Czechoslovakia alone, and that Seta should follow him on a different train the next day. Monte caught a tram to the train station on the last day of January, 1990. As his tram pulled away, Seta emptied a bottle of water onto the road and whispered: "Leave like water, return like water." This was an everyday gesture in Armenia, a gesture of good luck, harkening back to a pagan past.

The next day they met in the international post office in Prague and rented a room on the outskirts of the city. Two weeks later, Seta caught a train to Moscow and then flew from there to Yerevan. Now she was determined to try every last trick to get her fiancé to Armenia.

By March 15, Monte was back in Yugoslavia. He spent another month at a cheap *soba* in the town of Budva, south of Dubrovnik, finishing his long-delayed *Self-Criticism* on the black-sand beach. When the *Self-Criticism* appeared as a photocopied pamphlet, it was not well received. Ara Toranian felt it was an act of public masochism, while Shishko assumed it was an exercise in self-promotion. For my part, I couldn't understand why Monte had invested so much time and energy in a long-winded description of a flare-up at a Secret Army camp seven years earlier — especially while earthquake survivors in northern Armenia were still clawing themselves out of rubble, and shotgun skirmishes in Mountainous Karabagh were escalating into all-out war. In any case, the *Self-Criticism* was entirely true to Monte's character: he was an archaeologist who trusted the judgment of future generations, as long as they were presented with accurate records.

Back in Yerevan, Seta knew that her fiancé and his increasingly testy comrade Shishko were running out of money and time. She would have to get them to Armenia soon, before Interpol caught up with them. Or before they came to blows. In early June 1990, she walked into the yellow limestone headquarters of the Armenian National Movement on Baghramyan Street, to meet with Khatchig Stamboultsyan, one of the leaders of the pro-independence movement in Armenia. Perhaps he or one of the other new national leaders could help arrange for Monte and Shishko to come to Armenia.

With his bushy salt-and-pepper beard, Stamboultsyan looked like an Old Testament prophet in a sports jacket. He introduced Seta to Babgen Ararktsyan, another member of the Karabagh Committee, and then he introduced her to a tall, gaunt figure whom Seta immediately recognized as Levon Ter-Petrosyan, the popular leader of the Armenian National Movement. Ter-Petrosyan remembered her, too, from six or seven years earlier, when she had delivered letters and books from his relatives in Beirut.

Like Monte, Ter-Petrosyan was a son of a cabinetmaker. His father, Varbed Hagop, had been an anti-Nazi guerrilla and a founding member of the United Communist Party of Syria and Lebanon, before relocating from Aleppo, Syria to the Land of the Soviets in 1946. Since then, Varbed Hagop had worked in a furniture factory and raised five children in a modest Yerevan home. Speaking of his third son, Levon, Varbed Hagop smiled ironically: "He's against communism. And me, I'm a communist." When Seta had visited the Ter-Petrosyan home back in 1990, Varbed Hagop had asked, "When are you going to bring Monte over, so we can get to know him?" Before he died, the tall, soft-spoken octogenarian wanted to meet the Californian who shared his hope for a future society with neither class divisions nor standing armies. In Yerevan at the time, this was a rare hope indeed.

Levon Ter-Petrosyan already knew about Monte and Shishko's plight: earlier that year, on a visit to Paris, Ara Toranian had spoken with him for two hours, urging him to arrange for asylum for the fugitives. Now, months later, Seta assured Ter-Petrosyan that Monte and Shishko would make themselves useful in Armenia if only they were allowed to enter the country. After a moment of reflection, Ararktsyan suggested simply sending the two fugitives official invitations to Armenia, using the aliases in their false passports. Ter-Petrosyan liked the idea and agreed to expedite the invitations.

Seta left the meeting elated, but the more she reflected on Ararktsyan's plan, the more she worried. For one thing, the KGB might harass Monte if they found out that Ter-Petrosyan and his anti-Soviet associates had invited him to Armenia. Ter-Petrosyan, on the other hand, might use the favor as an excuse to curtail Monte's political independence. For lack of any other option, though, Monte and Shishko would have to settle for Ararktsyan's plan.

Seta sold her jewelry for traveling money and then she booked a flight to Moscow. From there, she caught a train to Yugoslavia, to discuss Ararktsyan's plan and to take the next step. Monte and Shishko met her at the Belgrade train station at noon on June 14. Neither looked happy. They discussed Ararktsyan's proposal until dusk, then Shishko surprised Seta by bidding her adieu and boarding a train for the town of Rijeka, 300 miles to the west. When the train pulled out, Monte explained that Shishko and he had just had a bitter argument about the publication of *The Right to Struggle*, and that as a result their friendship had come to an end. Shishko had accused Monte of grandstanding, of publishing information that could compromise their work and their security, and of presenting his own personal opinions as if they were the collective views of all of their comrades. In response, Monte had pointed out that most of the material in the book had already been published, and he objected on principle to Shishko's attempt to silence him: like any other comrade, he had a right to speak his mind.

Fifteen months had passed since Yemen. Money had disappeared, former friends had wandered away, and now Monte's closest comrade, Shishko, couldn't stand to look at him anymore. Monte's falsified passport had accumulated visas like the barnacle-laden hull of a listing ship, and all the while he had not taken one irreversible step closer to Armenia — where bad news had turned into worse news, and then into even worse news.

On September 8, Monte and Seta boarded a train to Sofia, the capital of Bulgaria, and bade a final farewell to the Socialist Federal Republic of Yugoslavia. The country had changed right before their eyes: the sons and daughters of the free-loving Belgradians Monte remembered from twenty years earlier were now filing into stadiums where a demagogue named Slobodan Milosevic was fanning embers of Serbian resentment. Monte watched the rainy landscape slide over the train car window like a procession of ghosts. "This country's headed for war," he thought out loud.

Arriving in the Bulgarian capital, Monte and Seta rented a room in an old lady's house until September 15, when Seta returned to Yerevan. Monte wangled a Soviet visa in Sofia and then made his way to Varna, where he booked a seat two weeks in advance on the penultimate flight of the season to Yerevan.

Although he had his ticket, his chances of arriving in Armenia were fading. The bureaucrats in Yerevan were taking longer than expected to fill out Timothy Sean McCormick's invitation to Armenia, and it was starting to look like he would not receive his travel papers before his September 30 flight reservation. Monte had neither the money nor the confidence in his phony Irish passport to reroute his flight from a different city, and the next flight from Varna to Yerevan—the last flight of the season—had been fully booked weeks in advance.

Seta had become more than anxious, too. When September 30 came and passed, she met with Stamboultsyan and convinced him to telex McCormick's invitation directly to the Soviet embassy in Bulgaria. Monte picked up the telex, obtained the visa, and then begged an Armenian woman working at the Aeroflot counter in Varna to put him on the last flight of the season to Yerevan. She bumped someone else off the roster to get him on, but he felt more relief than guilt when he took his seat on the plane. In his pocket he carried fifty-seven dollars, his entire fortune.

Meanwhile, in Yerevan one of Seta's acquaintances, a young man with wavy hair and swollen eyelids whom Seta called KGB Armen, informed her that his bosses had taken a keen interest in Monte's plans. After hearing rumors of a death threat against Monte from Secret Army supporters in Yerevan, the KGB had asked Armen to meet the fugitive at the airport if and when he arrived in Armenia, to provide security.

At noon on Friday, October 5, Seta met her friend Ashken near the Graduate and Faculty Dormitory on Mashdots Boulevard in Yerevan, where Seta had moved after completing her undergraduate work in 1987. Ashken's eyes grew wide as Seta rehearsed her itinerary: she was going with a KGB agent to pick up Monte at the airport. If Ashken did not hear from her in three days, she should ask Stamboultsyan to start searching for them.

PART FIVE

Armenia at Last

Bitter Bread

A fter scanning the sky through a crack in the curtains of a minibus for what seemed like an eternity, Seta fixed on a dot near the horizon. The plane swung down and skidded across the runway of Yerevan's Zvartnots Airport. Seta pressed her face against the window of the van, as one by one the passengers ducked out of the Tupelov airliner onto the unloading ramp and descended the stairs. Finally, a clean-shaven figure wearing jeans and a blue cotton shirt emerged from the plane with a flight bag on his shoulder and an old leather jacket over an arm. Twelve years after leaving the country of his birth, Monte Melkonian, alias Timothy Sean McCormick, finally set foot on the "homeland" he had imagined every day of his adult life but had never seen.

KGB Armen followed Monte into the terminal and handed him a note of introduction in Seta's handwriting. Monte squinted at the stranger in the tie. Was this a trick? Was he about to be arrested and imprisoned? There was nothing to do but follow the stranger out of the terminal. The minibus door opened, and Monte beamed when he saw Seta. Hugging her, he whispered that he was nervous: he knew he was in the hands of the KGB.

Monte spent his first days in Armenia as a "guest" of the KGB in a former rest home in the wild Hrazdan River Gorge, and then in a rest home in the mountains of Dilijan. He discussed developments in Armenia with his hosts, Armen and his tall, balding supervisor: two months earlier, on August 4, an overwhelming majority of Armenia's voters had elected Levon Ter-Petrosyan—the same Ter-Petrosyan who had helped arrange Timothy Sean McCormick's invitation to Armenia—as

President of the Supreme Soviet and the country's first non-communist leader in seventy years. About a month after that, the Supreme Soviet of Armenia had published a declaration announcing "the beginning of the process for the establishment of independent statehood." Legislators in Yerevan had adopted a new flag and national anthem, and had renamed the Armenian Soviet Socialist Republic "the Republic of Armenia." Meanwhile, Azerbaijan's Supreme Soviet followed suit with its own tricolor and its own equally Wagnerian anthem.

After nearly two weeks of discussions and long walks on country roads, Monte could no longer hide his impatience. He insisted on meeting with the new leaders in Yerevan without further delay, to discuss his permanent residence in Armenia. Armen's supervisor heaved a sigh, and then he left for Yerevan to arrange the meeting. When Armen came to pick Monte and Seta up for the meeting, his passengers were dressed and ready to go. Armen looked worried, though, and as they headed to the car he pulled Seta aside. Her fiancé, he reminded her in a low voice, was on his way to meet the highest leaders in the country. Could she have him change into something a bit dressier than faded corduroy pants, running shoes, and the same blue cotton shirt he had worn on the flight to Yerevan? Seta smiled apologetically: her fiancé was wearing the best clothes he owned. After an embarrassed well-what-can-we-do? smile, Armen drove his guest to Yerevan.

Monte shook hands with Levon Ter-Petrosyan's advisor, Babgen Ararktsyan. They discussed Monte's plans in the country, and Ararktsyan was satisfied with what he heard. When Monte returned to Dilijan, the KGB men rubbed their faces and finally agreed to release their "guest" on his own recognizance. Armen drove them back to Yerevan, and Monte registered at Seta's dormitory under the name "Simon."

Over the next several days, Monte accustomed himself to the novel feeling of living in the open, more or less. For the first time in years, he was neither in jail, nor in hiding, nor on the lam. Monte was one month short of his thirty-third birthday, and Seta was twenty-seven. They sauntered down boulevards arm in arm and stopped at a Polish cafeteria for oily noodles, meatballs, and fried potatoes, all the while discussing their next steps in Armenia.

Several times a week, a vast crowd of demonstrators gathered in the plaza around the gray basalt Opera House, just two and one-half blocks down Mashdots Boulevard from Seta's dorm window. Monte hadn't seen crowds like this since the heady days of the Iranian revolution.

The demonstrators denounced decades of Kremlin favoritism towards Baku, epitomized by the award of Mountainous Karabagh and the Armenian-populated region of Nakhichevan to Azerbaijan. "Karabagh is *ours*! Karabagh is *ours*!" the crowds chanted, each time more hoarsely.

Meanwhile in Baku, other demonstrators vented fury against Kremlin favoritism towards Armenia, the spoiled child of the Caucasus. Speakers railed against Stalin for handing the Azeri-populated district of Zangezur to Armenia, for the sole purpose, it seemed, of driving a wedge between Nakhichevan in the west and Mother Azerbaijan, to the east.

Back in Yerevan, Monte surveyed the multitude at Opera Square. Here, most assuredly, were "the people" in whom he had invested his faith and they overwhelmingly supported the establishment of a "Free, Independent, Armenia." Monte never recanted his opinion, stated so stridently throughout the 1980s, that secession from the multi-ethnic, multi-national Soviet Union would lead to disaster for Armenia. But by the time he had arrived in Yerevan, news of botched earthquake relief efforts and Moscow's intransigence on the Mountainous Karabagh issue had shaken his faith in the Soviet leadership. After a couple of weeks in Yerevan, it had become clear to Monte that the Soviet Union had already died in everything but name and that it was too late for a peaceful resolution of the conflict. The madness he had witnessed in disintegrating Yugoslavia had preceded him to the Soviet Union, as Gorbachev's *perestroika*, or "restructuring," had already become *perestrelka* — "crossfire." Armory doors were flung open, local regiments ignored orders from Moscow, and rocket bursts now punctuated skirmishes in Mountainous Karabagh. In Dear Everyone letters, he described a country in convulsions and swooning under a tight rail-and-road blockade by Azerbaijan. Saboteurs in the Republic of Georgia had bombed gas pipelines to Armenia; Yerevan endured electrical blackouts for all but several hours a day, and affordable food was in short supply. "This place is a *mess*," Monte concluded, shaking his head.

Even as tens of thousands of the wealthiest and best-educated residents of Yerevan were selling their houses and heading to Los Angeles, Monte was trying frantically to avoid expulsion from Armenia. The visa he had obtained in Bulgaria the year before had expired, and so he lived under constant threat of being seized by the KGB and deported. Finally, he managed to finagle a student residency permit as a researcher at Yerevan's Ethnology Institute.

By this time, Monte and his comrades had stopped referring to the disputed region as Mountainous Karabagh, and had switched instead to the word *Artsakh*, the preferred Armenian name for roughly the same territory. "The only real future for Artsakh is to be reunited with Armenia," Monte stated more than once, in writing and in conversation. To this end, he was determined to share his years of military experience with the beleaguered defenders in the mountains of Karabagh. He pored over Soviet military textbooks and US Army field manuals, and he received permission from the head of the paramilitary Defense Committee in Yerevan to form a partisan "detachment," or *chokat*.

Headquartered at the former Stepan Shahumyan Conference Palace in Yerevan, the Defense Committee was the embryo of Armenia's national army, which would soon supplant the disintegrating Soviet Army in the country. The head of the Committee, thirty-one year old Vazgen Sargsyan, was unusual among his peers, both for his easy smile and for the large white teeth it revealed. Under his loose charter, forty to fifty "detachments" of varying size, training, and discipline were already active in and around Mountainous Karabagh. The terminology, standard at the time, was misleading, though: none of these "detachments" could boast more than two dozen fighters in the field at any given time, and most consisted of fewer than ten full-time members. Moreover, they had no command-structural connection with platoon-size or larger units, and they were not even components of a larger army, in anything but the most lyrical sense of the word *army*.

Initially, Monte's detachment consisted of a total of seven volunteers, each with an olive drab uniform from the Committee. Other detachments adopted titles that evoked mythological and historical heroes from Armenia's ancient past: epic hero David of Sassoon; ancient king Tigran the Great; warrior leader Vartan Mamikonian, and so on. At Monte's urging, though, his group adopted the prosaic title, "Patriotic Detachment" (*Hairenasiragan Chokat*).

During a meeting in the Kabranian–Melkonian dorm room, Monte asked Seta to make a list of detachment members. After she had recorded the *noms de guerre* of all the members except Monte, he asked her to add "Avo" to the bottom of the list. Seta knew that *Avo* was the shortened form of *Avedis*, meaning "Good News," but she doubted that Monte had settled on his *nom de guerre* for that reason. When she asked him why he had chosen the *nom de guerre*, his explanation was characteristically practical: "It's a common name," he said, "and it's short and easy to recognize over a walkie-talkie."

"Avo" returned frequently to Sargsyan's office at the Defense Committee, to arrange for rifles and to ask permission to join the fighters at the front. Sargsyan liked the newcomer, with his strange accent and his threadbare jeans, but he knew that it would be too risky to send him to the front in Mountainous Karabagh: the Soviet Ministry of Internal Affairs, the MVD, still manned roadblocks and patrolled the towns there. With bad luck, they might seize Monte, a convicted "international terrorist," at a roadblock or during a routine document check on the street, and this would greatly embarrass authorities in Yerevan. So instead of sending him and his detachment straightaway to Mountainous Karabagh, Sargsyan asked him to undertake an inspection tour along the northeastern border of the Republic of Armenia, where there was less risk of arrest or capture. Since the Patriotic Detachment was so small, it would be combined with another small detachment, the self-titled Specially Designated Group, led by a good-looking captain named Vova.

Monte was more than happy to accept his first assignment in Armenia. In early March 1991, he and the combined detachments climbed into a hard-sprung truck, and for the next month they bumped over dusty roads along the Republic of Armenia's eastern border with Azerbaijan, from the town of Noyemperyan in the north to the town of Goris, 150 miles to the south. Along the way, Monte spoke with local defenders, inspected trenches, and jotted notes about the meager defense preparations he saw.

When they arrived at the village of Aykebar-Chinar in the northern district of Tavush, the locals asked their would-be defenders to leave. At first, Monte thought he was misunderstanding their village dialect. The locals explained that if the fighters were to attack their Azeri neighbors in nearby villages, a war would result, and they did not want that. They hadn't asked for a war, nor had their Azeri neighbors. Monte replied that a war was already at hand whether they wanted it or not, but his argument had little effect. He was still shaking his head in disbelief as the truck pulled out of the village, headed south to the district of Vardenis.

In the second half of April, Yerevan TV began airing video clips of dragon-like MI-24 attack choppers firing rockets into Armenian-populated villages north of the Mountainous Karabagh Autonomous Region. Monte scoured newspapers and television screens, to catch the latest news from the area: on April 21, troops from the predominantly Azeri 23rd Motorized Rifle Division of the Soviet 4th Army, together with gray-suited troops of the OMON, a paramilitary police associated with the Interior Ministry, launched an offensive dubbed Operation Ring. By June 12, almost all of the Armenians in the area around Getashen and Martunashen villages, some 5,000 villagers and farmers in all, had been deported. Azeri attackers then advanced several kilometers south to the Shahumyan district, an area in which 85 per cent of the 20,000 inhabitants were Armenians. On July 13, the attackers delivered an ultimatum by megaphone to the villagers of Bozluk, Manashid, and Erkej: either abandon your homes or be destroyed. The next day, the villagers wrapped lumps of their native earth in handkerchiefs, pushed the handkerchiefs into their pockets, and staggered away under the burden of whatever belongings they had thrown into the bedsheets that now served as gunny sacks. Helicopters and light tanks fired over their heads, motorized infantry from the 23rd Division rolled in, and looters brought up the rear. When the attackers had completed their work, they raised their flag over the village—not the red flag of Soviet Azerbaijan, but the tricolor of the nominally independent Republic of Azerbaijan. In all, they emptied twenty-three villages in and around the Shahumyan district, expelling 17,000 Armenians from their homes. The simple analysis of a local farmer appeared to be accurate enough: "The Turks want to take our land and drive us out of here."

Leaders in Baku had already rescinded the autonomous status of Mountainous Karabagh, and rising opposition figures in Baku now spoke openly of expelling all Armenians from the mountains. Monte was not alone in the belief that if the enemy were to succeed in capturing Mountainous Karabagh, they would advance further west from there, into the Republic of Armenia itself. "Even if we lost Artsakh we shouldn't think that the fighting would stop," he reflected. He had heard that "intellectuals" in Baku had formed a committee dedicated to annexing Zangezur, the narrow arc of land that connected Armenia to Iran. If Azerbaijan were to win a victory in Mountainous Karabagh, Monte concluded, "The next will be Zangezur." And if Azerbaijan were to annex Zangezur and thereby cut Armenia off from Iran, its only friendly neighbor, Armenia would be reduced to little more than a satellite of Azerbaijan's ally, Turkey. Indeed, the scenario could get even worse, as Monte pointed out at every opportunity: supporters of the nationalist Azerbaijani Popular Front, the ascendant opposition party in Baku, were printing maps on which the city of Yerevan itself—the capital of Armenia and the residence of one-third of its population—appeared as "Iravan," within a greater Azerbaijan.

To Monte, then, what was at stake in Mountainous Karabagh was nothing less than the survival of the Armenian nation on even the small portion of his homeland that the Turks had not yet managed to swallow. In a letter to a friend in Paris, he stated his conclusion: "The loss of Artsakh could be the loss of Armenia."

But even as he resolved to help defend the front, other matters demanded his attention. "One of our objectives while here," he had written in his first letter to his parents from Armenia, "is to finally organize and execute formal wedding plans." Time and money were short, but he agreed with Seta that a quick civil service would not do: after so long without seeing his parents and siblings, the least he could do to acknowledge their support throughout the years in jail and on the lam was to invite them to a church wedding.

When Mom, Dad, Maile, Marcia, and I arrived at Zvartnots Airport in late July 1991, Monte met us in his usual jeans and rubber sandals. We hugged, and then I held his shoulders at arm's length and remarked that he looked just the same as when I had last seen him ten and one-half years earlier in Beirut. "Oh yeah?" he said, dipping his head and comically jabbing at his thinning pate with an index finger, "What about *this*?"

Monte had rented an apartment for us several kilometers outside of Yerevan, in a maze of unfinished but already-crumbling high-rises faced with pink tufa stone. In the days and evenings that followed, my brother and I strode mile after mile through this maze, as he launched into a detailed account of the demise of the Secret Army. Even as battles raged along Armenia's borders, and even as his wedding preparations were in full swing, the duty to "go on record" about the Secret Army, and especially about the circumstances of Garlen and Aram's deaths, overrode all other obligations. From time to time, he would raise his eyes to the sky or wince to conjure a name or a date from his super-human memory, then he would fix his eyes on the road again as he strode forward, as if he were reciting lines written on the horizon.

Among other things, I learned that Monte now doubted his earlier assumption that Shishko's boys had killed Hagopian. Janet Hagopian, the Secret Army chief's widow, would soon confirm Monte's suspicion that Hagopian's own cohorts had pulled the triggers: in an article dated September 1991, she would pin the assassination on four of Hagopian's closest aids: Hovsep A., Vartan G., Garabed K., and Albert "Sultan-Minas" A. Six years later, Hagopian's old protégé, the writer Kevork Ajemian, would support Janet Hagopian's accusation: the assassins were indeed the very men who still emblazoned their communiqués with the slogan: "Hagop Hagopian lives! We are all Hagopians!" And yet these same four men would continue to condemn Monte and his comrades for their earlier opposition to the very same Hagopian they themselves had finally blasted with boar slugs on a sidewalk in Greece!

I noticed that Monte never discussed weighty issues indoors, and that there were events he never mentioned even out-of-doors. When I asked him about a scar on his right forearm, for example, he reflexively pulled the arm back, covered the scar with his left hand, and shrugged "Aw, nothin'." He never mentioned the girl in the back seat of the car in Athens, either.

I also noticed that he had stopped making sport of adversity. He was salting his food as he hadn't done for years, and having always had cold showers since his teens, he now heated water in a pot on the stove for his bath. I was most surprised, however, to see that after finishing the crust of the local bread he would leave the doughy center on his napkin uneaten. I had seen others do this, but I never would have guessed that Monte would adopt the custom: he had always eaten everything on his plate, and bread in particular was something sacred, not to be thrown away. When I asked about it, he claimed that he had almost cracked a molar on a stone once, and that Seta had picked bits of wood, metal, and bugs from her bread. "If you'd ever tasted this kind of bread in Iran," he added, "you'd know how it's *supposed* to turn out."

Bread had become a metonym for the shabby state of the country. Monte was not alone in presuming that the *nomenklatura* ate only fluffy bread baked from fine white flour. And so it was with most of the other artifacts at hand: after lamenting the sad state of the telephone service in Yerevan, Monte dismissed piecemeal improvement with a contemptuous *puh!* and a grumble: "They've got to pull the whole system out and start all over again." City streets, highways, hospitals, and apartment blocks — according to him, they all required demolition right down to the foundation before replacement. When I asked him to revise an article he had written in June 1990 entitled *Socialism, Confusion, and Our Homeland,* he sadly conceded that socialism had foundered everywhere except Cuba, but he reaffirmed the wish that appeared in the original draft of the manuscript: "All we can hope," he wrote, "is that we'll get things right next time."

One of those days, while Monte and I were going through papers at his dorm room, two bearded men sauntered in with jocular salutations.

They were wearing military fatigues, and one was toting an AKSU sub-machine gun—an accessory that had neither the range nor the accuracy for the battlefield, and which therefore no one needed except a show-off, a ne'er-do-well, or a "businessman's" bodyguard. Monte introduced me to his fellow detachment members. The darker one bore the nickname *Kechel Sergei*, "Bald Sergei," for his shiny dome. One glance at Kechel's glazed eyes and I knew he was a killer. We bantered for a while, and then they left. As soon as their footsteps faded down the hallway, I turned to Monte. "Nice guys," I said in English, "But you know very well that if you give them half a chance, they'll 'do' an Azeri village—they'll kill everyone in sight, men, women, and children."

Monte considered the medium distance for a couple of beats without disputing the point. "We can forget about internationalism and all the rest of that stuff," he said in a level voice. "The first thing we need to teach these people is: *don't kill civilians.*"

It had been more than a decade since Monte had quit his job at Torossian Junior High School in Lebanon, yet he had never abandoned his calling as a teacher. It would take him a while, though—too long, as it turned out—to realize that the Kechel Sergeis on both sides of the conflict were in no mood to learn lessons.

One morning not long after meeting Kechel, I accompanied Monte to a gated building on Octobrist Boulevard (soon to be renamed Tigran the Great Boulevard) to ask Ovir, the Directorate of Visas and Registration, to stamp the wedding guests' visas for an extended stay. On the sidewalk in front of the gate, we pushed ourselves into a crush of bodies, the Armenian version of a queue. Most of the supplicants jostling us on all sides had come for emigration papers. I scanned the crowd: these were Monte's compatriots; the people he had killed for; the people his comrades had died for; the people for whom he had spent four years in prison. And now here they were—hundreds of them that morning and thousands that week—almost literally stampeding to leave their newly "independent" homeland.

The scene embarrassed both of us. It was like being cursed on the street by a madman. Standing in that crowd, I couldn't bring myself to ask Monte if it bothered him that so many of his compatriots could shout themselves hoarse in the city squares demanding "*Our lands!*" one evening, and then show up at the Ovir the next morning to beg for visas to Los Angeles. Later on, I asked him about this as gently as I could. "Just because people leave doesn't mean they're not sincere patriots," he replied in a soft but higher-than-usual voice. The response struck me as so pathetic, so endearingly loyal that I had no heart to challenge it.

A couple of days before the wedding, I pushed Monte in front of a full-length mirror in the hallway of our apartment and demonstrated one or two simple dance steps. We both knew that all eyes would be on the bride and groom when they kicked off the first dance at the reception, and I knew that Monte had been dreading this prospect. He hadn't spent many moments of his life in front of a mirror, and he hated it. To make matters worse, his attempts to follow the dance steps were dismal. "Lost child!" Seta exclaimed when she came upon the scene. This was charitable of her: he danced more like a circus bear than a lost child. To this day, I cannot fathom how Monte—with his poise on the pitcher's mound and his ability to run like a greyhound and swim like an otter—could have been such a bad dancer.

On the morning of the wedding, August 3, I accompanied Vahram, a friend of the family, to the river at the bottom of the Hrazdan Gorge, to wash his green "Villis," an open-top jeep that would serve as the bride and groom's limousine. After Maile and one of Seta's sisters taped roses and white ribbons to the vehicle, Vahram chauffered the bride over a dusty road that wound through the mountains to Geghart, a 1,000-year-old monastery carved into a cliff of volcanic rock. Seta was wearing a European-style wedding dress that a sister had sewn for her, and Monte was wearing a simple European-style jacket and trousers, tailored a few days earlier from black fabric. It was the first suit he had owned in over ten years. He had borrowed a tie for the day, too, and for lack of a timepiece of his own (he had long since discarded his engraved Seiko wristwatch when it had ceased to tell time), he wore an old Citizen watch that Seta's grandmother had bequeathed. Inside the cave-like chapel, I held the traditional cross over the head of the bride and groom, while the priest conducted the ceremony. When the newly-weds finally emerged into sunlight, a drummer and a reed flautist led the guests, trilling and twirling down a dirt road, to a reception hall in a restaurant perched above a rocky gorge.

Later that evening, Monte rose from the head table and stood at military attention, his gaze fixed on some distant point beyond the walls of the reception hall. The music stopped, and every guest in the room fell silent. Monte raised a glass of a clear liquor called *oghi* and dedicated toasts to Alec and "other comrades who aren't with us today." Here, even on this most joyous of Monte's days, Garlen and Aram were almost palpably present. In the wake of the ensuing silence, Seta sang *The Lamentation of Karabagh*, a lilting folk song that was one of Monte's favorites.

The drums beat into the night and wine flowed until the early hours of the morning. At Dad's insistence, the newlyweds spent their honeymoon night at the Dvin Hotel in Yerevan.

A couple of days after the wedding, I accompanied Monte on what was supposed to be a short visit with some "good guys" in Masis, a squat town of 10,000 at the end of a road ten miles south of Yerevan. The townsfolk had recently evicted their Azeri neighbors and had elected a young, nationalistic town council. The purpose of our jaunt was to arrange for his Patriotic Detachment to use a certain two-axle military truck, a GAZ 66 that had probably been confiscated from an evicted Azeri neighbor. I had heard about this famous truck before: Monte was convinced that it would be the first of a formidable fleet of military vehicles at the service of his detachment.

Soon after arriving in Masis, we found ourselves seated on a bench along the wall of a municipal office, while half a dozen local functionaries in their twenties and early thirties sipped soda and debated the form of the post-Soviet regime. The leading contenders were either monarchy or an Israeli model, in which Armenia would make itself a garrison at Uncle Sam's service. Monte kept silent, as they droned on and on about Armenia's glorious future in the New World Order. At one point, I cut into the conversation to ask whether they had considered the possibility that Armenians might soon find themselves in the same predicament as the inhabitants of ten dozen other impoverished capitalist "democracies" in Asia, Africa, and Latin America. "Eh," a young official said, flicking his fingers as if to remove a bit of lint, "Those monkeys will have to climb down from the trees first, before they learn to walk."

I glanced over at my brother, who had sunken into his chair and was avoiding eye contact. He knew what I was thinking, and he knew that I knew what he was thinking.

After a dozen more bottles of soda, Monte finally interrupted the debate and repeated his original question: *what about the truck?* At that, one of the discussants replied that they hadn't had any luck locating the truck, and they were sorry about that. We excused ourselves and headed to the car. As our Lada crunched over the gravel road out of

Masis, I noticed a GAZ 66 rusting at the edge of a field. All four tires were flat, grass was growing under it as high as the differentials, and I'm not sure there was even an engine under the hood.

"Is *that* your truck?" I asked my little brother, who was sitting next to me in the back seat, following the jalopy with his eyes as we passed. "Yeah ..." he said, with an equal dose of embarrassment and surprise. The response threw me back many years, to an evening in Beirut when Monte had taken me to the apartment of a certain "good guy" who was supposed to join my brother in a revolutionary conspiracy of some sort. Instead of revolution, though, the "good guy" had treated us to an afternoon of excruciating spaghetti westerns on Super-8 film. "Well, *that* was a wasted afternoon ..." Monte had said with the same tone of embarrassment and surprise, as we had headed home. Now, twelve years later, I dropped an arm around my brother's shoulders. However quixotic, there was something poignant about his faith in these hopeless people.

"Call Me Avo"

A wakening on the morning of August 19, 1991, Monte clicked the dial on his transistor radio and listened with knitted brow to a BBC report from Moscow. Yerevan residents tuning in to Moscow stations that morning heard Tchaikovsky—putsch music. A Moscow TV channel showed a deer on a film loop drinking from a pond for hours, while another channel screened the movie *Planet of the Apes*. In the several days since I had left Yerevan, three high-ranking Soviet officials—KGB chief Kruchkov, Minister of Defense Yasov, and Vice-President Yanayev—had launched a coup against General Secretary Gorbachev, whom they had accused of ruining the country.

Even as armored personnel carriers took up positions at intersections around Yerevan, Levon Ter-Petrosyan denounced the coup and threw his support behind the emerging leadership of Gorbachev's rival, the President of the Russian Federation, Boris Yeltsin. After a couple of uneventful days in Yerevan, the coup collapsed for lack of popular support. Soon, Yeltsin would complete his counter-coup against Gorbachev and hoist the white, blue, red flag of imperial Russia over the Kremlin. In Yerevan, meanwhile, the red, blue, orange tricolor of the first Armenian Republic (which flickered into existence in 1918 and expired in 1920) was again flying over government buildings, after seventy-one years in mothballs.

Monte stood quietly at the window of his dorm room and watched the morning traffic revive in the street below. Writing from Poissy Prison a couple of years earlier, he had described the demand for Armenian independence (a word he could not resist putting in quotation marks) as a call for "national self-termination," "a catastrophe," and "a nightmare in disguise." "In spite of the current criticisms expressed from every quarter," he had written, "it is a fact that the inhabitants of the Armenian Soviet Socialist Republic today enjoy a higher standard of living and more security than Armenians have ever enjoyed at any other time in their three thousand-year history." But now, in the wake of the August coup attempt and Yeltsin's successful counter-coup, there was little to do but to make the best of a *fait accompli*.

Russian forces and the MVD hauled down the red flag and closed shop in Mountainous Karabagh. Just as soon as the Russians moved out, the field was clear for an all-out contest of arms between Armenians and Azeris. On September 2, 1991, a joint session of the Mountainous Karabagh Regional Council and the Governing Council of the Shahumyan District proclaimed the establishment of the Mountainous Karabagh Republic, an Armenian mini-state independent from Azerbaijan. (And why not? If it had been all right for Azerbaijan to secede from the Soviet Union in the name of self-determination, why shouldn't Mountainous Karabagh secede from Azerbaijan for the very same reason?)

Ter-Petrosyan, however, was in no position to officially recognize the upstart mini-state just to the east of "Mother Armenia": his Republic of Armenia had already been ravaged by seismic and social upheaval, and he could not afford to take a step that would amount to a declaration of war against Azerbaijan. Still, the leaders of Azerbaijan were not much impressed by Ter-Petrosyan's attempt to take a diplomatic distance from events in Mountainous Karabagh. They knew that Ter-Petrosyan's cohorts in the Armenian Ministry of Defense were providing fuel, food, and fighters to the secessionists in Mountainous Karabagh, so they tightened their crippling blockade of the Republic of Armenia. If they could strangle Armenia economically, they wagered, the rebellion in Mountainous Karabagh would sputter out.

At the same time, generals in Moscow seized on the rebellion as a stick to beat wayward Azerbaijan and its oil fields back into the Russian sphere of influence. Russian troops — "our blonde brothers," as an Armenian officer once described them to me with an ironic half-smile — remained at their posts in and around Yerevan.

A few days after Russia's imperial flag rose over the Kremlin, another face from the past appeared at Monte's door in Yerevan. Myriam Gaume was a pretty investigative reporter who had been covering the aftermath of the coup for the French publication *L'Evénement*. Monte had first met her at the Palais de Justice in Paris, just days before his final expulsion from France. During their twenty-minute interview back in January 1989, Gaume had been surprised to discover that the fearsome terrorist leader was in fact attentive, funny, and smart—a far cry from the bellicose fanatic she had expected. Now, less than three years after their first meeting, she had come to visit him in Yerevan. When Monte offered to accompany her to the mountains of Karabagh as her interpreter, Gaume gratefully accepted the offer.

On September 12, Seta tossed a glass of water into the street as her husband left for the military section of Erepuni Airport on the first leg of his first trip to the mountains of Karabagh. A short while later, Monte and Gaume lugged their daypacks across the tarmac and took seats on a bench in the tunnel-like fuselage of an old MI-8 helicopter. The flutter of the rotors rose to a high-pitched whine. Monte turned to Gaume and shouted over the rotors, but not too loudly: "Call me Avo now." He would be leaving his given name behind in Yerevan, and with it, his Secret Army past.

Gently swaying, the overloaded chopper chugged its way east, over the narrow, craggy gap separating the Republic of Armenia from Mountainous Karabagh. To elude anti-aircraft gunners, it shadowed the rising ridges just above the highest pines, rising to 3,000 feet above sea level. The chopper swung around to the left, flying north to an Armenian-populated area just beyond the northernmost frontier of Mountainous Karabagh. This was Gulistan, the "Land of Roses."

The chopper settled on a stubbly hill, as peasants mobbed it in the rising squall. Leathery, unshaven mountain people in threadbare suit jackets shouted greetings above the whirling rotors, while teenage girls in ill-fitting frocks and stocky women in blue, cream, and yellow flowered headscarves pressed forward like ghosts in the blowing dust. Shouting peasants unloaded Katyusha rockets, a skittish horse reared, and a fatigue-clad father pushed a little girl with a white pom-pom in her hair through a porthole.

Monte grabbed his daypack and hopped from the chopper. Looking down at the horizon from where he stood, it seemed as though he could make out the curvature of the Earth. He had spent a quarter of his life in dark, narrow spaces. Now, he stood on a wind-whipped hill, with nothing above but blue sky and nothing around but sunlight.

Monte and Gaume clambered into a minibus, which jostled over unpaved roads, past women digging potatoes and children with twine for belts. The Azeris had long since cut electricity and fuel to the district, in advance of the refugees from villages just to the northwest. "I couldn't believe how much poorer and more backward that area is than even the worst of villages in Armenia," Monte recalled a couple of weeks later, "It was almost like being in the mountains of Afghanistan."

When they entered the village of Shahumyan, it was bustling with men, perhaps 200 of them, loitering or squatting in faded suit jackets and beat-up, smooth-soled shoes. Monte identified fighters from a couple of small detachments, interspersed with about forty volunteers from villages nearby. Some had youthful wisps on their chins, while others had gray whiskers. Most lacked boots, many lacked uniforms, and some lacked guns. Even the uniformed ones were perfectly mismatched in a rag pile of fatigues, camouflage, and track suits. The exceptions were two huddles of dangerous-looking men in black wool uniforms and with up-curled moustaches. Daggers and bayonets dangled from their belts. These were the fighters of the Arabo and Aramo detachments, two itinerant groups that showed up when there was killing to be done. They were known to notch their gunstocks and to twist gold teeth from the gums of their victims.

That night, in the headquarters at Shahumyan village, Monte, now alias "Avo," pulled a mattress off a droopy cot, flopped it to the ground, and stretched out to think before dozing off. Men shuffled in the darkness, clinking and rattling ammo belts. Monte listened. This was too much bustle for merely defensive preparations. These were the sounds of fighters girding for an attack. Someone must have decided to attack OMON positions, rather than to evacuate the residents of Shahumyan. Monte winced: how unfortunate that he had arrived in these mountains empty-handed, wearing only track shoes!

The next morning, Monte and Gaume accompanied Gor, a skinny fighter in his early twenties, to the weapons depot. There, rusty old Mosin-Nagant rifles leaned against a wall next to shiny new assault rifles, as well as Katyusha and Alazan rockets, rocket-propelled grenades, and a 14.5-mm anti-aircraft gun. The arsenal was considerably more lethal than the hunting rifles and shotguns of the previous stage of the conflict. Gor watched Monte shoulder the guns one by one and inspect them, noting manufacturers and serial numbers. Monte shouldered a grenade launcher: "*Jboo! Jboo! Jboo!*" he imitated the sound of the weapon belching fire. "Ha! What a great gun! What a great gun!" he enthused, "I might well have fired this gun before, in Lebanon ... Or this one here."

Gor smiled. They could always use another fighter in Shahumyan, and Monte looked like he could handle a rifle. Gor introduced the newcomer to his fellow fighters. In a snapshot taken that day, Monte stands in the middle of a group of them, behind sandbags in the shadow of a gutted cottage. Monte is the only figure without a rifle, but his camouflage shirt is tucked under his belt. His transformation from interpreter to fighter was almost complete.

For the first five hours and forty-five minutes of Saturday, September 14, the fighters, 120 in all, scurried through cropped wheat on the outskirts of the village of Verishen. Azeri snipers fired tracer bullets from the opposing hills, but the Armenian fighters did not return fire. Monte and Gor pulled a small cannon on a two-wheel carriage more than 500 meters up a hill, and set it in place. Aside from rockets and a couple of locally produced light mortars, their 72-mm cannon was the only piece of artillery on the Armenian side. The gun was a relic of the Great Patriotic War that the Soviet Army had donated to a *kolkhoz*, where it had fired silver iodide rounds into the sky to seed rain clouds. This morning, it would be firing live ammunition.

By five in the morning, the jangling and whispering had ceased, as the fighters peered over trenches and sandbags at the invisible enemy in the high grass and poplars on the slope several hundred meters away. The aroma of wild mint wafted through the trenches. The Azeris, including remnants of the 23rd Division of the Soviet 4th Army, had a deadly 100-mm cannon out there, well positioned. Just beyond that lay Monte's comrades' first goal—four hills overlooking the road from Verishen to the village of Bozluk. On the hillside five or six kilometers to the west lay their second, third, and fourth goals, the villages of Bozluk, Manashid, and Erkej. Three months earlier, the OMON had deported Armenians from these villages. Now it was time to take them back.

At 6:20, just as the sun began glowing above the mountains to the right, Monte jerked the cannon's trigger cord, producing a deafening blast that sent partridges into flight low over the close-cropped field. The counter-offensive had begun. The back-and-forth rat-a-tat of automatic weapons merged into a roar, and the smell of black powder and cordite overwhelmed the mint. After dozens of rounds, Gor joined index finger with thumb, to signal that they had finally scored a direct hit on the Azeri cannon. By 8:30 they had repulsed the Azeri's forward position, although the enemy still held the heights.

The Armenians reloaded and pressed on through the mint and yellow wildflowers. Before long, their enemy began retreating under a storm of bullets, to the top of the hills. Within the first four and one-half hours of fighting, Monte's comrades managed to take three of the four peaks they wanted, as well as the village of Bozluk. Enemy soldiers retreated to the fourth peak, and Armenian attackers surrounded them. The enemy soldiers were now fighting for their lives, as Monte explained in his letter of September 27, so they "put up a very stiff resistance." At 1:00 p.m., an Azeri helicopter suddenly appeared, then whirled around under fire and disappeared behind a ridge, to lift the surviving OMON fighters off the last peak. By 1:30 p.m., the battle of Bozluk was over. It had lasted seven hours and ten minutes.

Shrapnel littered the road rising from Verishen to Bozluk on the ridge, and the smell of burned flesh now overwhelmed the cordite and wild mint. Three Armenians had been killed, including Edik of Arabo. On the Azeri side, thirteen had been killed, all of them fighters except for one looter. Monte inspected the scene. An OMON soldier clenched the air with upraised arms, his nose in the mud, and his torso stretched like taffy by the force of an exploding shell.

In his letter of September 27, Monte described the day's events blandly, writing that "the battle was well planned and rather organized." But later, in a lecture videotaped in Yerevan on January 25, 1992, he would describe the battle in more sweeping terms: "And so for the first time in modern Armenian history, the Armenians were able to retake territory." Armenians were not used to celebrating victories: most of the battles they commemorated, from the Battle of Avarair in 451 AD to the seizure of the Imperial Ottoman Bank in 1896, had been lost. Back in his Berkeley days, Monte had read the lines from Shahan Shahnour's novel *Retreat without a Song*, and had accepted the writer's words as his own:

> Parents, sons, uncles, and sons-in-law, retreat. Customs, conceptions, morals, and love, retreat. The language retreats, the language retreats, the language retreats. And we are still retreating in words and deed, willingly and unwillingly, knowingly and unknowingly.

The Battle of Bozluk had put an end to the retreat.

Entering the village, the fighters found little to salvage. Fleeing Azeri squatters had smashed what they had not been able to take with them: furniture, curtains, mattresses, plates, and jars of pickles and preserves. They had even shot the dogs. Gaume watched a returning villager wipe tears from her eyes and keen: "It took so many years to build my house

... my whole life! And now look, look what they've done!" The scene at the desecrated Armenian cemetery was even worse: amid shattered gravestones, cadavers leered from toppled tombs.

After a hot meal with Arabo fighters, Monte and Gaume billeted with other fighters in a big house in Bozluk, surrounded by the crests of mountains tinged by the moonlight. It had been a long day and it would be a sleepless night. Some men stood guard in shifts, while others slept fitfully in the trenches, awakened periodically by gunfire.

The next morning, Gaume snapped a photo of Monte sleeping on a wooden bench in the courtyard of the headquarters. *Drôle de garçon*, she thought to herself. He "constantly scrutinizes maps and ceaselessly consults his watch," she wrote in her notebook. "He spends the night on the ground in his sleeping bag, even when there's a bed. As soon as he opens his eyes, he turns on his radio, BBC, every morning, even in the trench. And he doesn't say a word before having eaten and washed."

At four in the afternoon and at a signal from the scouts, a group of fighters began advancing on Manashid, a cluster of houses along both sides of a road to the north. Entering the village without resistance, they pulled down the Azeri flag and tore it into ribbons that they tied to the barrels of their guns for luck.

The weather changed for the worse, as the sky filled with gray-white clouds. The dirt-caked men in the trench hardly spoke any more. Suddenly, a voice broke out. It was Monte, just returned from Bozluk. "I'd *never* operate a mortar like that one," he drawled, fixing on a locally produced mortar in the trench. "A friend of mine died thanks to that same kind of mortar. He was twenty-two years old."

The other fighters in the trench hardly bothered to shrug off Monte's warning.

The next day, September 16, Monte and his comrades beat off two Azeri counter-attacks. At the approach of noon, just as it became clear that the enemy would not breach Manashid, news arrived that the Azeris had begun shelling Karashinar, an Armenian village fifteen miles to the east. The leader of the Arabo fighters, Manvel, folded the blanket; Slavik hoisted an ammo crate onto his back; Valeri threw the mortar over a shoulder, and they all filed out of the trench, rejoining the road to the Karashinar front. With eyelids drooping over red eyes, but with few words and no complaints, they trudged through ravine passes and orchards fragrant with wet walnut leaves, pomegranates, and the smoke of distant fires.

Karachinar was a village of crushed walls and collapsed roofs. In better days, these houses had been repositories of family fortunes and legacies for future generations. These were not huts: they had been spacious homes with parquet floors, tile kitchens, balconies, and arbors. Now, even as crowds in Yerevan mobbed the Ovir for exit visas to Los Angeles, the villagers of Karachinar squatted in the forest outside their village, waiting to return to their hearths. "Why should we leave our land?" an ash-smudged youngster in a too-tight shirt asked, quite unrhetorically. "Where would we go?" another asked. "I'll *never* leave," a tousle-haired mother announced, "I want to die here." For them, these mountains were "our land, our whole life," as they put it, and Monte admired them for this.

The defenders dropped their packs and began setting up firing positions behind the walls of gardens facing the Azeri village of Shafak, on the northern outskirts of Karachinar. Valeri Ghambaryan, a forty-three-year-old volunteer from the village of Chailu in the Mardakert district, slid a round into the mortar. A blinding flash and a loud CLANG tore his left hand off and peppered his torso with shrapnel. In a haze of cordite, his comrades sprang forward to stanch the spurting blood with rags and tourniquets, then they bore him off to the hospital in Shahumyan, where he bled to death, leaving four orphans behind.

The shelling of Karachinar continued for three days, smashing and burning much of the village, but claiming only two casualties. As news of the battles filtered into the international wire services, Mom resumed the apprehensive mode she had assumed back in the Secret Army days. "I lay awake nights, so many nights," she later told a journalist for the *Fresno Bee* newspaper: "The dear boy, he doesn't deserve this life. We were all rooting for him, and he tossed it all away."

In Karachinar, Monte manned the light cannon again, but by September 18, when it had become clear that the Azeris were not going to take the village any time soon, he joined his comrades on the Manashid front, twenty kilometers to the west. That day they advanced on their third and final goal, the abandoned village of Erkej, where apples rotted in the orchards. After the battle, Monte headed back to Karachinar, to pay his respects to Valeri.

"Where's the exploded mortar?" Monte's jaw clenched under his beard.

The other fighters cast their eyes to the ground. Monte contracted and released his fists, then strode off to find the mortar. Vladimir told him that one of Valeri's friends had become enraged at the sight of the mortar's ripped-open muzzle, and had tossed the weapon into the latrine pit behind the hospital building that served as a barracks.

Rummaging through a wood shed, Monte found a metal wire that he tinkered into a trawling hook. Ten minutes later he returned, accompanied by a foul stench and brandishing the metal tube he had snagged from a shit-filled hole. The muzzle, already rusted under the shit, was curled open like a wilted black orchid.

"*Yallah!* I have it." Monte had not sounded so triumphant when he had entered Bozluk. The other fighters watched with dull eyes as Monte washed his hands and wiped dry. Gaume described the scene:

"I'm going to make a video with this, and a photo of Valeri. To explain to the boys that this is totally dangerous, this junk here." He turned the burst muzzle to his audience. "There, you see? It doesn't have an air bypass hole. And right there, the base should be chromed. If not, it explodes. A hundred guys are already dead because of this lousy equipment."

Roubo shrugged. "So what! It's good enough to fight with. We don't have anything else."

Monte glowered at him dangerously. Hoisting the mortar by the wire snag, he sprayed it off at a faucet in the courtyard and wound it into an old rag. Then he folded Valeri's shredded jacket, soaked with blackened but still-moist blood, and tucked the bundle away safely, near his pack.

On September 20, Gaume and Monte scrunched into a Yerevan-bound chopper, she to witness the referendum on Armenia's independence from Moscow, and he to "collect guns." In the roar of the rotors and the dusty squall, wounded fighters kissed their rifles goodbye, as their comrades hoisted them into the chopper. Meanwhile, other fighters offloaded the same sort of homemade mortar that had killed Valeri.

Arriving at his dorm room in Yerevan, Monte opened the window and laid Valeri's fatigue vest on the sill. It was still damp with blood, and he wanted to dry it out. When Seta entered the room that evening, a stench of rotted blood hit her, and a bat flitted around the room. She chased the animal out the window with a broom. The next day, September 21, Monte stood between a blackboard and a video camera at the auditorium on the third floor of the dorm, and made a pitch for money. He was dressed in a tee shirt and jeans, and on a table in front of him lay Valeri Ghambaryan's blood-soaked vest and the grotesquely twisted mortar. Several black-and-white snapshots of Ghambaryan and other victims of faulty weapons stood on the edge of the table.

In the videotape, Monte lifts one end of the mortar and explains in his calm voice that some of country's best youth—men and women who were willing to sacrifice everything in defense of their homeland— were dying not from enemy shrapnel or bullets, but by their own faulty weapons. The future of Mountainous Karabagh, he says, will depend on the ability of Armenian fighters to establish an overland link between the Republic of Armenia and Mountainous Karabagh at their closest point, through the village of Lachin. But to do this they will need reliable weapons. And reliable weapons cost money—more money than he and his comrades had.

When I received the videotape in Chicago, I edited it together with battle footage and mailed dubs to the comrades in San Francisco. With money from them and from comrades in Paris, London, and Yerevan, Seta bought arms and ammunition, some from Russian military personnel in Armenia, and some through a contact in neighboring Georgia.

Three days after Monte had returned to Yerevan, on Monday September 23, the Armenian parliament issued an official declaration of independence of the Republic of Armenia. Of the eligible voters 95 per cent had gone to the polls, and 99 per cent of them had cast ballots for independence from Moscow. Meanwhile, Boris Yeltsin and Kazakh President Nazarbayev arrived in Stepanakert to co-sign documents declaring an end to the conflict in Mountainous Karabagh.

The more Monte studied the maps, the more he worried. The defenders in Mountainous Karabagh had no reliable overland connection with the Republic of Armenia, and the only fixed-wing landing strip in Mountainous Karabagh, the airstrip at Khojalu, was in Azeri hands. Even in the summer, helicopters formed only the frailest link between Mountainous Karabagh and the Armenian Republic. Now, as winter approached, fog was settling on the mountains, making helicopter flights even more perilous. The Azeris, by contrast, enjoyed unbroken logistical lines all along the front, from the north to the south, in the east and the west. They could bring up munitions, reinforcements, armor, and heavy guns from the towns of Agdam, Ganje, and even Baku, on paved roads through flat land and rolling hills.

"We've got to secure the positions before winter," Monte concluded. If not, and if the enemy were to push their way south from Shahumyan before the snows, then they would be free to reinforce positions all winter and advance on Stepanakert as soon as the passes were free of spring runoff. The same danger existed in Hadrut in the south and in Martuni to the east. As long as Mountainous Karabagh remained an island cut off from the Armenian mainland, this would be the case.

Monte needed to return to Shahumyan as soon as possible. But this time he would not go empty-handed. Since the Patriotic Detachment had exhausted its meager funds, Monte needed to collect money for supplies, and he needed to do it fast. When Seta asked him about a figure that he had entered into the detachment's accounting book, he shrugged: "Oh, we've promised three hundred dollars to the detachment." When she asked how much money they had to their name, he laughed: "Three hundred and sixty-five dollars." That was before the donation.

A few days later, Monte was unloading crates under the whistling rotors of another MI-8 helicopter. He had landed in Shahumyan again, but this time he had brought boxes of bullets with him, as well as fifty rocket-propelled grenades, a couple of B-7 grenade launchers, and a couple of comrades from the Patriotic Detachment. They trudged with packs and rifles down a dirt road through the mountains, to join local volunteers in trenches around the village of Karachinar.

Monte gave combat directions to the assembled fighters: Don't open fire first. Don't fire if you don't see anything. Don't shoot at any target further than 200 meters. Don't fire at anyone who doesn't have a gun. Never abandon weapons or ammunition. His voice grew stronger with each order he gave, and the locals seemed to feed off of his confidence. They had no idea what would happen in the hours and days ahead; they only knew that the lives of their parents and their children, their homes, their land, and the graves of their ancestors were at stake. They needed a leader, someone strong and decisive who knew what he was doing. Or at least someone who *looked* like he knew what he was doing.

When it came to strength and confidence, Monte did not disappoint. Patriotic Detachment members Hovsep and Artoosh related the following story, which another detachment member confirmed in a slightly different form: during Monte's second stint in Shahumyan, a couple of local fighters confronted him with an empty vodka bottle and demanded to know where he had dumped the contents. Monte reminded them that he had already laid down the law: no drinking on the front lines. The fighters responded that if they had no right to drink, then at least they had a right to smell the vodka that he had dumped. At that, Monte sauntered to a nearby tree, unbuttoned his pants, and pissed at the foot of the tree where he had dumped the vodka.

"We drink before eating," a fighter protested, "This is our custom here. Our forefathers have always done this."

"Then your forefathers were jackasses, too!" Monte growled back.

Monte returned to Yerevan on December 14, to raise money, recruit new fighters, and buy munitions. Armenia's capital had become a city of refugees and soup kitchens. Azerbaijan had tightened its blockade of fuel shipments to Armenia, and saboteurs regularly dynamited rail links and natural gas pipelines to Armenia through Georgia. Now, as the days grew colder, residents picked up shovels and revisited Victory Park to uproot the stumps of trees they had chopped down the previous winter for firewood. This winter they would burn the roots. Other residents took hatchets to school benches and pried parquet from government buildings for kindling. Buses rusted in the yards for lack of fuel. Shampoo froze in useless showers, and infants, pensioners, and medal-studded veterans of the Great Patriotic War expired in lightless rooms. Someone had even broken into the Yerevan Zoo to slaughter a rare native deer for meat. It was just as well: the zoo animals were starving to death anyway.

Armenians were confused: where were all of those wealthy compatriots they had heard so much about, the tycoons from the diaspora who were supposed to lift the nation into American-style prosperity in the post-Soviet era? "The millionaires had better send us something quick or we're going to starve to death," a Western journalist quoted an Armenian as saying.

On New Year's Eve 1992, Monte and Seta drove around Yerevan in a borrowed car, delivering bags of candy, raisins, and balloons to the children of their Patriotic Detachment comrades. At midnight, they made their way to Opera Square, where thousands of revelers were dancing to keep themselves warm. Turning to Seta with a mixture of apprehensiveness and eagerness, Monte asked, "Want to dance?"

In Mountainous Karabagh, 1992 began with the wrong sort of bang. Azerbaijan's President Ayaz Mutalibov, under pressure from ultranationalist opponents, announced that the time was right to crush Mountainous Karabagh with an iron fist. Artillery duels escalated along Armenia's eastern border, and new enemy concentrations took up positions along battle lines winding from Shahumyan in the north of Mountainous Karabagh to Hadrut in the south. Then, beginning on January 10, Azeri commander Rahim Gaziev unleashed long-range rockets and artillery shells against Stepanakert, a refugee-choked city of 70,000. Gaziev's firing platform was in Shusha, an Azeri citadel of 20,000 inhabitants, perched on cliffs four miles south of Stepanakert. Soon, SU-25 ground attack fighters began looping overhead, safely out of range of the defenders' antique anti-aircraft guns, and dropped 250- and 500-kilogram bombs on Stepanakert. But the deadliest weapon was the Grad rocket complex, consisting of up to three dozen 122-mm rockets, with a range of twenty-two kilometers. The "flying telephone poles," fired in a quick succession of whooshes like a bundle of huge bottle rockets, fell in a checkerboard pattern, smashing into classrooms, kindergarten playgrounds, and densely packed apartment blocks.

The hellfire that rained on Stepanakert that year claimed the lives of over 2,000 residents and refugees, and crippled more than 2,500 people, many of them children. Bombs and rockets damaged nearly every building in the city, driving its residents into cellars and basements, and creating more terror than any previous operation by either side. Schools and factories remained empty. Water pipes, the sewage system, the gas, the electricity—everything in Stepanakert was broken. The city's main hospital, its top floors leveled by the bombardment, had only sporadic electricity and no running water. Surgeons in candle-lit cellars amputated limbs with vodka and shell shock as anesthetics, while flies crawled on open wounds.

Monte had seen it all before, ten summers earlier in Beirut.

"It seems the future of the region will be determined this year," he wrote in one of his last Dear Everyone letters. In a lecture videotaped in his dorm room on January 25, he repeated a theme he had expressed in conversations and letters: "The Azerbaijan government has clearly decided to empty the Armenians out, and therefore there is no choice but to resist." "So we don't have the right to lose in this case," he said in his quiet, level voice, "We must win this time. We must win."

But how could tiny, landlocked Armenia fight and prevail against oil-rich Azerbaijan, a country more than twice as large in territory, with twice the population, and the support of mighty Turkey? How could Armenians defeat 30,000 soldiers of Azerbaijan's National Army, as well as 10,000 OMON troops, and thousands of additional volunteers from the Azerbaijani Popular Front?

"A lot of Armenians don't understand that we can win," he acknowledged in his January 25 video lecture, but the example of Vietnam showed that a smaller military force *could* win against a much stronger force, if it were determined and well organized. In any case, Monte and his compatriots had no choice but to fight, regardless of the odds against them: in a taped interview with British journalists conducted a year and a half later, he would summarize the situation on the ground: "The Karabaghsis know that either they'll fight or they'll be slaughtered. So they choose fighting."

In the face of such a desperate situation, every fighter counted. Monte urged his friends to join the Patriotic Detachment. One of these friends was a dark, good-looking environmental engineer named Hrair. In better days, Hrair had worked to reduce air pollution in Yerevan. "You don't have anything to do anymore," Monte half-joked: Yerevan's air quality had improved considerably, thanks to the fuel embargo and economic disintegration. Hrair thought for a moment, and then he joined the detachment.

Stepanakert was under siege, but the six or seven overworked MI-8 helicopters and the two MI-20 choppers that constituted the air bridge between Yerevan and Mountainous Karabagh could not bring in enough food, fuel, and medicine for the city. If they only had somewhere to land their YAK-40 transport planes, they could bring in the supplies they needed to ease the suffering and to bolster the defense of Stepanakert. The only airstrip for fixed-wing aircraft in Mountainous Karabagh, however, was located next to the Azeri town of Khojalu, and Khojalu remained in Azeri hands.

Monte braced his forehead with his fingertips and studied the map.

Discipline Problems

O n the morning of February 4, 1992, Seta stood with her husband under the rotors of a battered MI-8 helicopter at Erepuni Airstrip, just outside Yerevan. With them stood seventeen other fighters from Monte's detachment, including Hrair the environmental engineer, five new volunteers from the town of Ashdarak, and shark-eyed Kechel Sergei. Their detachment was headed to a place called Martuni, one of the six main districts under Armenian control in Mountainous Karabagh. Aside from that, no one knew much more in the way of details.

The rotors started whirling. Suddenly, a runner arrived at the helicopter and summoned Monte to the shed that served as the airstrip office. When he returned from the shed forty minutes later, he paused before climbing into the chopper and whispered to Seta that he had just spoken by phone with Vazgen Sargsyan, the head of the Ministry of Defense. What he didn't tell her was that Sargsyan had just promoted him to the position of *Shtabee Bed*, or Chief of Headquarters, in Martuni. At first, Monte had refused to accept the promotion, protesting that he had never stepped foot in Martuni before, and that he knew nothing about the district. Sargsyan had countered that times were desperate, and that he knew of no better candidate for the job. Finally, with the phone receiver in one ear and the chopper whistling in the other, Monte had relented, but he had made it clear that he would only accept the assignment temporarily, until Sargsyan found a more suitable candidate.

But why had Sargsyan appointed Monte, of all people, to this post? Monte didn't know the lay of the land; he knew nobody in Martuni, and he could barely understand the local dialect. Sargsyan knew Martuni, though: it was an exposed district, partially occupied by Azeris and ripe for an enemy offensive. It was also a district ruled on the Armenian side by competing clans and fierce loyalties. An outsider like Monte, with neither kin nor cronies in the district, would have a better chance of skirting local jealousies and infighting.

Seta poured water from the bottle she was holding onto the tarmac, and the rotors whipped it into a mist. The helicopter bounced gently, lifted into the air, and then swung around and tilted forward, towards Mountainous Karabagh. Martuni, in southeastern Mountainous Karabagh, was a wild, mountainous area of 200 square miles populated by 28,000 mountain people, many of them farmers and vintners. The district jutted into the surrounding lowlands of Agdam and Fizuli like a peninsula surrounded on the north, east, and south by well-armed Azeri forces. It was the weakest link in the defense of Mountainous Karabagh.

When the chopper touched down, Monte and his detachment hitched a ride on a truck full of bagged salt. After a bumpy ride, the truck pulled up to a low concrete building on a rocky slope about three kilometers west of the town of Martuni, the capital of the district that took its name. In better days, the building, known as Dor Atzel, had belonged to the Soviet Road Construction Department. Now it would serve as a barracks.

As soon as Monte stowed his pack at the new barracks, he slung binoculars around his neck and headed out the door to conduct reconnaissance. The Defense Committee in Stepanakert wanted to "clean out" Karadaghlu, a well-to-do Azeri wheat-farming village of about 1,200 inhabitants, located on the only paved road from Stepanakert to Martuni. In the months leading up to the war, the Azeri OMON had stopped cars at the Karadaghlu turn-off, beating and abducting Armenian motorists. In one case, they had burned a family in a car. Azeris in Karadaghlu had protested more than once to OMON officers, saying that their cruelty would lead to no good, but the officers had waved them away. Later, when the OMON had withdrawn from surrounding villages in the face of mounting attacks, the residents of Karadaghlu found themselves surrounded by increasingly hostile Armenians. Finally, helicopters had arrived to evacuate women and children, so that by the time Monte's superiors in Stepanakert had asked him to prepare a plan to attack the village, most — but not all — of the remaining inhabitants were armed defenders.

As Monte and the several other members of his recon team began descending the snowy slope from the Armenian village of Haghorti towards neighboring Karadaghlu, Armenian villagers nearby began shouting at them. The team halted its descent and fell into an argument with the villagers. An attack against Karadaghlu would bring war to Haghorti, the villagers explained. "Leave," they said, "We don't want war here." Monte replied that it was too late for these sorts of sentiments: they already were *in* war. They had no option now but to face this fact and to finish the business as quickly as possible. The villagers remained unconvinced, though, and voices grew louder. Finally, Azeri sentries in Karadaghlu, apparently alerted by the argument, put an end to the debate by taking potshots at the squabblers, who scrambled for cover.

After the aborted recon operation near Haghorti, Monte traveled from village to village in the Martuni district, with a pen and a wad of notepaper in his breast pocket. He would simply show up at a village or a frontline position, and without bothering to inform anyone that he was the new Headquarters Chief, he would begin asking questions: how many men were on duty? How many reserves were available for call-up? What about their defensive positions, their trenches, the disposition of enemy forces? How many rifles, shotguns, rounds of ammunition, and liters of diesel did each local leader have on hand?

After repelling invaders for centuries, the mountain people of Karabagh were wary of strangers asking questions. To make matters worse, there was a rumor that a visiting journalist had provided information to the enemy. So when an outsider speaking a barely intelligible version of the mother tongue showed up at the headquarters in the frontline village of Pertashen with a head full of questions, the locals were evasive. Nelson, the subcommander there, matched every one of the stranger's questions with a lie, which Monte carefully transcribed into his pad. Nelson was a wiry man who wore an enormous Stechkin pistol on his hip. The gun was a *trofei*, booty he had stripped from the corpse of an Azeri officer in the debris of a downed helicopter. As Monte copied Nelson's lies into his notepad, Nelson studied him through a squint: the stranger's head was elongated at the back, more in the manner of a Turk than a Karabagh Armenian. Nelson would be keeping an eye on him.

The former Chief of Headquarters in Martuni, an ex-Soviet Army captain named Anastas Aghamalyan, was not surprised when Monte flatly introduced himself as his replacement. Aghamalyan had dug trenches and laid mines along sections of the front, but his superiors worried that he lacked expertise in defense preparations. He took his demotion in stride, but he left Monte with a bit of advice: beware of treachery among his own men at headquarters.

In mid-February, Monte and his Patriotic Detachment bivouacked at Mehdishen, a village just north of Stepanakert and well outside of the Martuni district, to conduct more reconnaissance, this time for a planned attack against the nearby town of Khojalu. With 6,000 inhabitants, Khojalu was the second-largest Azeri town in Mountainous Karabagh, after the citadel of Shusha. The Azeris in Khojalu controlled Mountainous Karabagh's only airstrip, and gunners there cut off two main roads through the area, one to the east and one to the north. For the most part, though, the armed presence in Khojalu was defensive. It consisted of about forty OMON fighters plus a "self-defense group" of anywhere between sixty and 200 men, mostly conscripts with little training.

On February 16, Monte's recon operation came to a halt when he received an urgent summons from his superiors in Stepanakert. He put the caps on his binoculars and raced off to the Defense Forces headquarters, located in a former train station on Freedom Fighter Boulevard in Stepanakert. While he listened slack-jawed, Artur Mkrtchyan, the bespectacled President of the Mountainous Karabagh Republic, explained that the Arabo and Aramo detachments had just attacked the village of Karadaghlu on their own initiative and without permission, and that Azeri defenders had repulsed them, killing one of the attackers in the process. Mkrtchyan knew that Monte had conducted reconnaissance at Karadaghlu, and so he asked him to finish the operation that the renegade detachments had botched.

"Collect your stuff right now," Monte announced when he skidded into the Patriotic Detachment bivouac at Mehdishen, "We're leaving." By mid-afternoon, as their UAZ troop carriers approached Karadaghlu, they met Arabo and Aramo fighters on the road. The battle was over, the black-clad fighters said: the village had been captured, and now the attackers were pulling out. Hearing this, most of the Patriotic Detachment members wheeled around and returned to their barracks at Dor Atzel, but Monte continued towards Karadaghlu, to confirm the report. A short while later, he burst into the barracks at Dor Atzel and shouted "Get ready!" The report had been false: Karadaghlu remained in the hands of its Azeri defenders.

By six the next morning, a dozen members of the Patriotic Detachment were crouching in brown grass and snow on a promontory overlooking the Azeri's stone block defense center on the southwest edge of Karadaghlu. Local fighters from the Martuni headquarters crouched on either side of Monte, while the Arabo and Aramo brigades had taken up other positions around the village. Neither the attackers nor the defenders had the benefit of tanks, artillery, or any other weapon larger than a grenade launcher.

Nine years earlier, Monte had written in his *Manual for the Training of a People's Fighter* that: "The command to open fire in an ambush should be given by the commander in the form of his own firing on the enemy (it is preferable to begin firing with a B-7 grenade launcher or any other weapon that will cause immediate heavy losses, if such a weapon is available)." Now, he coolly shouldered a B-7, lined up his sights, and squeezed the trigger. With a white flash, the first round roared straight through the second-story corner window of the defense center and burst inside, sending a yellow flame back out the window. With that, the attackers began pouring lead into the village. Nelson, the subcommander from Pertashen, watched round-eyed as Monte fired, lowered the B-7 to observe his forces advance, shouted orders to the subcommanders (for lack of a walkie-talkie), and then coolly reloaded and fired again.

Under a hail of bullets, the Azeri defenders radioed for backup, informing their commanders on the Agdam Plain a few kilometers to the north that they could not hold out much longer against the attack. From Monte's position overlooking the Azeri defense center, he could hear gunshots inside the building. It occurred to him that the defenders, unable to agree on their course of action, were shooting at each other. When the defenders ceased returning fire, Monte laid down the B-7 and watched his fellow attackers swarm into Karadaghlu from several sides.

By five in the afternoon, the detachments had achieved their military goals. Only one fighter had been killed on the Armenian side that day, while two enemy fighters lay dead and forty-eight captured Azeris were herded into the bed of a truck. The captives would be transported to Stepanakert, where they would be held until they could be exchanged for Armenian hostages in Azeri hands. It appeared as though Karadaghlu, the first battle Monte had officially been charged with commanding, had proceeded smoothly to its conclusion.

Soon, however, things changed. Arabo and Aramo fighters shoved thirty-eight captives, including several women and other noncombatants, into a ditch on the outskirts of the village. One of the captives in the ditch pulled the pin from a grenade concealed under a bandaged hand and tossed it, taking off the lower leg of one of his captors, a recent Patriotic Detachment recruit named Levon. The Arabo and Aramo fighters there had already been hankering to "avenge" the death of another comrade the day before, so as soon as the grenade had gone off they began stabbing and shooting their captives, until every last one was dead. Shram Edo, one of the five Patriotic Detachment "boys" from Ashdarak, had joined in too, dousing several wounded soldiers with gasoline and tossing a match to burn them alive. By the time Monte came across the ditch on the outskirts of town it was a butcher's scrap heap.

Monte had given strict orders that no captives were to be harmed. The veins on his neck stood out like braided hemp, and he hollered until he was hoarse, but the black-turbaned Arabo captain didn't even shrug as he turned away from the stammering nuisance and resumed loading booty.

The Arabo and Aramo detachments hauled off all the weapons captured that day—seventy-eight rifles plus thousands of rounds of ammunition—and they emptied the village warehouse, too, dragging out tons of bagged wheat to sell. After the looting, they set the village ablaze.

A total of fifty-three Azeris were killed in and around Karadaghlu during those two days, compared to three killed on the Armenian side, including a sixty-year-old villager in Haghorti who had been hit by a stray bullet.

As news spread that Karadaghlu had been "cleaned out," several delegates arrived from the village of Krasnyi Bazar, fifteen kilometers to the south. Two years earlier, local Azeris in OMON uniforms had stopped four Armenians from Krasnyi Bazar, including a woman, and burned them alive in their car. Now, their fellow villagers politely requested four of the Azeri captives for *madagh*—a blood sacrifice. It was written, after all: an eye for an eye. Monte scowled them down, and they left empty-handed.

More than fifty Azeri captives had been butchered at Karadaghlu. But it was not the butchery that damaged Monte's reputation among the Karabagh mountain people. On the contrary, vengeance ran deep in the mountains, and the loudest voices on both sides demanded blood for blood. What damaged Monte's reputation, rather, was the fact that the butchery at Karadaghlu had taken place *against his orders*. Kechel Sergei, who had been evacuated to a hospital with a bullet through the back, could not have cared less about Azeri casualties; what infuriated him were reports that Monte had not prevented Arabo Manvel from hauling off the Patriotic Detachment's split of the captured munitions. Karadaghlu only confirmed what Kechel and everyone else seemed to know: Avo, the new Headquarters Chief, was a weakling. The Martuni locals were lying to him and cheating him blind. In time, even Monte himself acknowledged as much: after Karadaghlu, a fighter asked him why he had taken "0-0" as his radio code. "I'm less than zero," he replied.

Monte realized that if he ever were to exercise authority in Martuni, he would have to gain that authority not by decree from Stepanakert, but on the battlefield. On February 22, he led a successful lightning attack against Azeri positions on the strategic heights of Vesalu. But a few days after the victory at Vesalu, he faced even more brazen insubordination, with even bloodier results than Karadaghlu: on February 26, he stood on a slope near Khojalu, the site of his first recon operation three weeks earlier, and surveyed a trail of bloody shawls strewn across the brown grass and snow. As soon as he had arrived at Khojalu in response to reports of fighting, he had begun piecing together the story of the massacre that had just wound down, perhaps only an hour before his arrival.

At about 11:00 p.m. the night before, some 2,000 Armenian fighters had advanced through the high grass on three sides of Khojalu, forcing the residents out through the open side to the east. By the morning of February 26, the refugees had made it to the eastern cusp of Mountainous Karabagh and had begun working their way downhill, toward safety in the Azeri city of Agdam, about six miles away. There, in the hillocks and within sight of safety, Mountainous Karabagh soldiers had chased them down. "They just shot and shot and shot," a refugee woman, Raisha Aslanova, testified to a Human Rights Watch investigator. The Arabo fighters had then unsheathed the knives they had carried on their hips for so long, and began stabbing.

Now, the only sound was the wind whistling through dry grass, a wind that was too early yet to blow away the stench of corpses. Monte had arrived in Martuni twenty-two days earlier, and since then he had staggered across two killing fields soaked with the fresh blood of captives and unarmed peasants. When it came to adult males, fighters on both sides seldom distinguished between combatants and noncombatants. But until Khojalu, Armenian fighters had spared women and children, either releasing them or holding them hostage for prisoner exchanges. On this score, they had a better track record than their enemies. The attack at Khojalu, however, had gone some distance to even the score.

Monte crunched over the grass where women and girls lay scattered like broken dolls. "No discipline," he muttered. He knew the significance of the day's date: it was the run-up to the fourth anniversary of the anti-Armenian pogrom in the city of Sumgait. Khojalu had been a strategic goal, but it had also been an act of revenge. Monte knew that enemy fighters would retaliate in kind, and sure enough, when Azeri forces overran the Armenian village of Maragha the next month, they slashed and burned Armenian captives.

Convinced of the supremely high stakes in Mountainous Karabagh, Monte had accepted the ends-justifying-means calculations of all "political realists," East and West: the Arabo and the Aramo were bloodthirsty, yes, but they were also brave fighters, at a time when there was a desperate need for brave fighters. After Khojalu, though, what shocked Monte was that they were unwilling to set vengeance aside, even for the sake of Armenian hostages in Azeri hands. Eventually, Monte would convince his superiors in Stepanakert to expel the Arabo and Aramo Detachments from Martuni. But he never succeeded in convincing them to disband these brutal detachments or to expel them altogether from Mountainous Karabagh before they killed again.

Insubordination only increased after Khojalu. The same defiance that the Arabo and Aramo fighters had demonstrated at Karadaghlu was spreading like a virus among the native fighters in Martuni: reservists didn't bother to show up at the trenches; road repair crews dwindled, and tanker trucks full of diesel vanished into the black market. Even Monte's closest staff at the headquarters lied to him and ignored his orders. One sunny day in early March, four of his fighters, including a local nicknamed Tsav (or "Pain"), requisitioned a jeep on a lark and set out across no-man's land to scavenge booty abandoned on the battlefield. As they approached a knocked-out enemy tank, their jeep blew on a mine, injuring the treasure hunters and tearing off Tsav's lower leg.

When Monte heard the news, his jaw dropped in disbelief. This act of insubordination, so quick on the heels of Khojalu and Karadaghlu, was the last straw: either Monte would take steps to shore up his eroding authority, or the defiance would spread and he would be hounded out of Martuni. And if that happened, his replacement, whoever it would be, would have an even harder time filling the trenches with fighters.

Tsav's bandages had not yet dried when Monte shouted him down and ordered the Patriotic Detachment—his own detachment and the last one within his jurisdiction—to leave Martuni.

Kechel was still recovering from his bullet wound when he learned that his former comrade had ordered him and his detachment out of Martuni. Monte, he concluded, was "going crazy" with his newfound authority, neglecting old friends and trusting treacherous locals. But if Monte wanted him out of Martuni, then so be it: he would serve elsewhere, under a stronger, less gullible leader.

Monte, for his part, was glad to be rid of one more headache. Later, he would find out just what sort of person he had embraced as a comrade-in-arms: back in November 1990, Kechel had kidnapped a young Azerbaijani Popular Front activist from a village across the border, stealing his car, a red Jhiguli, in the bargain. The young Azeri, Syed, spent a month chained to the wall of a cottage near Yerevan. On New Year's Eve 1991, Kechel and a couple of buddies, including a local police officer and their friend Ardag, dragged their captive to the top of Yeraplur, the burial hill near Yerevan. There they kicked Syed to his knees under a spreading tree next to the grave of a fellow fighter named Haroot. Then Kechel, a father of three children, began cutting Syed's throat with a dull knife. At first Syed screamed, but after a while the screaming gave way to moaning and gurgling. Finally, when Ardag could no longer listen, he pushed a knife into Syed's chest, putting an end to it. They drained Syed's blood on top of Haroot's grave and then left. Not long afterwards, a friend asked Kechel to be his daughter's godfather. As the priest's voice rose in hymn during the baptismal liturgy, Kechel heard Syed's moans echoing through the church. Swooning, he interrupted the ceremony. "Could God ever forgive a person who had killed a dog out of revenge?" he asked the priest. The priest lowered his miter. "That depends," he said, "Was it a four-legged dog or a two-legged dog?"

On March 24 or 25, Monte propped his rifle against a table at the headquarters and took a seat facing a delegation of town elders. In better days these elders had been the leaders of the local soviet, but when war had come to Martuni, younger men in camouflage had pushed them aside. Today, they had come to introduce themselves to the new Headquarters Chief, to find out what sort of man he was and what they could expect from him. One of the grayhairs, an old man with a big bumpy nose, rose from his seat to bring up the subject of the warehouse manager, Marad, who was pilfering food from the municipal stocks. Monte already knew about the dispute, but a local police officer, Mavrik, had advised him to steer clear of it: Marad was from an influential family, and he had many friends in Martuni. Against Mavrik's advice, Monte had ordered Marad to surrender the keys to the warehouse and to hand over the rifle that the headquarters had issued him. Needless to say, Marad ignored the order. It was time for a showdown.

Monte and the delegates stepped out of the headquarters onto an escarpment overlooking a football field. Before them stood the larger part of the adult male population of Martuni – hundreds of men who had responded to Monte's summons for an assembly. A video camera caught the scene:

Monte holds up his hand, and the crowd becomes quiet. "Every Armenian," he says, "every single Armenian has a right to be in Martuni, to have a voice in Martuni, to work in Martuni and defend it."

Ignoring the scattered applause, he continues. "Now, my guys want to know: *do you want us here or not?*"

Two matrons in headscarves at the top of the slope throw their hands up: *yes!*

Monte touches the fingers of his right hand to his forehead in a salute: "Very well. We're *very* happy about that." But, he says, they'll have to demonstrate their support by their deeds. They'll have to accept that friends, neighbors, and even family members who refuse to obey orders will be punished, no matter how many connections they have in high places. Monte illustrates his point with the case closest at hand: their neighbor Marad has abused his position as warehouse manager and has refused to step aside when ordered to do so.

Suddenly, a gaunt figure strides through the crowd and mounts the escarpment where Monte stands. It's Marad, the warehouse manager, who has just been indicted in front of his family, his neighbors, and his native village. Monte steps back to permit him to speak. Marad addresses his fellow villagers in their own dialect, waving an unlit cigarette and invoking his brother's record of military service. Hadn't his brother fought bravely?

"Yes, he fought bravely," Monte responds. "But that was your brother. What have *you* done?"

Marad changes the subject, reminding the assembled townsfolk of the mishap with Tsav in the jeep. One might think that he is trying to discredit Monte by portraying him as incapable of controlling even his closest subordinates, but this is not Marad's point. Rather, he is implying that, by punishing his closest comrades so severely and banishing them from Martuni, Monte has shown that he cannot be trusted to remain loyal to anyone else in Martuni. The mountain people of Karabagh place a high premium on loyalty to friends, and Monte has shown that he lacks this quality.

"Wait a minute!" Monte shouts hoarsely, "He said something quite right ..." His voice rises and he lifts a finger like a prophet: "My closest comrades — *my closest comrades* from *my own* detachment — didn't follow orders, drove where they had no business driving. They hit a mine. One lost a foot, and another one was wounded ..." His index finger hangs in the air, then it falls like an axe: "... and we *punished* them! We *punished* them!" Monte's voice is ferocious now; veins stand out on his neck and his eyes burn like coal: "*Whoever does wrong will be punished! WHOEVER DOES WRONG WILL BE PUNISHED!*"

Shouts of approval sweep over the assembled villagers, and then the audience erupts in applause. This newcomer, Headquarters Chief Avo, may have shown disloyalty to his closest friends, but clearly he is loyal — *fiercely* loyal — to something else: he is loyal to the land. To *their* land.

After the showdown with Marad, some people in Martuni began telling visitors "Our leader is Avo." Others weren't sure what to think. Monte removed Marad from his position and replaced him, but he would soon have to replace the replacement, and as it turned out he never would find an honest warehouse manager.

On one of the last days of March, Vazgen Sargsyan made the long trip to Martuni to promote Monte to the rank of Commander of the Martuni District, one of the six basic defense districts in Mountainous Karabagh. Throughout a sleepless night of discussions, Sargsyan endured Monte's objections to the promotion, and pointed out again and again that the Defense Committee had found no better candidate for the job.

Some locals were not pleased to learn about the promotion. When Sargsyan called subcommanders and headquarters staff together to introduce them to their new District Commander, Nelson's eyes narrowed to slits: surely the local stock could have provided its own military leaders! After all, their forefathers had been defying caliphs, shahs, and tsars for centuries. Even the armies of Genghis Khan and Tamerlane had failed to wrest autonomy from Nelson's ancestors. This pile of rocks had given the Soviet Union three marshals, thirty generals, twenty Heroes of the Soviet Union, and even an admiral. With this martial legacy, how could Vazgen Sargsyan or anyone else expect the mountain people of Karabagh to follow an outsider into battle on their own land?

Nelson's sentiments, however, were not unanimous. Many civilians in Martuni had come to view their new leader not so much as a mediator of local conflicts — conflicts which, after all, he could not be expected to understand — but rather as a pure, almost unearthly presence. He was a compatriot, yes, but he might as well have been an angel or a Martian, floating above the feuds, clan loyalties, and bribery in Martuni and Stepanakert. Grandmothers dubbed him "our holy son" and pressed jars of buffalo yogurt into his hands as he passed through their villages in his staff car. Mothers brought him folded loaves of flat bread cooked with *jingal* — a mixture of seven wild grasses that grow on the mountains he had pledged his life to defend. Old women in smocks and headscarves kissed the commander's forehead and intoned a benediction in the mountain dialect: *Klkhavt shoor kyem*, "I walk around your head."

In early May, Monte attended a briefing at the former railway station in Stepanakert, where square-jawed General "Komandos" Ter-Tatevosyan was finalizing the plan to capture Shusha. For weeks, Komandos' forces had been "softening up" the Azeri citadel with Grad rockets and cannons, in anticipation of a final assault on it. Meanwhile, Azeri helicopters had been flying in and out of Shusha since late February, delivering ordnance and evacuating women and children. Leaders in Baku were determined to avert another Khojalu.

When Komandos finished his presentation, Monte and several other fighters stepped forward to volunteer for the assault on Shusha. Komandos fixed his eyes on Monte and shook his head: when news of the attack on Shusha were to break, Azeri forces would launch counterattacks all along the eastern front of Mountainous Karabagh, including Martuni. And that's where Monte should be, ready to repel a retaliatory attack. Monte listened quietly, and then he left the office without argument and returned to Martuni.

In the early morning hours of May 9, Komandos' forces attacked Shusha from several directions. Monte didn't participate in the attack, but his former comrades of the Patriotic Detachment did. Moolto died during the attack; Hovsep was wounded, and Kechel was one of the fighters who howled into Shusha after scaling a cliff on an approach to the city that was so steep that the Azeris, considering it impassable, had left it undefended. The capture of Shusha would go down in the annals of local lore as the most glorious victory to date, and General "Komandos" Ter-Tatevosyan would go down as one of the most daring and brilliant military leaders in Mountainous Karabagh.

While the victors were celebrating in Shusha, the mood was different in Martuni. It was just as Komandos had foreseen: as soon as news of the attack at Shusha broke, Azeri generals hurled their men and armor against Armenian defenses all along the Martuni front. The Martuni fighters held their positions and then counter-attacked: on May 15, Monte led several hundred troops and a couple of tanks against Azeri artillery positions in the Gulabli Valley, north of Martuni. Azeri forces in the valley outnumbered Monte's fighters several times; their helicopter gunships raked Monte's trenches, and they laid down an incessant fusillade with artillery and tank guns all along the line. Though short on ammunition, diesel, and battlefield experience, Monte's fighters captured a tank, destroyed an enemy cannon, and downed an Azeri Krokodil helicopter, which trailed smoke like a dragon, drifted behind a ridge, and skidded into grass. When the dust settled, Monte had lost half a dozen fighters, while enemy corpses littered the valley.

Despite the large enemy losses, Monte counted the May 15 counter-attack at Gulabli as a military failure. His fighters had pushed the enemy back, but they had failed to capture the village of Gulabli, and everyone knew that Azeri gunners would regroup there to rain rockets and tank shells on Martuni again. Even more depressing was the news that one of the casualties on the Armenian side was Ashani Armen, a quiet, brave youth whom Monte had described to Seta as "a *real* good guy."

The shrapnel was still falling on Gulabli when Monte's fellow commanders followed up their victory at Shusha with an attack on Lachin, a Kurdish town that straddled the winding road that connected Mountainous Karabagh to Mother Armenia. Ever since the fall of Shusha, panic had seized the 5,000 inhabitants of Lachin, and many of them fled their homes in advance of the Armenian attack. After four days of fighting, the attackers seized Lachin on May 18, and set it ablaze.

When news of the losses at Shusha and Lachin reached Baku, thousands of red-faced demonstrators took to the city squares to shout down Azerbaijan's President Ayaz Mutalibov, whom they accused of bungling military operations in Mountainous Karabagh. Under a gale of jeers, Mutalibov ceded power to a national council composed mostly of deputies from the opposition Azerbaijani Popular Front.

Until Lachin, my brother had managed to convince himself that Kurds in Azerbaijan supported Armenian demands in Mountainous Karabagh. He was surprised, therefore—and even *angry*—to learn that the Kurds of Lachin had not welcomed the Armenian offensive. "The Kurds were used against us in Lachin," he later told an interviewer with a tone of bitterness, "and that had absolutely nothing to do with their own interests." But surely the Kurds of Lachin had an interest in self-preservation! It seems never to have occurred to Monte that they might have been justifiably reluctant to place their lives in the hands of the Kechel Sergeis or the heroes of Khojalu.

On May 28, high-stepping soldiers in smart new uniforms stomped past a reviewing stand in Yerevan filled with Armenia's political and military brass: Babken Ararktsyan, the new President of Parliament, was there, as was Minister of Interior Vano Siradeghyan, long-bearded Khachig Stamboultsyan, bright-smiling Vazgen Sargsyan, and stone-faced Arabo Manvel. It was Armenia's Independence Day, and there were victories to celebrate: Khojalu, Shusha, and Lachin.

But Commander Avo was nowhere to be seen. Military parades were a waste of time and diesel. Besides, now was not the time to leave the front. Monte knew that the enemy could match and exceed every battle tank and every heavy gun that trundled past the reviewing stand, as well as every MiG-23 and every Krokodil helicopter roaring overhead. The new weapons on parade only meant new panoramas of killing. Frowning through binoculars from a windswept trench on the heights of Martuni, he watched a storm gathering.

PART SIX

Distant Mountains

A Proper Army

In the spring of 1992, when rivulets of melted snow narrowed and muddy ruts hardened into mountain roads, war season was upon the mountains of Karabagh. Monte scanned the horizon from north to south. He knew that Azeri tank crews were out there setting their sights, revving their engines, and awaiting the order to roll. Twisting his sleeve, he glanced at the old watch that his wife's grandmother had bequeathed. He had been timing many things: travel between villages, the mustering of troops along trenches, the arrival of reinforcements, and intervals between flashes of muzzles and thuds of shells. Time itself was as much the enemy as were Azeri tanks, and Monte was convinced that his side was losing to that enemy.

Between 10,000 and 15,000 Azeri fighters and support personnel encircled the Martuni district of Mountainous Karabagh on the north, east, and south sides, compared to 4,000 Armenian defenders in Martuni, including reservists. The Azeri fighters carried more ammunition than the defenders, and they were more likely to wear boots. They also had around 300 battle tanks, 800 armored fighting vehicles and personnel carriers, and 330 heavy artillery pieces, compared to a far smaller total in each category on the Armenian side. And finally, the Azeris controlled the sky, with forty-five combat aircraft, including armored helicopters, SU-24 low-altitude bombers, and MiG-21 ground attack fighters. Mountainous Karabagh, by contrast, had no air force to speak of, and although the Republic of Armenia had several warplanes, including a couple of SU-24s, most were old SU-17s that rusted in back lots for lack of spare parts and pilots. In an interview with a foreign journalist months later, Monte summarized the situation: "We're outnumbered, out-armed. Our enemy has much more ammunition, better quality arms, everything. Mathematically speaking, we should have lost long ago."

If the mountain people of Karabagh had not yet lost the war, this had nothing to do with superior training. Indeed, Monte had been astonished by the lack of martial expertise in Mountainous Karabagh, and in Yerevan as well. Few of the fighters he had met, including detachment leaders and Defense Committee members, could honestly claim any previous combat experience at all. Even Military Chief Vazgen Sargsyan, who now held the title of State Defense Minister of the Republic of Armenia, had been a swimming instructor before the war. And the situation was no better at the bottom of the military hierarchy. Often, the first time an Armenian soldier fired an assault rifle was in battle. Teenagers who barely knew how to drive automobiles were driving heavy tanks into battle. They would either master the skills of a tank captain in their first battles, or they would die under the hatch.

The same was true on the Azeri side, except that the Azeris had more money to throw at the problem: anticipating quick profits from Caspian oil contracts, they hired mercenaries, mostly Ukrainian and Russian leftovers from the 4th Army, but also British and American trainers. Former Turkish Army officers were helping to train Azeri fighters, too, while Chechen tank commanders and Turkish volunteers from a fascist group called the Gray Wolves fought on the front lines. According to rumor, mercenaries from Pakistan and Afghanistan, some of the latter with CIA training, had also joined the Azeri effort.

Faced with a decided enemy advantage of firepower and manpower, Monte was quick to recognize his one advantage: motivation. Unlike most of the enemy fighters, his men were fighting for their hearths and for land sown with their ancestors' bones. This difference became apparent on the battlefield: time and again, Monte had seen Azeri fighters balk in the heat of battle, and some of his fighters claimed to have witnessed Azeri officers shooting their own men in the back when they refused to advance.

But as the battles ground on, his men's motivation was ebbing, and he knew that this crucial advantage would vanish unless the detachments were merged, post-haste, into a proper army with a centralized chain of command. Field communications would be crucial to the effort to revamp defense forces and set up a proper system that connected trenches and front-line positions with the headquarters. But more than that, Monte needed to establish his authority as a leader.

Meanwhile, in Baku, demonstrators brought down the two-month-old interim government and propelled Azerbaijani Popular Front leader Abulfez Elchibey into the office of the Presidency. The new president was Ankara's first hope in the region, and as such he was the enemy not only of Armenia and Russia, but also of Iran. Now that the Soviet Union had collapsed, Elchibey predicted, Iran would be the next empire to implode. And this would pave the way at last for a Greater Azerbaijan, uniting his newly independent Republic of Azerbaijan with the 10 million ethnic Azeris across the border in "southern Azerbaijan," currently northwestern Iran.

On June 12, 1992, the day Elchibey took office, Azeri officers launched their largest offensive yet. The Azerbaijan national army, joined by OMON fighters and tank crews from the Russian 104th Division based in Ganje, leapt forward along the northern and eastern fronts. At the head of the Azeri forces stood a diminutive but handsome young colonel named Surat Huseinov. The thirty-three-year-old colonel had trained and outfitted his own private army, the Ganje Brigade, with the proceeds from his wool concern in the northeastern Azerbaijani city of Yevlakh.

Huseinov's forces recaptured the Shahumyan district, including the villages of Manashid, Bozluk, and Erkej, which Monte and his comrades had fought so hard to capture the previous fall. After a few more days of fighting, the Mountainous Karabagh line of defense in Mardakert collapsed, too. By this time, 30,000 Armenian refugees had piled onto donkeys, rickety buses, tractors, and dump trucks, or had simply slung their belongings over their shoulders, cast a backward glance at their burning houses, and begun trudging south. Soon, Huseinov's men had overrun almost half of Mountainous Karabagh, including most of the Mardakert district. "You love the land?" they taunted as they shoved dirt down their hostages' throats, "Then eat it!" It looked like only a matter of time before Huseinov and Elchibey would succeed where Genghis Khan and Tamerlane had failed: it looked as though, for the first time in two millennia, every Armenian would be driven out of Mountainous Karabagh.

Rockets and tank rounds rained on Martuni. A Grad hit a cottage, incinerating the family in a flash. Mothers tore their hair and grabbed Monte, begging him to take their children to safety in Stepanakert. When he shook his head no, the mothers stared at him as if they were in the presence of a madman. "The most important thing for your children is to save their land," Monte responded. If parents left Martuni with their children, then who would clear the roads? Who would tend the fields? Who would bake bread for the troops?

In early June, Nelson requisitioned buses to evacuate women and children from Pertashen. When Monte heard about this, he flagged down the subcommander's staff car and explained calmly but firmly that if civilians were allowed to leave Martuni, then their fathers, brothers, and sons would soon follow them out. And without civilians at their backs, the defenders who remained in the trenches would waver.

When Monte set up roadblocks to stop refugees from leaving Martuni, he had raised the stakes as high as they could be raised: enemy columns were already marching through Mardakert in the north, pushing dazed and dust-streaked refugees ahead of them like rabbits before a range fire. If he allowed the enemy to vault his trenches in Martuni, every mother and every child buried under rubble would be billable to his account, and he would then have become a murderer of his own captive population.

The advancing enemy must be stopped. But to stop them, Monte would have to fight their armor with armor. Before battles, Monte would instruct his soldiers to knock out enemy tanks without "melting" them, as he put it. He didn't want enemy tanks so irreparably burned that his men couldn't drag them away with their armored caterpillar, repair them in the yard of the retooled agricultural machinery works in Martuni, and then turn them around against their former owners. More heavily damaged tanks would end up at the repair station in the Stepanakert train station, while optical instruments, quantum sights, and night vision instruments went to the condensation plant in Stepanakert for repair.

But the captured tanks were useless without fuel. Diesel, Monte said, was more precious than gold. Indeed, diesel was more precious than tanks, since so many tanks lay idle for lack of it. Monte would have to pool the district's diesel and ration it, liter by liter.

Thanks to Monte's fuel stinginess, as well as the roadblocks, his popularity waned. One morning, about an hour before noon, as a phalanx of enemy artillery and armor jockeyed into firing positions around Martuni, a worker from the Martuni fuel storage depot approached the commander hesitantly and mumbled something in a low voice. The large cylindrical storage container which hours earlier had held sixteen tons of precious diesel was now empty! Thieves had backed a tanker truck up to the spigot, filled up, and driven away, leaving the remaining diesel to spill onto the ground through the open spigot.

So this was how it would be: a contest of stubbornness! These mountain people were stubborn to the point of self-destruction. But Monte
was more stubborn than they were, and he'd prove it. He picked up an
empty oil can that had been lying around the yard, and then he squatted by the puddled diesel and began ladling the amber liquid, a splash
at a time, into a larger can. A depot worker began scooping cupfuls, too,
and then a couple of soldiers who had arrived on the scene joined them.
When the grit in the scooped-up diesel had settled, they poured the
several liters of salvaged fuel from the larger can back into the empty
storage container.

Monte scrambled back and forth to Stepanakert, trying to make up
for the stolen diesel while Grads from enemy positions screamed overhead. After ten months of intermittent bombardment, half the houses in
the town of Martuni had been blown to rubble or gutted by fire. And
now enemy gunners were softening up Martuni for a final assault. In
defiance of Monte's orders, locals began pushing aside the roadblocks
in a slow-motion stampede, to join tens of thousands of fellow refugees
in Stepanakert. Some reservists followed their families out, too, and
morale among the remaining defenders was sinking.

On or just after June 20, a blue staff car skidded into the yard in front of
the headquarters and out stepped a man in a Soviet colonel's uniform.
He placed a kepi on his head and straightened the visor. The visitor,
clearly, had been a career Red Army officer. He even looked Russian,
with his auburn hair, clean-shaven chin, crisp khakis, and tie. He also
looked to be at least ten years older than the rumpled, unshaven commander who greeted him. The colonel saluted the commander smartly.
Instead of returning the salute, the commander extended his hand and
asked in a strange dialect, "What's your short name?" The colonel
informed him curtly that he had no "short name." He should be
addressed, he said, as "Colonel Haroyan." For lack of anything else, the
colonel addressed the commander by his "short name," Avo.

The Ministry of Defense of the Republic of Armenia had assigned
Colonel Hemayag Haroyan and four other officers the task of building
an officer corps in Mountainous Karabagh. By this time, Monte was
used to advisors arriving from Yerevan, biding their time at the headquarters, and then leaving as soon as their one-month commission
expired. "They don't even stay a thirty-first day," he once lamented to
Seta. Colonel Haroyan looked like another one of those.

The Colonel went about his business, while Monte gathered intelligence about the disposition of enemy forces. On or about June 23, two of Monte's scouts tripped a mine while crawling back towards Armenian lines in the early hours of dawn. One of the scouts was blown to pieces, and the other, Mirza Valo, dragged himself back with a gashed chest, throat, and head. As his comrades carried him to a hospital in a semi-swoon, he asked over and over if his partner Aram had spoken with Commander Avo. For the sake of Mirza Valo's morale, his friends did not reveal that the mine blast had killed Aram. "Yes," they told their friend, "he's talked to Avo." Mirza Valo was not convinced. Arriving at the hospital, he asked someone else, who admitted that Aram had not returned from the minefield to tell the commander anything. "Get Avo," Mirza Valo choked. They summoned Monte, and Mirza Valo sputtered a few words into his ear through gritted teeth.

Monte dashed into the office of the Prime Minister of the Mountainous Karabagh Republic, dialed Seta on one of the few direct phone lines to Yerevan, and apologized. He would not be coming to Yerevan for her birthday. Only later did he fill her in on the details: Aram and Mirza Valo had set out on their recon mission in the pre-dawn darkness. They had crawled through a minefield to get behind enemy lines, and then crouched beneath a window at an Azeri command base. There, they had heard enemy officers planning a massive offensive against Martuni within the next several days.

Monte raced back to Martuni, put his fighters on alert, and called up reserves. He ordered them to bolster redoubts, to dig more trenches, to dig them deeper, and to bring up anti-tank rockets. Their test began on June 27, 1992. Twenty heavy tanks and armored vehicles leapt forward all along the Majgalashen front, from Alibali to Krasnyi Bazar, followed by hundreds of enemy infantry. Monte's fighters met the attack and stuck to their trenches among the thistle and wild asparagus. Despite their inexperience and substandard equipment, they drove the attackers back into the oak forests. Colonel Haroyan heaved a sigh of relief.

The next day, June 28, Azeri forces on the Jardar front joined the attack, and there, too, Monte's thinly-spread fighters stayed put in their trenches. At one position, a dozen defenders faced six enemy tanks and scores of infantry in a vineyard. One of these defenders, a twelve-year-old boy from the village of Jardar named Mooshegh, was shorter than the rocket-propelled grenade he wielded. Crawling from one trellis to another, Mooshegh fired a total of sixty rockets, stopping two enemy tanks single-handedly. At one point, from a distance of less than ten meters, he aimed his weapon at the fuel tank in the back of a BMP light tank as he had heard Monte once advise, and pulled the trigger. The BMP burst into flames, and his comrades mowed down the crew as they bailed from the hatches. Fighting without reinforcements for five hours, the Martuni fighters finally retook a position the enemy had captured earlier that day.

Every day for the next week, the enemy mounted attack after attack all along the front, flailing against the defenders' trenches and revetments. July passed in a torrent of blood and shrapnel, and with it Colonel Haroyan's thirty-day assignment. Yet he remained in Martuni. Monte noticed this, and he also noticed that, unlike the other officers who had rotated through Martuni, Haroyan had been spending more time at the trenches than at his desk. "Wipe down the barrel with a liter of diesel," he would tell artillery gunners, before snapping off a salute and heading to the next position.

For his part, Colonel Haroyan had noticed that the commander of Martuni had taken full charge of all aspects of defense there, right down to handing out individual boxes of all-weather matches to frontline fighters. He noticed that the commander was a stickler for rules, too, and he liked that: when one or another committee or ministry in Stepanakert sent piles of forms to fill out in triplicate, Monte agreed with Colonel Haroyan that the exercise was petty and pointless, but he sighed, "The big shots sent it, so we should fill it out." Haroyan also noticed that, unlike other commanders, Monte took the time to explain to his men what role they were playing within the larger defense strategy in Mountainous Karabagh, and within the unfolding history of their nation. "If we lose this land," he would tell them, "we turn the last page on Armenian history."

The commander of Martuni continued leading fighters into battle daily, and Colonel Haroyan joined him in the trenches. There were battles at Ghajar on the southern front (August 9), Vesalu on the eastern front (from August 15), and Gulabli, Avdal, Avdur, Tavabeli, Norshen, and Myurishen, on the northern front (mid-August). Some of these battles droned on for days, pitting hundreds of fighters and tens of tanks against each other, and scattering scores of corpses across fields, forests, and hills. Counter-attacks, probing operations, and skirmishes filled the days between the major battles. Through the smoke, Monte and Haroyan observed the enemy carefully, noting their tactics, maneuvers, deployment of troops and tanks, what sort of air support they summoned, and the fortitude and élan of their fighters. Once, when enemy fighters captured a crucial trench system called Dzover, on the highest hill to the north of Martuni, Colonel Haroyan observed through binoculars that they started celebrating, dancing, and singing. The Martuni fighters spoiled their celebration with a mortar barrage and then followed up with a successful counter-attack.

In the heat of battle, Haroyan and Monte saved precious time by dispensing with explanations. They dashed from one front to another, exchanged a few words in trenches, and then charged off in different directions. Before long, they were moving against each other synchronously in opposite directions, like cogs in a precision machine. Each seemed to know instinctively from one moment to the next where the other was going and what he was up to.

They had no time to waste on risk assessment, either. In the third battle at Vesalu on August 15, 150 Mountainous Karabagh fighters fought off four enemy tanks and 420 fighters attacking from three directions. Monte conducted recon two days later from a hill just above the village of Vesalu, very close to an enemy position. Binoculars in hand, he crawled to the precipice. Suddenly, he turned his head and whispered over his shoulder to the three fighters behind him: "Boys, they've seen us!" As soon as the words left his lips a single sniper's bullet grazed his scalp, passed through the thigh of the fighter next to him, and hit the fighter behind them, fatally piercing his liver. The last fighter, a native of Jardar named Sergo Hairabedyan, would die from his wound later that day. After evacuating the casualties, Monte returned to headquarters and vomited. The bullet had left a neat wound that looked like a knife cut on his scalp. At Haroyan's insistence, Monte took a two-hour nap at the hospital, before returning to his maps and binoculars.

Nelson might have been thinking of this incident when, in an interview six years later, he portrayed Monte as a hypochondriac who demanded medical attention for every little scratch. Or perhaps Nelson had been thinking of an earlier incident, when Dr. Gasparyan, the Russian-speaking surgeon, had pulled a shard of plasticized glass from the commander's arm. It had been a memento from Rome, a fragment of Gokberk Ergenikon's bullet-proof window, which Monte had carried in his arm for twelve years. In any case, the rumor that Monte's father used to wash underwear and cook meals ("wearing a long white apron," as Nelson later embellished the story for an interviewer) only confirmed Nelson's opinion of the commander as a pantywaist. On top of everything else, Nelson noticed that Monte had the annoying custom of scrubbing his teeth every morning with a little brush that he kept for that purpose.

Monte had neither the time nor the inclination to defend himself against charges of being a sissy. Although Azeri fighters had sustained heavy losses on the Martuni front, their fellow fighters were still advancing rapidly on the Mardakert front to the north. News of the advances in Mardakert must have reinvigorated the Azeri officers who had been laying siege to Martuni. The fighting rolled into September without respite, as enemy gunners and pilots continued hammering the mountains with artillery and warplanes. It began to look as though the Azeris would bury the defenders under shrapnel, if they couldn't broach their defenses.

At the height of the enemy offensive, Monte began turning heads with a new word: *victory*. "There will be peace only with *our* victory," he told a video interviewer. Haroyan took up the victory-talk too, repeating it in his slightly weary voice, but Monte put the colonel's faith to the test by showing him a wall-size contour map on which he had traced his vision of "revised borders" for the Mountainous Karabagh Republic. Monte's red marking pen circumscribed all of the land separating Mountainous Karabagh from the Iranian border to the south, and to the west it took in all of Kelbajar, the craggy landmass separating Mountainous Karabagh from the Armenian Republic. The "revised borders" would encompass twice the territory of Mountainous Karabagh. All of this land, according to Monte, was part of the Armenian homeland that had been forcefully depopulated of its rightful inhabitants.

Staring at the map, the thought occurred to Colonel Haroyan that Monte had lapsed into insanity. But there was no time to dwell on doubts. In the face of counter-attacks on September 4, Haroyan stayed at Gulabli, while Monte dashed off to command defenders at the Majgalashen front, twelve kilometers to the south. There, an enemy column of 500 soldiers and thirty armored vehicles drove straight into Monte's guns. The attackers lost seven battle tanks, three light tanks, and so many dead that no one had the time to count them. But Monte's men had paid a high price, too: the tiny mountain village of Majgalashen, with 200 inhabitants in all, lost ten of its best sons that day.

The next day, Monte raced back to the Gulabli front in the north, where the enemy pounded his positions with 100-mm and 120-mm guns, then hurled sixteen tanks, six helicopters, and hundreds of infantry into the fray. Monte and Haroyan calmly led the defense. When the enemy withdrew, they left tanks, munitions, and scores of corpses, many of them so badly torn up by tank shells that it was impossible to take an accurate body count. The day after that, the Commander and the Colonel split up again, to rally defenders against yet another big attack against the Jardar–Majgalashen front in the south, and to shore up defenses in the face of a day-long barrage against Gulabli in the north. By the end of the day, the attackers had failed to breach their positions, and had sustained great losses once again.

The next two days, September 7 and 8, Azeri fighters launched simultaneous counter-attacks at the narrow, scrub-colored valley of Gulabli in the north, and also at the Agdam front in the east, and at Majgalashen again, in the south. As usual, Monte fought on the front lines. His ability to get his fighters to charge into this tornado of fire and iron depended on his courage and the strength of his personality. A Martuni schoolboy described it this way: "Avo doesn't say *Charge!* He says *Follow me!*"

By mid-September, the Azeris had regrouped on the Agdam Plain and began hurling even more infantry and ordnance against Martuni. Azeri SU and MiG warplanes went back into action against civilian targets throughout Martuni, and Azeri gunners in the nearby villages of Amiranlar, Mughanlu, and Kurapatkino lobbed Grads, artillery rounds, and tank shells onto their neighbors in the town of Martuni. On September 20, several hundred Azeri infantry launched another attack on the southern front, in the groves of twisted mulberry trees near the ruined fourth-century monastery of Amaras. Monte and Haroyan led Majgalashen fighters to meet the attack. A witness, local writer Seyran Kamalyan, reported that tank commanders and infantry "were performing acts of great courage," and that grandparents volunteered to carry ammunition and weapons: "Women were asking God to protect their sons—No, God forgive us!—they were thinking about Avo … They're asking about Avo. They say Avo is with the boys on the battlefield. Avo won't let the enemy set foot on our land."

Their faith was not misplaced. The retreating Azeris left behind nine tanks, three other armored vehicles, and scores of corpses.

But even before the dust had settled on the southern front, hundreds of enemy infantry and eight tanks had begun advancing once again into the Gulabli Valley in the north. From an opening on the Agdam Plain, the valley jutted deep into Mountainous Karabagh, to within seven kilometers of Stepanakert. To Azeri commanders still buoyed by their advances throughout the summer, the valley looked on the map like a dagger pointed at the heart of Mountainous Karabagh: if they could push into Gulabli and position artillery on the heights to the west, they could sever two roads from Stepanakert to the east and the south, forcing a wedge into Mountainous Karabagh's midsection and bringing them within accurate artillery and Grad range of Stepanakert.

But to Monte, the Gulabli Valley looked like a trap waiting to be sprung. Crouching on the heights with binoculars, he watched Azeri armor roll into the valley. The deeper the enemy advanced — the more distance they put between themselves and the narrow mouth of the valley that opened onto the Agdam Plain — the more completely they were encircled. When Monte gave the signal to open fire, his gunners immediately hit two tanks and halted the Azeri advance. The battle continued for another eight hours. Throughout the night, Azeri artillery and tank guns kept up a steady barrage against Armenian positions on the heights, and at daybreak they attacked again. From the heights, Martuni tanks began pouring even more iron into the valley. When they hit two more Azeri tanks, the enemy infantry started to fall back, but in that narrow valley there was no room for an organized retreat. The Armenians' 125-mm tank guns cut down scores of enemy fighters, like wool from a sheared sheep.

The next day, September 23, 300 enemy soldiers, five heavy tanks, and two light tanks massed in the fog for yet another attack, this time against positions to the north of the valley. When the enemy reached within 200 meters of the defenders' trenches, two of their tanks blew on mines, and then seventeen-year-old Felix Arstomyan hit another tank with a rocket-propelled grenade. A gust of lead and shrapnel sent the enemy's front line tumbling to the ground, and the survivors beat a hasty retreat.

The morning after that, Azeri infantry advanced on Gulabli yet again, crawling through vineyards undetected. By this time, Monte had redeployed his tanks in revetments and behind redoubts, in case of just such a sneak attack from that direction. Almost as soon as the first shots crackled, Monte's men hit four enemy tanks and the attackers began falling back again, in a chaotic retreat. Their only route of escape was over open ground, where tanks that had been theirs only a few days earlier lurched forward and cut them to pieces. The battle was quick, but by the time it was over the attackers had lost six more heavy tanks, three light tanks, and seventy fighters.

Until Gulabli, Monte had never imagined how devastating a tank could be when properly deployed. He described the scene in the valley after the battle: "Everywhere — a foot here, a hand there. All over the fields, pieces of meat everywhere."

The next day, September 25, Azeri commanders threw six heavy tanks, two light tanks, and two battalions of young and inexperienced soldiers into yet another attack, this time at the heights of Aghboolagh. Once again they advanced, only to turn under the Martuni tank guns and stumble over their own casualties as they retreated. After the battle, Monte's men lifted ID cards and other documents from enemy corpses, before burying them where they had fallen. Checking the IDs, Monte noticed that "a very high proportion of the bodies" were not Azeri, but were from the non-Turkic Talish and Lezgi minorities in Azerbaijan. From his perspective, these boys had been tricked into dying for the cause of Azeri chauvinism, a cause in which the Talish and the Lezgi had no stake.

"That reminds me of the Turkish policy at the beginning of this century and the end of the nineteenth century, where they used the Kurds against the Armenians," he later told a Western journalist:

> They used the Kurds to massacre the Armenians, and then once the Armenians were pretty much massacred, they started deporting the Kurds and massacring Kurds. In other words, they're setting non-Azeri national minorities against us in this war, knowing that the more of those youth that are killed, the better for the chauvinist Azeri authorities.

In August and September, the Martuni fighters had scored one victory after another. To Monte and Haroyan, however, the avalanche of battles had only highlighted the shortcomings of their forces, notably their lack of a central command. Each village in Martuni still had its own detachment, whose fighters could — and often did — refuse to join battles to defend neighboring villages or the village just down the road.

Throughout the summer and into early fall, Haroyan and Monte had set out to remedy this weakness by redistributing their forces and improvising a new ground-force structure. Each main front-line position would be manned by thirty to sixty fighters organized into a battery (a *dasak*). For every active battery, there would be another battery on reserve and a third battery on leave. This way, reservists could plough, plant, and harvest their fields when not in the trenches. Each of these positions had its own subcommander, who answered to a sub-district or municipal headquarters.

Haroyan and Monte organized nine municipal and sub-district headquarters in the district of Martuni: two at the town of Martuni, two at the village of Jardar, one at Krasnyi Bazar, one at Majgalashen, one at Pertashen, one at Ashan, and one at Gishi. Each of these municipal or sub-district headquarters was accountable to Monte's headquarters in the town of Martuni. The Martuni headquarters, in turn, was one of the six Mountainous Karabagh District headquarters, all of which fell under the command of the newly organized Defense Committee of Mountainous Karabagh, in Stepanakert. Every few days, Monte would arrive for consultations at the Defense Committee Headquarters in Stepanakert and clomp in his dusty boots across three layers of looted carpets in the office of Commander-in-Chief Samvel Babayan.

Back in Martuni, Monte's men graded roads, to move their patched-up tanks to front-line positions quickly, and Haroyan organized specialized mobile units under the direct command of the Martuni headquarters. The mobile units included motorized infantry and tanks, as well as communications, logistics, reconnaissance, artillery, air defense, sappers, a tank repair crew, and cooking staff. Thanks to the road improvements and the new mobile units, the Martuni fighters were able to compensate for their shortage of armor by concentrating their forces rapidly.

This, then, was the new command and ground-force structure that Haroyan and Monte implemented in the heat of battle. By October 1992, this structure was more or less in place, and at long last Monte could announce, *Amen mart eer kordzuh*, "Each man to his job."

By this time, too, Russian-trained anti-aircraft batteries had swung into action in Mountainous Karabagh, with mobile-mounted Strella-10 multiple rocket launchers, as well as shoulder-fired Strella-4 and Igla heat-seeking rockets. Within the next months, Mountainous Karabagh fighters would shoot down some twenty enemy warplanes and helicopters, thereby ensuring that, in Mountainous Karabagh at least, valor rather than avionics would decide the day.

Monte leaned over the rose that he kept in a cup of water on his desk and inhaled deeply. The time had come to capture enemy firing bases on the surrounding heights, to break the encirclement of Martuni by Azeri gunners. One of the Azeri firing bases was in the ghost village of Amiranlar, which was so close to the town of Martuni (500 meters) that from the town one could hear the buzz of a motorcycle in the village. On October 2, Monte and Haroyan set up their command post at Ghoo-roochoogh Peak, in preparation for an attack against Amiranlar and the nearby Azeri villages of Mughanlu and Kurapatkino. The operation started at 6:50 a.m. A fair-haired young officer named Mavo led one group of attackers towards Amiranlar, and another subcommander named Merujan led another group towards Mughanlu. The two groups advanced smoothly and swiftly, overrunning their respective villages in less than an hour, and then joining forces, to attack and capture the last village, Kurapatkino.

Exhausted attackers resting in front of the captured Azeri headquarters at Kurapatkino were startled when a staff car jerked to a stop and the bearded driver jumped out and shouted in Azeri Turkish that the Armenians were poised to capture the village. The Armenian fighters who had beaten this officer to his destination jumped to their feet and leveled their guns. "Come over here," one of them growled, before taking him into custody.

Haroyan viewed the victory at Kurapatkino as a turning point, and Monte marked October 2, 1992 as the day the Azeri bombardment of Martuni ceased. Their fighters registered two dead in this battle, compared to forty-seven enemy dead and two enemy tanks.

At times, Monte didn't know whether to strangle the fighters under his command or to hug them. He was constantly exasperated by their pettiness and stupidity, but their bravery left him brimming with affection. Between battles, he visited hospitalized soldiers with shattered limbs, third-degree burns, fractured skulls, and missing eyes, who hoisted themselves by their elbows, grabbed traction bars, and wagged stumps, begging to rejoin their comrades on the front lines before the next battle. It was not unusual to see bandaged amputees and thrice-wounded combatants limping back to the trenches.

Each soldier killed under Monte's command took a little something from him. He later recalled to Seta the death of one of his favorites, the young commander of the mountain village of Majgalashen, another quiet youth named Armen. In the early morning hours of October 8, as his troops had girded for an attack on Azeri positions on Ghajar, Monte had noticed an uncharacteristic sadness on the young man's face. By the end of the day, Armen lay dead, hit by Grad shrapnel during the attack. "They probably can sense when they're going to die," he later reflected to Seta. From then on, Armen personified the brave village of Majgalashen, home of so many martyrs.

On November 1, Monte moved his headquarters from the old technical school to a dacha on the eastern outskirts of the town of Martuni, at the end of a poplar-lined driveway. In better days, the two-story concrete and tufa building had been the vacation home of Heydar Aliev, former first deputy chairman of the USSR Council of Ministers and protégé of Soviet leaders Brezhnev and Andropov. Monte's new office was a small room on the second floor, with an alcove hardly larger than a booth, where he put his cot. Haroyan moved into the larger office on the same floor, after sealing the windows with cinder blocks and cement.

Thanks to all of the enemy armor that they had captured and repaired, the fighters in Martuni had thirty main battle tanks in working order by late 1992, as well as twenty light tanks, four mobile Grad platforms, twenty heavy artillery pieces, several amphibious armored personnel carriers, and other assorted "technicals." Four-fifths of this weaponry had been captured from enemy forces. In some cases, the dried blood of enemy tank-crews still speckled the portals and instruments of the tanks, and some still bore Azeri flags, crescents, and slogans splashed in white paint across the turrets. "We're tank-rich," Monte reported to wounded fighters during a visit to a hospital. After noting that most of his tanks had been captured from the enemy, he concluded that "The Azeris are arming two armies — theirs and ours." "May God keep Elchibey in good health," his fighters joked, referring to the bellicose President of Azerbaijan who had unintentionally supplied them with so many tanks.

On December 5, the Martuni forces used these tanks to capture the Cheyl Heights, a line of hills overlooking the village of Merzuli on the Agdam Plain. After the battle that evening, Monte squinted through binoculars from the captured heights and watched 400 enemy soldiers, two heavy tanks, a light tank, and heavy guns converging on a farm near Merzuli. They were preparing a counter-offensive.

Under cover of night, Monte led 400 of his fighters, as well as four heavy tanks and four light tanks, down from the mountains to the northwest of the Cheyl Heights. Before darkness had lifted, Monte's men had connected with the asphalt Martuni–Agdam road and circled behind the Azeri staging base. When the Martuni fighters attacked, they hit hard from two directions, taking the Azeris by surprise. An Azeri warplane swooped down to cover the enemy's retreat.

Monte emerged exhausted and depressed from the two days of fighting: he had lost nine fighters on December 5 and 6, including the subcommander, Valod. On the other side of the ledger, his fighters had pushed the enemy back three kilometers east of Merzuli, leaving 150 enemy corpses on the battlefield.

After the capture of the Cheyl Heights on December 5, word spread that the area around the nearby village of Pertashen was quiet and secure. Villagers began returning to their homes and farms and the menfolk joined reserves in the trenches. With families and neighbors at their backs, the defenders stiffened their resolve. Thanks to the greater security, farmers returned to their fields, truck traffic increased, and bakeries and wineries returned to full production. Soon, it was easier to eat well in Martuni than in Yerevan. Greater economic activity, in turn, attracted more refugees back to their abandoned homes and farms, including young men of fighting age, who joined the reserves and rotated through the trenches on the front lines.

Despite the roadblocks and Monte's stinginess when it came to fuel, he had become "a favorite of the people," as Bulgarian filmmaker Svetana Paskaleva described him. Mothers rocked babies and cooed: "Avo's with us. Wherever Avo is, there will be victory." Even more than courage (which, after all, was not a rare trait among the mountain people of Karabagh), Monte's persuasive power derived from his incorruptibility. The commander of Martuni conducted himself in conformity with Ibn Khaldun's negative dictum: "The decay of sincere intentions causes the decay of military defense." Monte was the personification of sincere intentions. He ate with his men, he slept on a cot a few steps from his desk, he picked up shovels to dig trenches and fill potholes, and he handed over his monthly salary from the Defense Committee to the families of wounded soldiers and to the more efficient cooks and cleaning women at the headquarters.

The locals loved to share stories about Monte's kindness to animals. They'd describe the commander scooping snakes off roads with the barrel of his rifle, or hopping out of a troop carrier to pour a bucket of water into a drying puddle of tadpoles, or shouting down a soldier who had nailed a dead hawk to the lintel of a bunker. Hélène Hakopyan, a Martuni native who was not yet in her teens, described the commander as "amazingly kind, with an almost naïve simplicity."

Not everyone was impressed by these antics, though. Nelson blew smoke through his nose and squinted. Americans are crazy: they level cities with their bombers and then they fawn over a puddle of tadpoles ...

Azeri Secretary of State Panakh Huseinov (no relation to Surat) began the new year by announcing that the question of Mountainous Karabagh would be resolved not in Moscow or Washington, but on the battlefield. Negotiations over the future of Mountainous Karabagh had been taking place for months, in Minsk, Rome, and Geneva. The United States, Russia, and nine other countries had been involved (the list notably excluded Iran), but they had achieved next to nothing.

Monte could not have agreed more with Secretary of State Huseinov: the question would be resolved on the battlefield. On the night of January 4, his fighters pushed Azeri forces several kilometers further to the east of Martuni town, all the way to Kizilkaya, or "Red Rock," a peak on the eastern edge of the mountains. Martuni did not lose a single fighter during the battle, but afterwards, a tank from the Jardar front detonated a mine on Red Rock. Believing that their tank was the target of an incoming volley of Grads, the crew bailed and scattered across a field that turned out to be laced with anti-personnel mines. Monte showed up at the scene before the wounds had been bandaged and counted eight crewmembers dead and six injured. He stumbled back to head-quarters and flopped into his cot at 3:00 a.m., but the hissing radio woke him two hours later. It was a report from the front: the enemy had launched a strong counter-attack, recapturing Red Rock, along with seven Martuni fighters from Krasnyi Bazar. As other defenders retreated in a light tank, they too hit a mine. The tank rolled onto the arm of a soldier, who escaped by cutting his hand off with his own bayonet.

Monte grabbed his jacket. Before the sun rose, his fighters had knocked out two enemy heavy tanks, captured a light tank and a 100-mm anti-tank gun, and killed sixty enemy soldiers. Nevertheless, the enemy had succeeded in recapturing the peak, killing six more of Martuni's best fighters, and capturing four more fighters from Krasnyi Bazar, whom they tortured and eventually executed.

By this time, Monte's right arm was twitching like a dying fish, and no one who came into contact with him could ignore his constant blinking. What he needed more than anything else was what he was getting the least of: sleep.

On the evening of January 16, Monte girded for yet another battle. But this time, the battle would be verbal and his adversaries would be his own men. Around 100 officers and heads of specialized units clomped up the stairs at Martuni headquarters and took their seats in the wide second-story corridor that served as a meeting hall. The main item of discussion was Colonel Haroyan's presence in Martuni. It seems that the Colonel had run afoul of a local clique when he had ordered an inventory of the assets of a nearby *kolkhoz* that had been paying protection money to the clique. The clique's leader was an Afghan War veteran named Artik, who saw himself and his buddies as the first champions of Martuni. In retaliation against Haroyan, one of Artik's buddies had stolen his blue staff car and refused to return it until the Colonel left Martuni.

Monte rose to his feet and reminded his fellow fighters of Haroyan's extraordinary record defending the people. He defended the Colonel until he was hoarse, but Artik's friends were adamant, and few locals were willing to side with Haroyan against native sons, even if the latter were thugs.

After the meeting, almost everyone left the headquarters building, fearing that a showdown was looming between Haroyan and Monte on the one hand and Artik's clique, on the other. When Monte and Haroyan propped their chins on their elbows at the dining-hall table that night, they sat with only two other people: Seta and Rashid "Saribeg" Mardirosyan, a good-looking tank captain who, in the local expression, "had spit for" the opinions of gossips and thugs. The four figures around the table were gloomier than they were angry. When Saribeg tried to convince Haroyan to stay, the Colonel just smiled sadly.

"My work is finished here," he said.

Come in, Zero-Zero

B y early March, 1993, Monte had begun to feel that, despite smoldering defiance from Artik's clique, his Martuni fighters had gained enough discipline and confidence to get along without him. Now it was time to put his Deputy Commander, a young Red Army veteran from Stepanakert named Mosi, to the test, to see how he would fare as Commander Avo's successor. As Monte stated in a video message to his parents, it was time to start settling his accounts in Martuni and to move on to another front.

He secured some diesel and raised a mobile detachment for a vaguely described operation in the north. The detachment would consist of about seventy volunteers from Martuni and an equal number from the southernmost district of Hadrut. Monte's driver Gomidas signed on, too, as did Saribeg and another stalwart officer named Abo, along with fighters from the village of Gishi and another group under the subcommand of fair-haired Mavo. Two former Secret Army comrades from Iran, Vahig Sh. and Masis Sh., also joined, as did Marad, the errant warehouse manager, who had had a change of heart since his public arraignment a year earlier and now counted himself as a loyal fighter under Monte's command. Nelson found himself in the detachment, too, in part perhaps to make sure that Commander Avo didn't receive all the credit for any victories they might win along the way. The detachment also included several women who were nominally medics but who carried rifles, as well as a light tank crew from the martyr village of Majgalashen, plus about 130 other volunteers. Few of these volunteers had any clear idea how long they would be on the road, nor where the road would lead.

A couple of refurbished battle tanks, several light tanks, and a few troop carriers bristling with volunteers bumped into first gear early on March 5, before rumors had a chance to spread. The next day, outside the ruined Armenian village of Haterk, Monte stood in front of a video camera and asked Norair Tanielyan, Mardakert District Commander, to document the discarded enemy provisions scattered in the scrub grass at their feet.

"Munitions were brought from Iran, Turkey, Arab countries ..." he said, omitting to mention Israeli *matériel* and technical assistance to the stridently anti-Iranian Elchibey regime. The wind crackled on the microphone, drowning out his voice.

Monte interrupted and shook an open palm at the discarded enemy provisions: "Just say what you *see!*"

Tanielyan repeated his line about Muslim countries providing aid to Azerbaijan.

Monte interrupted again: "What do you see? Just say what you *see!*" he shouted, exasperated.

Tanielyan mumbled a few unintelligible syllables, then Monte took the camera and zoomed in on the blue and black Hebrew lettering across the plastic wrapping material of the abandoned enemy supplies. Tanielyan might have wished to appease a Western audience by ignoring the facts, but here at his feet was evidence that Azerbaijan was receiving provisions from Israel.

Monte's fighters rode into battle the next day, pushing the enemy out of Haterk, on the north shore of the Sarsang Reservoir. The day after that (March 8), they pushed five kilometers farther west, to the abandoned village of Kedavan, where they billeted in a stone-block schoolhouse perched at a dirt switchback on a steep slope. From there they backtracked, to join battles to capture the peaks at Janyatagh, on the eastern front in Mardakert. After hard fighting, they captured the peaks on March 17. Three days later, the Azeris launched coordinated counter-attacks east and west of Mardakert, and north and south of the Lachin Corridor, too. Monte's fighters repulsed the counter-attacks in eastern Mardakert and advanced towards a strategic hill called Pushken Yal.

At 7:29 the next morning, machine guns announced that the battle for Pushken Yal had begun. Just before eight o'clock, the video camera caught Monte shouting hoarsely, "First aid! First aid! They hit our BMP-2!" The camera swings around, to catch the commander hunched over and bellowing so hard that his hands tremble: "*First aid! First aid! We hit our own BMP-2!*"

Minutes later, seven or eight fighters in tan fatigues sprint down the slope to meet the tank that is evacuating a wounded member of the BMP-2 crew. They hoist a limp figure from the turret hatch. It's Vartan, a slender fighter with an angelic face and the thin beard of youth. "Let me die, boys," he groans, wincing. One of his comrades lashes out at the video camera in helpless rage: "*Get the fuck out of here!*"

Later that day, the Martuni fighters threw open the doors of barns and privies as they advanced to the summit of Pusken Yal. The hill was not easy to keep, though. Azeri counter-attacks droned on until March 25, when Monte left Pushken Yal in the hands of Tanielyan's forces. At this moment, it might have appeared as though Monte's fighters would head south, back home to Martuni and Hadrut. But instead, they followed their commander down the road headed west.

On March 26, the Martuni fighters marched with weapons and ammo on their backs over fifteen kilometers of steep mountains, before they reached the point where they attacked the militarized village of Aghdaban, thirty kilometers due west of Janyatagh. After hard fighting and stiff Azeri resistance, they broke the line of defense and advanced several kilometers further west, to the western edge of Mountainous Karabagh.

The next day Monte launched an attack on the ruined village of Charekdar, which straddled the only asphalt road from Mardakert leading west. Meanwhile, another Armenian fighting group advanced from Aghdaban a few kilometers to the north, and a third group took up positions several kilometers to the south of the main group, at the village of Nareshtar. By this time, it must have been clear not only to Monte's fighters but to enemy commanders as well, where the road was leading. The Azeris now faced a threat that had been unthinkable a few days earlier: an Armenian push into Kelbajar, the 3,000-square-kilometer maze of canyons and mountains that separated Mountainous Karabagh from the Armenian Republic, "Mother Armenia."

Earlier that year, a video camera had been running while Monte clomped into his office with muddy boots, to debrief a delegation of pro-Ter-Petrosyan parliamentarians from Yerevan. Like a professor arriving late for class, he launched straightaway into a lecture on defense preparations in Martuni. At one point he turned to a map that covered a large part of the wall behind him and placed an open palm on it, between the borders of Mountainous Karabagh and the Armenian Republic. "This area ..." he said, "this area is very important." After a moment of incredulous silence, one of the parliamentarians, Pakrat

Asatryan, muttered under his breath, but audibly for the video camera behind him: "Nice dreams."

Two months had passed since then. Now, poised at the entrance to the stone maze of Kelbajar, it seemed that he would try to realize his "nice dreams."

The forces at Aghdaban and Nareshtar advanced, but not Monte's fighters at Charekdar—not on March 27. Azeri commanders had thrown their best-trained and most determined fighters, including Ukrainian and Chechen tank commanders and Turkish volunteers, onto the front defending Charekdar. As soon as Monte's lead tank rounded a blind bend in the road at the foot of a cliff, an enemy Sagger rocket hit it, killing all three crew members, young men from the village of Herher. His best fighters, it seemed, were always the first casualties. Monte shouted to halt the advance, then he sent scouts to the top of the cliff to reconnoiter.

Meanwhile, just to the west of Kelbajar, near the town of Vardenis in the Republic of Armenia, a fourth force composed of fifty smartly uniformed fighters had already begun trudging through the knee-high snow of the Mrav Mountains, towards Kelbajar. At the head of this group was a stocky man in a red beret, an Armenian from the West who spoke the same strange dialect as Monte.

Back at Charekdar, Monte's fighters re-launched their attack on March 28. Finally, after eight hours of fighting and one casualty on the Armenian side, they vaulted the defenders' trenches and captured two light tanks and a heavy tank with a crescent-and-star stencil on the barrel. The captured armor joined the lengthening column that clattered across the Tartar River, which twisted into Kelbajar. When they reached the opposite bank, Monte and his fighters jumped from the tanks and continued their march. Quiet, unsmiling, and covered with yellow dust, even the youngest of Monte's fighters was a hardened veteran of a dozen battles.

The same day, local journalist Baghryan caught up with Monte near the abandoned village of Vankvan. The commander faced his interviewer in full battle dress, with an ammo vest over a flak jacket, but no helmet. Silhouetted on a ridge in the distance was the medieval Armenian monastery of Tativank.

"Now we've reached the Kelbajar road," he announced. "When we want to, we'll advance. The issue is whether or not we want to. We'd prefer if the peaceful population gets out of this place safely, and then we'll advance. But it looks like their soldiers won't allow it. So maybe we'll start up again."

But why advance into Kelbajar? No Armenians lived there.

Monte later claimed they "*had* to take Kelbajar," because Azeri gunners in the area had launched artillery barrages against Armenian villages. But to him, the operation was not purely—nor even primarily—based on security considerations. "This is an historical issue," he told Baghryan: current demographics and political borders notwithstanding, Kelbajar was part of the Armenian homeland. "*Of course* this is historical Armenia!" he said, pivoting and pointing to the monastery in the distance, "And we'll vindicate that reality with our guns. Unfortunately! It would be nice if the Azeris would understand that reality is reality, agree and say OK, it's yours, and that's that."

Never mind the fact that the population of Kelbajar was half-Azeri and half-Kurdish: for the sake of understanding that "reality is reality," they should either accept living as minorities within an Armenian state or leave their homes. But the Armenian fighters had already foreclosed the former option, as Monte himself acknowledged to a Western reporter just before the offensive: "A lot of blood has been spilled on both sides," he observed, "The emotions are high and that isn't conducive to living together in the near or medium future." It would seem, then, that all options were closed except mass expulsion.

By March 31, Monte's fighters had advanced another nine kilometers along the two-lane road that traced the twists and turns of the Tartar River. Suddenly, they found themselves at the bottom of a narrow and winding canyon with a sheer 100-foot vertical rise on either side. Monte recorded the scene on a video camera: the brown water of the river Tartar churns over boulders, and rays of sunlight slant over the stone face of the cliffs, rising straight up. "What a pretty place it is," Monte says as he follows the river with the video camera, "It's still winter, there's not much foliage, but when it gets green it'll be a really pretty place."

Another twenty kilometers of this terrain separated his column from the town of Kelbajar, the capital of the district of the same name. From the top of the canyon, Monte's scouts peered down at an intersection with the only road leading south to Lachin. Cars and trucks laden with bundles headed out of Kelbajar, bumper to bumper. Monte ordered his column to halt, to allow the traffic to pass.

They watched and waited for twenty-four hours. Finally, on April 1 at 2:00 p.m., when the scouts reported that the refugee traffic had thinned to a trickle and then dried up entirely, the Mountainous Karabagh fighters resumed the offensive, punching into the intersection near the entrance to a tunnel leading south at Zufulgarli. Suddenly, a military-green GAZ-52 truck barreled out of the tunnel towards them. Monte's fighters swung around and opened fire with assault rifles and rocket-propelled grenades. It did not occur to them that the truck was anything but a military transport. But when they approached the smoldering hulk, their jaws dropped: it contained twenty-five Kurds and Azeri *kolkhoz* workers, and not a single soldier. Most of the occupants had bullet holes, burns, or shrapnel wounds, and four of them, including the driver and his daughter, lay dead.

Monte ordered the survivors to be evacuated to the hospital in Stepanakert. Several of them, perhaps as many as eleven, would die of their wounds. Later, in an interview with a British journalist, Monte explained in a sad, halting voice that by the time his soldiers had reached the mouth of the Zufulgarli Tunnel, they had assumed that the last of the refugees had crossed the intersection. His fighters had been tired and jumpy when they opened fire on the truck as it charged towards them out of the tunnel.

Monte's column advanced a few kilometers further west, then halted just short of another intersection, this time with a new primary road leading north to Ganje, Azerbaijan's second-largest city. Monte's goal, the town of Kelbajar, was fifteen kilometers beyond the intersection, to the southwest. From the top of the canyon wall, his scouts watched a bumper-to-bumper caravan of cars and trucks wending north towards Ganje, while overhead, Azerbaijani MI-8 helicopters fluttered back and forth, overladen with refugees.

Monte ordered his fighters to wait forty hours before advancing. This time, he would make sure that they did not repeat their terrible mistake at the Zufulgarli Tunnel. They would wait for the refugees to clear the intersection, even at the cost of permitting Azeri fighters to move into the area to reinforce their positions. Monte's Azeri-Turkish-speaking officer, Abo, radioed the governor of Kelbajar, who identified himself by his radio code name, Khan. "Put your arms down," Abo told him. "You're free to leave until April 2 at 14:00 hours. You and all the civilians."

"We're never going to leave," Khan responded, "We'll fight to the end."

Monte ordered Abo to point a loudhailer at the intersection, to communicate directly with the fleeing population, in the hope that they would relay the information to family and neighbors who were not yet on their way out of Kelbajar. Abo announced five times, in Russian and Azeri Turkish, that anyone who did not want to get caught in the crossfire had until 14:00 hours on Friday, April 2 to leave the area without fear of attack. The message echoed down the canyon, to the intersection and beyond.

By the evening of April 1, the helicopters had flown their last loads of refugees to safety in Yevlakh, about one hour away. In the meantime, Azeri tanks and infantry had arrived at the intersection and dug in, bracing for the inevitable attack. At 2:45 p.m. on April 2, Monte's forces burst into the intersection, firing straight into the dug-in Azeri forces. Minutes later, charred armor and enemy soldiers littered the intersection, along with four of Monte's fighters.

Before they had finished scavenging enemy munitions, a ZIL troop carrier and several other vehicles laden with Azeri fighters and fuel hurtled around a blind bend just ahead of Monte's forces, towards them. One of Monte's fighters happened to be recording the scene on video: the camera swings around to catch Monte for less than an instant, as he almost casually charges his rifle without bothering to take cover. He puts a knee to the road, aims and fires, all in one smooth motion, as if he did this out of habit, the way another man might rub his elbow. In that same instant, the camera swings back towards the bend, as a round from a Martuni BMP hits an enemy fuel tanker, rolling sixty enemy soldiers into a huge orange fireball that flares across the camera frame, whiting it out.

When the flames had dwindled to embers at the Ganje intersection, Monte took the video camera to record the debris-strewn scene: buckled and charred machines litter red clay at the foot of a high stone cliff. The camera floats up to scorched corpses flung akimbo, then pans across bloody faces and mouths gaping at the sky.

"There's one thing I want everyone to note well." Monte's voice emerges from behind the camera: "There are no boots on their feet. Our boys don't have boots, so when we hit an Azeri, we take his shoes ..."

Sure enough, the corpses are all in stocking feet. Monte zooms into a light-haired corpse lying face-up on the side of the road, then he pans to another one: "Russian," he says from behind the camera: "One Russian ... Two Russians who were with them." Just beyond them, the lacy skeleton of a melted light tank totters on a precipice, while on the other side of the road a troop carrier smolders, surrounded by charcoal figures frozen in death like so many torn tires. Monte pans on the intersection, strewn with perhaps seventy enemy corpses, and then he points the camera down the road: "The farther you go down this road," he says, "the more corpses you'll find."

After the wounded soldiers had been evacuated to Stepanakert, Monte took a head count: he now commanded only about sixty fighters. As far as he knew, another group of diehard enemy defenders might be lying in ambush somewhere along the last fifteen kilometers of road between the Ganje intersection and Kelbajar town. He needed reinforcements, but the sun was on its way down, and if he were to wait for fresh troops to arrive, his men would lose their momentum. Monte gave the order, and trucks and tanks lurched forward, trailing black exhaust.

The video camera recorded meetings with Azeri and Kurdish stragglers along the last stretch of road: a downcast enemy soldier with a bandaged hand and a burned leg rides up on a donkey and surrenders. An old man in a faded jacket studded with medals from the Great Patriotic War weeps before leaving his home forever. An elderly woman in a black *yazma*, waving a torn sheet on a stick, greets Monte and Abo in Azeri Turkish, then suddenly kneels to the ground to kiss Monte's feet. Surprised and awkward, Monte tries to pull back. *Yok!* he shouts, "No!" He reflexively bends over and brings the woman up by her arm. "What are you doing?" he asks in Anatolian Turkish, "Don't *ever* do that!"

Not long after that, the video camera is still running as Monte and a group of his fighters, all of them grinning ear to ear, pass around a bottle of the local *Isdi Soo* mineral water. They have just received word by radio that troops advancing from another front had taken Kelbajar town. "Kelbajar is ours!" Monte shouts. Nelson takes a big swig and hands the bottle to Monte. The outsider may be crazy, but this time he has led them to victory.

When Monte entered Kelbajar town on Saturday, April 3, he found a row of neat but bleak storefronts and a few chickens. The townsfolk must have been in such a rush to leave that they had not bothered to grab the chickens as provisions for the road. The only other sign of life was a BMP idling in the middle of the road through the center of town. "Congratulations!" Monte shouted to a fighter sitting atop the light tank. He was a member of one of the fighting groups that had entered the abandoned town just ahead of Monte's fighters.

The fighters from Vardenis were among those who had beaten Monte to Kelbajar town. As it turned out, the leader of the group, the commander with the strange dialect and the red beret, was an old acquaintance of Monte's. Shishko had arrived in Armenia two and a half years earlier, just twenty days after his former co-conspirator, "Timothy Sean McCormick," had arrived. The Marseillais had entered

Armenia on one of his forty-seven passports, this an Italian one under the name of Angelo Rossetti, "Little Red Angel." Since the beginning of the Kelbajar offensive, Monte had been hearing rumors about Shishko's expedition, but to his great relief he did not cross paths with his estranged former comrade.

The canyon was quiet. The Kelbajar offensive was over. In one fell swoop, the Armenian fighters had secured the entire western flank of Mountainous Karabagh, from the Mrav Mountains in the north to the Lachin Corridor, ninety kilometers to the south. With the seizure of Kelbajar, they now held sway over the entire 3,000-square-kilometer swath of canyons and mountains between Mountainous Karabagh and Mother Armenia. Thus, Monte and his fellow fighters had united Mountainous Karabagh with the Republic of Armenia, while dramatically filling in their defensive lines to the north. With new, impregnable positions on the commanding heights, 200 fighters could secure the Mrav Mountain passes against an Azeri counter-offensive, relieving the remaining Karabagh forces for redeployment on fronts to the south and east.

They had captured Kelbajar, but the victory had cost the lives of forty of Monte's best fighters. Azeri sources reported that 100 of their fighters had died in the same four-day period, but they had probably under-counted: around seventy Azeri defenders had died at the Ganje intersection on April 2 alone. Whatever the precise figure, one thing was clear: civilian casualties on the Azeri side were considerably higher than military casualties. Monte told a British interviewer that the only civilian casualties had been the fifteen *kolkhoz* workers in the truck that had barreled out of the Zufulgarli tunnel, but the true casualty count was much higher. By capturing the Ganje intersection, Monte's fighters had thereby cut the last paved road out of Kelbajar. And when the last helicopter had left, the remaining refugees had no choice but to flee over the Mrav Mountains, on a footpath through the wind-whipped Omar Pass. Refugees from fifty Kelbajar villages, laden with bundles of whatever possessions they could throw on their backs, draggled through the pass on a rut through frozen mud and hip-deep snow at 10,000 feet altitude. According to a Reuters report of April 5, 1993, some 200 exhausted refugees slumped into snowdrifts on the pass and froze to death, while others made it to safety with severe frostbite.

Throughout most of Monte's adult life—in Tehran, Kurdistan, Bourdj Hamoud, Kfar Tibnit, Fresnes Prison, and Shahumyan—Monte had put himself on the side of the underdog. But the roofless ruins of

Karadaghlu, Khojalu, Shusha, Lachin, and now Kelbajar showed that Monte was no longer on the side of "the" underdog: he was on the side of one underdog against another. And since his side happened to be winning at the moment, they were less the underdog.

Whenever one side, Armenian or Azeri, suffered reversals on the battlefields, orators and ministers in Yerevan or Baku blamed it on Russian support for the other side: after Azeri offensives, Armenians accused Russia of siding with Azerbaijan; and after Armenian offensives, Azeris accused Russia of siding with Armenia. So after Kelbajar, it was not surprising when Vafa Guluzade, Chief Presidential Advisor to Azerbaijan's President Elchibey, claimed that, "The Armenian army is weaker than ours. But as always, it is the Russian army that fights." Guluzade was mistaken, however: the only Slavs fighting in Kelbajar during the offensive were mercenaries fighting on the Azeri side. Russians did not fight on the Armenian side in Kelbajar, nor did Russians plan the offensive: the latter task fell to white-haired Colonel-General Daribaltayan, of the Defense Ministry of the Republic of Armenia.

This is not to say, however, that the Kremlin did not welcome news of the Armenian push into Kelbajar. The Armenian offensive came at a time of escalating military threats to Russia: Washington was eager to push NATO right up to Russia's western doorstep, to set up military bases in Central Asia, and to abrogate the Anti-Ballistic Missile Treaty. Chechnya teetered on the brink of secessionist rebellion in the high Caucasus, while Armenia's northern neighbor, the newly independent Republic of Georgia, was tearing itself up in three civil wars. And now Azerbaijan, the former Soviet Republic, once again turned its eyes towards Russia's age-old enemy, Turkey, whose leaders were waxing lyrical about transforming the Caucasus and Central Asia into a launching pad for Ankara's century of the Turks. Only Armenia held out any promise as a reliable Russian ally in the southern Caucasus.

When Monte's fighters began blasting their way through the Tartar River Canyon, they put an abrupt halt to the US-sponsored "consultations" in Geneva over the future of Mountainous Karabagh. The Kelbajar offensive turned the balance of power in the southern Caucasus to Russia's advantage, at the expense of Ankara. "What happened today radically changes the military and geopolitical situation in the area," declared Azerbaijani Defense Ministry spokesman Khafiz Gaibov on April 4: "The territory occupied by the Armenian forces is as big as Mountainous Karabagh itself." President Elchibey ordered men aged from eighteen to twenty-seven to report for military duty and imposed press censorship, a curfew, and a ban on strikes and demonstrations, as part of a sixty-day national state of emergency.

Meanwhile in Yerevan, guards at the presidential palace got busy ushering grim diplomats bearing protest letters into Ter-Petrosyan's office. The US State Department was one of the first to register a "sharp rebuke," on Monday, April 5. "The United States government condemns this offensive," crowed Secretary of State Warren Christopher— a man who brimmed with euphoria when it came to Turkish offensives in Iraqi Kurdistan and Israeli offensives in Lebanon. Then the European Community and the United Nations Security Council followed suit. Turkey and Pakistan co-sponsored UN Resolution 822, calling for the immediate withdrawal of "ethnic Armenian forces" from Kelbajar and the "immediate withdrawal of all occupying forces from the Kelbajar district and other recently occupied areas of Azerbaijan." The resolution passed unanimously.

Turkish UN Ambassador Mustafa Aksin declared that Turkey would "not allow Azeri territory to be occupied by anyone—by anyone!" His colleagues in Ankara recognized the name of the commander who had led the main force in the Kelbajar offensive. The previous July, the Turkish newspaper *Hurriyet* had reported that Monte Melkonian, the Secret Army militant who had attacked Turkish embassy officials in Rome and Athens, had been commanding Armenian forces in Mountainous Karabagh, and a couple of days after the *Hurriyet* story, on July 23, 1992, the Turkish daily *Milliyet* announced in a front-page, block-letter headline: "An Armenian Assassin Has Recently Become a Commander."

Statements from Ankara became increasingly bellicose. "Turkey must show its teeth to Armenia," Turkish President Turgut Ozal announced in early April. Then, as Turkish helicopters, tanks, and infantry massed on the border with Armenia, Ozal wondered out loud, "What harm would it do if a few bombs were dropped on the Armenian side by Turkish troops holding maneuvers on the border?" Almost a year earlier, just after the fall of Shusha, General Yevgeny Shapashnikov, Military Chief of the Commonwealth of Independent States, had already answered Ozal's question when he warned of "a third world war, if Turkey becomes involved in Mountainous Karabagh."

As if to mock Russia's warnings, Ozal set out on a five-country tour of the former Soviet Republics of Central Asia, to muster support for Azerbaijan. At an April 14 news conference in Baku, the Turkish President announced: "We will take whatever steps are necessary if the fighting between Azerbaijan and Armenia does not stop, including the formation of a military alliance with Azerbaijan."

Three days later, on April 17, Ozal died of heart failure aged sixty-six. Officials in Ankara suggested that the Turkish President's hectic tour had brought on his death. Monte, the former Secret Army militant, could now congratulate himself for having helped to trigger the death of Turgut Ozal, a Turkish leader he had long despised.

Meanwhile, neighboring Iran was trying to maintain its official neutrality, while at the same time it joined other nations in condemning the Armenian offensive in Kelbajar. Iran was already choked with refugees from Afghanistan and Iraq. The last thing it needed was tens of thousands of refugees from Azerbaijan arriving in the ethnically Azeri areas of northwestern Iran, to foment Azeri nationalism in the Islamic republic. Iran's president, Hashemi Rafsanjani, threatened without elaboration to "take a more severe stand" if the fighting continued.

Armenian President Ter-Petrosyan had been visiting Tehran when the guns had begun booming down canyons in Kelbajar. Judging from his startled reaction, he had not been informed of the offensive until the tanks had rolled into the Tartar River Canyon. As soon as the news had reached him, he fired off an angry letter to the defense forces' leadership. The offensive, he believed, would only lead to Armenia's diplomatic isolation, impede all-important trade agreements with Ankara, and further complicate peace negotiations that were necessary to establish stability in the region and to attract foreign investment.

Ter-Petrosyan had begun his presidency determined to appease the West by snubbing Moscow, keeping his distance from Tehran, and sidling up to NATO Turkey. But now, after two years of diplomatic overtures and concessions to Ankara, it was clear that Ter-Petrosyan's "new thinking" had failed: in the wake of the Kelbajar offensive, NATO Turkey slapped Armenia with an economic embargo and threatened to invade the country.

The fact that the West was unwilling to moderate Ankara's hostility may have surprised Ter-Petrosyan and his well-tailored advisors, but it did not surprise Monte. In a video interview just hours before the attack on Charekdar, the former school teacher cleared his throat and summarized the situation:

> The United States has extremely tight relations with Turkey. They count on Turkey for a lot of things. Turkey is sort of their little puppet in the region. Turkey does more or less what they want it to do. It has a strong army. The United States wants to use that army to police the

Arab states, to police Iran, to enforce U.S. policy in the region. And due to that, the United States is willing to totally ignore the rights of an awful lot of people, including the Armenian people.

Thus, in seven quick sentences, Monte identified Armenia's main foreign policy challenge more clearly and realistically than a file cabinet full of essays by Ter-Petrosyan's advisors.

But geopolitics was the last thing on Monte's mind when he stumbled up the steps to the Martuni headquarters on April 5 at 5:40 a.m. He had left Martuni exactly one month earlier, on March 5, and for the last week of that month he had caught no more than a few furtive hours of sleep in the back seat of his banged-up staff car. Now he was looking forward to stretching out for a few hours of uninterrupted slumber. As it turned out, though, he couldn't find the keys to the room with his cot. So the commander who had just brought Russia and Turkey to the brink of war unrolled a sleeping bag in a hallway and crawled in.

Twenty minutes after shutting his eyes, one of his men shook him awake: the enemy had attacked Hovik 1 trench and taken it. Monte jumped up, buckled his belt, and threw his fighters back into battle. In the days that followed, the fighting continued without interruption: at Hovik 1 and Sevan trenches (April 8 to 9); at Kzilkaya Peak (starting April 10); at Valod and Raffo 5 trenches (starting April 13); at Hovik 1, Sevan 4 and Valod trenches (starting April 14); at the Krasnyi Bazar and Majgalashen fronts (from April 16), and so on. "Our side killed many Azeris," Monte wrote in his calendar after the April 13 battle at Valod trench. But these victories cost the lives of twenty more of his fighters, and as usual, the best were always the first to die.

When local journalist Vartkes Baghryan ran into Monte in Stepanakert in the last week of April and invited him for an impromptu TV interview, the commander shook his head and tried to step away: "I'm really rushing." Baghryan pressed the point, assuring him that the interview would take only half an hour. Monte glanced at his watch and then relented: "Alright, let's go." A moment later, he faced his interviewer across a dais at the TV studio. Baghryan was determined to reveal something about the man behind the legend of Commander Avo.

"What do you think about when you're alone with yourself?" he asked.

Monte hunched his shoulders apologetically and replied: "In general, I think about my work. Really. The work is so heavy that there's only time to think about that ..."

Undeterred, Baghryan asked, "Do you have any spare time, and if you do, what do you do?"

"No, I don't have any spare time," Monte responded with another apologetic shrug.

Before ending the interview, Baghryan asked his guest if there had ever been incidents that had made him regret having come to Mountainous Karabagh.

"Let's not say I've regretted it," Monte replied,

> ... but of course there have been times when, thanks to the lack of discipline and the low level of consciousness on the part of some people, the nerves have been brought to a point where they were about to burst. There have been a lot of incidents like that.

Other incidents were soon to follow. On May 4, Monte met his old comrade Colonel Haroyan in the ruins of the village of Lachin, to conduct reconnaissance for another planned offensive. This time, the target was to be Gubatli, the pocket of land south of Lachin, between Kelbajar to the north and the Iranian border to the south. After eighteen hours of hiking over the grassy hills south of Lachin and squinting through binoculars, they headed back to the staff car in a light rain. On the drive back to Lachin, a drunken soldier at a checkpoint leveled his rifle at the staff car and fired. Gomidas braked, and Monte bounded out of the staff car, charging his rifle. The soldier and Monte approached each other, guns drawn, until they were face to face. Haroyan hopped out of the vehicle and grabbed the barrel of the drunk's gun, but when he pulled the muzzle down, the gun discharged, sending two bullets through the Colonel's left thigh. After pummeling the drunken soldier, Gomidas drove Haroyan to a clinic in a nearby village. From there, Haroyan was transferred to Yerevan to recover.

Colonel Haroyan's convalescence from the bullet wound delayed preparations for the Gubatli operation. In the interim, Monte received a summons from the Ministry of Defense of the Republic of Armenia. When he arrived in Yerevan on the night of May 25, however, he discovered that the meeting at the Ministry of Defense had been postponed for a couple of days. For the first time in months, Monte and Seta found themselves together with time on their hands to discuss their plans.

At night in bed, and then in the morning over breakfast, Monte broached the subject of children. Back in December, he had believed they should wait until the war was over before having their first baby. But in the months since then, it had become clear that the war was not about to wind down any time soon. They resolved to start a family in June, before the second anniversary of their wedding. Seta would then join her husband in Martuni for the duration of her pregnancy.

They would have to find time to prepare their "nest" before the new arrival. Although Monte preferred Mountainous Karabagh, they agreed that they should buy a house in Yerevan, where Seta's university and friends were. A piece of Yerevan real estate had already caught their eye: it was half of a stone-and-concrete duplex just off Baghramyan Boulevard, with three small bedrooms, a shoulder-width hallway, and a garden the size of a parking space. It was a cramped hovel, but when Monte first gazed from the kitchen window at the snow-capped peak of Mount Ararat looming above the haze of Yerevan, he announced, "This is a good house."

Although Monte had become a homeowner, he was a long way from settling down. "What will you do when the war here ends?" a visiting journalist from the *Fresno Bee* had asked him recently. "Go to the next one," he answered without skipping a beat. When Seta asked him where he would prefer to go from Martuni, he mentioned the nearby districts of Hadrut or Mardakert. One destination was out of the question, though—namely, the country of his birth, the United States of America. Back in fall 1991, Monte had written to Dad, asking him to stop lobbying his congressman for the issuance of a US passport. "I couldn't care less about their 'allowing' me to go to the U.S. or not," he wrote. "I am very comfortable and happy where I am." Besides, he could get by without an American passport, since he already carried two neatly forged Soviet-Russian passports, and one of them even bore his real name and his actual birth date.

On May 27, Monte picked up Haroyan on the way to their meeting at the Defense Ministry of Armenia. Vazgen Manoogyan, the Defense Minister of the Republic, cleared his throat and told them to call off the planned offensive in Gubatli. Manoogyan explained that representatives from Yerevan and Baku had just announced acceptance of a Russian-brokered peace plan, and that a new offensive would destroy whatever credibility the Ter-Petrosyan government had managed to salvage after Kelbajar.

Monte listened quietly. He was not happy to hear the news, but there was never any doubt that he would abide by the decisions of his superiors. Leaving the Defense Ministry building, he was sure now that his work was finished in Martuni, and that it was time to move on. The new command structure was in place, and everyone, from the officer corps to the reservists, was battle-hardened and confident. As if to confirm this, news reached Yerevan that the Martuni fighters had just captured the peak of Ulyan Dagh, in southeastern Martuni. To remove any remaining doubts that the Martuni fighters could win without Monte's leadership, Seta suggested that he go to the next battle not as a commander but just as an observer.

That evening, their last evening together before Monte was to head back to the front, he accompanied his wife to a play at the Baronyan Theatre at Republican Square. For some time, he had been feeling guilty that Seta and he seldom did the sorts of things she liked to do. After the performance, they shared a bag of street-vendor popcorn—a rare treat in post-Soviet Yerevan—as Gomidas drove them to the dorm. Monte clomped up the stairs, grabbed his backpack and gun, and headed back to the waiting car, for the return trip to Martuni. Seta followed him downstairs with a wine-bottle full of water. Before climbing into the car, he turned to Seta:

"Sure you don't want to come with me?"

After a beat, Seta said, "Yeah, I'll come."

Monte smiled. "Nah ... nah, it'll only be a couple of days," he said on second thoughts. "I'll go and come right back."

Gomidas pulled away from the curb onto Mashdots Prospect and shifted gears. As the car disappeared into the darkness, Seta poured water from the bottle onto the street. "Leave like water, return like water ..."

Leave Like Water

S oon after returning to Martuni on May 28, Monte discovered several hectares of cultivated hashish near the killing field of
Karadaghlu. Artik's buddies, he suspected, had planted the field
as an export crop. The news worried Seta. Ever since the confrontation
with Marad, she had been begging her husband not to get mixed up in
the local "family businesses." He was a military man, she reminded
him, not a cop. Despite the advice, Monte was determined to burn the
field. But before he had found the time between skirmishes to do so, his
old friend Ara Toranian phoned Seta with an urgent message. Their
former comrade Shishko had asked Toranian, who was visiting from
Paris at the time, to relay a message to Monte: somehow, the Marseillais
had learned that whoever had planted the hashish in Karadaghlu had
also planted mines around the field, to make an example of trespassers.

Since there was no direct phone connection from Yerevan to Martuni, Seta had to phone the Defense Ministry in Stepanakert and ask
them to contact Monte by radio. He drove to Stepanakert that evening
to return Seta's call, and she repeated Shishko's message. When she had
finished, she heard a thoughtful "Hmmm … Hmmm" on the other side
of the line. It was not the news of the mines that had given Monte
pause: he had already discovered the danger and had made alternative
arrangements for burning the field. What had impressed him, rather,
was that his estranged comrade Shishko had gone to the trouble to
inform Seta of the danger.

Monte rode in the tank that crossed the minefield into the hashish
and set the field ablaze. But as the smoke rose, the danger only
increased: the field was still smoldering when Gomidas suddenly lost

control of Monte's staff car, which seemed for a moment to want to leap into a ravine and certain death. Gomidas and Monte hopped out of the vehicle, to discover that one of its wheels had almost flown off the axle. Someone had loosened all the lugs on the wheel, and whoever had done it must have known what most adults in Martuni knew, namely that the commander's staff car crossed perilous terrain every day.

The diesel thieves were back at work in Martuni, too, and border skirmishes continued unabated. As usual, Monte was not getting much sleep at night, and what sleep he got was interrupted by the ringing phones and buzzing walkie-talkies that he kept next to his cot. His blinking was getting worse, and the nervous twitch, which had disappeared during his few days of rest in Yerevan in late May, had returned to his arm.

After an especially ferocious bout of roaring at a wayward subordinate, one of the officers at the headquarters convinced Monte to get some fresh air. The officer, an Iranian-Armenian named Vartan, set out walking with Monte in the vineyards behind the headquarters. They walked for a while in the waning afternoon sun, when Monte spotted a little bird with blue and orange wings. It was a common species, but for some reason, this particular bird couldn't fly. Monte caught it and gently stroked its head. A peaceful smile transformed his face. Vartan walked away without a word, leaving Monte petting the bird.

Monte's voice sounded sad on June 10, when he phoned Seta from the front: headquarters staff had returned to their villages to take in the spring harvest, he explained, and Mosi, his second-in-command, had taken his sick aunt to Yerevan for medical treatment. That left Monte alone in the headquarters and unable to return to Yerevan as soon as he had hoped. The soonest he would be able to leave on vacation, he said, would be Wednesday, June 16. On that date they would disappear for a few days to celebrate Seta's thirtieth birthday. They had already reserved a room at the Aralez Hotel in the town of Vanadzor forty miles north of Yerevan, and they were keeping the reservation secret.

Seta felt the impatience in her husband's voice. Even with no end to the war in sight, it was time to start a family. They would be together soon, but Monte had a small job to take care of first.

On the night of June 11, Monte skipped dinner, drank a glass of yogurt in the kitchen of the headquarters, and retired to his cot uncharacteristically early.

A week earlier and eighty miles to the northwest, several hundred rebel fighters in Surat Huseinov's 709th Battalion near the Azeri city of Ganje had begun marching on the main road headed east towards Baku. Azerbaijan's President Elchibey had demoted Huseinov in a dispute over responsibility for the debacle in Kelbajar and dispatched troops to the rebels' garrison near Ganje, in a bloody attempt to capture the renegade war hero. The attempt had failed, however, and now Huseinov would get his revenge: the young commander vowed to seize Baku unless Elchibey resigned his post as President of Azerbaijan. Fearing civil war, Western oil companies started pulling their employees out of Baku just days before Elchibey was scheduled to sign a $10-billion contract between the State Oil Company of Azerbaijan and a consortium of Western oil companies, including Amoco, Unocal, BP, Pennzoil, and other giants.

With the enemy temporarily diverted and split, Monte's fighters in Martuni turned their sights on Agdam, an Azeri town with a pre-war population of 50,000, on the plain of the same name. Agdam, a district capital, was the third-largest city in Azerbaijan, after Baku and Ganje. Before the war, it had been a rich farming town of fountains, tea houses, and mansions. But all of this had changed in the past several years. In the early days of the war, Azeri gunners in and around the town had loosed hellfire on Stepanakert and other Armenian towns and villages within range of their cannons and Grad launchers. Later, when Mountainous Karabagh forces captured the heights a couple of kilometers to the west of Agdam, they unleashed their own version of hellfire in the opposite direction. As a result, craters pocked the pretty town of arbors and gardens, and many of its houses were empty. Now, if Mountainous Karabagh fighters could capture Agdam and the surrounding plain, they would drive home the point to Baku at last: you have lost the war. Cut your losses and accept Mountainous Karabagh's secession from Azerbaijan.

In the early morning of June 12—the first anniversary of the Azeri offensive that had reduced the largely Armenian town of Mardakert to rubble—Gomidas greeted his commander at headquarters. Monte was wearing a green tee shirt, camouflage pants, locally produced running shoes, and an LED wristwatch that a comrade in France had sent him. As usual, he wore no hat and no jewelry except for his wedding band. He drove with three companies to positions along a ridge overlooking the Agdam Plain and began setting up at about 3:00—a little later than he had wished. His fighters and tanks were to attack enemy firing positions in the Azeri ghost village of Merzuli at the foot of the ridge, and chase enemy gunners out of the area. Their longer-term goal was to establish a foothold in the Agdam Plain, as a first step towards capturing the depopulated town of Agdam.

If two months earlier Monte had tried to convince himself that his forces only entered territory that comprised Armenia's "historic homeland," he could no longer sustain that claim. Nobody even pretended that Agdam was part of the Armenian homeland. Even the contours of the expansive "Historic Homelands" map that Monte had drawn in the late 1980s veers clear of the Agdam Plain. From Monte's perspective, then, the battle for Agdam would be a battle for a bargaining chip, not a battle to defend the homeland.

Monte toured the front-line positions, to confirm that his fighters were clear about their orders: after "softening up" the area with artillery and tank rounds, subcommanders Mavo, Merujan, and Nelson would take their fighters down the ridge, and then split into their three respective companies. Mavo's company would proceed with their four tanks to Yusufjanli, a village of 600 houses about seven kilometers east of Agdam. Merujan's company would proceed to the neighboring village of Kiamatlu, while Nelson's company would proceed to the village of Merzuli. Backed up by Mountainous Karabagh forces from the Askeran district to the west, each company would chase the remaining enemy troops out of the area, and then torch the villages to deprive the enemy of cover, in case they should return to try to set up firing positions again. Upon completion of their tasks, the companies were to regroup at an intersection near Merzuli, to await further instructions.

After an hour of issuing battle instructions, Gomidas drove Monte, Saribeg, and a radio operator to the command post on the Cheyl Heights, a position designated Trench 08. They opened radio communications at 3:30 a.m. Monte had always preferred being on the front line during a battle, but this day he would stay behind at the command post. It was time for his fighters to get used to fighting without his leadership on the front line.

At four in the morning, an Azeri commander roused his troops from sleep at their bivouac at the bridge over the Gargar River on the plain, just to the east of the town of Agdam. There were around sixty soldiers in the fighting group, as well as a heavy tank and two light tanks, a BMP-1 and a BMP-2. The Azeri commander informed his young recruits that the enemy would attack that morning. They began packing their gear.

On Monte's order, cannons and tank guns shattered the silence of the dawn like dry boards breaking. After leveling much of Agdam and the surrounding Azeri villages, Martuni tanks and troop carriers trundled down from their mountains into the gently rolling Agdam Plain and joined a two-lane asphalt road that curved through abandoned orchards and wheat fields towards Merzuli. At an intersection just before Merzuli, they split into their three companies and headed to the targeted villages. Nelson's company, with a heavy tank at the lead, entered Merzuli from the south. By ten in the morning smoke was spiraling from Yusufjanli and Kiamatlu. Mavo's company had left five villagers dead in Yusufjanli, including an eighty-year-old woman, two younger women, and a thirty-four-year-old man who had been crushed by a tank as he had tried to flee. As soon as Monte had absented himself from the front line, it seemed, his fighters' conduct had degenerated.

From his position on the ridge, Monte frowned into binoculars while his radio fizzed with reports from his subcommanders on the plain below. His allies in the Askeran forces to the northwest had been out of radio contact for awhile. One of their tanks had either hit a mine or had been hit by an explosive round. In either case, the explosion had caused casualties and had halted the column before they had finished chasing enemy troops from the area north of Merzuli. As long as the possibility existed that enemy forces lurked nearby, it would be risky for Mountainous Karabagh fighters to take up positions in Merzuli. Monte contacted Askeran forces by radio and suggested that his own fighters complete their part of the operation. Meanwhile, Saribeg had stretched out for a nap in nearby bushes.

By then, the Azeri commander of the fighting group that had broken camp at the Gargar River had told his soldiers, quite inaccurately, that no Armenian forces had entered Merzuli. A party of Azeri scouts in a light tank entered Merzuli from the northeast, crossing terrain that Askeran forces were supposed to have captured and cleared, according to Monte's original battle plan. Unbeknownst to either side, the dust in the wake of Nelson's tank must have barely settled on the main road through Merzuli when the Azeri light tank rolled onto that same road just behind Nelson, from a dirt track leading into fields to the northeast. The light tank wheeled around and proceeded a short distance to the south end of the village.

From the north end of Merzuli, Nelson radioed Hovik, an ox-like subcommander from Jardar village, to report that he had captured an abandoned battle tank and a truckload of munitions. Hearing this,

Hovik turned to Monte and asked permission to take his staff car with Gomidas down into the plain, to confirm Nelson's claim. Since Nelson had crossed Merzuli from one side to the other, it would seem that it was now safe to enter the village.

"No, I need the car," Monte retorted. Hovik pressed the point. Finally, Monte relented: "OK, wait. We'll go check on Nelson together." Monte was just as eager as Hovik to confirm Nelson's claim of captured armor and munitions. Perhaps there was enough time to check it out before regrouping with his three companies in Merzuli, and then proceeding to clear the fields to the north of the village, as the Askeran fighters had failed to do.

The sun was directly overhead as Hovik, Monte, and the officer from Iran named Vartan climbed into the staff car with Gomidas and headed into the dun-hued plain, following the route that their tanks had just traversed. Just then, Saribeg shook himself awake. When it dawned on him that Monte and the others had left without him, he grabbed a walkie-talkie, hailed Gomidas, and told him he wanted to ride to Merzuli with them. Gomidas glanced sidelong at Monte as they jostled down the slope in the staff car. Monte had heard Saribeg's request crackle through the radio, but he didn't respond one way or the other. Gomidas downshifted and stopped the vehicle to wait, as Saribeg loped down the ridge towards them. When he hopped into the staff car puffing, they resumed their descent to Merzuli.

At the foot of the ridge, they picked up Saro Yeremyan, a huge-eyed subcommander who had just hitched a ride into the plain in a private car to fetch batteries for Monte's Alinco "mother" radio. Gomidas steered the staff car onto the road that curved across the plain towards Merzuli, in the north. At this point, he was driving five passengers: Saro, Saribeg, Vartan, Hovik, and Monte. When they approached a tractor station just south of Merzuli, they slowed down to greet Merujan and a small group of his fighters, who were loitering around an armored personnel carrier parked on the side of the road. Merujan's fighters hid a snake they had just killed, lest the sight of the creature provoke Monte's wrath. Even on a smoke-swept battlefield, the Martuni fighters knew by now not to tempt Commander Avo with evidence of a gratuitous killing.

As Monte congratulated Merujan on a successful operation, a three-axle truck barreled towards them from the opposite direction. Monte hopped out of his staff car and flagged the truck down, to discover that it was loaded with captured munitions, including twenty-five tank rounds. Was this the captured munitions that Nelson had reported earlier? A moment earlier, the truck had passed within a few meters of a light tank idling at an intersection about a kilometer up the road. Both parties, the Armenians in the truck and the light tank crew, must have assumed that the other vehicle was manned by friendly troops.

Monte instructed Merujan to reload two of his tanks with the captured rounds, to have the tanks lead the way into Merzuli, and then to proceed a couple of kilometers to the northwest, to the Gargar River. If the enemy were to infiltrate the area, Monte reckoned, they would come from that direction. The tanks were low on fuel, though, so Merujan's men would have to return to Martuni to fill up first, before catching up with Monte's staff car in Merzuli.

It was about 2:00 p.m. when the staff car and its six passengers passed the first cottages on the outskirts of Merzuli and approached an intersection fringed by yarrow, thistle, and sage. Suddenly, as they passed a stone fence, a BMP-1 loomed into view. The light tank was idling in a gravel turnoff, no more than twenty meters away. Three or four soldiers wearing an unfamiliar type of camouflage lounged on top of it, and several others loitered around it.

Asonk ov en? Monte asked, as Gomidas slowed down, "Who are these guys?"

Since Martuni headquarters had no BMP-1s, Gomidas assumed that the fighters and the light tank were back-up forces from Askeran, while Saro assumed they were from Pertashen. Gomidas pulled the staff car to a stop in the middle of the road and climbed out, automatically grabbing his rifle as he did so. Monte climbed out, too, walking around the front bumper to the driver's side. The young fighters lolling around the light tank paid little attention to them. Gomidas was wearing his favorite fatigue shirt, a war trophy with an Azerbaijani flag on the shoulder. He took several steps towards a soldier standing a few meters from the group, near the stone wall, and shouted in the local dialect of Armenian, *Elli ari esdegh*, "Come over here."

The soldier staggered back a step, with a confused expression.

Gomidas' eyes flashed. "*Boys, they're Turks!*" he shouted, as he charged his rifle and fired a burst at the soldiers scurrying to take cover behind the BMP-1. Behind him, the four remaining passengers jumped from the staff car and ran for cover under an instant hail of lead.

What happened in the next several seconds is not altogether clear: testimonies differ in details. Saro claimed that three or four enemy fighters fell to the ground, and Gomidas reported seeing several bodies fall, too. Monte might have returned fire at this time with his Kalashnikov while stepping backwards to take cover, or he might have dived to the road to avoid being hit, and then returned fire.

While Azeri soldiers riddled Monte's staff car, Saro and the others also fired back, revealing their positions in the process. The enemy fighters re-sighted, hitting Saro three times in the arm and side. He dragged himself to a gully to the east of the road and pressed his body to the ground. By this time, the enemy turret gunner had loaded and aimed his smoothbore cannon. Whistling like a train in a long tunnel, the 73-mm round flew high of the staff car and burst against a white stone fence on the opposite side of the road, knocking a hole in it and throwing up a cloud of dust.

As Gomidas dashed to take cover behind a stone wall, a second explosion knocked the corner off the wall and threw him to the ground. Turning, he squinted through the swirling dust, looking for Monte. Suddenly, he made out Monte's figure lying on his right side ten meters away, a few steps behind the staff car. He was not moving.

Gomidas ran a few steps towards Monte, but felt his left knee give way and a hot pang shot up his thigh. He had been hit in the knee with shrapnel. He shouted to Hovik to come and see what had happened to Monte, then he dragged himself into a shallow gully just a few meters from the enemy tank, between the stone fence and the road, and tried to cover himself with dry grass.

Hovik had been hit in one leg, too, but this did not prevent the hulking fighter from run-limping into the middle of the street, directly in front of the BMP-1, to pull Monte out of the line of fire. As he ran up, he saw Monte lying on the ground with a peaceful expression on his face. He lifted Monte by the shoulders to remove his walkie-talkie strap, but then dropped him when he saw the crushed side of his forehead, just above the right ear, and thick blood pooled under it. A large piece of shell casing had hit him from behind, probably over his right shoulder, as he was facing the Azeri tank with his back toward the wall. (Alternatively, the ricochet from the stone wall behind the staff car might have hit him over his left shoulder, as he momentarily turned his head back, towards the wall.)

Hovik stood in the middle of the road and wailed, *Avon cheega!* "Avo's gone!"

"He sort of forgot about the enemy," Vartan recalled to Seta four years later. "He stood in the middle and started yelling, screaming. I will never forget that voice."

"Kill me!" Saro moaned.

Hovik unstrapped the Alinco radio from Monte's shoulder. Weeping and rocking back and forth, he shouted into it: "*We need help!*"

Nelson's voice crackled through the hiss of the radio: "I'm on my way."

The Azeris continued firing, and the base radio in the staff car continued hissing, as it had throughout the confrontation. Finally, after perhaps fifteen minutes, the BMP-1 lurched forward and left the scene, accelerating down the road and then turning down the dirt track leading northeast, towards Azeri-controlled territory.

The wounded fighters from Martuni stayed put, waiting for the promised help. After five to ten minutes, they heard the squeal of tracks approaching from the direction in which the BMP-1 had just disappeared. It was another enemy light tank, this time a BMP-2, which jolted to an idling stop at the gravel turnoff next to the stone wall, just where they had encountered the first light tank. Suddenly, about twenty enemy infantry fanned out around the BMP-2, and Saro thought he heard a soldier shout in Turkish: "*You're finished! You're ours!*"

After several long minutes, Gomidas felt the ground tremble under the tracks of another approaching tank, but this time it was approaching from the south, the Armenian side. The commander of the idling Azeri light tank gunned the engine and retreated in the same direction as the first light tank, as a column of vehicles, including two BMPs from Martuni, approached the turnoff from the opposite direction. Abo jumped from one of the Martuni tanks and sprinted towards Gomidas, as enemy fighters covered their retreat with assault rifles, light machine guns, and rocket-propelled grenades.

"Avo's dead," Gomidas groaned, as Abo dragged him a couple of meters through the yellow grass, into the shade of a small tree. While Abo splinted Gomidas' leg with his rifle and an elastic band, four more Martuni tanks arrived. Vartan spread a handkerchief over Monte's head and helped Abo lift the body onto their tank.

Meanwhile, other Martuni fighters discovered Saribeg leaning against the foot of a pomegranate tree, clutching a grenade. The barrel of his rifle was still hot. He had a wad of shrapnel in his abdomen, and he was losing blood through a bullet hole in the leg. On the way to the hospital in a Martuni light tank, he cursed, begged for water, and moaned, "It's burning." By the time he arrived at Martuni Hospital in the basement under the kindergarten, he was unconscious. He died of blood loss shortly thereafter, leaving his five children without a father and his impoverished family without a breadwinner.

Earlier that day, Seta had awakened to dazzling sunshine slanting through her dorm room window in Yerevan. A few hours later, as she sat at a reception for the wake of a friend, someone sighed, "All the world is a lie." "No," Seta objected: "For my part, I've got Monte." When she returned to her dorm room and saw Haroyan waiting for her with his kepi under his arm, her breath caught.

"Where's Monte?" she asked.

"He's injured."

"Injured?"

"Heavily injured. In the head."

Seta's eyelids drooped: "You can tell me."

"He's dead."

Her next question was the same as mine: who had killed him?

Seta recalled a letter her husband had sent from prison: "I know that if nothing happens to me in my work, it's possible that I'll live long," he had written. But in a short article from 1978, he had quoted a line from the writer Shahan Shahnour: "We are Orientals, and we believe in what is called fate—what is written on our forehead." Dying of old age was not Monte's destiny, his *jagadakir*—literally, that which is written on one's forehead.

The next morning, June 13, Seta arrived by helicopter in Martuni. There, the entire town pressed into Opera Hall, where Monte, their Avo, lay in state on the stage in a shallow casket of unfinished wood, his forehead wrapped in white gauze. Women in headscarves and black dresses wailed, *Avo, vai vai vai! Vai Avo-jan vai vai!*

More than one of the locals begged Seta not to take Monte back to Yerevan, but to bury him in Martuni instead. He had died a Martuni fighter, and Martuni people bury their fighters in their own native land, not in distant cemeteries. There were others who believed that the remains of his body, like the relics of a saint, would ward off evil. Seta shook her head: no, Monte would be buried in Yerevan, the capital of Armenia.

The commander's fighters slid his open casket into the helicopter, followed by the casket lid. The chopper blew up a squall as it ascended, then it circled the mourners in the field three times clock-wise, in the direction of life, before heading west, towards Yerevan.

When the chopper set down in Yerevan an hour later, someone came up behind Seta and put his arms around her. Even before she turned to look at him, she knew it was Shishko. He lowered his face to her shoulder and wept.

Mom, Dad, Monte's childhood friend Joel, and I arrived in Yerevan without visas on the next flight from Paris, on June 17. Maile arrived via Moscow the next day. There, we met up with a contingent of Monte's old Parisian comrades, including Ara Toranian.

A visit to the morgue the next day settled one of the questions that had occupied my mind ever since Maile had telephoned me five days earlier with the bad news: had Monte suffered before dying? The trough above his eyebrow was deep, extending from his forehead to well behind his ear. It did not take a pathologist to figure out that he had died either immediately or within a couple of seconds, at most. This was a relief, as was Seta's report that when she had examined the body she had looked for evidence of mutilation, but had found none.

In addition to relief, however, another feeling swept over me, a feeling of déjà vu: the wound on the right side of my brother's forehead was the same wound that had appeared in my nightmares twelve years earlier, when Monte had writhed in slow motion under a hail of bullets, and the intolerable thought had occurred to me: *we're dying like dogs.*

"What a waste ..." Mom sighed in English, as she received unintelligible condolences from yet another delegation of mourners. "When I think of what he could have done as an archaeologist ..."

At that, Joel flashed me a sardonic smile and mused: "Yeah, he could have been a really *great* man ..."

On the morning of the burial, June 19, at daybreak, we followed the ambulance-hearse from the morgue to a small stone row house on a dirt street just off Marshall Baghramyan Boulevard. Until that morning, I had not seen the famous house that Monte had described so reverently, as if it were a palace. I was surprised, therefore, to step into little more than a pile of rocks framing out a few small rooms. The house had neither running water nor heat. But the kitchen window did indeed frame Mount Ararat.

Monte's rough wooden casket lay on a table in the largest room, and the camouflage-clad body lay in it, hands crossed at midriff as tradition dictated. Those hands looked too familiar, too young and supple to be the hands of a corpse. Reflexively laying my hand on them, however, a chill pulsed through my arm: they were as cold as stone.

Dad had been quiet all morning. He looked drawn and gaunt. Turning away from the casket, he said in English, half to Maile and half to himself: "This will reduce a man to nothing."

Joel plucked the long pinion of a redtail hawk from the band of his doffed cowboy hat and laid the feather in the coffin. Then pall-bearers in crisp fatigues hoisted the casket to their shoulders and bore it into the dirt street in front of the house. They turned the casket three times clock-wise, then slid it into the ambulance, to begin its final journey from house to grave, a short journey that would take up most of the day.

The sun had risen on a day too hot for a tie, but Dad, Joel, and I were wearing them anyway. For lack of a black dress, Mom wore a dark blue one. Maile would endure the day in black. More out of listlessness than deference to custom, I had not shaven since leaving Chicago. Only later did it occur to me that I was wearing the same suit jacket and pants that I had worn at my brother's wedding two years earlier.

According to tradition, the lid of the casket was not to be closed until the casket was lowered into the grave. I knew that the funeral would drag on throughout the hottest part of the day, and I was worried about my brother's body holding up. I had heard stories about the funerals of other martyrs, whose corpses had so badly decomposed that mourners gagged through their tears. This day, a woman from the morgue was following Monte's casket, periodically daubing his face with some sort of powder she kept in a little metal box. As it would turn out, the powder wasn't necessary, since Monte's skin never sank or spotted throughout that long hot day.

When we entered the Officers' Hall, a set of droning reed flutes (*duduks*) played *Siretsee Yares Daran*, "My Dearest Love Has Been Borne Away." Colonel Haroyan and the funeral committee had arranged for the music and for every other detail of their comrade's funeral. General Daribaltayan, the mastermind of the Kelbajar offensive, entered the hall almost unnoticed, and removed his kepi. Abo, Masis Hrair, Mosi, and the other fighters saluted their departing commander.

In death, Monte's compatriots were now referring to him as "General Avo," using the honorific title *Zoravar* for "General." During his lifetime, though, Monte never even achieved the rank of a full colonel. Just a couple of weeks before his death, in late May, Seta had learned that the Defense Committee in Stepanakert had promoted her husband to the rank of lieutenant colonel. When she mentioned it to him, he shrugged and said, "Won't make much difference to me." It wasn't the first time he had received a commission at that rank: a dozen years earlier, in the Lebanon days, Zaher al-Khatib had promoted Monte to the rank of lieutenant colonel in the Workers' League militia.

The reed flutes droned on. Two soldiers leaned a wreath of red carnations against the catafalque. The wreath, which had been ordered from Beirut, bore the message: *Ton viel ami Alec*, "Your old friend, Alec."

I estimated that 12,000 mourners, mostly haggard common folk, filed silently by that morning and early afternoon. For lack of suit jackets, they had donned threadbare sweaters in the heat, and for lack of presentable dress shirts, they wore their best tee shirts. The President and Vice-President of Armenia, their Ministers, parliamentary deputies, and Russian military officers paid their respects, too, and even infants in arms were quiet.

After what might have been a couple of hours, a Defense Ministry officer ushered our row of close family and friends out of the pew and led us to a room in the back for tea. When we returned to our pew perhaps twenty minutes later, we learned that the US Ambassador, Harry Gilmore, had made his appearance and left in our absence. I wondered whether Colonel Haroyan, ever attentive to details, had orchestrated this non-meeting, so as to avoid an awkward confrontation that day. The thought also occurred to me that this was the ambassador's last opportunity to peek into the coffin, to confirm Monte's death for the FBI.

At about two o'clock, we followed the honor guard and pall-bearers from the Officers' Hall, into the searing light. I blinked and surveyed the thousands of mourners who filled Republican Square. An amphibious scout car pulled the caisson to final rites at the seventeenth-century Church of St. Zoravor, and thence through streets and overpasses lined with mourners, to the military cemetery on the rocky hill of Yeraplur. Since the beginning of the war, young men had been coming to this hill to choose their own grave sites before leaving for battle in Mountainous Karabagh.

At the top of the hill, a single reed flute droned into the open grave, as censers rattled and black-clad women keened and ululated. The carnations and roses that mourners had piled on the tumulus were wilting under the sun. Brandishing a crucifix, the priest repeated the words of the fifth-century chronicler, Yeghishe: "Death knowingly grasped is immortality."

I'm not sure what sort of burial Mom had expected, but this day she was overwhelmed. Throughout his years underground, in prison, and on the run, she had had little to report about him to the proud mothers of realtors and attorneys at her garden club. But now, on the day he went to his grave, the son finally redeemed himself in his mother's eyes: the red carpets, the epaulets, the high-stepping honor guard in riding boots, the guests from nine countries, the generals in kepis and ribbons, the silver-haired dignitaries in tailored suits, the television cameras, the washed streets with freshly-filled potholes — but more than anything else, the endless queue of adoring mourners — all of this conveyed the message that in death at least, her son was no longer a convicted terrorist: he was a national hero, as she would now get used to saying.

Seta poured sand from Martuni into the coffin, and then Monte's soldiers closed the lid and lowered him into the earth he had died defending. Dust billowed from the open grave. Standing there under the hot sun, surrounded by hundreds of other graves and the stumps of trees chopped for firewood, Colonel Haroyan's low voice echoed in my head: "May Armenia's blessed earth rest lightly on your ashes."

The following morning we were chugging over peaks and gorges in a battered MI-8 helicopter overloaded with fighters, a prostitute wearing a crucifix, and 250 gallons of gasoline. Down below, a battle raged for the ruins of Mardakert. Meanwhile, 150 miles to the east, Surat Huseinov's rebel army, marching in the opposite direction from the battle, had approached within five miles of Baku. Two days earlier, before Monte had been buried, Azerbaijan's embattled President Elchibey had fled Baku for his native village of Keleki, in the isolated region of Nakhichevan, near the Iranian border. He had been in office one day short of a year. Earlier Azeri defeats at Shusha and Lachin had toppled President Mutalibov and brought Elchibey to power. Now the aftershocks of the rout in Kelbajar had toppled President Elchibey and cleared the way for the return of his rival, the wily former Soviet boss, Heydar Ali-Reza Aliev. Thus, Monte, the commander of the Kelbajar offensive, had done as much as anyone else — as much as Huseinov, Aliev, or any general in the Kremlin — to bring down Abulfaz Elchibey, Ankara and Washington's best hope in the Caucasus.

When we arrived at Martuni headquarters, an empty chair, plate, and glass had been set for the deceased commander in the buffet where he had taken his meals. On the nightstand next to his cot lay a paperback edition of Machiavelli's *The Prince* and a well-thumbed French edition of Sun Tzu's *The Art of War*. On the desk in his office, beneath the huge military map upon which Monte had traced new borders, lay his bloodstained fatigues, neatly folded. Next to the fatigues lay a surprisingly

large helix of shell casing, wrapped in gauze. In Yerevan, mourners had
clicked their tongues and sighed "If only he were wearing a helmet ..."
Examining this jagged chunk of shrapnel, however, it occurred to me
that he was lucky that he had *not* been wearing a helmet at that intersection a week earlier: by deflecting the full impact of such a large piece of
shell casing, a helmet might only have prolonged his suffering.

Colonel Haroyan confirmed the rumor that a member of the fighting
group that had killed my brother had been captured the day of Monte's
death and was being held in the Martuni jail. The following morning,
Seta and I met Haroyan at the municipal jail. We didn't know what to
expect when we took our seats around a table in the office. A moment
later, guards lead a porcelain-pale eighteen-year-old into the room and
grunted, to indicate that he should stand in front of us. He was a waif,
hardly more than a boy. Despite the thin scraggle on his chin, his yellow teeth, and the crud on his black wool pants and shirt, he was a
good-looking kid, with high cheekbones and fine features. I don't recall
the color of his eyes, but I'll never forget his dilated pupils. His eyes furtively darted right and left, and he was shaking. I imagine he expected
to be killed, or perhaps tortured first and then killed.

I motioned with my hand to the chair across the table. After he was
seated, I pointed to the black-and-white snapshot of my brother that I
had pinned to the chest pocket of my fatigues. One of the guards, a local
police officer in a gray uniform, translated from Azeri Turkish: "This is
a snapshot of this man's brother, this woman's husband. He was killed
the day you were captured."

The prisoner leaned forward and squinted at the snapshot. "Have
you ever seen him before?" the translator asked. The young man shook
his head. I asked a few more questions about what had happened in
Merzuli on June 12, but he didn't have much information about that,
either. To this day, I'm not sure why his fighting group had remained
behind in Merzuli, and I take it the prisoner was not clear about that,
either. Perhaps they had been on a scouting mission, or they might simply have lost their way.

"I hope you return to your family soon in good health, and that we
can all live in peace," I told him, pinning the snapshot back on my shirt
pocket. "Yes," he nodded with rheumy eyes, "Peace."

They ordered him back to his cell, and a guard pulled him up from
his chair. As he rose, he watched me rise, too, shifting my brother's rifle
on its sling. He must have been aware of the local custom, practiced by
nearest-of-kin on both sides in this war, of "sacrificing" enemy captives

on the graves of loved ones. As the guard led him out of the room, he was trembling like a man who believed he was being led to a gruesome death. I reached forward to steady his right shoulder. When my hand touched his arm, he jumped, as if he had received a jolt of electricity.

"Take it easy," I whispered in a language he didn't understand, "Take it easy."

Only later did it occur to me that neither Seta nor I had asked this young man his name.

In the jailhouse hallway, I had a few words with the ranking official in charge: "Bathe this kid and get him some clean clothes," I said. "And if you respect Avo's memory, please trade him for an Armenian hostage as soon as possible. Get him back to his parents in good health." I paused to make sure the jailer was looking me in the eye: "If you respect Avo's memory, do that." He nodded yes.

By this time, barely a week after the commander had fallen in the presence of four surviving witnesses with conformable testimonies, his death had already become enshrouded with rumors of betrayal and treachery. It's not surprising that Turkish newspapers have insinuated that Monte's own fighters had betrayed him. But even in the Armenian diaspora, in Yerevan, and in Martuni there are those who cleave to the belief that Monte was a casualty of "Armenian mafiosos who were angry with him for dumping their contraband wine or burning their cannabis fields," as an Armenian Heroes website phrased it. Others have whispered that the commander had been killed by the same pro-Ter-Petrosyan gunmen who had killed the late Artur Mkrtchyan, President of the Mountainous Karabagh Republic, and who ambushed and killed Norair Tanielyan, the twenty-seven-year-old commander of Mardakert, shortly after Monte's death.

And then there are those who have convinced themselves that an Armenian had tipped off the enemy about Monte's approaching staff car. The testimony of the young POW at the Martuni jail subverts this scenario, however, as do eyewitness testimonies that the Azeri fighters standing around the light tank in the turnoff had not been prepared for a confrontation, and had not even recognized the Armenian fighters as enemies until Gomidas charged his rifle. Despite the evidence, however, I am surprised how many Armenians cling to the belief that Monte had been the victim of a conspiracy.

According to other rumors, Monte had not died at all; rather, his reported death had been another ruse, a story planted to cover his disappearance underground, and his transfer to another front. Months after Monte's funeral, FBI personnel continued to doubt the reports of his death. In a secret teletype dated February 25, 1994, the FBI Field Office in Los Angeles wrote:

> Although Melkonian's death and funeral were widely reported in the news media, it is noted that the remains that were buried as his have never been officially confirmed by any means of positive identification as identical to the subject by any representative of the United States Government. Indeed, U.S. Embassy personnel were not allowed to view the body prior to burial.

The rumors and conspiracy theories continue to proliferate. But for my part, I'm convinced that Monte and Saribeg died in a chance encounter with Azeri fighters. My interviews with Gomidas, Saro, Hovik, and other eyewitnesses, and my visits to Merzuli have dispelled initial doubts about that. What happened on that road on June 12 was a skirmish between two groups of enemy fighters who surprised each other. And in this confrontation, one side, the Azeris, happened to have the advantage of armor and a 73-mm cannon.

An FBI special agent, one William O. Heaton, once described Monte to *Los Angeles Times* writer Mark Arax as "a soldier of fortune." But if this were the case, no one has yet discovered where he hid his fortune: he left no will-in-testament, no credit card, and no bank account. He never owned a car, and at the time of his death, the only rifle he carried belonged to the defense forces of the Mountainous Karabagh Republic. In fact, Commander Avo didn't even own a pistol or a bayonet as personal property. (Once, when one of his men had asked him why he never carried a pistol, he shrugged: "It's just extra weight.")

What others might have described as self-abnegation, Monte called *simplicity*. While his compatriots looked longingly to the West for "the finer things in life," Monte viewed simplicity as one of the finest things. Back in March 1981, he told Alec the following story: one morning a year earlier, while he was hurrying to work at Torossian High School in Beirut, he suddenly felt especially light, happy, exhilarated. For a moment he couldn't figure out why—until suddenly he noticed that instead of his usual shoes and socks, he was wearing only flip-flops! This was Monte, the man who coined that most un-American of slogans: "The less I have, the better I feel."

Since even Monte's worst detractors could not accuse him of doing what he did for money, I suppose FBI agent Heaton was compelled to

ascribe some other unsavory motive to him: "Some people just like killing people, don't they?" he quipped to *Los Angeles Times* writer Arax.
Bulgarian video journalist Svetana Pascaleva, a person who actually
knew Monte, described him rather differently: "He had the mentality of
a professional soldier, concern for his surroundings, good will, and an
uneasy conscience," says the narrator of one of her documentaries.
Monte himself recognized, perhaps better than his worst enemies, that
scores of civilians had paid with life and limb for his miscalculations
and blunders. His victims had included the casualties of the car bomb
in Beirut, nine casualties of a November 9, 1980 bombing in Rome, and
the fourteen-year-old girl in the back seat of the car in Athens. Then
came Karadaghlu and Kelbajar.

But the record should reflect that Monte had saved lives, too. It
would be preposterous, of course, to try to draw up a double-entry ledger of lives he had saved compared to lives he had taken. Nevertheless,
the fact remains that in addition to having killed, Monte had also
defended the defenseless. He had done so in Bourdj Hamoud between
1978 and 1980, at Kfar Tbnit in 1981, and during the Israeli invasion of
Lebanon in the summer of 1982. He had opposed Hagopian's "blind
terrorism," too, and for a while he had done so in the full expectation
that he would die in the process. Later, he and his fellow fighters had
defended the population of Shahumyan against the OMON, the Gray
Wolves, and the National Army of Azerbaijan. And in the last year of
his life, he and his fighters pushed murderous artillery and Grad rockets out of range of towns and villages in Martuni.

Though it may sound outrageous to survivors of Karadaghlu and
Kelbajar, the record should also reflect that, whenever he had an opportunity to do so, he thwarted reprisals against Azeri civilians and against
enemy prisoners and hostages. He directed fire away from Azeri villagers, and he tried to spare noncombatants suffering even more than they
had already endured. Just after the Kelbajar offensive, Kourken
Melikyan, an Iran scholar from Yerevan, spoke with a mother and her
two children sitting in an idling car in Stepanakert. They were Kurds
from Kelbajar, hostages on their way to the border to be exchanged for
Armenian hostages held by the Azeris. The mother blessed Avo by
name. "He saved our lives," she said, "If it weren't for him, I'm sure the
others would have killed us." In the course of researching this book,
I've encountered many such stories.

Shortly after his death, Monte's pacifist friend from the Berkeley
days, Armen S., wrote to Seta about her late husband: "He makes me

ashamed of myself," Armen said. Like Armen, I too "live so comfortably here in the United States, a nation based on genocide and conquest," as he put it. And like my fellow citizens, I too pay my taxes and try to ignore the torrents of blood that the CIA, the Pentagon, and Uncle Sam's dozens of death squads annually release in my name and with my tax dollars. This is the closest FBI agent Heaton and my fellow Americans, with their lazy abhorrence of "terrorism," have ever come to keeping their hands clean. My brother, at least, refused to let others do his killing for him.

Monte died at the age of thirty-five and one-half years, 110 years after his great-great-uncle Jacob Seropian had died at the same age. Separated by five generations, they crossed paths in opposite directions. "I am here a stranger and a pilgrim," Jacob had written after arriving in America. Monte, too, was a pilgrim of sorts. But unlike Jacob, Monte did not consider himself to be a stranger anywhere on Earth. And unlike Jacob, his long road had led him home.

The View from Yeraplur

I lug the bucket from the cistern and pour water over the gravestone. Bees buzz in the white petals of cherry saplings that grow
where, a few springs earlier, only stumps had escaped the fate of
firewood. As I pour the water, Seta wipes the slab, leaving shiny gray.
Swallows squeak in their looping flight as the afternoon sun goes
down.

There must be 700 graves at Yeraplur now, most of them marked
with headstones of polished gray basalt bearing portraits of martyrs
sandblasted into their surfaces: there are teenagers with the faces of
children; a couple of women in camouflage; one or two Yezidi Kurds
clutching rifles; a few faces I recognize, and many others I don't. One of
the first graves on this hill belongs to Haroot, the Arabo soldier who
died on August 20, 1990. This is the grave where Kechel Sergei "sacrificed" the Azeri captive, Syed. The tree irrigated with Syed's blood has
been cut down for firewood.

For all the graves here, Yeraplur contains only a small fraction of the
war dead. Monte's driver, Gomidas, for instance, is buried in his family
gravesite in Martuni. He was one of seven comrades who died on the
night of October 31, 1996, when they detonated an anti-personnel mine
while returning from a reconnaissance mission.

But not all of the dead were killed by Azeris: eighty steps to the south
of Monte's grave lie the bones of Garlen Ananian and Aram Vartanian.
Garlen's father dug up their grave in Iran with his own hands, and in
early 1994 he at last managed to transfer their remains to Armenia. In
this way, the elder Ananian fulfilled his son's last request, expressed in
Garlen's letter of July 1983, to be buried in Armenia. Next to Garlen and

Aram lies the grave of Tavit Tavitian, the young man who had set in motion the events that had led to their deaths. After years of restless wandering from Sweden to Sudan, Nepal, and Japan, he had finally settled in Yerevan before Monte's death. On the morning of October 29, 1997, someone shot him in the head while his three-year-old son looked on. "They put a hole in Daddy's head," the little boy told a visitor after the funeral. Ballistic evidence established that the bullet that had killed Tavitian had been fired from the same gun used fourteen months earlier, on August 9, 1996, to kill his former Secret Army comrade Khalil, who is buried next to Tavitian.

Just to the right of the entrance to the cemetery, the mortar has barely set on a stone monument dedicated to the martyrs of the Secret Army. Among these martyrs is Hagop Hagopian, the man who had tortured and killed Garlen and Aram. Thus death, ever indiscriminate, has brought the executioner into communion with his victim.

After June 12, 1993, the Martuni district defense command was divided into two headquarters, one headed by Mosi and the other by Nelson. In October 1993, these forces helped occupy all Azerbaijani territory south of Mountainous Karabagh to the Iranian border, creating another 200,000 Azeri refugees in the process. Azerbaijan launched a counter-offensive in late 1993, and the fighting raged for weeks. Three hundred Armenian fighters died and perhaps 4,000 Azeri fighters, before the counter-offensive sputtered out and a Russian-brokered ceasefire went into effect in May 1994. By then, the six years of fighting had created over a million refugees, perhaps two-thirds of them Azeris, and Human Rights Watch estimated that some 25,000 people had died in the war on both sides. Since the ceasefire, Azerbaijan's President Heydar Aliev has turned his attention to long-term diplomatic and economic isolation of Armenia, supported by the lure of Azerbaijan's oil resources in the Caspian.

The 1994 ceasefire continues to hold, more or less. But every week, new graves bloom on this hill. Today, at the edge of the graveyard, six new graves gape like open mouths, ready to swallow victims of a helicopter crash in Mountainous Karabagh.

Seventeen steps east of Monte's grave lies the grave of Vazgen Sargsyan. The war hero and former Defense Committee leader had just been appointed Prime Minister of Armenia when five gunmen burst into the parliamentary debating chamber in Yerevan on October 27, 1999. Shouting "Enough of drinking our blood!" they swung Kalashnikovs out of trench coats, and by the time the smoke had cleared Sargsyan and seven fellow parliamentarians lay dead.

The attack on parliament was only the most extreme expression of rising anger over poverty and corruption in post-Soviet Armenia. Back in September 1990, when Monte had first arrived in Yerevan, the city squares had radiated a hope that is now dead. The warm bodies packed together in Opera Square, the cracking voices, and a breathlessly urgent series of tasks had swept Monte into the embrace of a national unity that he had dismissed a few years earlier as a mere chimera. In Yerevan he had joined the processions, sung the anthems, and permitted himself to believe the four-column headlines and the angry eulogies.

But even as Armenians and Azeris were mauling each other in the mountains of Karabagh, several hundred "family businessmen," government ministers, and local brokers for foreign capital were plundering the country Monte would die defending. Since then, his compatriots have discovered a form of destitution that they had dismissed a few years earlier as a mere hobgoblin of the commissars. The rich have grown richer, of course, even as infant mortality and morbidity, unemployment, and suicide rates have soared, and income levels, life expectancy, marriage rates, and birth rates have plummeted. Beggars with Soviet-era college degrees panhandle in front of new pizza restaurants full of foreigners, while "entrepreneurial" young women hardly more than girls save up for the bus fare to seek their fortunes in the brothels of Istanbul.

In a published interview, Hemayag Haroyan recalled Monte's response to the question: how do you see Armenia's future? "One might have thought that he would have responded 'victorious' or 'with secure borders,'" Haroyan reported. "But no. He responded: *'Without corruption and just.'*" In the final decade of the twentieth century, the country has skewed further and further from that vision. What surely would have alarmed Monte most is the catastrophic level of emigration since Armenia returned to the capitalist fold: after a decade of "free market reforms," the population of the republic has fallen by one-quarter—down from 4 million in 1991 to less than 3 million in 2001—and emigration has reduced the population of Mountainous Karabagh to around 65,000, or less than half of its Armenian population at the end of the Soviet era.

As Seta and I finish washing Monte's gravestone, we notice a middle-aged man in a shabby jacket standing at a respectable distance, with folded hands. We don't know him, but it's clear that he has come to Yeraplur today to place flowers on the grave of a friend, perhaps, or a family member. Now, standing at Monte's grave, tears puddle in the hollows under his red-rimmed eyes.

Et mart ooreesh er, he whispers through gold teeth, "That man was different."

Here in the shadow of Mount Ararat, where Noah's Ark of salvation ran aground, I recall the Armenian proverb: the flood passes, the sand remains; the man passes, the name remains. Monte, it seems, is the only post-Soviet hero who has endured in Armenia. Nationalists, Communists, liberals, and the politically apathetic majority—they all revere him and claim him as their own. President Ter-Petrosyan declared him posthumously one of seven National Heroes of the Republic of Armenia, and he has received the highest honors in Mountainous Karabagh, too, including the Military Cross, First Order (on November 25, 1993) and the Golden Eagle medal (one of five recipients, on September 21, 1999). Today, new recruits take their oath in the plaza in front of Martuni's town hall, facing a heroic-scale marble statue of Commander Avo, with his walkie-talkie, binoculars, and rifle. Seven years after the commander's death, five out of seven of Mountainous Karabagh's District Commanders are soldiers who had served under Monte in Martuni.

Meanwhile, Armenia's erstwhile heroes have fallen, one by one: the first President of the post-Soviet republic, Levon Ter-Petrosyan, resigned in disgrace after accusations of election-rigging and the violent suppression of opposition demonstrators. His rival, Vazgen Manoogyan, the candidate who many believe had won an election that Ter-Petrosyan stole, has since joined Babgen Ararktsyan, Khachig Stamboultsyan, and the other former heroes in oblivion. Ter-Petrosyan's colleague, Vano Siradeghyan—a former mayor of Yerevan who had posed as a paragon of anti-Soviet virtue—is under indictment for the murder of his opponents, and has fled the country. Grinding poverty, corruption, and human rights abuses have also eroded the popularity of Ter-Petrosyan's successor, President Robert Kocharyan. Meanwhile, in Mountainous Karabagh, police have arrested thirty-five-year-old Samvel Babayan, recently promoted to the rank of general, and charged him with a March 22, 2000, ambush that wounded NKR President Arkady Ghukasyan and killed his driver. And so it goes on.

Some of Monte's admirers have claimed that he demonstrated the decisive influence that one individual can have on the fate of a nation.

But reviewing the sad condition of Armenia today, one could just as well conclude that even the most exceptional individuals cannot re-route a nation's fate. Others, admirers and detractors alike, may draw any number of lessons from Monte's example: one observer might discover in Monte's life proof that exceptional individuals, great heroes and villains, make history. Another might discover that his life illustrates the maxim that great men and women are themselves products of history. One observer might conclude with Saint Matthew that "all they that take the sword shall perish with the sword"; another might concur with the ancient chronicler Yeghishe that "Death knowingly grasped is immortality."

I myself am not sure what to make of the conflicting morals drawn from Monte's life, the incongruous pictures, the claims and counter-claims. But I do know that whatever lessons we draw will reflect as much about ourselves as about Monte.

I turn to scan the hazy horizon. Standing on this hill in this last year of a brutal century, I follow the green stretch of the Ararat Plain, the field of a hundred battles, beyond the watchtowers that mark the Turkish border. Perpetually ice-covered Ararat, the Mountain of Pain, towers above the plain. And the roads and rivers wind into the distance, far beyond what we can see.

Yerevan,
April 15, 2000

Notes

Preface to the Paperback Edition

page

viii "illegal to deny the Armenian genocide": In October 2006, the lower house of the French parliament passed a bill making it a crime to deny the Armenian genocide.

viii "Nubar Yalimian": Yalimian was shot in November 1982, in the Dutch city of Utrecht, allegedly by an operative of Turkey's National Intelligence Organization, the MIT.

Prologue: Funeral, 1993

page

xii "soldier of fortune": Mark Arax, "The Riddle of Monte Melkonian," in *Los Angeles Times*, October 9, 1993, pp. A1, A16. The reference appears on p. A16.

xii "the best god": Raymond Bonner, in an article with the dateline "Martuni, Azerbaijan," in *New York Times*, August 4, 1993, p. A3.

xii "the most battle-hardened fighting force": Thomas Caufield Goltz, *Azerbaijan Diary: A Rogue Reporter's Adventures in an Oil-Rich, War-Torn, Post-Soviet Republic* (Armonk, NY, and London: M. E. Sharpe, 1998), p. 392 (henceforth Goltz 1998).

xiii *Slayer of Soviets in Afghanistan*: Afghan war veteran General Anatoli Zinevich made this claim several times, including at least once in a televised interview in Armenia, and once in a 1998 interview that appeared in *Azk*, a Yerevan newspaper.

I: Small Town Kid

page

4 "strange that I stayed alive": *Self-Criticism* (*Eenknaknatadootioon*), (London: Kaytzer, 1990), p. 8 in the Armenian-language typescript. Approximately 14,000 words in length, the *Self-Criticism* was originally written in the winter of 1989–90 and circulated among a small number of Monte's comrades as a thirty-two page single-spaced typescript. The passage cited is from Seta's English-language translation of the text.

7 *Baseball terminology*: Juan Marichal, Willie Mays, and Roberto Clemente were famous baseball players during Monte's childhood. *Slider, change-up, knuckle-ball, curve, fastball*: Ways of throwing a baseball to make it more difficult for a batter to hit as it crosses home plate. *Catcher*: The player who squats behind the batter, to catch the ball when the pitcher throws it (assuming the batter doesn't hit the ball into the field). *Inning*: A division of a baseball game in which each team takes a turn at bat, ending with the third out. A game typically lasts nine innings.

2: A Riddle

page

13 *California Robin Hoods*: The venerable historian Hubert H. Bancroft shared our view that, "Murieta had higher aims than mere revenge and pillage," *The Works of Hubert Howe Bancroft, Vol. XXXIV: California Pastoral: 1769–1848* (San Francisco: The History Company, 1888), p. 646.

3: Stories of Forebears

page

20 "the first Christian Nation": According to the stories Monte read, his ancestors had been Christians since 301 AD, when King Drtad III of Greater Armenia hauled Saint Gregory, Bringer of Light, out of the dungeon hole where the king had entombed him for fourteen years. The saint promptly cured the king's disease — possibly lycanthrophy, "assuming a wolf-like mien" — and out of gratitude, Drtad proclaimed Christianity the religion of prince and people.

21 "culture rather than genetic lineage": "Our Origins: True and False," a short article that appears in Monte Melkonian, *The*

Right to Struggle: Selected Writings by Monte Melkonian on the Armenian National Question, 2nd edition (henceforth *RTS*) (San Francisco: Sardarabad Press, 1993), pp. 3–6. The quote appears on p. 5. Monte wrote "Our Origins" in 1981, but the sentiments pre-date the article by many years.

22 "I consider myself an Armenian": "Our 'Indo-European' Roots," in *Asbarez* (a bilingual newspaper published in Los Angeles), May 24, 1978, p. 2.

22 "secret Armenian revolutionary society": That "society," as it turns out, was the Social Democratic Hunchakian Party.

22 *Jacob's arrival in Fresno*: The date is not certain, but according to Jemima Kiramidjian, he arrived several years earlier than the 1881 date cited by numerous sources (including the author's daughters' fourth-grade California history textbook). Jacob's unpublished diary confirms Kiramidjian's testimony.

24 *Homesick, self-pity*: This is the clear impression that Jacob has conveyed in his diary, an accounting book containing 117 pages of family history, travel notes, favorite recipes, and hymns of his own composition, written in Armenian and unsteady English. Jacob began writing the diary some time after he arrived in Massachusetts in 1872, and continued until his death in 1883, at the age of thirty-five and one-half years. "All the years are past as fast as a gleam/It does seem to me just like a dream," he wrote in his *New Year's Day Song*, "But I am sank in Loneliness yet." Monte never read his great-greatuncle's diary; indeed he did not even find out about it until his early twenties, when I mentioned it to him in a letter.

25–6 "They tortured their victims": Rev. George H. Filian, *Armenia and Her People, or the Story of Armenia by an Armenian* (Hartford, CT: American Publishing Company, 1896), p. 243.

4: The Open Road

page

34 "diasporan Armenian": In a 1984 essay, Monte defined an *Armenian* as: "anyone (a) whose ancestors have been Armenian, and (b) who considers herself to be Armenian, or (c) who is more attached to Armenian culture (as a whole, not just in its religious, linguistic, or other aspects) than to any other culture" (*RTS*, p. 27). A *diasporan Armenian*, as the essay goes on to state

on the next page, is simply an Armenian so defined who resides outside the "homeland."

36 "Sooner or later": From a letter to the author dated September 3, 1987. The passage appears in *RTS*, p. 15.

37 "Who can forget": Judy Sanoian, "Hye Profile: Monte Melkonian," in *Hye Times*, No. 2 (March 1978), p. 2.

37 "too many Fs": *UCLA Daily Bruin*, October 4, 1977, p. 1.

37 "Entente propaganda mills": Stanford J. Shaw and Ezel Kural Shaw, *History of the Ottoman Empire and Modern Turkey, Volume 2: Reform, Revolution, and Republic: The Rise of Modern Turkey, 1808–1975* (Cambridge: Cambridge University Press, 1977), pp. 315–16.

37–8 *Paragraph 30*: When the UN Subcommission presented the final study to the Special Rapporteur on September 12, 1978, its 187 pages did not contain a single reference to the Armenian genocide.

39 "you should live through it": Letter to Seta Kabranian dated June 19, 1988.

39–40 "everything was so simple": *Self-Criticism*, p. 4.

5: Pilgrimage

page

41 "some sort of Mexican shirt": The account of Monte's 1978 visit to London is based on his personal correspondence and conversations with the author, as well as conversations and telephone interviews with Nejdeh Melkonian conducted by the author between October 1991 and 2000.

42 "I just looked at a world map": Letter to Armen S. dated April 25, 1988.

44 "difficult to gain the confidence": *Self-Criticism*, p. 10.

45 *Young avengers*: Arshavir Shiragian (1900–73): Under the direction of the Armenian Revolutionary Federation, the Dashnak Party, Shiragian and five or six other young men carried out Operation Nemesis, a campaign to assassinate top Turkish leaders responsible for the genocide against Armenians of the Ottoman Empire between 1915 and 1918. Beginning in 1921, Shiragian assassinated former Turkish Grand Vizier Sayid Halim Pasha, Committee of Union and Progress leader Behaeddin Shakir Bey, and Jemal Azmi Pasha, the Governor-General of Trabzon. Soghomon Tehlirian (1897–1960): In 1921, Tehlirian

assassinated Talaat Pasha, Minister of Interior and head of the Committee of Union and Progress, the ruling Ottoman clique during the Armenian genocide. A German court tried Tehlirian and found him not guilty.

47f *Monte's trip to Afghanistan*: The next year, on December 24, 1979, Soviet tanks rolled into Afghanistan. In a letter to his folks dated February 12, 1980, Monte wrote: "The Soviet invasion of Afghanistan is, in the long run, going to hurt the USSR in immeasurable ways."

47 "most amazing things ... kissing the police": Letter dated September 24, 1978, written soon after his return to Beirut, but postmarked from Syria.

48 *The massacre at Jaleh Square*: William Sullivan, US Ambassador to Tehran from June 1977 to April 1979, suggested that "over two hundred demonstrators were killed" in the square that day (Waheed Uz-Zaman, *Iranian Revolution: A Profile* (Islamabad: Institute of Policy Studies, 1985), p. 64). Other Western observers have upgraded the body count to 1,000 fatalities or more (refer, for example, to: Barry Rubin, *Paved with Good Intentions: The American Experience and Iran* (New York and London: Penguin Books, 1981), p. 214, and Dilip Hiro, *Iran under the Ayatollahs* (London: Routledge & Kegan Paul, 1985), p. 77). Another pro-Washington pundit has written that the shah's troops killed "many thousands of innocent demonstrators" that day (R. K. Ramazani, *Revolutionary Iran: Challenge and Response in the Middle East* (Baltimore and London: Johns Hopkins University Press, 1986), pp. 164, 205). Opposition figures in Iran claimed that over 4,000 demonstrators were killed in Jaleh Square, a figure said to be confirmed by the number of burial certificates issued at the Behisht-e-Zehra Cemetery (Ali-Reza Nobari (ed.), *Iran Erupts* (Stanford, CA: 1978), p. 196; Uz-Zaman, p. 64, citing an eyewitness report that appeared in *Le Figaro*, September 9–10, 1978). On p. 159 of Ramazani's book, the author mentions the charge that Israeli soldiers had been present in the square and had joined the shah's troops that had fired into the demonstration. In a letter from Iran, Monte reported this charge as a fact.

48 "I straightened them out": Letter dated September 12, 1978, addressed to Dear Everyone. The account of Monte's short-lived career at the Iran-American Association is based mostly on the

author's conversations with Monte, and on a June 14, 2003 interview in Yerevan with Tehran native Vahig Sh. Several months after the strike, in 1979, a bomb gutted the Association's building and the school closed its doors.

51 "the most crucial years": Both Alec and Monte used this phrase more than once in conversations with the author.

52 "the white massacre": *RTS*, p. 6.

56 *Yeghishe the Chronicler* (Latinized form: Elisaeus): Monk, purportedly a warrior under Vartan Mamikonian, and author of *The War of Vartan and the Armenians*. (Refer to the entry "Avarair, Battle of," in the Glossary.)

57 "the hard way": Letter to Armen S. dated April 25, 1988.

6: Time of Turmoil

page

60f *The journey to Haftvan and Mahabad*: This account is based in large part on the author's interviews with Raimond Kevorkian (Paris, April 1, 1997) and Vahig Sh. (Yerevan, April 22, 2000), as well as Monte's letters and conversations.

60 *Destitution of village life*: Quoted passages in this paragraph are from Monte's Dear Family letter of September 9, 1979 from Iran.

62-3 *A Phalangist began shouting*: The account in this paragraph is based in part on Seta's interviews with Manushag and Hagop Stepanian (New Jersey, August 25, 2000).

64 "As a very minimum": The passage is from an article entitled "The Question of Strategy," which first appeared in 1984. (The article was included in *RTS*, pp. 53–72; the passage quoted appears on p. 59.)

65 *The confrontation at Nazo's house*: This account is based on the author's conversations with Monte and Cousin David not long after the event took place, and on a conversation between Seta and Vartkes in the late 1990s.

66 *Marxism as a fashionable jargon*: This appears to have been a common view among Monte's admirers in Armenia, and it was Sarkis Levonian's opinion, too, in a published interview with H. Jack Aslanian ("Home at Last: Monte Melkonian," *Armenian Observer*, October 12, 1994, pp. 7–11).

67 "an eventual change of address": Dear Everyone letter from Fresnes Prison dated January 10, 1987.

7: Underground

page

76ff *Hagopian's biography*: The information in the following paragraphs was drawn from interviews with former Secret Army members who must remain anonymous, as well as the following three texts authored in whole or in part by Monte: *History of ASALA (HOA)* (in particular, the section entitled "Who Is 'Hagop Hagopian'?" pp. 88–151); *The Reality*; and the previously cited *Self-Criticism*. (*History of ASALA* was published without Monte's consent by unknown persons, supposedly in Lausanne, Switzerland in 1990. *The Reality*, 17,000 words in length, was compiled collectively in 1984, and then updated in January 1985 and circulated in photocopy form in the English version. After another revision in early 1991, an Armenian translation was published in Yerevan in 1992, together with two other texts, under the imprimatur of "ASALA-Revolutionary Movement.") Other sources include: Seta's 1996 conversation with "Holandaee" Vartan, a former schoolmate of Hagopian's from Mosul; back issues of the Secret Army journal, *Armenia* (from the first unnumbered issue of fall 1980 to the commemorative issue entitled *ASALA: 1975–1995*); published interviews with the Secret Army chief, and a critical reading of the *Memoirs of Hagop Hagopian*, published as a pamphlet in English translation in Beirut (no date; no publication information).

76 *Haddad's group dismantled itself*: Even after the Foreign Operations Branch dissolved, Haddad continued planning operations independently, including the December 21, 1975 seizure of seventy hostages at the Vienna headquarters of OPEC by a group calling itself "The Arab Revolution." The Vienna operation was led by the Venezuelan "Carlos."

76–7 *Abu Iyad*: In 1959, Abu Iyad (*nom de guerre* of Salah Khalaf), then about twenty-five, co-founded *al-Fateh*, the largest Palestinian guerrilla group, together with Yassir Arafat (Abu Ammar), and Kalil Wazir (Abu Jihad). After King Hussein's September 1970 massacre of Palestinians in Jordan, Abu Iyad formed the "Black September" guerrillas who killed eleven Israeli athletes (many of whom had been reservists in the Israeli army) at the 1972 Munich Olympics. Israeli operatives assassinated Abu Jihad in 1988 and killed Abu Iyad and two colleagues in Tunis on January 14, 1991.

78ff *Secret Army activities*: The account in this and the following
chapters is drawn from many sources, including first-hand
observations, eyewitness testimonies, Seta's reminiscences of
Monte's stories, newspaper clippings, and a critical reading of a
small library of published and unpublished material. The published material includes back issues of a variety of periodicals,
notably the Secret Army journal *Armenia* and Ara Toranian's
tabloid, *Hay Baykar* (issue Nos. 1–124, published between 1978
and 1988), as well as texts authored in whole or in part by
Monte. The latter category includes the collectively written
studies, *A Critique of Armenian Armed Action from the Early 1970's
until December 31, 1983* (distributed in the mid-1980s by the
Kaytzer group in London as a photocopied 126-page book
under the imprimatur of "ASALA-Revolutionary Movement"),
and *A Critique of Armenian Armed Action from 1985 to 1987* (distributed in 1988 by the Kaytzer group as a photocopied
seventeen-page pamphlet under the imprimatur of "ASALA-
Revolutionary Movement"), along with Monte's handwritten
corrections and addenda to these texts.

81 *Monte's plan to visit Armenia*: In a letter of February 22, 1980 to
his sister Maile, Monte had written of his plan to be in Soviet
Armenia by June 18 of that year: "Of course, these are my plans
as of now," he had written, "There are months ahead of me
which could affect these plans."

82 *Kohler*: "a Bavarian Neo-Nazi who belonged to no organization," and "a lone wolf without an organization". The phrases,
respectively, are from: George Rosie, *The Directory of International Terrorism* (Edinburgh: Mainstream Publishing, 1986), p.
206; and Hans Josef Horchem, "Terrorism in Germany: 1985," in
Paul Wilkinson and Alasdair M. Stewart (eds.), *Contemporary
Research on Terrorism* (Aberdeen: Aberdeen University Press,
1987, pp. 141–63), p. 150.

82 *Freikorps Adolf Hitler*: Refer, for example, to Horchem, "Terrorism in Germany" (in Wilkinson and Stewart), pp. 154–5. Later,
when Hagopian had a falling out with Abu Iyad, the Secret
Army journal *Armenia* exposed the Hoffman gang's relations
with the Palestinian leader (*Hayastan*, No. 77–8, 1983, p. 58).
West German police arrested Hoffman in February or March
1981 in connection with the murder of two Jewish writers in
Erlangen, Germany on December 19, 1980. The presumed trig-
german, Uwe Behrendt, committed suicide in Lebanon in 1981.

82 *Neo-Nazis at the Fatah base*: Beirut-based journalist Robert Fisk
has raised the question of Hoffman's ties with the Lebanese
Phalangists (*Pity the Nation* (New York: Atheneum; Oxford:
Oxford Paperbacks, 1990), pp. 169–72). It should be pointed out
that more representative Palestinian leaders, including George
Habash of the PFLP, Nayef Hawatmeh of the Democratic Front
for the Liberation of Palestine, and Abu Jihad, deputy to Yassir
Arafat in Fatah, rejected any association with neo-Nazis.

82 *Fascists our father fought*: During World War II, Staff Sergeant
Charles Melkonian flew twenty missions over Nazi-occupied
Europe as a radio operator and side gunner on an Army Air
Corps B-17 Flying Fortress, in the 8th Air Force, 385th Bomb
Group. Dad rarely mentioned his wartime experiences, and he
never showed us the Air Medal and the other little medals he
kept in a box with his cufflinks. Nevertheless, referring to his
father's example during World War II, Monte once explained
that "It was that inspiration—not the stories of the 'Old Country'
that my grandfathers whom I had never known used to tell—
that gave me the conviction to struggle against fascist occupation and oppression" (*Armenia*, No. 21–2 (March 1982), p. 66).

83 *Carlos Marighella (1911–69)*: A former Communist militant,
Marighella is best known as the author of *The Mini-Manual of the
Urban Guerrilla*. In the mid-1960s, he helped found an underground group called Action for National Liberation, which
fought the brutal US-supported dictatorship that had over-
thrown the government of populist leader Joao Goulart in a
March 1964 coup. Brazilian police shot and killed Marighella in
1969.

84 "dark glass windows": Monte Melkonian, *HOA*, p. 198. Eventually, Monte would come to regret shooting the attaché's wife,
too (author's April 1997 interview with Alec Yenikomshian).
Also refer to: *A Critique of Armenian Armed Action from the Early
1970's until December 31, 1983 (CAAA)*, p. 38, and *Self-Criticism*,
p. 28.

Monte wrote *HOA* in English in late 1985, but he quickly had
second thoughts, and destroyed what he believed was the only
version of the manuscript in existence. Five years later, he was
surprised and angry to discover that someone somehow had
published an unauthorized version of the book. The published
version contained no publication information, aside from the

dubious claim that it had been translated into Armenian by one "Azad Mardirosian" and printed in Lausanne in 1990.

87 "keep your gun after getting it": From "A Message," in *Armenia*, No. 10–11 (July–August, 1981), p. 98.

88 *Rita Porena*: In an interview published in *Milan Panorama* (September 1, 1980, pp. 62–5), Porena described the Secret Army as "the most mysterious and best-organized armed formation operating in the Middle East and Europe." Though her accuracy left something to be desired, Monte admired her dedication and sincerity.

88 "anarchistic and Mafia-like": *CAAA*, p. 29.

94 *Alec at Yanta*: This account is based largely on Alec's testimony, as well as Monte's recollections to Seta in 1989 and to the author in late July 1991.

8: Terrorist Suspect

page

95 "historical and cultural attachment": *RTS*, p. 179 (emphasis in the original).

96 *Devastatingly accurate barrages*: Jonathan C. Randal, *Going All the Way: Christian Warlords, Israeli Adventurers, and the War in Lebanon* (New York and London: Viking Press, 1983), p. 242. Israeli military commanders described the July 16, 1981 Palestinian rocket counter-attack as "one of the most intense in recent years" (*New York Times*, July 16, 1981, p. A3).

96 *July 1981 casualties*: Casualty figures for the invasion are drawn from Western sources, notably the *New York Times* (which has tended to minimize Arab civilian casualties). One Israeli airstrike alone — a strike on Fakhani on July 17, 1981 — killed 350 civilians and wounded hundreds of others (see, for example, Douglas Watson's report in *Baltimore Sun*, July 22, 1981).

96 "little or no military damage": *New York Times*, July 25, 1981, p. A4.

97f *The takeover of the Turkish consulate in Paris*: This account is based on numerous sources, including: published reports from the French press; back issues of *Hay Baykar*; Monte's description of the operation in conversations with the author in Yerevan in July 1991; the author's April 1997 interview with Ara Toranian in Paris, and a conversation with Vazken Sislian, Hagop Julfayan, Seta; and the author in Yerevan in late April 1997. The

Secret Army journal *Armenia* dedicated much space in two issues, No. 16 (October 1981) and No. 17–18 (January 1982), to this operation and its aftermath.

98f *Rome, Milan, Paris*: This account is based on numerous sources, including: the author's conversations with Monte in Yerevan in July 1991; Seta's conversations with Monte (reported to the author in Yerevan, April 1997); and the testimony of several former Secret Army members who must remain nameless. Written sources include relevant passages in *HOA*, *CAAA*, *The Reality*, and *Self-Criticism*.

98 *Absorbed in thoughts about architecture*: Monte described the scene to Seta in 1989, complete with interior dialogue. Seta related his account to the author in April 1997, in Yerevan.

99ff *The Georgiu affair*: The account is drawn in large part from Monte's serialized report, "Orly and the Georgiu Affair," which appeared in *Armenia*, No. 21–2 (March 1982), pp. 60–6; and No. 23–4 (April–May 1982), pp. 56–62.

102f *Family visit to the Seventh Floor*: This account is based on Monte's recollections to Seta, as well as the author's interviews with Charles, Zabelle, Maile, and Marcia Melkonian.

103 "What could we do?": John D. Cramer, in *Fresno Bee*, September 20, 1992, p. A14.

104 "in front of everyone": *Self-Criticism*, p. 21.

105 *Lebanese and Palestinian defenders*: According to a Western journalist who visited the region at the time of the invasion, the defenders consisted of a total of 11,200–12,200 Palestinian fighters, Lebanese militiamen, and Syrian troops (Michael Jansen, *The Battle of Beirut: Why Israel Invaded Lebanon* (Boston: South End Press; London: Zed Books, 1982), p. 4). With few exceptions, the estimated 1,200 Syrian troops avoided fighting with the vastly superior Israeli military. *The Jerusalem Post* of June 7, 1982 estimated that PLO forces in south Lebanon numbered 6,000 armed men — about one half of the PLO's total strength in Lebanon.

105 "retreat with no losses": *CAAA*, p. 30. The account of the 1982 Israeli invasion is drawn largely from Seta's conversations with Monte, the author's conversations with Monte in Yerevan in July 1991, and the following texts: *HOA*, *CAAA*, *The Reality*, and *Self-Criticism*. During the invasion, the author compiled a large file of clippings from major US newspapers. Other published sources include: Noam Chomsky, *The Fateful Triangle: The*

United States, Israel, & the Palestinians (Boston: South End Press; London: Pluto Press, 1983); Fisk; Walid Khalidi, *Conflict and Violence in Lebanon* (Cambridge, MA: Center for International Affairs, 1979); Selim Nassib and Caroline Tisdall, *Beirut: Frontline Story* (London: Africa World Press, 1983); and Randal.

106 *Casualty figures*: Fisk, p. 418. Incomplete Lebanese government figures put the toll from the first eighty days of fighting at 19,000 killed.

106 *Habib's pledge to defend refugees*: Refer to the account in Fisk, pp. 333–4.

107 *"greatest of ease"*: HOA, p. 252.

108 *Over 1,000 corpses*: Fisk, pp. 389–90; Randal, pp. 15–16; Chomsky, pp. 369–70.

108 *Air Force "liaison officer"*: HOA, p. 66. The officer in question might have been either Colonel Haithan Said, head of the Intelligence Department of the Syrian Air Force (Gaidz Minassian, *Guerre et terrorisme arméniens* (Paris: PUF, 2002), p. 79), or Mohamed Khouli, secret service chief of the Syrian Air Force. Khouli was close to Syrian President Hafez al Assad's younger brother, Rifaat. The younger Assad, who commanded Syria's elite Defense Brigades, was one of Hagopian's benefactors (as an Agence France-Presse report of February 13, 1986 accurately conjectured), but only until President Assad banned him from public office. The author has not found any evidence that President Assad ever endorsed Rifaat's relationship with Hagopian; indeed, the Syrian leader probably did not even know about the relationship at the time. Hafez al Assad was an instinctively cautious leader who tried hard to resist the provocations of his hostile and enormously more powerful neighbors, Israel and Turkey.

108 *one and the same organization*: Hagopian's communiqué appeared in *The Armenian Reporter*, Thursday, September 30, 1983, pp. 1, 14.

110 *"thought more quickly"; "unrealistic"*: Self-Criticism, pp. 23, 27, respectively.

9: Martyrdom

page

111ff This chapter is based in large part on Monte's detailed accounts in *HOA*, *Self-Criticism*, and *The Reality*, in addition to the author's conversations with Tavit Tavitian and the parents of Garlen Ananian, Mr. and Mrs. Hovsep Ananian. Other sources include Hagop Hagopian's videotapes of the events of July and August, 1983, as well as Monte's personal correspondence and his description of these events in conversations with Seta in Eastern Europe in 1989 and with the author in Yerevan in July 1991. Alternative accounts of events, as reported in the journal *Armenia* (notably Nos. 67–8 and 77–8, from late 1983), and other pro-Secret Army literature provide little in the way of reliable information.

114 "a very, very dangerous plan": The citations in this paragraph are from *Self-Criticism*, pp. 25–6.

118 *Karnusian's crippled Congress Movement*: The Reverend died in Moosseebordf, a suburb of Bern, on April 8, 1998, at the age of seventy-two. According to a report in an Armenian-American newspaper, he "ended his efforts on behalf of his people" and retired "a broken and frustrated man" (*Armenian Reporter*, April 18, 1998, p. 28).

119ff *Strangers approached Seta's father*: This account of events in and around Ainjar after July 15, 1983 is based largely on Monte's reminiscences to Seta, and on the testimonies of Seta's parents and sisters, as related to Seta not long after the events transpired.

123 "if guilty people should be punished": *Self-Criticism*, p. 28.

10: Good-Doers

page

137ff Much of this chapter was drawn from Seta's conversations with Monte and Levon "Shishko" Minassian in 1989 and 1990, as well as the author's April 1997 interviews with Ara Toranian and former associates and acquaintances in France, including Stepan Injeyan, Valerie Toranian, Zepur Kasbarian, Benjamin Keshishian, and Jeannette Samurkas. Written sources include *The Reality* and *Self-Criticism*, in addition to French police records, court documents, and clippings from French and Armenian-language newspapers and journals.

139–40 "highly unlikely … collective cultural life … possible re-unification": Letter of October 12, 1986 to Armen S.

141 "slightly elaborate process": In conversation with the author, July 1991.

142 "a haven for all murderers and traitors": Unsigned statement, *Armenia*, November 1985, p. 59.

145 "There's a rule among us": Alec was not the only comrade to have been injured while assembling a bomb: On July 30, 1982 — less than a year after the mishap at the Hôtel Beau-Site — a sickening bang summoned Khatchadour Gulumian into a smoke-filled cellar in the Paris suburb of Gagny, to find his brother, Pierre, slumped over a work bench splattered with his partially missing head. Noting that Pierre was an explosives expert, Monte ascribed his slip-up to his conflicted state of mind, after having received an order from Hagopian to place a bomb in the path of innocent passers-by (*The Reality*, pp. 22–3).

146ff *Monte's legal battles*: This account is based in part on the author's interviews with Ara and Valerie Toranian (in Paris in late March and early April, 1997), and with attorneys Henri LeClerc and François Serres (in early April, 1997), in addition to the relevant police reports and court documents. The author wishes to thank Myriam Gaume for her help procuring these documents.

146 *association de malfaiteurs*: In an open letter to *Hay Baykar*, Monte scoffed at the charge: "Benjamin Keshishian and Zepur Kasparian have been arrested because of alleged contact with me, and accused of association with *malfaiteurs*. It is therefore logical to conclude that I am the *malfaiteur*." At the same time, "the French government accuses me also of association with *malfaiteurs*. Who are the *malfaiteurs* this time? Benjamin Keshishian and Zepur Kasparian." "Here in France," Monte concluded, "patriotic activities have become crimes, and patriots criminals." (The open letter was dated February 5, 1986 and appeared in the February 25 edition of *Hay Baykar*, p. 5.)

148 "educated, intelligent, and nice": Dear Everyone letter of January 19, 1986.

149 *Mexican food*: In conversation with the author, spring 1980.

150 *Prieur and Mafart's fate*: A New Zealand court handed down ten-year sentences to the accused French agents. After less than two years in prison, they were sent to resort-style accommodations on France's Hao Atoll in the South Pacific, presumably to complete their sentences.

150-1 "Worst is yet to come": Dear Folks letter of February 8, 1986.

152f *Monte's trial*: This account is based largely on court documents, police reports entered as evidence in the trial, and Monte's personal correspondence at the time. Reports of the courtroom proceedings on November 28, 1986 appeared in the following issues of *Hay Baykar*: December 20, 1986 (a front-page story entitled "Proces Melkonian"); January 25, 1987 (pp. 3ff); and February 25, 1987 (p. 5).

152 *A police reporter present*: Author's interview with anonymous police officer in Paris, February, 1997. Thanks to Myriam Gaume, once again, for arranging this interview.

152 *Zepur in total isolation*: In a letter of July 9, 1988, Monte noted that: "Amnesty International had criticized the French government for putting dozens of political prisoners into total solitary confinement (as I was for four weeks in 1981 and for 7 weeks in 1985/86), which it accurately describes as a form of torture."

153 "absolutely amazed ... battle isn't over": Dear Everyone letter of December 13, 1986.

11: Serving Time

page

154ff Much of this chapter was drawn from Seta's reminiscences and from Monte's personal letters to her and to other correspondents, notably his family. Monte wrote hundreds of letters from prison, filling thousands of sheets of airmail stationery with small, spidery script on both sides of the paper.

154–5 "Many guards are very racist": Letter of July 28, 1986 to documentary filmmaker Ted Bogosian.

156 "almost an honor": Dear Everyone letter of July 26, 1986.

156 *Judges should spend time in prison*: Dear Everyone letter of May 23, 1987.

156 *Prison makes things worse*: Letter of November 28, 1987.

157 "reactionary marble heads": Dear Everyone letter of October 1, 1986.

158 "They're going to create huge problems": Dear Everyone letter of March 15, 1987.

158 *Prison rebellions*: The account is drawn from Monte's personal correspondence, as well as interviews and conversations with Seta and Valerie Toranian.

160 *Mountainous Karabagh*: English-language sources often refer to the region as "Nagorno Karabagh" or "Nagorno Karabakh." (Refer to: "A Note on Usage" in the Glossary, and to the Glossary entry "Artsakh.") In Azeri Turkish, *Karabagh* means "Black Garden," and the Russian modifier *Nagorno* translates as "High" or "Mountainous." Mountainous Karabagh is to be distinguished from the surrounding lowlands of Lower Karabagh, with its overwhelmingly Azeri-Turkish population.

162 *The massacre at Sumgait*: According to Human Rights Watch/ Helsinki, the massacre claimed thirty-two lives, mostly Armenians. (HRW/H, *Seven Years of Conflict in Nagorno-Karabagh* (New York, Washington, DC., Los Angeles, London, Brussels: HRW/ H, December 1994), p. 1). Also see: Samvel Shahmuratian (ed. and compiler), *The Sumgait Tragedy: Pogroms against Armenians in Soviet Azerbaijan: Volume I: Eyewitness Accounts* (New Rochelle, NY, and Cambridge, MA: Aristide D. Caratzas and The Zoryan Institute for Contemporary Armenian Research and Documentation, 1990).

165 *The strange emissary*: Highly redacted documents released by the State Department in response to the author's repeated Freedom of Information Act requests provide little insight into the identity of this visitor, and the National Security Agency has denied the author's FOIA requests for disclosure of files listed under Monte's name. (The NSA has cited several exemptions from disclosure, including Executive Order 12958, according to which the FOIA does not apply to matters that are to be kept secret in the interest of national defense or foreign relations.) Marvin Groeneweg, at the US consulate in Paris, might have provided some insight into the emissary's identity, but staff at the consular section of the US embassy in Paris claimed in late March 1997 that Mr. Groeneweg had passed away.

165 "the biggest murder hunt in history": Rodney Wallis, *Lockerbie: The Story and the Lessons* (Westport, CT, and London: Praeger, 2001), p. xiii.

166ff *Shishko fought Monte's extradition*: This account is based in large part on an interview that Seta and the author conducted with Shishko in Yerevan, late April 1997, and on the author's conversations with Monte in July 1991. The description of Monte's stay at the depot at the Île-de-la-Cité and at the Coqvert is based largely on the author's interviews and conversations with Ara and Valerie Toranian (Paris, April 1997), Myriam Gaume (Paris, April 1997), and CSAPP member Achod Schemavonian (Etape Coqvert, March 29, 1997), in addition to Seta's conversations with Monte.

Chapter 12: Wandering through Ruins

page

170 "warmer climate": Letter of September 10, 1988. Much of the information in this chapter and in the first pages of Chapter 13 is based on Seta's detailed testimony, which she related to the author over the course of more than one week in late April 1997. Other sources for this chapter include the author's conversations with Monte in July 1991, and his April 1997 interview with Shishko.

173 "blow the horn": Letter to author, dated January 10, 1987.

174 "stupid … very naïve" idea: *Self-Criticism*, p. 29.

174 "efficiency in certain necessarily centralized domains": The phrase appears in the collectively written "Charte politique provisoire du Front Patriotique pour la Liberation de l'Arménie" (unpublished, 1989), p. 5.

175 *public masochism*: Author's interview with Ara Toranian in Paris, March 23, 1997.

176 "And me, I'm a communist": Quoted in Myriam Gaume, *Les Invités de la Terre* (Paris: Editions du Seuil, 1993), p. 123. Gaume interviewed the elder Ter-Petrosyan in 1990.

178 "This country's headed for war": Seta's reminiscence. In an unpublished monograph entitled "Socialism, Confusion, and Our Homeland", which Monte completed in early June 1990, he lamented the dangerous chauvinism sweeping Yugoslavia, a trend that "has already cost hundreds of lives and is threatening the interests of all the Yugoslav peoples."

13: Bitter Bread

page

181ff The first pages of this chapter are based largely on Seta's reminiscences, as well as the author's interviews with Monte's comrades Hovsep and Artoosh (in April 1997 and April 2000) and other members of the Patriotic Detachment.

183 *Kremlin favoritism towards Armenia*: Refer, for example, to: Leila Alieva, "The Institutions, Orientations, and Conduct of Foreign Policy in Post-Soviet Azerbaijan," in Adeed Dawisha and Karen Dawisha (eds.), *The Making of Foreign Policy in Russia and the New States of Eurasia* (Armonk, NY, and London: M. E. Sharpe, 1995), pp. 286–308; p. 292; and Audrey L. Altstadt, *The Azerbaijani Turks: Power and Identity under Russian Rule* (Stanford, CA: Hoover Institution Press, 1992), p. 127. Altstadt and many Azeris resented the fact that Soviet officials had granted Mountainous Karabagh the status of an Autonomous Region within the Soviet Socialist Republic of Azerbaijan. To them, "the loss of Mountainous Karabagh" during the Soviet period was a loss to Azerbaijan, not to Armenia (Altstadt, p. 127).

184 *Stepan Shahumyan (1878–1918)*: Bolshevik revolutionary, comrade of Lenin, and leader of the Baku Commune (May–July 1918). After the fall of the Commune, Shahumyan and other leaders of the Commune (the famous "Twenty-Six Commissars") were captured in Turkmenistan and executed, probably by order of British occupation forces.

184 *Armenia's ancient heroes*: *David of Sassoon*: Mythical hero of an Armenian folk epic, who mounted his steed Jelali to fight the King of Egypt. The epic probably refers to the invasion of Armenia by Abbasid caliphs in the ninth century. *Tigran the Great* (ca. 140–55 BC): King Tigran II, one of two kings who ruled Armenia with Roman consent, briefly established an Armenian Empire stretching from the High Caucasus to the Galilee. By 69 BC, however, Pompey had stripped the upstart emperor of the land he had conquered, and Tigran the Great ended his reign as ruler of the small, landlocked kingdom he had started with. *Vartan Mamikonian* (ca. 400–51 AD): This general lead Armenian forces into unequal battle against the Persian army on the Plain of Avarair in 451 AD. (Refer to the entry "Avarair, Battle of," in the Glossary.)

185–6 *Operation Ring*: Accounts of the offensive appear in: David E. Murphy, "Operation 'Ring': The Black Berets in Azerbaijan," in *The Journal of Soviet Military Studies*, Vol. 5, No. 1 (March 1992), pp. 80–96; and Joseph R. Masih and Robert O. Krikorian, *Armenia at the Crossroads* (Amsterdam: Harwood Academic Publishers, 1999), pp. 32–3.

186 "Even if we lost Artsakh": The quote is from a video lecture of January 25, 1991. Monte expressed this view frequently, both immediately before arriving in Armenia and afterwards.

187 "The loss of Artsakh": Letter of January 26, 1992, to Myriam Gaume.

187–8 *Ajemian confirmed the accusation*: Not long before his death, Ajemian published a fictionalized account of Hagopian's assassination (*A Time for Terror* (Herndon, VA: Books International, 1997)). Shortly after the novel appeared, Ajemian confided (in an interview with the author in Los Angeles on October 24, 1997) that Hagopian's assassins had indeed been the same individuals who publicly posed as his greatest admirers.

188 *Socialism, Confusion*: Monograph dated June 8, 1990, approximately 35,000 words in length. An edited excerpt appears in *RTS*, pp. 233–8, but the monograph has never been published in full.

14: "Call Me Avo"

page

193ff Much of this chapter was based on Seta's reminiscences, as well as interviews with Myriam Gaume in Paris in 1997, and the testimonies of former members of the Patriotic Detachment.

193–4 "national self-termination," etc.: The terms appear in "National Self-Determination or National Suicide?" an article originally written in Armenian while Monte was at Poissy Prison. The article appeared in translation in the first edition of *The Right to Struggle* (San Francisco: Sardarabad Press, March 1990), pp. 163–9, but Monte had it excised from the second, "authorized" edition of the book. The quoted terms appear on pp. 164 and 168.

194 "In spite of the current criticisms": Ibid., p. 165.

196 "mountains of Afghanistan": Letter of September 27, 1991.

196 "*Jboo, Jboo!*": The dialogue appears in Gaume, pp. 176–7.

198 *Shahan Shahnour (1903–74)*: Born Shahnour Kerestejian in Constantinople, he authored many books, including *Retreat without a Song* (1929).

199 "*Drôle de garçon*": Gaume, p. 176.

200 "Why should we leave?": The quotes in this paragraph are drawn from conversations that the author overheard during visits to Mountainous Karabagh.

200 "he tossed it all away": John D. Cramer, "His lifework: fighting oppression," *Fresno Bee*, Sunday, September 20, 1992. The article bears the dateline "Martuni, Azerbaijan."

200 "Where's the exploded mortar?": Gaume, p. 163. The account of the mortar appears in Gaume, pp. 163–4.

202 "secure the positions before winter": Gaume, p. 175. Monte repeated the claim in private conversation with the author the previous summer.

204 "the millionaires": "Old Struggle Flares Anew in Bitter Kara-bakh Battle," in *Los Angeles Times*, February 23, 1992, p. A17.

205 "they choose fighting": Audiotape interview at Martuni and Ganzasar in the Mardakert district, conducted on May 15, 1993 by a British journalist accompanying a delegation headed by Baroness Caroline Cox, Deputy Speaker of the British House of Lords.

15: Discipline Problems

page

207ff This chapter is based in part on Seta's reminiscences, and on the sources listed in the notes below.

208 *The Defense Committee in Stepanakert*: A note on the tangled ter-minology of Committees and Ministries: The State Defense Committee in Stepanakert wielded broad governmental powers that were not limited to military defense. The Defense Ministry of the Republic of Armenia, by contrast, was a more specialized military body, which should not be confused with Vazgen Sarg-syan's State Ministry of Defense, also in Yerevan. The former was closer to the office of the Presidency of the Republic of Armenia, while the latter corresponds roughly to the Defense Department in the United States. Neither of these Ministries, in turn, should be confused with the Defense Ministry of the Mountainous Karabagh Republic (which was headed by Serge Sargsyan, until Ter-Petrosyan brought him to Yerevan in the summer of 1993 and promoted him to Vazgen Manoogyan's former post as Defense Minister of the Republic of Armenia).

209 *Elongated head*: May 27, 1998 video interview with Nelson, con-ducted in Martuni by Edig Baghdasaryan and Ara Manoogian.

210ff *Karadaghlu, February 16 and 17, 1992*: This account is based in part on interviews with the following eyewitnesses: Abo Hairapetyan and Vova Movsesyan at the battle site on April 25, 2000; Slavik, retired police (*militsia*) chief of Martini, on April 26, 2000; Patriotic Detachment members Hrair Karapetyan, Hovsep, and Artoosh in Yerevan on April 20, 2000; Patriotic Detachment member Edig Baghdasaryan, in Yerevan, April 1997. Published sources include: Ismet Gaibov and Azad Sharifov, *Armenian Terrorism* (Baku: Publishing House Azerbaijan, 1992), pp. 15–19; and United States Committee for Refugees, *Faultlines of Nationality Conflict: Refugees and Displaced Persons from Armenia and Azerbaijan* (Washington, DC: USCR, March 1994).

212 *Hollered until he was hoarse*: Author's audiotaped interview with Abo Hairapetyan at Karadaghlu, April 25, 2000. Edig Baghdasaryan confirmed the report in interviews and conversations, as did other eyewitnesses, including an anonymous former member of the Arabo Detachment, in conversation with the author in San Francisco, July 30, 1993.

213 *Casualties at Khojalu*: The figures vary widely, and Armenian sources contest them. Human Rights Watch/Helsinki investigators who visited the site in 1994 estimated that the Armenian attackers had killed more than 200 civilians, and perhaps as many as 1,000 (HRW/H, p. 5). Another sympathetic Western source reported that "at least 159 Azeris died in a massacre in the town of Khojaly; the remaining 2,000 fled" (Ellen Ray and Bill Schaap, "This Time, Armenians Are the Aggressors," in *Covert Action Quarterly*, No. 49 (Summer 1994), pp. 36–40, p. 39). At roughly the same time these figures appeared, an Azeri researcher, Leila Alieva, claimed that more than 800 civilians had been massacred in Khojalu (Alieva, in Dawisha and Dawisha, p. 293). Thomas Goltz, an American journalist with a pro-Baku tilt, who had visited Khojalu more than once and investigated the aftermath of the massacre, reported that "Scores, hundreds, possibly a thousand were slaughtered" (Goltz 1998, p. 122).

214 *Even his closest staff lied to him*: May 27, 1998 video interview with Nelson; May 27, 1998 video interview with Garo Tovmasyan, conducted by Edig Baghdasaryan and Ara Manoogian in Alibali; April 26, 2000 interview with Garo Tovmasyan, conducted by Seta and the author in Martuni.

215 *Kechel Sergei's fate*: After the 1994 ceasefire in Mountainous Karabagh, Kechel joined the ranks of the National Security Directorate, the renamed KGB in post-Soviet Armenia. He was

among those who clubbed demonstrators who were contesting Levon Ter-Petrosyan's announced electoral victory in the wake of the September 25, 1996 presidential elections. Not long after that, Kechel was arrested, tried, and imprisoned for kidnapping and murdering an Armenian university rector.

217 *After the showdown with Marad*: Mavrik Sargsyan, interview with Seta and the author in Martuni, April 25, 2000. The showdown took place on March 24 or 25, 1992.

219 *Aftermath of the battle at Gulabli on May 15*: This account is based on Seta's interviews with eyewitnesses on the Armenian side, including Artoosh of the Patriotic Detachment, Ashod of the Spendaryan Detachment, and Abo Hairapetyan.

219–20 *Mutalibov stepped down*: Refer to the accounts in: Shireen T. Hunter, *The Transcaucasus in Transition: Nation-Building and Conflict* (Washington, DC: The Center for Strategic & International Studies, 1994), p. 73; and Goltz 1998, pp. 131–48.

220 "Kurds were used against us": Video interview with New York-based journalist Esti Marpet, conducted at Jehar Hektar, Mountainous Karabagh, on March 27, 1993.

16: A Proper Army

page

223ff The battle reports in this chapter and the next one are drawn from numerous sources, including the interviews and video-taped testimonies cited (as well as scores of additional interviews with soldiers and civilians in Martuni, conducted by Seta and the author), and battle notes in Monte's handwriting. Published sources include: Seyran Kamalyan, *Avon Mer Achkerov* (*Avo with Our Own Eyes*) (Yerevan: Nairi, 1994); Masih and Krikorian (previously cited); Joseph Masih, "Military Strategy in Nagorno-Karabagh," in *Jane's Intelligence Review*, Vol. 6, No. 4 (April 1994), pp. 160–3; Vicken Cheterian, "De la guérilla à la guerre totale," *Les Nouvelles d'Arménie* (first, unnumbered, issue), Paris, June 1992, pp. 31–3; Max Sivaslian, *Le Jardin Noir: Karabagh récit de guerre 1992–1994* (Paris: UGAB/Editions Cape, 2001); Ara Tatevosyan, "Nagorno-Karabagh's New Army of 'Iron Will and Discipline'," *The Armenian Mirror-Spectator* (October 5, 1996), pp. 8–9; and a large file of clippings from the international press.

223 *Relative troop strength in and around Martuni in late spring 1992*:
These are the estimates of Colonel (later General) Humayag
Haroyan (interview with Seta and the author in Hrazdan,
Armenia, April 1997). The figures conform to the testimonies of
other Armenian officers who had served at the Martuni head-
quarters at the time.

223–4 "We're outnumbered, outarmed": March 27, 1993 interview
with Esti Marpet.

224 *Foreign mercenaries in Azerbaijan*: Alexis Rowell, "U.S. Mercenaries Fight in Azerbaijan," in *Covert Action* (Spring 1994), pp. 23–7;
Garine Zeitlian, "So There Are Mercenaries in Azerbaijan," in
AIM Magazine (May 1994), pp. 13–14; Hunter, p. 165. Also see:
Goltz 1998, pp. 270–9, and HRW/H, p. 64n. Goltz claimed to
have seen Afghan mercenaries "strutting around Baku in their
tribal regalia — and even in and out of the Ministry of Defense."
He added that, "The Americans, brought into Azerbaijan as part
of the revived MEGA Oil/force-multiplier project once associ-
ated with General Richard Secord, were harder to spot although
I succeeded in meeting a few" (Thomas Caufield Goltz, *Requiem
for a Would-Be Republic: The Rise and Demise of the Former Soviet
Republic of Azerbaijan* (Istanbul: The Isis Press, 1994) (henceforth
Goltz 1994), p. 499n). Also see: Goltz 1994, p. 432; HRW/H, p.
46n; Reuters, "Afghan Party Said to Aid Azerbaijan," in *Boston
Globe*, December 26, 1993; and Masih, "Military Strategy in
Nagorno-Karabagh," pp. 160ff (Masih's reference to "1000–1500
mojahedin from Gulbidden Hekmatyar's Hezb-i-Islami"
appears on p. 4 of the text-only back issue).

225 *Abulfez Elchibey (1938–2000)*: Before his June 1992 election as a
pro-Turkish President of the Republic of Azerbaijan, Elchibey
made his name as an Azeri academic and an anti-Soviet dissident. Born Abulfez Aliev, he took the name Elchibey, or "Envoy
of the People," in the late 1980s, when he became a leading figure in the nationalist Azerbaijan Popular Front. President
Elchibey served less than one year before his ousting in late
June 1993 and his eventual replacement by former Soviet boss,
Heydar (variants: Haidar, Gaidar) Aliev.

225 "You love the land?": Relatives of former hostages confirmed
this story, which appears in Gaume, p. 188.

225 "The most important thing": Seta's reminiscence.

226f *The story of the stolen diesel*: In a conversation of late April 2000, and in a telephone interview of December 2, 2000, Seta related these events as she witnessed them. Headquarters staff member Vova confirmed the story, in conversation with the author in Martuni, April 26, 2000.

228 *Scouts tripped a mine*: This account is based largely on Seta's testimony. Mirza Valo would survive, but henceforth he would speak in a sing-song voice, with elongated vowels.

228f *The June 27 and 28 battles*: This account is based in part on a conversation with Monte videotaped in his dorm room on November 26, 1992. The story of twelve-year-old Mooshegh is based in part on the author's conversation with a fighter at Martuni headquarters in June 1993, who pointed out the young man. A roughly contemporaneous Agence France-Presse report "facilitated" by Leo Nicolian also mentioned the incident.

229 "we turn the last page": The passage appears in Vartkes Baghryan, *Avo: Hooshabadoom* (*Avo: A Remembrance*) (Stepanakert: Mashdots, 1993), p. 34, and it was reprinted in the June 1993 edition of *Mardig*, the bulletin of the Mountainous Karabagh Defense Forces, No. 13 (June 1993), p. 1. Also refer to Philip Marsden, *New Statesman & Society*, December 10, 1993, (pp. 22–3), p. 22.

230 *Counter-attack at Dzover*: This account is based on the testimonies of General Haroyan (in April 1997 in Hrazdan) and Garo Tovmasyan (in April 2000 at the site of the battle). The author has not discovered reliable figures for casualty counts on either side.

230 *The sniper at Vesalu*: This account is based on the following sources: interview with Colonel Garo Tovmasyan at Alibali, Mountainous Karabagh on April 26, 2000; interviews with eyewitness Mosi Hakobyan, Deputy Commander of the Mountainous Karabagh Self-Defense Army (later Lieutenant General), in Martuni on April 25, 2000, and in the town of Abovyan on June 21, 2003; Seta's conversation with Haroyan on an uncertain date in 1996; interview with Dr. Gasparyan conducted by Seta and the author at the Avo Hospital in Martuni on April 25, 2000. The soldier who was wounded in the thigh was named Anastas (not to be confused with the former headquarters chief), from the village of Gishi.

230 "long white apron"; *little brush*: May 27, 1998 video interview with Nelson.

231 "only with *our* victory": Video interview with Vartkes Baghryan, October 3, 1992.

232 "He says *Follow me!*" (*Eem hedeveets!*): Unidentified sixth-grader from Martuni, in a short essay written for child psychologist Elianora Zarkaryan in 1994.

232 "acts of great courage … Avo is with the boys": Kamalyan, p. 158.

233 "a foot here, a hand there": Video interview shot on November 26, 1992 by Seta in their dorm room, Yerevan.

234 "Turkish policy … setting non-Azeri national minorities against us": March 27, 1993 interview with Esti Marpet.

237 "We're tank-rich": Maile's videotape, in Stepanakert hospital room, January 1993. "Azeris are arming two armies": Marsden, p. 23.

237f *The battle for Cheyl Heights, December 5 and 6*: The account is based largely on a December 6 (or 7) 1992 video interview with Monte on the Cheyl Heights, as well as Monte's handwritten notes on the battle.

238 "Wherever Avo is, there will be victory": Elianora Zakaryan, in conversation with the author, June 2003. Kamalyan made the same claim, in conversation with Seta in 1994.

238 *Ibn Khaldun, Abdurrahman (1332–1406)*: This North African Arab historian and political leader was the author most famously of the *Muqaddima* (final revision 1402), a brilliantly original work of historiography and political philosophy, which in some ways anticipated the work of Marx and Engels five centuries later.

238 *Scooping snakes*: Seta's reminiscence and interview with Garo Tovmasyan.

238 *Saved tadpoles*: Interview with eyewitness Haroyan. Nelson described the same event in his May 27, 1998 video interview.

238 *Dead hawk*: Seta's account, repeated by Martuni locals.

238 "Naïve simplicity": *Nouvelles d'Arménie*, No. 35 (July–August 1998), p. 28.

238 *Panakh Huseinov's announcement*: This appeared in an Itar-Tass wire service report of January 5, 1993.

239f *The January 16 meeting*: Seta's reminiscences and conversations with General Haroyan.

17: Come in, Zero-Zero

242 *Israeli assistance to Azerbaijan*: In an article that appeared in the November 17, 1992, issue of *Le Figaro*, reporter Pierre Rousselin confirmed President Elchibey's interest in military cooperation with Israel, and claimed that the Israelis were keen to provide weapons and military training to Azerbaijan. Israel has provided arms to Azerbaijan to bolster Turkish–Israeli relations against Iran (*Covcas Bulletin: Nationalities, Conflicts, and Human Rights in the Caucasus*, II 31 (November 5, 1992), p. 77; Hunter, p. 177).

244 "Nice dreams": Videotape shot by Maile Melkonian in mid-January 1993, during the meeting at the headquarters in Martuni. Eyewitness Hrair Garabedyan confirmed the story during a June 15, 2003 interview with the author in Yerevan.

244 *The battle at Charekdar*: The account is based on interviews with fighters, as well as Monte's handwritten battle report and his May 15, 1993 audiotape interview with a British journalist accompanying Lady Cox's delegation, at Martuni and Ganzasar.

245 "*had* to take Kelbajar": May 15, 1993 audiotape interview with British journalist at Martuni and Ganzasar.

245 "*Of course* this is historical Armenia!": Interview with Vartkes Baghryan near Vank, March 29, 1993. At least four years earlier, Monte had sketched a map (reprinted in *RTS*, p. 49), that shows the borders of "Historic Armenia" encompassing Kelbajar, as well as Mountainous Karabagh, Nakhichevan, and territories within the borders of the Republic of Turkey.

245 *Population figures for Kelbajar*: Before the war, the population of Kelbajar had been around 60,000, according to Baku's figures; however, local Azeri officials had reported that at the time of the offensive the population was closer to 45,000 (Goltz 1998, p. 344). During the offensive, the refugee collection center at Khanlar processed some 30,000 refugees, mostly Kurds from Kelbajar, while the center at Yevlak processed 3,000 refugees flown out by helicopter, and another center in the town of Dashkesen processed around 6,000. Thus, a revised Associated Press report of 20–30,000 refugees (AP report of April 8, 1993) was on the low side, while a Human Rights Watch/Helsinki figure of "an estimated 60,000 individuals" (HRW/H, p. 9), was probably on the high side. Also refer to demographic statistics

in Mehrdad Izadi, "You Too, Armenia?," *Kurdish Life*, No. 9 (Winter 1994), (Brooklyn: Kurdish Library), pp. 1–5.

245 "A lot of blood has been spilled": The quote is from *Boston Globe* correspondent Jon Auerbach's story, datelined "Martuni, Azerbaijan" (*Boston Globe*, March 9, 1993, p. 8).

246 *Casualties at the Zufulgarli Tunnel*: This account is based in part on the testimonies of eyewitnesses Vahig Sh. and another Iranian-Armenian volunteer, Masis Sh. (in conversation with Seta, March 2001), as well as on Monte's detailed account of the incident in his May 15, 1993 interview at Martuni and Ganzasar. The account of the attack as described in HRW/H, pp. 12–13 differs in some details.

249 *Civilian casualties in Kelbajar*: Monte's casualty figure is from his May 15, 1993 audiotape interview with a British journalist at Martuni and Ganzasar.

249 *Refugees from fifty Kelbajar villages*: HRW/H, p. 11. Also refer to Mehrdad Izadi, pp. 1–5. Figures for refugee casualties at the Omar Pass are cited in HRW/H, p. 15. (The Human Rights Watch/Helsinki report on the Kelbajar offensive appears at HRW/H, pp. 8–18.)

250 "it is the Russian army that fights": Guluzade was quoted by Faruk Arslan, in an article entitled "One Should Prepare for War, Says Vafa Guluzade," which appeared in the Baku newspaper *Zaman*, April 1, 2000, p. 5. Also see: Hunter, p. 88: "The Azerbaijanis firmly believed that the Armenian advances would not have been possible without Moscow's help." Hunter added, however—quite accurately—that, "Moscow was not in total control of Armenian military operations" (Hunter, p. 89). Also refer to: Daniel Sneider, *The Christian Science Monitor*, April 16, 1993, "The World: International" Section, p. 6; and Daniel Sneider and Colin Barraclough, "Turkey and Russia Back Rivals in Azerbaijan Power Struggle," *Christian Science Monitor*, June 30, 1993, pp. 1, 4.

250 *Nor did Russians plan the attack*: Colonel-General Daribaltayan confirmed that he was the chief planner of the Kelbajar offensive, as well as several other pivotal offensives in the course of the war (conversation with the author, June 20, 2003, in Yerevan).

250 *Century of the Turks*: Refer, for example, to Hunter, pp. 163–4.

250 *Consultations in Geneva*: Alieva, p. 294

250 "What happened today": Richard Boudreaux, "Armenian Forces Seize Key City in Azerbaijan," in *Los Angeles Times*, April 4, 1993, pp. A1, A20. The Gaibov quote appears on p. A20.

251 "sharp rebuke": On the morning of April 5, two days after the seizure of Kelbajar, Richard Lehman, heading a US congressional delegation in Yerevan, emerged from a private meeting with Levon Ter-Petrosyan and informed reporters that he had told the Armenian President "in pretty frank terms the State Department was upset about the escalation of the war and its effect on peace negotiations." The Warren Christopher quote: "U.S. Rebukes Armenia on New Drive in Caucasus," *New York Times*, April 7, 1993, p. A3.

251 *UN Resolution 822*: Three more resolutions were to follow: Security Council Resolutions 853 (July 29), 874 (October 14), and 884 (November 12). All of these resolutions called for Armenian forces to withdraw from occupied areas of Azerbaijan.

251 "by anyone!": *Fresno Bee*, April 7, 1993, p. A18.

251 "Turkey must show its teeth": *New York Times*, April 18, 1993, p. 46.

251 "What harm would it do?": *AIM*, April–May, 1993, p. 20.

251 "a third world war": "Turkey Warned in Enclave," *Boston Globe*, May 21, 1992, p. 2; Dmitri Trenin, "Russia's Security Interests and Policies in the Caucasus Region," in Bruno Coppeiters (ed.), *Contested Borders in the Caucasus* (Brussels: VUB Press, 1996), p. 97.

251–2 "whatever steps are necessary": Reported by Daniel Sneider, staff writer for the *Christian Science Monitor*, April 16, 1993, "The World; International" Section, p. 6.

252 *Tour brought on Ozal's death*: According to *New York Times* reporter Alan Cowell, for example: "Officials said the cause of death was heart failure and suggested that it might have been hastened by a grueling 12-day tour of Central Asia that ended two days earlier" (*New York Times,* April 18, 1993, p. 46).

252 "a more severe stand": The quote from President Rafsanjani appeared in the *New York Times*, April 13, 1993, p. A5.

252–3 *United States has tight relations with Turkey*: March 27, 1993 interview with Esti Marpet.

255 "Go to the next one": John D. Cramer, *Fresno Bee*, September 20, 1992, p. A14.

255 *The May 27 meeting with Vazgen Manoogyan*: This account is drawn from Seta's reminiscence, as well as Haroyan's testimony, in conversation with the author.

18: Leave Like Water

page

257 *Artik's fate*: In the first weeks of March 2003, police in Armenia arrested six men in connection with the December 28, 2002 assassination in Yerevan of Tigran Naghdalyan, Chairman of the Board of Armenia's Public Television and Radio. Most of the suspects were from Martuni, and at least two of them had been members of Artik's clique. Yerevan-based journalist and former Patriotic Detachment fighter Edig Baghdasaryan reported that Artik had been spotted in Yerevan at the time of Naghdalyan's murder, and had returned to Russia after the murder (Edig Baghdasaryan, "Who Gave the Order to Shoot?" online article posted on the Association of Investigative Journalists of Armenia website, www.hetq.am, on March 12, 2003). While the prosecutor general of Armenia requested Artik's extradition from Russia, investigators cast a wider net for suspects. On March 15, 2003, police in Yerevan arrested Armen Sargsyan, a younger brother of war hero Vazgen Sargsyan, and charged him with ordering Naghdalyan's murder. Serious questions remain about the motives behind the arrest: Sargsyan was a prominent opponent of President Robert Kocharyan, and ten months before his arrest US officials had accused him of having ties with Lizin, an Armenian biochemical company that allegedly sold sensitive equipment to Iran.

258 *Petting the bird*: Vartan described the story in conversation with Seta, and repeated it in conversation with the author in Yerevan, June 2003.

259ff *The June 12, 1993 offensive*: This account was compiled for the most part from eyewitness testimonies of fighters, medical staff, and Armenian civilians who had been present in Martuni and Merzuli that day. Sources include: audiotaped interviews with Gomidas Avanesyan and Saro Yeremyan, conducted by Hacob Mkrdchyan in Yerevan, June 1993; videotaped interviews with Abo Hairapetyan at the headquarters in Martuni, conducted on November 24, 1993, and with Abo and Gomidas at Merzuli the same day; an interview with Saro Yeremyan, conducted by Seta and the author in Martuni, April 26, 2000; an interview with Vartan, the eyewitness fighter from Iran, conducted with Seta not long after the incident; the testimony of Dr. Grisha Gaspar- yan and other staff at Martuni Hospital, April 25, 2000; the testimony of subcommander Hovik from Jardar, in conversa- tion with Seta and the author in Yerevan, June 1993; Seta's numerous interviews and conversation with Lilia Mardirosyan, the widow of Saribeg; and an interview with a captured Azeri fighter by Seta and the author in the Martuni municipal jail, June 21, 1993. Eyewitness testimonies were corroborated by the author's first-hand inspection of the Cheyl Heights and Merzuli (in June 1993, April 2000, and June 2003), as well as forensic evidence provided by the Ministry of Defense of the Republic of Armenia.

260 *Monte's "Historic Homelands" map*: The map appears in *RTS*, p. 49. (Refer to map of Armenia and the Middle East, above, p. xiii.)

260 *Bivouac at the Gargar River*: A young Azeri soldier captured that day in Merzuli told Abo Hairapetyan during interrogation that he was part of a detachment of about sixty fighters in the vicin- ity (Abo, in conversation with the author while touring the Spitakshen/Gulabli area, April 27, 2000). Saro Yeremyan con- firmed this account, in conversation with Seta and the author in Martuni on April 27, 2000.

261 *Azeri casualties in Yusufjanli*: HRW/H, pp. 23–5.

261 *No Armenian forces in Merzuli; Azeri fighters entered Merzuli from the northeast*: This was the testimony of the captured Azeri sol- dier during his June 21, 1993 interview. Members of Monte's party reported that they had seen an Azeri light tank retreat on that dirt track, and they described seeing another light tank enter Merzuli via the same track and then retreat using the same route.

262 "We'll go check on Nelson together": This was the testimony of Gomidas (in conversation with Seta shortly after Monte's death), as well as eyewitnesses Deputy Commander Mosi (interview with Seta and the author, Martuni, April 25, 2000), and Vova Movsesyan (conversation with Seta and the author in Martuni, April 27, 2000). According to Abo's videotaped testi- mony (November 24, 1993), Monte said, "Wait at the intersection. I want to check it out with my own eyes."

264 *Monte might have returned fire immediately or dived to the road first*: In either case, he must have returned fire at some point, since the author counted twenty-two bullets in the magazine of Monte's rifle when he inspected it later. Since Monte habitually reloaded at his first opportunity, it would be safe to assume that his magazine had been full when Gomidas had pulled the staff car to a stop at the intersection. Thus, he probably fired a total of eight shots.

264 *The first cannon round hit a stone fence*: This was Gomidas' repeated testimony, which was later confirmed by the author's on-site inspection: The stone wall behind the staff car bears clear evidence of an explosive impact. According to other accounts, the first round hit a nearby electrical pole, chopping it to splinters. The latter scenario is unlikely, though, since the splintered electrical pole was far wide of the line of fire from the tank to the staff car.

265 *Saribeg's death*: This account is based on interviews and conversations with Saribeg's wife Lilia conducted by Seta and the author, as well as interviews with Dr. Gasparyan, "Dr." Barseghyan (a physician's assistant at the Avo Hospital in Martuni), and two other hospital staff members named Margo and Areka, at the hospital in Martuni on Tuesday, April 25, 2000.

268 *Promotion to lieutenant colonel*: The head of the Defense Committee, Serge Sargsyan (no relation to Vazgen Sargsyan), confirmed this account in conversation with the author, June 19, 2003, in Yerevan. At the time of the conversation, Sargsyan held the office of Defense Minister of the Republic of Armenia.

269 *To confirm Monte's death*: Subsequent revelations have bolstered my initial suspicion: on June 16, 1993, the Los Angeles Field Office of the FBI requested that the Washington DC Metropolitan Field Office of the FBI notify the Department of State, Bureau of Diplomatic Security, Command Center, "and request that the U.S. Department of State, through official liaison at Yerevan, Armenia, confirm the death of Monte Melkonian, and attempt to obtain major case fingerprints for Interpol and FBI."

270 *The fates of Elchibey, Huseinov, and Aliev*: Turkey and the United States rued Elchibey's downfall; Russia and Iran did not (Alieva, p. 305; Hunter, p. 88; Goltz 1998, p. 252). The change of guard brought quick benefits to Russia: in September 1993, Baku announced that the Russian oil firm, Lukoil, would

develop one of Azerbaijan's Caspian oil fields, and that Russia would receive a 10 per cent share in the consortium. The same month, on September 20, the parliament of Azerbaijan adopted a resolution to join the CIS. Huseinov, however, benefited little from the Aliev regime he helped to install, and on February 16, 1999, after a seven-month trial, Azerbaijan's Supreme Court sentenced him to life in prison after finding him guilty on dozens of charges, including high treason. A year later, Abulfaz Elchibey, herald of the Turkish Century, died in exile in the isolated region of Nakhichevan. His successor, Heydar (or Geidar) Aliev, died on December 12, 2003, at the age of eighty. Aliev's son, Ilham, succeeded him in the office of the Presidency of Azerbaijan.

272 "If you respect Avo's memory": In the years since this meeting, the author has repeatedly enquired about this young man's fate. According to the most credible report, he was released in a hostage exchange within a year of his capture.

272 *Rumors of treachery*: After claiming to have met "any number of Azeris who claim credit for his death," a Western journalist added: "I have also been told by Armenians that he may have been the victim of assassination" (Goltz 1994, p. 499n).

272 *Norair Tanielyan's death*: The Mardakert commander was killed on October 19, 1993, when gunmen stopped his staff car between Stepanakert and Mardakert, and cut him down with a burst from an assault rifle. At the time, according to the rumors, he had been involved in a personal dispute of some sort with military strongman Samvel Babayan.

272–3 *A story planted to cover Monte's disappearance underground*: Refer, for example, to Goltz 1994, p. 499n.

273 *FBI teletype*: Several pages after the quoted passage, the document states: "Inasmuch as subject [Monte] is publicly reported as deceased, and there has been no evidence surfaced to date to contradict that reporting, this matter is closed by the FBI Los Angeles Field Office and considered referred upon completion."

273 *The flip-flops story*: Alec Yenikomshian recounted the story in conversation with the author in Yerevan, June 11, 2003. Monte related the story to the author when he returned from work that day in 1980.

273 "the less I have, the better I feel": Letter of October 12, 1986 to Armen S.

274 "He saved our lives": Interview with Kourken Melikyan, reported by Seta, May 30, 1997.

Epilogue: The View from Yeraplur

page

279 *A national unity that he had dismissed*: In a typical passage dating from 1985, for example, he had written that "Unity for unity's sake is a recipe for failure and disillusionment" (*RTS*, p. 173).

279 "Without corruption and just": *Nouvelles d'Arménie*, No. 35 (July–August 1998), p. 26. Haroyan was promoted to the rank of General in the armed forces of the Republic of Armenia in 1996, but he resigned his post in September of that year, when the Defense Ministry ordered him to put his men under alert, for possible deployment against opposition demonstrators in Yerevan. Reinstated in his post since then, he has been a reservist since 1997.

279 *Emigration from post-Soviet Armenia*: On February 15, 2002, Armstat, the Armenian national statistical service, released a report that claimed that in the ten years since the final collapse of the Soviet Union in 1991, the population of the Republic of Armenia had shrunk by almost 1 million, reducing the country's total population to a little more than 3 million. Armstat's population figures were the results of a nationwide census held in October 10 to 19, 2001 (Armenpress news service, February 15, 2002). These figures confirm earlier estimates by a number of institutions and publications, including: The United Nations Development Project's *Human Development Report: Armenia 1997*, p. 13; and S. Karapetiyan, "Migration from Armenia in the Post-Soviet Period, 1991–1995," a report to the UNDP, Armenia office, 1996 (cited in Marina Kurkchiyan, "Health Care in Armenia: The Human Cost of the Transition," CACP Briefing No. 16 (London: The Royal Institute of International Affairs, March 1998) p. 1); The United States Department of State, Bureau of Public Affairs ("Background Notes: Armenia" (Washington, DC: US Department of State, March 1996), p.1), as well as *CIA World Factbook* population, growth rate, and net migration rate estimates. Most Armenian emigration throughout the 1990s

took place for "economic reasons," and most of the traffic has been to Russia (Snark News Agency report of December 8, 1997). As of this writing, the population of Mountainous Kara-bagh is fluid, but officials in the Ministry of Defense and in the civilian administration of the region quoted the 65,000 figure during the author's visits in 2000 and 2003.

280 *Ter-Petrosyan resigned*: Other factors besides accusations of election rigging and suppression of demonstrators contributed to the former President's demise, including the common perception that Ter-Petrosyan was willing to capitulate on the issue of Mountainous Karabagh's independence from Azerbaijan. Ultimately, it was a "pro-Karabagh" section of the ruling circle that forced Ter-Petrosyan to resign.

|||||||||||||||||||||||||||||||||||||||||||||||||||||||||||||||||||

Further Reading

This list of sources, most of them book-length and in English, is intended as a guide for further reading. Although several of these sources appear as citations in this book, this is by no means a complete bibliography of sources consulted during the writing of this book.

Sources for Chapters 1 and 3: The History of the San Joaquin Valley

Arax, Mark and Wartzman, Rick. *The King of California: J. G. Boswell and the Making of a Secret American Empire*. New York: Public Affairs, 2003.

Daniel, Cletus. *Bitter Harvest: A History of California Farmworkers, 1870–1941*. Ithaca, NY, and London: Cornell University Press, 1981.

Garner, Van H. *The Broken Ring: The Destruction of the California Indians*. Tucson: Westernlore Press, 1982.

Heizer, Robert Fleming and Almquist, Alan F. *The Other Californians: Prejudice and Discrimination under Spain, Mexico, and the United States to 1920*. Berkeley: University of California Press, 1971.

McWilliams, Carey. *Factories in the Field: The Story of Migratory Farm Labor in California*. Santa Barbara: Peregrine Publishers, Inc., 1971.

Mitchell, Annie R. *Visalia: Her First Fifty Years*. Exeter, CA: self-published, 1963.

————. *Visalia's Heritage*. Visalia: Visalia Heritage, Inc., 1986.

Norris, Frank. *The Octopus*. New York: Bantam Books, 1963. (Historical novel, first published in 1901, now available as a digital download.)

Preston, William. *Vanishing Landscapes: Land and Life in the Tulare Basin*. Berkeley: University of California Press, 1981.

Secrest, William B. *When the Great Spirit Died: The Destruction of the California Indians, 1850–1860*. Sanger, CA: Word Dancer Press, 2003.

Sources for Chapters 1 and 3: Armenian Immigration to Central California

Avakian, Arra S. *The Armenians in America*. Minneapolis: Lerner Publications Company, 1977.
Bakalian, Anny. *Armenian-Americans: From Being to Feeling Armenian*. New Brunswick, NJ, and London: Transaction Press, 1993.
Bulbulian, Berge. *The Fresno Armenians: History of a Diaspora Community*. Fresno, CA: California State University Press, 2000.
Davidian, Nectar. *The Seropians*. Berkeley, CA: self-published, 1965.
LaPiere, Richard Tracy. "The Armenian Colony in Fresno County, California: A Study in Social Psychology". Dissertation, Stanford University, 1930.
Mahakian, Charles. "History of the Armenians in California". Thesis, University of California, 1935.
Malcolm, M. Vartan. *The Armenians in America*. Boston: Pilgrim Press, 1919.
Saroyan, William. *My Name is Aram*. New York: Dell Publishing Company, 1966. (Fiction.)
Wallis, Wilson D. *Fresno Armenians* (ed. Nectar Davidian). Lawrence, KS: Coronado Press, 1965.
Yeretzian, Aram S. "A History of Armenian Immigration to America with Special Reference to Los Angeles". Thesis, University of Southern California, 1923.

Sources for Chapters 2 and 3: The Armenian Genocide

Balakian, Peter. *The Burning Tigris: The Armenian Genocide and America's Response*. New York: HarperCollins, 2003; London: Heinemann, 2002.
Bryce, James and Toynbee, Arnold. *The Treatment of Armenians in the Ottoman Empire, 1915–1916: Document Presented to Viscount Grey of Falloden by Viscount Bryce* (uncensored edition). Princeton: Gomidas Institute, 2000.
Hewson, Robert H. *Armenia: A Historical Atlas*. Chicago and London: University of Chicago Press, 2001.
Hovannisian, Richard G. *Armenia: On the Road to Independence, 1918*. Berkeley: University of California Press, 1967.

Miller, Donald E. and Miller, Lorna Touryan. *Survivors: An Oral History of the Armenian Genocide*. Berkeley: University of California Press; Cambridge: Cambridge University Press, 1993.

Morgenthau, Henry. *Ambassador Morgenthau's Story*. Garden City, NY: Doubleday, Page & Company, 1919.

Permanent People's Tribunal. *A Crime of Silence: The Armenian Genocide*. London: Zed Books, 1985.

Raffi (Melik-Hagopian, Hagop). *The Fool: Events from the Last Russo-Turkish War (1877–1978)* (trans. Donald Abcarian). Princeton: Gomidas Institute; Reading: Tademon Press, 2000. (Historical novel, first published in Armenian as *Khente* in 1881.)

Riggs, Henry H. *Days of Tragedy in Armenia: Personal Experiences in Harpoot, 1915–1917* (ed. Ara Sarafian). Princeton: Gomidas Institute, 1997.

Sarafian, Ara (ed.). *United States Official Documents on the Armenian Genocide*, Vols. 1 and 2. Watertown, MA: Armenian Review Press, 1993.

Walker, Christopher. *Armenia: The Survival of a Nation*. New York: St. Martin's Press; London: Routledge, 1980.

Werfel, Franz. *The Forty Days of Musa Dagh*. New York: Viking Press, 1934. (Historical novel.)

Sources for Chapters 5 through 9: The Lebanese Civil War

Chomsky, Noam. *The Fateful Triangle: The United States, Israel, & the Palestinians*. Boston: South End Press; London: Pluto Press, 1983.

Fisk, Robert. *Pity the Nation: The Abduction of Lebanon*. New York: Atheneum; Oxford: Oxford Paperbacks, 1990.

Jansen, Michael. *The Battle of Beirut*. Boston: South End Press; London: Zed Books, 1982.

Khalidi, Walid. *Conflict and Violence in Lebanon*. Cambridge, MA, and London: Center for International Affairs, Harvard University Press, 1979.

Randal, Johnathan C. *Going All the Way: Christian Warlords, Israeli Adventurers, and the War in Lebanon*. New York: Viking; London: Vintage, 1983.

Sources for Chapters 6 through 11: "Armenian Terrorism" and Related Topics

Chaliand, Gerard, and Ternon. Yves. *The Armenians: From Genocide to Resistance* (trans. Tony Berrett). London: Zed Press, 1981.

Feigl, Erich. *A Myth of Terror: Armenian Extremism: Its Causes and Its Historical Context*. Edition Zeitgeschichte, nd.

Gunter, Michael M. *"Pursuing the Just Cause of Their People"*: *A Study of Contemporary Armenian Terrorism*. New York: Greenwood Press, 1986.

Gurriarán, José Antonio. *La Bomba*. Barcelona: Planeta, 1982. (Memoir.)

Hyland, Francis P. *Armenian Terrorism: The Past, the Present, the Prospects*. Boulder, CO: Westview Press, 1991.

Kurz, Anat and Merari, Ariel. *ASALA: Irrational Terror or Political Tool*. Tel Aviv: Jaffee Center for Stategic Studies, Tel Aviv University, 1985.

Melkonian, Monte. *The Right to Struggle: Selected Writings of Monte Melkonian on the Armenian National Question*, 2nd edition (ed. Markar Melkonian). San Francisco: Sardarabad Press, 1993. (The Armenian edition, *Baikareloo Eeravoonku* (Yerevan: Monte Melkonian Fund, 2003), includes a Foreword by Alec Yenikomshian.)

Minassian, Gaidz. *Guerre et terrorisme arméniens: 1972–1998*. Paris: Presses Universitaires de France, 2002.

Nalbandian, Louise. *The Armenian Revolutionary Movement*. Berkeley and Los Angeles: University of California Press; Cambridge: Cambridge University Press, 1963.

Shiragian, Arshavir. *The Legacy*. Boston: Hairenik Press, 1976. (Memoir.)

Ternon, Yves. *The Armenian Cause*. Delmar, NY: Caravan Books, 1985.

Villeneuve, Charles and Pèret, Jean-Pierre. *Histoire secrète au terrorisme*. Paris: Editions Plon, 1987.

Wilkinson, Paul and Stewart, Alasdair M. (eds.). *Contemporary Research on Terrorism*. Aberdeen: Aberdeen University Press, 1987. (Includes Khachig Tololyan's paper, "Martyrdom as Legitimacy: Terrorism, Religion, and Symbolic Appropriation in the Armenian Diaspora" (pp. 89–103).)

Sources for Chapters 11 and 13 through 18: The History of Azerbaijan

Altstadt, Audrey L. *The Azerbaijani Turks: Power and Identity under Russian Rule*. Stanford, CA: Hoover Institution Press, 1992.

Goltz, Thomas Caufield. *Azerbaijan Diary: A Rogue Reporter's Adventures in an Oil-Rich, War-Torn, Post-Soviet Republic*. Armonk, New York and London: M. E. Sharpe, 1998.

Shaw, Stanford J. and Shaw, Ezel Kural. *The History of the Ottoman Empire and Modern Turkey*, Vol. 2. Cambridge: Cambridge University Press, 1977.

Suny, Ronald G. *The Baku Commune: Class and Nationality in the Russian Revolution*. Princeton: Princeton University Press, 1972.

Swietochowski, Tadeusz. *Russia and Azerbaijan: A Borderland in Transition*. New York: Columbia University Press, 1995.

Van der Leeuw, Charles. *Azerbaijan: A Quest for Identity*. Richmond: Curzon Press, 2000.

Sources for Chapters 11 and 13 through 18: Mountainous Karabagh and "the Karabagh Movement"

Adalian, Rouben Paul (ed.). *Armenia & Karabagh Factbook*. Washington, DC: Armenian Assembly of America, July 1996.

Asenbauer, Haig. *On the Right of Self-Determination of the Armenian People of Nagorno-Karabagh*. New York: The Armenian Prelacy, 1996.

Bournoutian, George (ed.). *A History of Qarabagh*. Costa Mesa: Mazda Publishers, 1994. (Annotated translation of Mirza Jamal Javanshir Qarabaghi's *Tarikh-e Qarabagh*.)

Chorbajian, Levon (ed.). *The Making of Nagorno-Karabagh: From Secession to Republic*. New York and Houndmills: Palgrave, 2001.

Chorbajian, Levon, Donabedian, Patrick, and Mutafian, Claude. *The Caucasian Knot: The History and Geo-Politics of Nagorno-Karabagh*. New Jersey and London: Zed Books, 1994.

Cox, Caroline and Eibner, John. *Ethnic Cleansing in Progress: War in Nagorno-Karabagh*. Zurich, London and Washington: Institute for Religious Minorities in the Islamic World, 1993.

Dawisha, Adeed and Dawisha, Karen (eds.). *The Making of Foreign Policy in Russia and the New States of Eurasia*. Armonk, NY, and London: M. E. Sharpe, 1995. (Includes articles by Leila Alieva ("The Institutions, Orientations, and Conduct of Foreign Policy in Post-Soviet Azerbaijan," pp. 286–308) and Rouben Adalian ("Armenia's Foreign Policy: Defining Priorities and Coping with Conflict," pp. 309–39).)

Human Rights Watch/Helsinki. *Seven Years of Conflict in Nagorno-Karabagh*. New York, Washington, DC, Los Angeles, London, Brussels: Human Rights Watch, 1994.

Hunter, Shireen T. *The Transcaucasus in Transition*. Washington, DC: The Center for Strategic & International Studies, 1994.

Libaridian, Gerard J. (ed.). *The Karabagh File: Documents and Facts on the Question of Mountainous Karabagh: 1918–1988*. Cambridge, MA and Toronto: The Zoryan Institute, March 1988.

Libaridian, Gerard J. *Armenia at the Crossroads: Democracy and Nationhood in the Post-Soviet Era*. Watertown, MA: Blue Crane Books, 1991.

Malkasian, Mark. *"Gha-ra-bagh!": The Emergence of the National Democratic Movement in Armenia*. Detroit: Wayne State University Press, 1996.

Masih, Joseph and Krikorian, Robert. *Armenia at the Crossroads*. Amsterdam: Harwood Academic Publishers; London: Routledge, 1999.

Ministry of Foreign Affairs of the Azerbaijani Republic. *Information Bulletin on the Consequences of the Aggressions by the Republic of Armenia against the Azerbaijani Republic*. Baku, February 1994.

Shahmuratian, Samvel (ed. and compiler). *The Sumgait Tragedy: Pogroms against Armenians in Soviet Azerbaijan: Vol. I: Eyewitness Accounts*. New Rochelle and Cambridge, MA: Aristide D. Caratzas and The Zoryan Institute for Contemporary Armenian Research and Documentation, 1990.

Suny, Ronald Grigor. *The Revenge of the Past: Nationalism, Revolution, and the Collapse of the Soviet Union*. Stanford: Stanford University Press, 1993.

Swietochowski, Tadeusz. *The Problem of Nagorno-Karabagh: Geography versus Demography under Colonialism and in Decolonization in Central Asia*. New York: St. Martins Press, 1993.

United States Committee for Refugees (USCR). *Faultlines of Nationality Conflict: Refugees and Displaced Persons from Armenia and Azerbaijan*. Washington, DC: USCR, March 1994.

Walker, Christopher J. *Armenia and Karabagh: The Struggle for Unity*. London: Minority Rights Publications, 1991.

Biographical Monographs about Monte

Alexandrian, A. "*De Monte a Avo: Histoire d'une legende*," *Nouvelles d'Arménie*, No. 87 (June 2003), pp. 18–31.

———. "*Il est entré dans la légende*," *Nouvelles d'Arménie*, No. 35 (July/August 1998), pp. 24–9.

———. "*Itinéraire d'un enfant de la diaspora*," *Nouvelles d'Arménie*, No. 2 (June/July 1993), pp. 5–13.

Baghryan, Vartkes. *Avo: Hooshabadoom* (*Avo: A Remembrance*). Stepanakert: Mashdots, 1993.

Kamalyan, Seyran. *Avon Mer Achkerov* (*Avo with Our Own Eyes*). Yerevan: Nairi, 1994.

Vorbach, Joseph E. "Monte Melkonian: Armenian Revolutionary Leader," *Terrorism and Political Violence*, Vol. 6, No. 2, (Summer 1994), pp. 178–95.

Glossary

A Note on Usage: For the most part, foreign words have been transliterated with an eye to ease of reading and pronunciation, rather than strict conformity with standard systems of transliteration. Accordingly, the region appears as *Karabagh*, rather than the more accurate Azeri Turkish and Armenian transliteration, *Gharabagh* (and rather than the less-commonly used variants, *Karabakh* and *Qarabagh*), and the village appears as *Karadaghlu*, rather than *Gharadaghlu* (Chapter 15). For ease of reading, too, the region appears as *Mountainous Karabagh*, rather than the more official russified title, *Nagorno Karabakh*, and the district appears as *Kelbajar*, rather than *Kalbacar*, *Kel'badzhar*, or other variants. Similarly, the Turkish group appears as *Kurtulush*, rather than *Kurtulus* (Chapter 9), and the family name appears as *Mukurtchyan*, rather than *Mkrtchyan* (Chapter 15). Some exceptions to this rule include: *Çorum*, rather than *Chorum* (Chapter 2), and *Kharpert*, rather than *Kharberd*, *Harput*, or other variants (Chapter 3). These exceptions are concessions to place names as they commonly appear in authoritative English-language atlases.

adep-sus Uncivilized; uncultured. (Turkish)

Artsakh Ancient Armenian province, corresponding roughly to the borders of the former Soviet Autonomous Region of Mountainous Karabagh (4,388 sq. km.). Many Armenians today use the term to refer to Mountainous Karabagh and surrounding territories (see map of Armenia and Karabagh, p. xiv).

Askeran One of six main administrative districts within Mountainous Karabagh, located between the districts of Mardakert to the north and Martuni to the southeast (see map of Mountainous Karabagh, p. xv).

Avarair, Battle of (variant: Avarayr) In 451 AD, according to Armenian accounts, a Persian force of 300,000 fighters reinforced with elephants clashed with 66,000 Armenian warriors at Avarair, a field on the banks of the Teghmut River (presently in northwest Iran). Yazdegerd, the King of Persia, was determined to subdue the principalities of Armenia and to force their feudal princes (called *nakharars*) to embrace Zoroastrianism, the official faith of Persia. According to Armenian sources, the Persian side counted three times as many casualties as the Armenian side. Nevertheless, the Armenians lost their commander, Vartan Mamigonian, and the battle was counted as an Armenian defeat. Armenians continued to resist Persian rule, however. Eventually, in the Treaty of Nouarsak (484 AD), the King of Persia agreed to allow the Armenian princes to retain their Christian faith, in exchange for recognition of Persian sovereignty over Armenia. Armenians today view the Battle of Avarair as a heroic defense of their faith in the face of certain death.

chokat Detachment; group of partisan fighters, or irregulars. (Armenian)

chorbah Soup. (Turkish)

dasak (variant: *tasag*) Literally, a flock, herd, or troop. During the war in Mountainous Karabagh, it referred to a military group the size of a battery or a company. (Armenian)

Dashnak Party (variant: Tashnag) The Armenian Revolutionary Federation. Founded in 1890, this nationalist party helped organize self-defense efforts of Armenians in the Ottoman Empire and played a leading role in the first Armenian Republic (1918–20). Following the Sovietization of Armenia in 1920, its base of power shifted to Iran and Lebanon, and then to the United States, where it cast its lot with the West in the Cold War. After the collapse of the Soviet Union, the Party returned to Armenia, where it at first supported and then opposed the government of the first President of the newly independent Republic of Armenia, Levon Ter-Petrosyan.

duduk Middle Eastern reed flute, traditionally made of apricot wood. (Armenian)

Fatah (variant: *al-Fateh*) The largest Palestinian resistance organization, founded in 1959 by Yassir Arafat (Abu Ammar); Salah Khalaf (Abu Iyad), and Khalil Wazir (Abu Jihad), among others.

fedayee (variants: *fedahee, fidai,* etc.) Freedom fighter. (Arabic, Armenian, Farsi)

hamam Bathhouse. (Turkish, Arabic)

Jhiguli Small sedan of Russian manufacture.

keffiyeh (variants: *kuffiyeh,* etc.) Scarf, often with a distinctive checkered design, worn around the head, neck, or waist by peasants in some countries of the Middle East. (Arabic)

Kharpert (variants: Kharput, Kharberd, etc.; present designation: Harput) Largest city in the province (*vilayet*) of Mamouret ul-Aziz, in east central Anatolia. Commercial and agricultural center. At the beginning of the twentieth century, half the population of 30,000 was Armenian (see map of Armenia and the Middle East, p. xiii).

Komala Organization of Revolutionary Toilers of Iranian Kurdistan. Founded in 1969, the Sanandaj-based organization favors autonomy for Iranian Kurdistan. Just before the US invasion of Iraq in 2003, Komala established a nominal presence in northern Iraq, in an area controlled by Ansar al-Islam, a small Islamist group with alleged ties to Osama bin Laden's al-Qaeda organization.

Kurtulush "Liberation," in Turkish. Left-wing group that was active in Turkey in the late 1970s and early 1980s. Kurtulush has been described as an "independent left" group, in the sense that it revered neither Moscow nor Beijing.

laissez-passer Document permitting its holder to enter and pass through a country.

madagh Blood sacrifice, typically of sheep or roosters. (Armenian)

malahini A native Hawaiian. (Hawaiian)

Nakhichevan (variants: Naxichewan, Nakhijivan, etc.) Mostly mountainous area of 5,500 sq. km., bordered on the north and east by the Republic of Armenia, and on the south and west by Turkey and Iran. During the Soviet period, Nahkichevan became an Autonomous Soviet Socialist Republic that was part of the Azerbaijan Soviet Socialist Republic, although it shared no common border with the rest of Azerbaijan. After the collapse of the Soviet Union, the area became part of the independent Republic of Azerbaijan. In 1999, Nakhichevan's population was estimated to be 320,000 (see map of Armenia and Karabagh, p. xiv).

nomenklatura Soviet-era term for high officials appointed to their positions by the Party. The most privileged and best-connected strata of the old Soviet order, it included high-ranking Party functionaries, state bureaucrats, and managers of large enterprises. (Russian) *oghi* Clear liquor, similar to vodka. The Lebanese variety is anise-flavored. (Armenian)

Ottoman Bank Affair On August 26, 1896, twenty-five Dashnak Party militants stormed the Ottoman Bank in Constantinople, to demand that the Great Powers of Europe take action against Ottoman Turkish officials responsible for the ongoing series of massacres that would claim the lives of 250,000 Armenian subjects of the Empire. The militants threatened to blow themselves up, and the bank with them, if their grievances were not heard. After holding the bank for several hours, they agreed to leave under escort, and to be evacuated from Turkey. During the bank seizure, and for two days afterwards, Turkish mobs retaliated against Armenians in Constantinople, killing several thousand.

Phalange, Lebanese (*al-Kata'ib*) Right-wing paramilitary and political organization, founded in 1936 by Pierre Gemayel, a prominent Lebanese Maronite, under the inspiration of the fascist Spanish Falange (*la Falange Española*), Spain's single official party from 1939 to 1975. Thanks in large part to Western and Israeli largesse, the Lebanese Phalange was the largest and best armed force in civil war Lebanon.

Progressive Socialist Party A political party founded in the late 1940s by prominent Lebanese Druze leader, Kamal Jumblatt (or Joumblatt) (1917–77). During the Lebanese civil war (from the mid-1970s through the 1980s), the party and its militia were a leading force within the Lebanese National Movement.

Red Army Faction (*Rote Armee Fraktion*, also known as the Baader-Meinhof Group) The best-known of several small ultra-left-wing "front-line organizations" active in the Federal Republic of Germany during the 1970s and 1980s.

sadir Low cushions for sitting and lounging, often arranged against a wall. (Turkish)

Sevres, Treaty of (August 10, 1920) Post-World War I pact between the victorious Allied powers (excluding Russian and the United States) and representatives of Ottoman Turkey. The treaty removed Arab lands from Ottoman control, provided for an independent Armenia and an autonomous Kurdistan, and made territorial concessions to Greece. The new Turkish nationalist regime rejected the treaty, and in 1923 it was superceded by the Treaty of Lausanne, which made no mention of Armenia.

soba "Room." Also refers to a short-term boarding arrangement in a private house. (Serbo-Croatian)

tufa (or tuff) A porous sedimentary rock that is a common building material in Armenia.

tezoog Dwarf. (Armenian)

Vai! "Alas!" Thus, the passage quoted in Chapter 18, p. 266: *Avo, vai vai vai! Vai Avo-jan vai vai!* Would translate as: "Avo, alas, alas! Dear Avo, alas!" (Armenian)

Wehrsportgruppe Hoffman The "Hoffman Sport Group," a German neo-Nazi group that was active in the 1970s and 1980s.

yazma Women's headscarf. (Turkish)

Zangezur The mountainous southernmost region of the Republic of Armenia, bordered on the south and west by Iran and the Nakhichevan region of Azerbaijan, and to the north and east by the larger mass of the Republic of Azerbaijan (see map of Armenia and Karabagh, p. xiv).

Acknowledgments

This book is the product of too many hands and memories to list here, but several people must be mentioned.

Seta Melkonian has been more than a collaborator from the start, and she is to thank for whatever is best in these pages. She has cleared her schedule for my research trips, hosted me in Yerevan for weeks at a stretch, set up interviews, conducted dozens of interviews on her own, and reviewed draft after draft. Most indispensably, Chapters 11 through 18 are in large part the product of her archives, her advice, and her indelible memory.

I have also benefited greatly from Ara Alec Yenikomshian's testimonies and insight. Alec has always made time for this project, and the result is much better thanks to him.

In addition to the endless interviews he has endured, Charles Melkonian has cared for his granddaughters for weeks at a stretch while I was on the road doing research. And without Zabelle Melkonian's fastidious work as family archivist (a skill she has honed over the years as historian for the Tulare County branch of the American Association of University Women), these pages would have been less authoritative and interesting. I owe them this book, at the very least.

Over the course of seven years of research, Maile Melkonian and Marcia Bedrosian have also endured more than their share of interviews. Marcia has quietly compensated in childcare, too, and Maile has provided editorial assistance.

This book would have been considerably less readable if it were not for Nancy Kricorian and Mark Arax. Their criticisms have been right on the mark, and their encouragement has been vital. I also owe Nancy and Mark, each individually, a debt of gratitude for convincing me not to produce a conventional biography, as I had originally set out to do. Thanks in large part to them, *My Brother's Road* is as much a memoir as a biography.

Hanako Birks, my editor at I. B. Tauris, made painful cuts that had to be made. If this book appeals to that famous but elusive "intelligent general reader," then she deserves much of the credit.

The following people also deserve special thanks: Myriam Gaume, for her journalistic advice, research, and enduring friendship; Michael Burlingham, for encouragement and help through the first chapters; General Hemayag Haroyan, formerly of the Ministry of Defense of the Republic of Armenia, for his honesty and hospitality in Yerevan; Bedros Bedros, for his expertise with graphics software; Ashod Schemavonian and Geoff Goshgarian, for guidance in Paris; Edig Baghdasaryan, for assistance in Yerevan; and Levon Chorbajian, for invaluable comments and counsel on a variety of topics.

I am grateful also to scores of people in Mountainous Karabagh. In particular, I wish to thank Abo Hairapetyan, Garo Tovmasyan, and the Ararat Avanesyan family. So many natives of Mountainous Karabagh have been so helpful in so many ways that thanks are due to these good people *en masse*.

My friend Nareg Hartounian provided generous financial support at a make-or-break moment for this project, and he did so with neither fanfare nor strings attached. I want this book to stand as an expression of my gratitude.

And finally, I want to thank Suzy Melkonian for the extraordinary patience she has displayed throughout her husband's seven years of unremunerated moil.

Any errors of omission or commission are the sole responsibility of the author. Proceeds from the sale of this book will benefit the Monte Melkonian Fund, Inc., a California 501(c)(3) charity dedicated to helping the neediest of needy children in Mountainous Karabagh (www.melkonian.org).